HIGH AND MIGHTY

HIGH AND MIGHTY

SUVs — THE WORLD'S MOST
DANGEROUS VEHICLES AND HOW
THEY GOT THAT WAY

KEITH BRADSHER

PublicAffairs   New York

Book design by Mark McGarry, Texas Type & Book Works.
Set in Meridien.

Library of Congress Cataloging-in-Publication Data
Bradsher, Keith.
High and mighty: SUVs—the world's most dangerous vehicles and how they got that
way / Keith Bradsher.—1st ed.
p. cm.
Includes bibliographical references and index.
ISBN 1–58648–123–1 (hb.)
1. Sport utility vehicles—Crashworthiness.
2. Consumer protection.
3. Automobile industry and trade—United States.
I. Title.
TL230.5.S66 B73 2002
629.2'31—dc21
2002028722

FIRST EDITION
10 9 8 7 6 5 4 3 2 1

To my beloved wife and son

CONTENTS

PART THREE

THE FUTURE OF THE SUV

ACKNOWLEDGMENTS

A senior editor of business news at *The New York Times*, Glenn Kramon, called me from New York in February 1997 with an intriguing question. As the newspaper's Detroit bureau chief, I had been writing articles for more than a year that mentioned how affluent families were flocking to SUVs, and how the huge profits on these vehicles were bringing renewed prosperity to Detroit. But Kramon wanted to know about something that had little to do with business: What happened when SUVs hit cars. It turned out to be a big problem that regulators and automakers were almost completely ignoring.

With constant encouragement from Kramon, I wrote regularly about the problems of SUVs for the next four and a half years. In between, I did the meat and potatoes of auto industry reporting: writing about the management power struggles, marketing wars, quarterly earnings and monthly sales figures of the nation's biggest industry. The criticisms of SUVs infuriated auto executives, who denounced me in speeches and in interviews with other reporters.

But *The New York Times* consistently supported my coverage despite the criticism. Because the bulk of my articles had nothing to do with SUVs and a lot to do with subjects near to every auto executive's heart, like who would be the next CEO of Ford or General Motors, the industry's leaders had to keep talking to me, and they did.

The backing of *The New York Times* was also invaluable to me in tapping into the knowledge of mid-level auto engineers. The newspaper sent me to many auto engineering conferences, where I was usually the only reporter in attendance. I found the engineers spoke with remarkable candor, as engineers usually do. In one of my favorite "Dilbert" cartoons, a customer refuses to listen to a marketing employee of the company and demands to speak to an engineer, saying that engineers always speak the truth. In the cartoon, the engineer bluntly tells the customer that the product doesn't work. In real life, engineers say that SUVs are poor substitutes for cars when it comes to meeting the needs of most families.

This book is essentially a biography of the sport utility vehicle. Rather than quote outside critics, I have tried to quote the auto industry's own executives, the men and women who have designed, built and marketed SUVs despite their reservations about the vehicle's practicality and safety. Some of the quotes were gathered during interviews for *The Times*. Others were gathered during a book leave that *The Times* generously granted me for this project, a leave of absence that allowed me to explore the history and problems of SUVs in much greater depth, gathering a lot of new information. A few quotes and statistics in this book come from books and articles by other writers, and these sources are identified in the endnotes.

Rising executives in the auto industry commonly change jobs every year or two whereas the interviews used in this book span a period of six years. Unless otherwise specified, all quotes in this book are attributed to officials using the titles they held at the time they made the comments.

My literary agent, Freya Manston, helped me craft the initial structure of my manuscript. The painstaking work of my editor, Paul Golob of PublicAffairs, greatly improved the book.

I very much appreciate the support and advice I have received from *The Times* and especially from Glenn Kramon over the last six years. But this book is solely my project and all of the opinions expressed here are my own.

INTRODUCTION

Sport utility vehicles have taken over America's roads during the last decade, and are on their way to taking over the world's roads. The four-wheel-drive vehicles offer a romantic vision of outdoor adventure to deskbound baby boomers. The larger models provide lots of room for families and their gear. Their size gives them an image of safety. The popularity of SUVs has revived the economy of the upper Midwest and has helped power the American economy since the early 1990s.

Yet the proliferation of SUVs has created huge problems. Their safe image is an illusion. They roll over too easily, killing and injuring occupants at an alarming rate, and they are dangerous to other road users, inflicting catastrophic damage to cars that they hit and posing a lethal threat to pedestrians. Their "green" image is also a mirage, because they contribute far more than cars to smog and global warming. Their gas-guzzling designs increase American dependence on imported oil at a time when anti-American sentiment is prevalent in the Middle East.

The success of SUVs comes partly from extremely cynical design and marketing decisions by automakers and partly from poorly drafted government regulations. The manufacturers' market researchers have decided that millions of baby boomers want an adventurous image and care almost nothing about putting others at risk to achieve it, so they have told auto engineers to design vehicles accordingly. The result has been unusually tall, menacing vehicles like the Dodge Durango, with its grille resembling a jungle cat's teeth and its flared fenders that look like bulging muscles in a savage jaw.

Automakers are able to produce behemoths that guzzle gas, spew pollution and endanger their occupants and other motorists because of loopholes in government regulations. When the United States imposed safety, environmental and tax rules on automobiles in the 1970s, much tougher standards were set for cars than for pickup trucks, vans and the off-road vehicles that have since evolved into sport utility vehicles. Many of these loopholes still exist, and have spread to other countries that have copied American regulations. The result has been a public policy disaster, with automakers given an enormous and unintended incentive to shift production away from cars and toward inefficient, unsafe, heavily polluting SUVs.

No automotive safety issue has ever captured the nation's attention with such intensity as the many rollover crashes of Ford Explorer sport utility vehicles equipped with Firestone tires that failed. Ford and Firestone have been rightly condemned for cutting corners in the design and manufacturing of the Explorer and the tires, and for doing little for several years as some of their employees learned of problems with the tires.

Yet terrible as the tire-related crashes have been, killing as many as 300 people worldwide over the last decade, they are just a tiny part of the safety and environmental problems associated with sport utility vehicles. These problems are already needlessly killing thousands of Americans each year. Hundreds of people are also dying unnecessarily in other countries that are starting to use large numbers of SUVs.

The height and width of the typical SUV make it hard for car drivers behind it to see the road ahead, increasing the chance that they will be unable to avoid a crash, especially a multi-vehicle pileup. The stiff, truck-like underbody of an SUV does little to absorb the force of collisions with trees and other roadside objects. Its size increases traffic congestion, because car drivers tend to give sport utility vehicles a lot of room, so fewer vehicles can get through each green light at an intersection. Most of the nation's roadside guardrails were built for low-riding cars, and may flip an SUV on impact instead of deflecting it safely back into its lane of traffic. The trucklike brakes and suspensions of SUVs mean that their stopping distances are longer than for a family car, making it less likely that an SUV driver will be able to stop before hitting a car. And when SUVs do hit pedestrians, they strike them high on the body, inflicting worse injuries than cars, which have low bumpers that flip pedestrians onto the relatively soft hood.

For all their deadliness to other motorists, SUVs are no safer than cars for their own occupants. Indeed, they are less safe. The occupant death rate per million SUVs is actually 6 percent higher than the occupant death rate per million cars. The biggest SUVs, which pose the greatest hazards to other motorists, have an 8 percent higher death rate for their occupants than minivans and the larger midsize cars like the Ford Taurus and Pontiac Grand Prix.[1] How is this possible? SUV occupants simply die differently, being much more likely than car occupants to die in rollovers, as well as being much more likely to send other drivers to the grave.

SUV occupants also face a higher risk of paralysis. While no national studies have been done, statewide studies in Arkansas and Utah have found that rollovers account for nearly half of all cases of paralysis. Put another way, rollovers cause almost as many paralyzing spinal injuries as all illnesses, falls and every other form of traffic accident combined—even though rollovers make up less than 1 percent of all crashes.

Worst of all, we have only seen the beginnings of the SUV problem, which is certain to become much bigger and much deadlier in the years to come. The safety hazards of SUVs have been mitigated until now because they have mainly attracted the safest drivers in America. The principal buyers of SUVs in the 1990s and early 2000s have been baby boomers in their 40s, with some sales to people in their 30s and 50s. These affluent first owners of SUVs tend to be the most cautious drivers on the road, because they are mostly middle-aged people who have plenty of driving experience and still have acute vision, hearing and mental faculties. Half of them also have families, so they are much less likely to be out driving in the wee hours of the morning, when crash rates soar.

There are 20 million SUVs on the nation's roads and more than half of them are less than five years old. Three-quarters of the full-size SUVs, the largest models, are also under five years old. As affluent, cautious-driving baby boomers begin to sell their SUVs or turn them in at the end of leases, the used-vehicle market will be flooded with these vehicles. Falling prices will make them more attractive to younger drivers and drivers with poor safety records—including drunk drivers. The only thing more frightening for traffic safety experts than a drunk or young person behind the wheel of a new SUV is a drunk or young person behind the wheel of an old SUV with failing brakes and other maintenance problems.

Traditional SUVs, which use the same underbodies as pickup trucks, have climbed from 1.78 percent of new vehicles sold in 1982 to 6.7 percent in 1991 and 16.1 percent in 1997, and have since leveled off at about 17 percent. The change has been even swifter at the luxury end of the auto market, with SUVs rising from less than one-twentieth of the market in 1990 to half the luxury market by 1996. But SUVs still make up only 10 percent of the vehicles currently registered in the United States. Most of the automobiles built in the 1980s are still on the road, and these are mostly cars, so this has been holding down the percentage of all vehicles on the road that are SUVs. As older model years of vehicles are scrapped, however, they are being replaced with new model years in which a much larger proportion of the vehicles are SUVs. This will eventually make SUVs nearly twice as common as they are now.

SUVs are terrible not just for traffic safety but for the environment. Because of their poor gas mileage, they emit a lot of carbon dioxide, a gas linked to global warming. A midsize SUV puts out roughly 50 percent more carbon dioxide per mile than the typical car, while a full-size SUV may emit twice as much. The Sierra Club likes to point out that driving a full-size SUV for a year instead of a midsize car burns as much extra energy as leaving a refrigerator door open for six years. SUVs also spew up to 5.5 times as much smog-causing gases per mile as cars.

Automakers made surprising progress in the 1980s and 1990s in improving the fuel economy of cars, but these gains are being slowly erased by the rise of SUVs. Chrysler boasts that its full-size Concorde sedan now has better acceleration and exactly the same interior room as a 1978 Chrysler New Yorker luxury sedan, but gets nearly the same gas mileage as a 1978 Dodge Omni subcompact, 23 miles per gallon. Yet sales of the Concorde and other large cars have eroded, displaced by big SUVs like Chrysler's Dodge Durango—which get the same mileage as the 1978 New Yorker, about 14 miles to the gallon.

How many people is the SUV boom already needlessly killing? My best estimate is that the replacement of cars with SUVs is currently causing close to 3,000 needless deaths a year in the United States—as many people annually as died in the terrorist attacks at the World Trade Center in New York on September 11, 2001. Roughly 1,000 extra deaths occur each year in SUVs that roll over, compared to the expected rollover death rate if these motorists had been driving cars. About 1,000 more people die each year in cars hit by SUVs than would occur if the cars had been hit by other cars.

And up to 1,000 additional people succumb each year to respiratory problems because of the extra smog caused by SUVs.[2]

This conservative estimate excludes a lot of problems that are hard to calculate, like SUVs' harm to pedestrians, or their contribution to global warming. It also excludes the growing problems overseas, where SUV sales are also starting to rise, especially in Europe, South America and Australia.

SUVs are the world's most dangerous vehicles because they represent a new model of personal transportation that is inherently less safe for road users and more harmful to the environment than cars. SUVs also threaten to displace cars because of a phenomenon known as "network externalities."

This economic concept holds that if enough people start using a certain product, everybody else will start buying the same product just for the advantages of being able to work with people who already have the product. Consumers will do this even if the product chosen is technologically inferior to the alternatives.

The best example of network externalities lies in the computer industry. Once enough people started using Microsoft DOS, and later Microsoft Windows, then practically everybody had to use it, even though Apple arguably had a much better product in its Macintoshes.

Another good example of network externalities lies in VHS video recorders. They represent a less sophisticated technology than the Beta machines with which they initially competed. But once enough people owned VHS video recorders, most movie rentals became available in a VHS format and then everybody had to buy VHS machines.

SUVs are inferior to cars in safety, pollution, comfort and driving performance. Yet their sales have benefited from network externalities. It is becoming harder and harder to see down the road while sitting in a car, because of the impossibility of seeing through the tall SUVs, minivans and pickups ahead in traffic. At night, the glare from SUV headlights is blinding for car drivers. Backing a car out of a parking place between two taller vehicles has become an exercise in hope that no one is about to come barreling by. The sheer size and menacing appearance of SUVs inevitably make car owners feel less safe. The result has been a highway arms race.

If nothing is done to check this trend, automakers will gradually make more and more people feel as though cars are obsolete. The sale of SUVs is creating strong demand for yet more SUVs, as Ford Explorers and Toyota Sequoias displace Ford Tauruses and Toyota Camrys in garage after garage. Advertising reinforces this trend. The auto industry completely dwarfs every other industry in advertising, accounting for one in every seven dollars of advertising in the United States and bankrolling the nation's media to a remarkable extent, especially the television and magazine industries. The auto industry outspends on advertising the next three largest industries combined: financial services, telecommunications (including local, long-distance and cell phone service) and national restaurant chains. A big chunk of the automakers' ad money has gone toward ads that subtly or blatantly undermine people's confidence in cars.

Picking the most offensive SUV ad is hard, because there are so many candidates. My favorite is the nearly full-page newspaper ad that Cadillac ran for its huge Escalade in early 1999. The Escalade was photographed from a point about five feet in front and about two feet off the ground, so that the vehicle's huge grille looms over the viewer. The windshield above is entirely black, giving no hint of who inside is bearing down on the viewer. Trees are a blur of motion around the sides of the vehicle but the SUV itself is in perfect focus as it hurtles forward. It looks just like what you might see in the last second of your life as you looked out the side window of your car and suddenly realized that a big SUV had failed to stop for a red light.

The text of the ad is even more frightening. "YIELD," it commands at the top, in inch-high, underlined letters. In half-inch letters under the Escalade is another warning, delivered in parentheses: "(Please Move Immediately To The Right)" The large type text below continues in the same tone: "You might as well give in now. Because this is the new Cadillac Escalade. The one luxury SUV so powerfully built and intelligently equipped, it's designed to be, well, irresistible. With the standard go-everywhere support of the OnStar system, Escalade brings you virtually unlimited personal concierge services, emergency assistance and directions, right at your fingertips. And no other SUV in the world can make that claim. So tell the other luxury SUVs to yield the right of way. Because Escalade is coming through."

Underneath was the Escalade slogan, in white lettering against a solid black box. "Escalade: It's Good To Be The Cadillac."

You might be more likely to survive if you were in the Cadillac in the ad than in whatever lower-riding car it was about to hit. But few people reading the ad carefully could possibly conclude that "to be the Cadillac" was "good" in a moral sense. Nor is it good for public safety and the environment to have even some people "be the Cadillac" in the sense of this ad.

The ad's advice for other drivers to yield is actually pretty good advice, however, as the Escalade can be a hard vehicle to control even for an experienced driver. The steering is sluggish, the suspension vague and the brakes not as effective as car brakes. I climbed in one of the early Escalades in early 1999 at Detroit's airport for a test drive, but was so appalled by its unresponsive steering that I drove straight home. I called Cadillac and asked them to pick up the vehicle and take it away. Cadillac has improved the Escalade somewhat since I first drove it, but it still has the nimbleness and ride quality of a pig on stilts.

While the Escalade's sheer bulk may provide some protection in collisions with cars, that does not mean it is especially well designed for safety in other crashes. Regulators give it a so-so three-star rating (on a scale of one to five) for driver survival in a frontal crash with another vehicle of the same weight or with a solid object, like a bridge abutment. Many large cars and minivans now carry five-star ratings and the rest typically earn four stars. The regulators also took the extremely rare step of noting that while thigh injuries are not included in calculating survival odds, Escalade drivers are at unusually high risk of a fractured femur in a serious frontal crash.

Cadillac, a division of General Motors, rushed the Escalade onto the market in 1998, a little over a year after the Lincoln Navigator went on sale and was an instant hit. To make the Escalade, GM essentially put lots of chrome and optional equipment on a GMC Yukon SUV, which in turn is little more than a fancy version of a Chevrolet Tahoe SUV. The Tahoe, in turn, uses the underbody and a lot of other parts from the full-size Chevrolet Silverado pickup truck. So Cadillac was essentially taking a $20,000 work truck, tricking it up with lots of chrome, leather seats, and a fancy stereo, and selling it for close to $50,000. This is how automakers have earned enormous profits on full-sized SUVs.

GM and Ford have nearly seven times the sales of Microsoft, and each has been restored to financial health by SUV profits.

GM has been the most aggressive automaker over the last several years in stepping up sales of large, pickup-based SUVs. GM executives like to defend their decision to make vehicles like the Escalade by saying that they are simply building what Americans want. As long as gasoline prices remain low, government regulations remain tilted against cars, and Americans remain enamored of big, macho vehicles worthy of the American frontier, executives at GM and other automakers plan to go on making SUVs.

Harry Pearce, the powerful vice chairman of GM, put it best as he was leaving a press conference in August 2000: "If pigs are big and popular, I guess we'll make pigs."

PART ONE

THE BIRTH OF THE SUV

EARLY RUMBLINGS

At Henry Ford's mansion outside Detroit, the carved wood busts supporting the ceiling in the ballroom show the inventor of the Model T and three close friends, all famous: Harvey Firestone, founder of the tire company that bears his name; Thomas Edison, inventor of the lightbulb and phonograph; and John Burroughs, the naturalist. The four men loved to go on camping trips in the 1920s, accompanied by cooks and other servants in Ford's employ. Driving automobiles specially made in Ford factories, they would spend weeks at a time traversing the American West; they called themselves the Vagabonds.

The mansion, Fairlane, is now a museum, preserved much as it was in Henry Ford's day, and its large octagonal garage is what you might expect of an auto baron—or perhaps a railroad magnate, since the garage looks a little like an old railway roundhouse for steam engines. There are huge windows around the circumference, so that Henry Ford's automobiles can be admired in natural lighting. There is a turntable in the middle, to make it easier to put each car into its space against the walls.

Next to the door is a 1922 Lincoln camper that was custom made for the Vagabonds' trips. The Ford Motor Company put this vehicle on display at the Detroit auto show in 1997 when it unveiled the Lincoln Navigator full-sized SUV, contending that Henry Ford had created the first sport utility vehicle. But the camper looks nothing like any SUV today. There are no seats behind the front row, just a long, enclosed cargo area in the back for carrying camping gear. It is basically a pickup truck with a covered bed.

What is an SUV? There is no official definition—most government regulations simply have categories for "off-highway vehicles," which in turn are lumped in with pickup trucks and minivans as "light trucks." The auto industry has not settled on a definition either. My definition has five parts. An SUV is a vehicle that (1) has four-wheel drive available as either standard or optional equipment; (2) has an enclosed rear cargo area like a minivan; (3) has high ground clearance for off-road travel; (4) uses a pickup-truck underbody; (5) is designed primarily for urban consumers and marketed primarily to them, with a cushy suspension and other features that may even compromise some of its appeal to serious off-road drivers. In the last few years, automakers have begun taking car designs and making them considerably taller and adding four-wheel drive, so as to market the result as an SUV. These vehicles, like the Toyota Highlander, which is derived from the Camry sedan, are often described within the auto industry as crossover utility vehicles, not SUVs, because they are not based on truck underbodies. I follow this convention in this book.

General Motors contends that the Chevrolet Suburban, which was introduced in 1935, is the world's oldest sport utility in mass production. The Suburban also happens to be the oldest nameplate of any car, minivan, SUV or pickup truck in continuous production in the United States.

The early Suburban was a handsome vehicle, a big powerful automobile of the sort that Al Capone might have been proud to drive. It had a long hood with a tall grille on the front, and then a long, elegant passenger compartment with three windows on each side and two more in the back door.

To make the Suburban, Chevrolet engineers simply used the hood, engine, fenders and underbody of a pickup truck and fashioned an attractive passenger compartment to replace the pickup truck cab and bed. No one at GM can identify the father of the Suburban. Chevrolet officials say that the first Suburban was probably a minor project, viewed as a variation of an existing pickup truck design, and so its development did not merit any mention in the files that survive from that era. The name "Suburban" was not original either—another GM division, Cadillac, had sold an expensively upholstered, seven-passenger Suburban sedan from 1918 to 1927.

A 1936 Chevrolet truck catalog touted a "Carryall Suburban" available as either a passenger vehicle or as a light delivery truck, with side windows filled in behind the front row of seats. A photo of the passenger version showed a fashionably dressed woman stepping out of a Suburban while a liveried chauffeur holds the door. "Its utility is proved by its wide demand by private estates, country clubs, hotels, bus and transfer companies, airports, as well as operators who use it for business and pleasure," the catalog said.[1]

But until the 1960s, Chevrolet only sold the Suburban with one door on each side, a design that reflected the pickup truck model on which it was based. That made it hard to climb into the rear seats, and limited the demand for it as a family vehicle. What kept the Suburban in production for so many years was the delivery truck version, which was especially popular in one specialized market: funeral homes.

Undertakers discovered that with all but the front seats removed, the back of a Suburban was precisely the right length and height for carrying the dead, either in bags or in coffins. Suburbans were used as "first-call" vehicles to pick up the dearly departed at homes and hospitals and bring them back for burial preparations, while converted limousines were preferred as hearses for funeral processions. Suburbans were also popular for carrying flower arrangements and chairs, for bringing back coffins from coffin builders and for picking up human remains at airports, because the sturdy metal boxes that the airlines use for shipping corpses are actually bigger and heavier than many caskets.

Funeral home demand for Suburbans has been dwindling since the mid-1980s as Suburbans have became chic and the price has soared. But to this day, the height of the Suburban's rear cargo floor partly reflects an early effort by GM engineers to find a comfortable height for the loading and unloading of the dead, says James Hall, a longtime GM engineer who is now at AutoPacific, a big consulting firm.

It was not until 1967 that Chevrolet finally got around to offering a four-door Suburban. By then the Suburban had become a fairly bare-bones workhorse for cost-conscious funeral homes and other businesses rather than a station wagon for families. So early Suburbans were not really the first sport utility vehicles, as the term is understood today. That honor must go instead to a Jeep.

The American military began experimenting after World War I with lightweight vehicles that could replace its mules and reconnaissance motorcycles. The Army wanted a lightweight vehicle with four-wheel drive that could carry men and a heavy machine gun. In 1940, three weeks after Hitler defeated the French and the British had to evacuate Dunkirk, the Army got serious and put out a request for corporate bids to build huge numbers of such a vehicle. A nearly bankrupt company named American Bantam came up with the design that came closest to meeting the Army's specifications. But the Army had little faith in American Bantam's manufacturing ability and gave large contracts for a Bantam-like design to Ford and Willys-Overland as well. Willys-Overland improved the design with a better engine and ended up producing the bulk of the Jeeps made for World War II.[2]

Nobody knows for sure where the term "Jeep" came from. Some historians say it honored a character of that name in E. C. Segar's Popeye comic strip in the 1930s. Other experts suggest that it was derived from G.P., or general purpose vehicle. Other small military vehicles were briefly known as Jeeps at the beginning of World War II. But the Willys model quickly became the only true Jeep. The cartoonist Bill Mauldin sketched what may be the most famous single drawing of a vehicle, an old soldier from the horse-drawn era ending the suffering of his broken-axle Jeep by shooting it in the hood.[3]

Willys registered the Jeep name as a Willys trademark, making sure that the company would own the brand for the civilian market after World War II.[4] But Willys ran into a problem as the war ended. With government backing, it had been buying the exterior sheet metal for its Jeeps from other companies. But with the end of the war, there was a severe shortage of factories that could stamp out big pieces of steel for automobile bodies, and GM, Ford, Chrysler and their affiliated suppliers controlled most of the available factories.

Willys's response to this conundrum has haunted the SUV market ever since. Charlie Sorenson, who had become the president of Willys late in the war, found a former metal-stamping factory for the washing-machine industry that could stamp out the needed hoods, fenders, roofs, doors and so forth. The factory's shortcoming was that it could only stamp out fairly flat pieces of metal, of the sort that might be used to make the sides of washing-machines.[5] So while Willys had made fairly attractive, curvaceous cars in the pre-war years, all it could make after World War II were very boxy, straight-sided Jeeps with parts stamped at the former washing-machine factory.

The rest of the auto industry moved into the postwar years with an emphasis on rounded, even sensuous shapes that were meant to evoke the curves of women's bodies. The most famous examples are the chrome, conelike ends of the bumpers of Cadillacs from 1946 to

1959, which resembled women's breasts. But Jeeps would keep their very boxy look from their washing-machine factory roots for decades as successive owners invested little in the brand, until boxiness become one of the defining traits of sport utility vehicles.

Willys moved quickly into family vehicles after the war. It introduced the Jeep Station Wagon in 1946, and began offering it with four-wheel drive in 1949. But while the Jeep Station Wagon looked like a station wagon in that it had two rows of seats and a large storage area in the back, it still had only one door on each side, making access to the back seat difficult. Sales of the utilitarian, no-frills vehicle were slow at a time when Americans wanted elegance after the deprivations of World War II. Willys struggled.

Henry J. Kaiser, an industrialist who made his fortune building dams in the 1930s and ships during World War II, bought Willys-Overland in 1953 and renamed it Willys Motors. But he invested fairly little money in new factory equipment or new designs. Better roads, including the start of the interstate highway system in the 1950s, reduced the need for four-wheel drive. Most people did not see the need for a Jeep Station Wagon that looked too much like a modified pickup truck from the Depression.

Two utilitarian alternatives to the Jeep came on the market in Europe and East Asia in the years following World War II. Land Rover began making four-wheel-drive vehicles for the landed gentry to tour their muddy fields in Britain. In Japan, Toyota began building Jeeps under contract for the United States Army during the Korean War. When the contract expired, Toyota turned this expertise to the production of the very similar Land Cruiser, which was sold to police and forestry agencies operating in remote areas with few paved roads. Toyota shipped a single Land Cruiser to the United States in 1957, sold it easily, and began shipping Land Cruisers regularly in 1958 (over the course of many model changes, the Land Cruiser has become enormous and no longer looks much like a Jeep at all). But Toyota and Land Rover remained bit players in the American market for utility vehicles until the 1990s.

Jeeps started to face serious competition in 1961, when International Harvester introduced a small, four-wheel-drive vehicle known as the Scout, with an open bed like a pickup truck and a canvas top that was notorious for leaks. It had a single bench seat in the front and a windshield that could be folded down if it became too spattered with mud to be cleaned.[6] International Harvester never had much success with the Scout and finally abandoned production of it in 1980 to focus on its core business, the production of commercial trucks and farm equipment.

Willys Motors was renamed Kaiser Jeep in 1962, the same year it overhauled the Jeep Station Wagon and renamed it the Jeep Wagoneer.[7] The Wagoneer's passenger compartment was designed to some extent for family buyers and the vehicle had four-wheel drive. Unlike the Jeep Station Wagon, it was available with four doors as well as two. Magazine ads highlighted not just the military history of Jeeps but the availability of pink and white upholstery.[8] Yet the Wagoneer was a bulky, uncomfortable vehicle, and no amount of colorful upholstery could disguise that it was quite different from the station wagons on sale in the early 1960s. It was not well suited to the needs of family buyers and drew few of them.

Kaiser Jeep was only able to sell a few thousand Wagoneers a year—no more than a full-sized assembly plant of GM, Ford or Chrysler could make in a week. Stephen A. Girard, the president of the company from 1954 to 1969, says that the magazine advertisements notwithstanding, he had believed the vehicle would appeal to a limited number of families who really needed four-wheel drive for activities like hunting and fishing, and the company marketed the vehicle primarily to these customers. Moreover, Kaiser Jeep had factories or distributors in more than two dozen countries—the Brazilian and Argentine markets were the biggest—so it had to design rugged models that would be used for heavy-duty off-road driving every day in those countries. Even with the Wagoneer, Girard says, "We were providing four-wheel drive to people who needed it."

The Wagoneer nonetheless helped inspire competitors. Ford started selling fairly large, two-door Broncos in 1965. Chevrolet added a third door to the Suburban in 1967, a rear door on the curb side that allowed better access to the back seat. In 1969, Chevrolet started selling the very large, two-door Chevy Blazer, which was based on a full size pickup-truck underbody. But the Chevy and Ford offerings were even more trucklike than the Wagoneer. Nobody yet had the imagination to sell big four-wheel-drive vehicles as substitutes for cars.

At Kaiser Jeep, the practical approach reflected the extent to which engineers dominated the company while marketers took a back seat. Henry Kaiser had accumulated a global empire of industrial commodities firms before buying Willys-Overland in 1953. He had helped to organize the consortiums of construction companies that built the Hoover, Grand Coulee and Bonneville dams in the 1930s and early 1940s. During World War II, he owned seven shipyards on the West Coast that mastered the task of building freighters in as little as four and a half days. After the war, he expanded rapidly in steel and aluminum, selling to the colossi of Detroit. His only big failure before Kaiser Jeep was his attempt to sell an aluminum car, the Henry J, in the late 1940s and early 1950s.

What all of Henry Kaiser's successful projects had in common, unlike the Henry J and then the Jeeps, was that they involved selling to only a few buyers. Kaiser and his top aides knew how to woo state and federal officials who wanted to build dams. They knew how to talk the purchasing agents of shipping lines and automakers into buying freighters and steel. They knew a lot less about how to promote consumer products to 200 million Americans. Girard, himself an expert in building hydroelectric dams, recounted years later that he and his top aides at Kaiser Jeep had simply not understood the importance of salesmanship. "I had been there since Coulee, and none of us had any experience in marketing to the whole country," Girard said. The SUV boom would have to wait until someone came along who could do that.

*

As Kaiser Jeep struggled into the 1960s, a very different dispute was going on among a handful of trade negotiators and farm lobbyists in Washington, a disagreement that would later have an enormous effect on the development of the SUV market. Because of the dispute, foreign automakers were essentially shut out of the American market for pickup trucks until the late 1990s, ensuring that pickups and their descendants, SUVs, would be the virtually exclusive fief of Detroit automakers for more than a quarter of a century. In turn, this gave Washington a powerful incentive to go easy on SUV regulations even when it got tough on car regulations, as a way to mollify Detroit automakers and the powerful United Automobile Workers (UAW) union.

Yet the original trade dispute, oddly enough, had nothing whatsoever to do with automobiles. It involved, of all things, frozen chickens. Between 1957 and 1961, American farmers had quintupled their exports of frozen chickens to Western Europe. The European Economic Community, then just six countries, was developing a common agricultural policy but finding that chicken farmers, especially in West Germany, were in danger of going out of business because their costs were too high. The Community responded by imposing steep import taxes on frozen chickens, which made it too expensive for American farmers to keep selling them there.

The taxes were a flagrant violation of international free-trade rules that the Europeans had pledged to follow. The United States appealed the European taxes in 1962 to a panel of trade experts in Geneva, as part of an established arbitration process. The panel ruled in favor of the United States a year later, saying that the United States could raise import taxes on a value of imports from Europe equal to the value of the lost chicken exports, unless the European Community swiftly cancelled its chicken tax.

Kennedy Administration trade officials threatened in August 1963 to impose taxes on four imported products: high-priced brandy, potato starch, dextrin (a starch derivative used in adhesives

and certain foods) and light trucks. The Detroit automakers dominated the world market then, especially General Motors, and the
United States imported very few vehicles. But Volkswagen in West
Germany was shipping to the United States a small number of
Kombi panel vans and a few pickup trucks. The Kombi vans only
had side windows for the front seats, and were marketed as delivery vehicles to flower shops, donut stores and other small businesses. Since West Germany was the main country responsible for
imposing the chicken tax, threatening retribution against Volkswagen seemed like a natural choice.

The Europeans remained intransigent in the following months.
When Lyndon Johnson took office after the assassination of President Kennedy on November 22, 1963, the trade dispute was one of
the first issues on his desk.

Johnson was in frequent contact from the day after the assassination with Walter Reuther, the president of the United Automobile Workers union, according to secretly recorded tapes that have
since been released by Johnson's presidential library. Johnson soon
began wooing Reuther energetically, for he especially wanted to
discourage Reuther from staging a national strike when the UAW's
labor contracts with the Big Three expired in September 1964, less
than two months before the presidential elections.

Reuther, in turn, wanted Johnson's help. He was concerned that
the Big Three were ignoring the market for small cars, allowing
Volkswagen to sell its Beetle with increasing success. Reuther asked
Johnson's help in getting the Big Three to build small cars, if necessary through a joint venture, which would require a special dispen-
sation from antitrust laws. Johnson consulted repeatedly with his
attorney general, Robert Kennedy, and his defense secretary,
Robert McNamara, who had briefly been the president of the Ford
Motor Company before joining the Kennedy Administration.

Yet at least among the taped conversations, there is no record of
the light-truck tax being raised, even though it also involved Volkswagen products. When I asked McNamara, the only one of the

group still alive today, he said that the light-truck tax had simply never been seen as important. Nobody seems to have realized at the time how important a light-truck tax might become. Families drove cars, so cars were important; trucks were for a few workmen and farmers.

President Johnson finally imposed the threatened taxes in January 1964, including a 25 percent tax on imported trucks. Volkswagen promptly stopped shipping Kombi vans and pickups to the United States, because the tax made them so expensive that they were no longer competitive.

Under international trade rules, however, the new tax applied to imported light trucks from anywhere in the world, not just Germany. And whereas the taxes on brandy, potato starch and dextrin were later lifted, there has never been a cease-fire in the chicken war of the early 1960s. The light-truck tax persists to this day, although its scope has narrowed somewhat over the years through various court decisions. Japanese automakers subsequently took over a huge chunk of the American car market in the 1970s and 1980s. But cracking the American truck market would take far longer, and require the building of factories in the United States to get around the tariffs.

Because of the chicken dispute, light trucks would remain the almost exclusive turf of Detroit automakers all the way into the late 1990s. Time and again, government regulators would soften the blow of new rules by applying them first to cars and only later, if at all, to the Detroit-dominated market for light trucks.

The first steps on the road to persuading Americans that light trucks were viable substitutes for cars were taken on a private duck-hunting preserve in southern Ontario in the 1960s. Located an hour's drive from downtown Detroit, the preserve offered a rustic retreat for the nation's auto barons, and was the property of a rising executive at American Motors, Roy D. Chapin Jr.

Chapin was a second-generation American industrial patrician of the sort who ruled Detroit in the middle of the twentieth century. Roy D. Chapin Sr. was one of the founders of the Hudson Motor Car Company in 1909 and had been Hudson's president for many years and then chairman, before resigning to serve as Commerce Secretary in the Hoover Administration. His son grew up in one of the largest and most beautiful mansions in Grosse Pointe, Michigan, and attended Hotchkiss, an elite New England boarding school. Roy Chapin Sr. died suddenly in 1936, while his tall, socially poised son was still at Yale. When the younger Chapin graduated from Yale a year later, he immediately became an engineer at his late father's company, in which he had inherited a huge block of stock. When Hudson Motor merged with Nash-Kelvinator in 1954 to form the American Motors Corporation, Chapin was invited to join the board of directors even though he was still a junior executive. He began to rise swiftly through AMC's management ranks.

Chapin moved in an elite circle of wealthy bankers and industrialists who liked to hunt and fish on remote rivers and ponds in Canada and on Nantucket Island, where the Chapin family had a summer estate. Hidden in the woods of Chapin's hunting preserve in southern Ontario, several hundred yards from the marshy fringes of Lake St. Clair, was a large, well-furnished cabin with a kitchen, dining room, living room and four small bedrooms for Chapin and his hunting friends. During the autumn hunting season, there was always a woman present to cook the ducks and one or two handymen to help with the expensive shotguns and the black Labrador retriever dogs. Roy Chapin's son, William R. Chapin, recalls that an aging Jeep was parked outside the cabin, and was used to reach outlying duck blinds.

A frequent guest was Chapin's close friend Stephen Girard, who worked at Kaiser Jeep's administrative headquarters in Toledo, Ohio, next to the sprawling Jeep factory there. Whenever Girard had meetings in the autumn in Detroit, 40 miles northeast of Toledo, he would call Chapin and arrange to spend the night at the cabin before returning to Toledo the following morning. The two men, sometimes joined by a few of Chapin's friends, would stay up much of the night talking, then awake before dawn and head for the duck blinds in the hope of shooting a few teals and mallards before going back to work.

In 1965, the Kaiser family decided to sell the Jeep business, and it was Girard's job to find a buyer. He tried General Motors, Ford and various foreign automakers, especially Renault, which shared some factories with Jeep overseas. Not one of these companies was interested. One of the executives who turned him away, Girard recalls, was Lee Iacocca, who was a top Ford executive at the time.

Americans wanted cars, not Jeeps, automakers believed then. Worse, the Jeep distribution system was a disaster, with tiny rural dealerships that had no money for advertising. Labor relations at the Toledo factory were terrible, with periodic strikes and even vandalism of unsold vehicles. The Jeeps themselves used technology and factory equipment that dated back to the 1940s, because the Kaisers had not invested much money. Jeep sales had languished through the 1960s, while the rest of the auto industry was booming.

As it happened, Girard really wanted to sell Kaiser Jeep to his hunting buddy, Roy Chapin, who was AMC's executive vice president. "Roy and I were so close and we got to talking about it, and he always thought Jeep would make a good combination, and I helped him to that idea," recalls Girard. "Chapin, he was my big shot to make a deal."

Chapin was eager. His wealthy friends on Nantucket and elsewhere drove Jeeps at their hunting clubs and summer homes, and Chapin was convinced that the brand could have broader appeal. He lobbied AMC's president, Roy Abernethy, to buy Kaiser Jeep and even negotiated a tentative deal with Girard. But the deal fell apart when Henry Kaiser demanded a steeper price and Abernethy refused. Nobody else wanted Kaiser Jeep, so Girard had to take it off the market.

But circumstances changed in 1967. Chapin became chairman and president of American Motors while Henry Kaiser died and his son, Edgar, inherited the family empire. Edgar Kaiser, a friend of Chapin's who had run Kaiser Jeep during the first year after his father bought it, wanted to stop building Jeeps, a business that he deeply disliked because of frequent disputes with local union leaders in Toledo. He was more interested in various business opportunities for the family in Asia, notably mining ventures. "He didn't like the automotive business, he didn't want to be in it," recalls Carlyn Kaiser Stark, the eldest child of Edgar Kaiser. "He got pushed into it by his father and it was a very unhappy experience."

In this new, more receptive environment, Chapin and Girard worked out the outlines of a new deal in a series of meetings in late 1969. Chapin flew out to San Francisco to present it to Edgar Kaiser over lunch at an inexpensive restaurant where they were unlikely to be noticed. American Motors would buy Kaiser Jeep for just $10 million plus a bundle of AMC stock and IOUs optimistically valued at another $60 million. Without any investment bankers or lawyers, the two men worked out the deal on a restaurant place mat, according to Roy Chapin's son, William.

"Like a lot of place mats in history, I wish it had been saved," he said. "It may not have meant much at the time to the people writing on it, but it certainly had some historic significance."

Although nobody even dreamed it then, the Kaiser Jeep deal was the beginning of a huge shift in what people would drive on roads across America and, eventually, around the world. American Motors would transform the public perception of Jeeps, executing successfully the strategy of turning Jeeps into family vehicles that Kaiser Jeep had tried but failed to implement. After decades on the fringes of the auto industry, the world's most famous brand of off-road vehicles had finally come into the possession of an automaker with real marketing ability.

The fact that American Motors bought Kaiser Jeep instead of Ford or General Motors made antitrust regulators happy. But the purchase would have disturbing consequences for the sport utility vehicle market that would later develop.

American Motors was the smallest and weakest of the Detroit automakers. While it had a bright sales staff and an extensive network of dealers, it lacked the financial and engineering resources of its rivals. American Motors struggled even during the 1960s, a golden age for the American automobile industry. When gasoline prices soared, the United States economy stumbled and auto regulations became more stringent in the 1970s, American Motors would barely survive. It would look to Washington for relief again and again. Too often, that relief would take the form of exempting Jeeps from rules aimed at making highways safer, making the air cleaner and making the American economy less dependent on foreign oil.

REVIVING A CORPSE

It was only much later, more than 30 years later, that Gerald Meyers began comparing himself to Dr. Frankenstein, the scientist who breathed life into a corpse, only to create a monster he could not control.[1]

Meyers was the vice president of vehicle development at American Motors when it acquired Kaiser Jeep. Late in the autumn of 1969, just after the deal was struck with Edgar Kaiser, Roy Chapin asked Meyers to conduct a preliminary evaluation of Jeep's factory equipment, vehicle designs and marketing operation for the next meeting of AMC's board, just a few days away.

Meyers was immediately hostile to the idea, sharing the perception of most auto executives that Jeep was a disaster. He drove to Toledo and was dismayed by the sullen workforce. He flew to the Jeep factory in South Bend, Indiana, in a little, propeller-driven Cessna that American Motors sometimes chartered and was unimpressed by the aging factory equipment. He already knew that Jeep dealerships were mostly mom-and-pop operations in rural areas with no money for advertising, and had little use for them. Worst of all, Kaiser Jeep faced huge legal expenses to settle the many lawsuits filed by the families of people killed or paralyzed when their tippy Jeeps rolled over.

Meyers returned to Detroit just before the board meeting and bluntly told Chapin that he would recommend to the directors that American Motors not buy Jeep. As far as Meyers was concerned, Jeep was a corpse, soon to follow Studebaker, Packard and many other companies that had already entered the graveyard of American automakers.

But Chapin was not so easily dissuaded. He told Meyers of one more detail he had not mentioned before. Meyers recalled, "Roy said I'd become executive vice president and get to fix Jeep if I supported it. I said to myself, 'I'm a vice president, an executive vice president is pretty good,' so I supported it."

The directors rubber-stamped Chapin's deal and American Motors formally agreed to buy Kaiser Jeep on December 2, 1969. Despite the cheap price tag, a local magazine columnist dubbed the transaction "Chapin's folly," and many questioned whether American Motors, already struggling for survival, could have spent its money better. No one, not even Chapin, realized that Jeep had been one of the best buys in the history of the auto industry.

As a newly minted executive vice president, Meyers moved quickly to overhaul American Motors' new Jeep subsidiary. He began with the small CJ5, which was the direct descendant of the Jeeps of World War II. The CJ5 rolled over so easily that it was one of the deadliest vehicles on the road to drive, according to insurance industry statistics. When American Motors bought Kaiser Jeep, the CJ5 was still being sold with military-style canvas seats and a canvas roof. It was marketed to outdoorsmen and people who needed it for work—the last catalog produced by Kaiser Jeep, in late 1969, showed a photograph of a CJ5 being used to pull the stump of a tree out of the ground.

AMC began producing hard metal roofs for the CJ5. To attract affluent young residents of urban areas, the company replaced the canvas seats with leather bucket seats from cars, and licensed the right to emboss a distinctive Gucci pattern on the leather. AMC replaced the CJ5's noisy aluminum engine with one of American Motors' heavy, cast-iron engines, which made the vehicle more powerful and slightly less prone to tip over. AMC also began mounting the wheels wider, so that the tires actually stuck out slightly from under the sides of the vehicle, further improving the vehicle's stability. Roll bars were installed, making rollovers less deadly for the small minority of occupants who wore seat belts and were not thrown from their vehicles during crashes. The four-door Jeep Wagoneer was also made a little fancier to increase its appeal to urban buyers.

AMC's marketers looked at what kinds of cars were parked in the same driveways as Wagoneers. They found, as Roy Chapin already knew, that they were Mercedes, Porsches and other luxury cars that had nothing in common with the blue-collar heritage of the Wagoneer. AMC executives soon developed a new vision of who would buy Jeeps, and why.

The marketers found that there were many Americans living in cities who admired the Jeep's military heritage, liked its utilitarian image and wanted to ape the automotive fashions of the horses and hunting set of Nantucket and other wealthy enclaves. These affluent urban customers especially liked the fact that Jeeps had four-wheel drive, which sounded like it could be useful in bad-weather driving and gave an air of adventure to the vehicles.

AMC promoted the Jeep's four-wheel drive even though its engineers and executives knew that it had little value for urban buyers. Four-wheel drive is designed for extracting vehicles from deep mud or thick snow. But it has little value on paved roads that are simply wet, or that are plowed of snow before the flakes become more than a few inches deep. "All of the SUV market was psychological, there was no actual customer need for four-wheel drive," said William Chapin, Roy Chapin's son, who rose through the ranks to became a senior marketing executive of Jeep while AMC owned it.

William Chapin made the same mistake as many of his customers. He chose a Jeep in the 1970s as his free company car, thinking he might need it during snowy winters in Detroit. But he found that the snow was almost always plowed from roads before it became deep enough to require four-wheel drive. "I didn't need it," he concluded.

But before AMC could begin marketing Jeeps to affluent young urban buyers, it had to address a problem. Kaiser Jeep had relied on a network of tiny, poorly financed dealerships located in small towns where people actually needed four-wheel drive for hunting, fishing or work.

It is hard to overestimate the importance of dealers to the success or failure of an automaker. State franchise laws essentially bar automakers from owning dealerships except briefly during the transfer of a franchise from one dealer to another. So after spending hundreds of millions or even billions of dollars on the design and engineering of a new model, manufacturers must entrust the actual sale of the vehicle to independent car dealers around the country. Successful car dealers invest millions of dollars of their own money in extensive local advertising, fancy showrooms and large lots. Automakers help by lending large sums to these well-capitalized dealers, so that they can afford to keep a wide selection of new cars and light trucks on display.

Kaiser Jeep had taken the low-budget approach of relying on a motley collection of little rural dealerships that catered to local businesses and outdoorsmen. Many of these little dealerships belonged to middle-class families without a lot of money to invest. They could not afford to buy showrooms and big lots in cities, nor could they afford to advertise much. They even lacked the money to keep a large number of vehicles on hand while waiting for customers to show up.

Instead, they often operated out of gas stations, small auto repair shops and Main Street storefronts, with perhaps a single vehicle or two on hand to show prospective customers. Buyers were expected to order their vehicles from a catalog and wait for the factory to build it and ship it. But while the factory-order system still prevails today for selling automobiles in some countries, notably Japan, delayed gratification in car buying had become hopelessly outdated in the United States by 1970, as big dealerships became the rule. Americans came to expect the instant reward of walking into a showroom, buying a car and driving it away the same day.

After a lengthy review of the problem, American Motors stopped shipping Jeeps to many longtime dealers. AMC instead insisted on buying back the franchises for tiny sums from small-town families without the money to hire lawyers and go to court to protect their businesses.

William Chapin joined his father's company straight out of college in 1972, and his first job was to visit some of these families and persuade them to sign the necessary papers. "Most of these Jeep dealers were little holes in the wall, places that looked like you'd need a tetanus shot to go in," he said. "As I was having the father sign the termination agreement, the mother was crying."

After buying up the franchises, AMC redistributed them to hundreds of its biggest urban dealers around the country. These dealers began displaying Jeeps in spacious showrooms and at the street curbs of big crossroads in large cities. They advertised them heavily in local newspapers. Consummate networkers, the dealers described Jeeps enthusiastically to their many friends on the boards of local Little Leagues, charities and religious institutions.

Jeep sales quadrupled during the 1970s. *Time* magazine dubbed the basic Jeep "a macho-chic machine." The corpse of Jeep was definitely stirring. But a huge obstacle still remained for Meyers: government regulation.

Jeeps, and the many sport utility vehicles that would follow them, were inherently less safe, less fuel-efficient and more polluting than cars. Their high, heavy, stiff underbodies, designed to take the punishment of scaling muddy mountain tracks, made them hard to stop during emergency braking and made them guzzle gas. They had virtually no crumple zones to absorb the force of impacts. Their extra height made them prone to tipping over. The combination of their height, stiffness and lack of crumple zones made them unusually deadly to their own occupants and to the occupants of cars that they hit. The large, fairly primitive engines of SUVs also spewed huge quantities of smog-causing gases linked to respiratory diseases.

The 1970s were the years in which the American auto industry ceased to be a freewheeling collection of industrial giants that could pretty much build what they wanted. In his 1965 exposé, *Unsafe at Any Speed*, Ralph Nader had persuaded the country that automotive safety and pollution had to be addressed, and auto manufacturing gradually became a heavily regulated industry. Each year brought another batch of new rules, from safety and fuel-economy regulations to air pollution controls. Had Jeeps been more than a tiny niche of the market, their many drawbacks might have attracted close scrutiny. But safety and environmental activists ignored the then-tiny Jeep market, focusing on cars instead.

American Motors was the smallest and sickest of the Detroit automakers. Rather than enact regulations on Jeeps in the 1970s that might put AMC out of business, Washington politicians and regulators repeatedly chose the politically expedient course of taking it easy on Jeeps.

As executive vice president, and later as chairman, after Chapin retired in 1977, Meyers practically commuted to Washington. His goal, in numerous regulatory fights, was the classification of Jeeps as light trucks, not cars, because light trucks were being subjected to far less stringent rules.

Light trucks in those days tended to be commercial vehicles, and made up less than a fifth of all vehicles sold. They were pickup trucks and big, two-door vans with few windows on the side that were used by plumbers, builders, farmers and other small business owners. Businesses used light trucks to tow heavy loads and traverse muddy fields, tasks that required powerful engines. Business owners were less inclined to worry about the poor fuel economy and heavy air pollution that went with big engines. Small businesses also packed a lot of political clout with politicians and regulators. They used that clout during the economic stagnation of the 1970s to make sure that their vehicles did not have to carry the same safety and environmental equipment that was contributing to rising car prices.

As it happened, AMC was building Jeeps on the same underbodies, or chassis, as it was building pickup trucks, so it was possible to argue that Jeeps should be regulated the same as pickups. In each of a series of regulatory fights, Meyers made this point first to members of Congress from Ohio and Michigan, then to representatives and senators from other states. Finally, when he had gathered considerable political support, he went to the regulators themselves. Never mentioned was that American Motors was already moving at top speed to make its Jeeps as luxurious as possible, effectively entering the market for family vehicles while largely abandoning the market for trucklike, bare-bones vehicles used by outdoorsmen and small businesses.

"We made damn sure they were classified as trucks, we lobbied like hell," Meyers recalls.

It did not hurt that in the 1970s, AMC was a big employer in a highly visible, politically powerful domestic industry that was already attributing its troubles to excessive government regulation rather than poor quality, poor labor relations and other shortcomings. AMC had extra clout because the bulk of its workers, and the workers of its hundreds of suppliers, were in Michigan, Ohio and Wisconsin. Michigan and Ohio residents in particular are so evenly divided among Democrats and Republicans that these states are crucial in every presidential election that is not a landslide. This makes Washington particularly sensitive to auto-industry concerns.

The pattern of special treatment for Jeeps started with air pollution, and the rules that the Environmental Protection Agency drafted to enforce the Clean Air Act of 1970. AMC did not have the engineering know-how to build cleaner engines for its Jeeps, and rival automakers, notably GM, were reluctant to sell cutting-edge emissions technology to AMC. So the EPA decided in late 1973 to count Jeeps as light trucks, not cars.

"We had to find a way to keep the Clean Air Act from being blamed for putting AMC out of business, so we reached for the truck chassis definition," recalls Eric Stork, who was the deputy assistant administrator of the Environmental Protection Agency for vehicular pollution at the time.

The next big decision came in 1975, when Congress, frightened by soaring gasoline prices and shortages in 1973 and 1974, decided to force the auto industry to improve fuel economy. Detroit automakers and their most powerful ally in Congress, Representative John Dingell, a Michigan Democrat, fought the new federal rules. But the industry owed much of its political influence to its employment of nearly 2 million heavily unionized workers. To the surprise of many, the United Automobile Workers union quietly supported the legislation.

The union's leaders were sympathetic to public calls for energy conservation, improved safety and cleaner air. The union had even donated $10,000 to the organizers of the first Earth Day in 1970. Union leaders distrusted top auto executives, who had repeatedly said through the 1960s and early 1970s that pollution reductions and especially safety improvements were impractical or too costly. Time and again, the automakers had been able to make the changes easily as soon as regulators or Congress mandated them. So when the automakers asked for help in fighting fuel-economy standards, union leaders turned them down. While union officials did not actively lobby for the law, and did not favor a specific amount by which to raise standards, they did tell anyone who asked that they thought the government had a role in making sure that gas mileage improved.

"There was real skepticism on our part, on my part anyway,

about what the auto industry was telling us, and that started with the safety standards, where the industry resisted every step of the way, to the point that Washington didn't trust them either," recalls Douglas A. Fraser, who was a top UAW official in 1975 and became the union's president two years later.

The automakers wanted any fuel-economy standards to be set by regulators, not by Congress. Their reasoning was based on the fact that once Congress passes a law, it is extremely difficult to undo it, whereas regulators have to follow elaborate procedures to assess the technical feasibility of any future improvements. Regulators could also be lobbied to set less stringent standards later, once politicians and consumers were less worried about gasoline shortages.

Automakers were alone in favoring regulatory standards, instead of legislated standards, for cars. But they had powerful allies on their side in favoring regulatory standards for light trucks, which were still mostly pickup trucks. Environmentalists had paid virtually no attention to these vehicles, reasoning that they served a legitimate business purpose. Farmers, small businessmen, boaters and horse owners all wanted to be able to keep buying large, powerful pickup trucks for carrying and towing heavy loads, even though the pickups got poor gas mileage.

In the end, Congress required the auto industry to double the average fuel economy of cars, to 27.5 miles per gallon by the 1985 model year, a standard that has endured ever since. But Congress left light-truck gas mileage standards to be set by regulators at the Transportation Department. It was a big win for the auto industry. "You fight for whatever you can get, and if you've got better allies on the light-duty trucks, you win those and you don't win the others—there aren't many organizations that weigh in on passenger cars," said Jim Johnston, then a senior auto-industry lobbyist.

The 1975 law gave the Transportation Department broad discretion in dealing with light trucks. The law vaguely stated that the department "shall, by rule, prescribe average fuel economy standards for automobiles which are not passenger automobiles."[2]

The Transportation Department confronted a problem: As it drafted regulations in 1976 to implement the law, nobody had any trustworthy data on fuel economy—except for Stork at the EPA. An automobile engine produces 19.5 pounds of carbon dioxide for every gallon of gasoline that it burns, as 5.3 pounds of carbon in the fuel combine with 14.2 pounds of oxygen coming through the grille. Stork's staff had been making detailed measurements of auto exhaust to assess emissions of smog-causing gases like nitrogen oxides and unburned gasoline vapors, and had measured the amount of carbon dioxide too. The EPA used the carbon dioxide measurements to calculate the fuel economy of each model for the Transportation Department.

Using the EPA data meant a natural tendency to adopt the EPA's definition of light trucks, too—including the decision that utility vehicles were trucks rather than cars. There was, moreover, a powerful lobby that wanted this done. While American Motors had been alone in 1973 in seeking to have utility vehicles counted as trucks for emissions purposes, it was joined by the rest of the auto industry when the same question came up for fuel-economy regulations. Raising the gas mileage of cars to an average of 27.5 miles per gallon would be especially difficult if big, gas-guzzling Jeep Wagoneers, Chevrolet Blazers and Ford Broncos were included in the average, the automakers argued. "The industry wanted to keep those in the light-truck category, absolutely," said Jim Johnston, who had become GM's top lobbyist in 1976 and would keep that job until his retirement in 1994.

The Transportation Department ended up adopting the EPA definition of a light truck with very few changes, and published the rules in the Federal Register in 1977. The rules plunked Jeeps and other utility vehicles in with pickup trucks and cargo vans as meeting the law's category of "automobiles which are not passenger automobiles."

The regulations would later feed the trend toward taller SUVs. While pickups are automatically classified as light trucks, an SUV only qualifies as a light truck if its manufacturer vouches that it is what the regulations describe as "an automobile capable of off-highway operation." Off-road driving requires considerable ground clearance, which tends to mean a high-riding vehicle.

The Transportation Department decision ensured that fuel-economy standards for SUVs, along with other light trucks, would be set in an annual or biennial regulatory review of light-truck standards that would later become rife with lobbying. After watching how fuel-economy standards hurt the sales of Detroit's big cars and helped sales of imported cars from Japan, the UAW joined the automakers in opposing further increases in fuel-economy standards. Undoing the legislation on cars was politically impossible, but the union and the automakers would see to it that fuel-economy standards would never rise nearly as high for light trucks as for cars.

Emissions rules and fuel-economy standards in the 1970s also covered only those light trucks that were quite light indeed. To classify trucks, the auto industry as well as road and bridge builders had long used something called "gross vehicle weight." This is the truck's weight when fully loaded with the maximum weight recommended by the manufacturer. Federal laws gave the EPA and the Transportation Department the authority to set rules for light trucks with a gross vehicle weight of up to 10,000 pounds. But regulators at both agencies initially refrained from setting rules for the larger light trucks because these tended to be very large pickups used for serious work. So the initial emissions and fuel-economy regulations only covered light trucks with a gross vehicle weight of up to 6,000 pounds—the equivalent of a Ford Explorer SUV today.

Automakers quickly spotted the loophole. By beefing up the suspensions of their pickup trucks so that they could carry more cargo, they could push the pickups' gross vehicle weight over 6,000 pounds and escape regulation. When the emissions rules took effect in 1971, they covered two-thirds of the light trucks being sold. By 1977, the emissions rules and the newer fuel-economy rules covered only a third of the light-truck market.[3] In other words, automakers shifted to beefier, less energy-efficient pickups even in a time of rising gasoline prices rather than try to meet regulations that they deemed too stringent.

When Jimmy Carter became President in 1977, he named an experienced regulator with an activist bent, Joan Claybrook, to oversee traffic safety and fuel-economy issues at the Transportation Department. Claybrook and her staff were aware that automakers were evading the fuel-economy rules by making their light trucks heavier and set out to address the problem. But in doing so, she made a big mistake that has attracted little notice to this day, with harmful consequences for the environment and safety alike.

In 1978, Claybrook and her staff set the fuel-economy standards for light trucks in the 1980 and 1981 model years. While they were at it, they considered raising the weight limit all the way up to 10,000 pounds, as provided for by the law. But the law also said that fuel-economy averages could only be raised in increments that were technically feasible. So Claybrook had a choice: she could raise the limit all the way to 10,000 pounds and set a modest increase in how many miles the average light truck would be required to go on gallon of gas, or she could raise the limit only to 8,500 pounds and raise the mileage standard a little more.

There were only a handful of vehicles being sold between 8,500 pounds and 10,000 pounds, and the automakers assured Claybrook that an 8,500-pound limit was, as GM put it, "a reasonable cut off between the commercial and mixed personal/commercial use vehicles."[4] Claybrook and her staff accepted this argument and established a new 8,500-pound limit. They announced it in the Federal Register with a statement that mentioned, "the light truck category could be further expanded [i.e., to 10,000 pounds] to avoid circumvention of the fuel-economy standards."[5] The EPA subsequently raised its weight limit to 8,500 pounds too.

In the years since then, however, the category has never been expanded, and automakers now sell a wide range of pickups and some SUVs with gross vehicle weight ratings of 8,550 to 8,600 pounds, neatly escaping all fuel-economy regulations and many emissions rules. Not withstanding GM's statement in 1978, many of these large pickups and SUVs are now being sold for personal use. "I was trying to set the highest number that I could" for the number of miles to the gallon that new light trucks would have to achieve in the 1980 and 1981 model years, Claybrook said ruefully two decades later. "It never occurred to me at that time this would be such a permanent precedent."

While the car mileage standard rose swiftly to 27.5 miles per gallon for the 1985 model year, as dictated by Congress, the light-truck standard leveled off at 20.5 miles per gallon in the 1987 model year. For automakers, the message was clear: If gasoline prices ever fell and Americans ever returned to their love of large, powerful vehicles, they would have to build light trucks.

The tax code also ended up favoring gas-guzzling light trucks. Congress voted in 1978 that cars with gas mileage that was 5 miles or more per gallon below the federally mandated standard should be labeled as "gas-guzzlers" and be subjected to a new tax, which remains on the books to this day. The tax now adds as much as $7,700 to the price tag of some of the most powerful, fuel-gulping sports cars.

But when the House Ways and Means Committee was drafting the new tax, there were pleas to exempt light trucks—not just from Congressmen from auto-manufacturing states, but from rural districts too. "The feeling was the farmer's pickup truck should be exempted, because it was both a personal and business vehicle," recalls Albert Buckberg, a retired senior economist with the Joint Tax Committee of Congress who worked on the gas-guzzler tax then. The rural lawmakers prevailed: Automakers could build light trucks as large as they wanted and not have to worry about stiff taxes on them. And because Congress did not try to redefine what was a light truck, the exemption from the gas-guzzler tax would cover SUVs as well.

*

The auto industry also won more lenient safety regulations for light trucks. Light trucks were initially exempt from new rules requiring headrests to prevent whiplash, and requiring steel beams inside car doors to minimize injuries during side-impact collisions. They were also allowed to have longer stopping distances during emergency braking than cars, and they were allowed to have less durable tires.

One crucial decision involved bumper-height regulations. Cars were required to have bumpers that could withstand impacts between 16 and 20 inches off the ground. Light trucks were simply exempt from this rule, so that they could drive up steep inclines during off-road driving without scraping their bumpers the way cars often do when they start up a steep driveway. But the exemption would also mean that when automakers later started designing pickups and SUVs so that drivers could ride higher off the road, there would be no regulatory pressure to keep the front ends of these vehicles down at the same height as the front ends of cars.

Some of the many safety loopholes, including those for headrests and steel beams in the doors, were later closed, and light trucks were forced to meet the same regulations as cars. Other loopholes, like those in the tire and bumper rules, remain to this day. SUVs were counted as light trucks for all these safety rules.

Most important, American Motors fought off government efforts to address vehicle stability, the bane of Jeeps from their earliest days. The Transportation Department's National Highway Traffic Safety Administration, better known as NHTSA, announced plans in 1973 to regulate how prone vehicles were to rolling over. But when the department had trouble measuring stability and the auto industry fought the idea vigorously, the department dropped the idea of issuing regulations.

Soon after the Transportation Department retreated, the Federal Trade Commission (FTC) grew alarmed at AMC ads that showed drivers careening off tall sand dunes in CJ5s and then driving off into forests. The federal commission told AMC that it wanted not only to ban the ads but also to declare the CJ5 itself unsafe because of its tendency to roll over.

Meyers fought back. His company had only a handful of models, not dozens, and the CJ5 was one of the few successes. "We were American Motors, not General Motors," he recalled. "We said, 'We can't stop this, we live on this stuff, we've got 27,000 people and they live all over the country.'"

Jeeps and other off-road vehicles represented a little less than 1 percent of the American market, hardly a big enough target to justify a huge fight by regulators.[6] The FTC backed off trying to ban the CJ5 when NHTSA put forward a plan that automakers be required to put a warning sticker on the sun visors of all SUVs with a wheelbase (the distance front to back between the wheels) of less than 110 inches. The plan started with the CJ5 and took effect for other short-wheelbase SUVs with the 1984 model year, and the stickers have been attached to the sun visors of small and medium-sized sport utility vehicles ever since. They cost automakers pennies per vehicle to attach and have been found by numerous studies over the years to be singularly ineffective in preventing rollovers.

"I said, 'Is that all we've got to do? Sold!'" Meyers recalls.

The stickers even became a selling point for American Motors, giving an aura of danger to the vehicles. "Guess what happened? Sales soared, the kids loved them, it added to the excitement," Meyers said.

Jeeps also won protection from foreign competition, although that took longer. When Japanese automakers began selling small pickup trucks in the United States in the late 1960s and early 1970s, they did not want to pay the 25 percent tax still on the books from the chicken war of 1964. So they shipped the cabs and chassis of pickups separately, paying the negligible taxes on auto parts instead and then bolting the vehicles back together on the docks of Long Beach, California.

When the American economy fell back into recession at the end of 1979, Detroit asked Washington for help. In early 1980, the chairmen of the Detroit automakers and Fraser, who had become president of the UAW, gathered in the West Wing of the White House to discuss their troubles with President Carter. Most of the auto executives griped about high interest rates, which were making it hard for many Americans to afford car loans. But Carter could do nothing about that—the independent Federal Reserve guided interest rates, and the central bank's chairman, Paul Volcker, was not at the meeting.

Meyers had served as a senior manager in Chrysler's European operations in the early 1960s and was well aware that the chicken tax was still on the books. When it was his turn to speak, he made a personal appeal to the President to apply the tax to the disassembled pickup trucks. Fraser quickly added his support then, too. Fraser and Meyers both recall that Carter expressed surprise that he had the discretion to take such a big step unilaterally.

As it happened, the White House had its own reasons for trying to appease the UAW. Fraser was supporting Senator Ted Kennedy, not Carter, in the Democratic Presidential primaries that spring, because he believed that Kennedy's plans for national health care were more closely aligned with the interests of auto workers. But Fraser also wanted the 25 percent tax on disassembled pickups from Japan, and let the White House and Carter himself know it. "They were trying to accommodate me and find some way," Fraser recalls.

The United States Customs Service ended up announcing on May 20, 1980, that the 25 percent import tariff on light trucks covered partially disassembled light trucks, too. It was a big victory for Detroit, because it meant that any foreign automaker that wanted to enter the American pickup truck market would have to go to the enormous risk and expense of building an entire assembly plant in the United States to build it. Pickup trucks, especially full-size pickup trucks, are a peculiarly American phenomenon. They have not been nearly as popular in Europe or most of East Asia, where they are viewed strictly as work vehicles. There are so few big markets for pickup trucks that the world's second-largest demand for them, after the United States, is in Thailand, a small market where tax rules give preferential treatment to vehicles with open beds. After the Customs Service's decision, Asian and European automakers continued building some small pickups for the markets in their respective regions. But they did not invest in designing full-size pickups, for which the only real market was in the United States.

President Ronald Reagan took office in January 1981 and froze most auto regulations in place for years to come. Even American Motors executives were amazed by then that their Jeep division had almost completely dodged the preceding decade's regulatory ferment. Countless trips to Washington by Meyers and his lieutenants, as well as considerable lobbying by General Motors and other automakers on the fuel-economy issue, had spared the Jeep division from spending billions of dollars on engineering work, if the division had been able to find scarce engineers at all.

"It escaped regulation—we didn't have to worry about fuel economy much at all, we didn't have to worry about bumper height standards, we didn't have to worry about side-impact standards, we didn't have to worry about emissions standards," Meyers said. "So you see, it was a dream for us—we didn't have the money to do anything, and we didn't do anything. . . . I wasn't doing the sociological thing, I was keeping a dying company alive, I had the blinders on."

Other auto executives instrumental in creating the early SUV loopholes are less apologetic. GM's Jim Johnston dislikes SUVs now because he still drives cars, but regrets none of his lobbying. "It just annoys the hell out of me when I get behind one, I can't see anything, but I'd still, like they say about free speech, fight like hell for the right of people to buy one," Johnston says.

But as the 1980s began, AMC started bracing itself for tougher competition. For decades, Ford and GM had not bothered building small pickup trucks, preferring to manufacture more profitable full-size models with beefy V-8 engines. This meant that neither automaker had a small pickup truck underbody that could double as the underbody for a small SUV. So Ford and GM left the small SUV market to Jeep and International Harvester, while making huge, unwieldy Ford Broncos and full-size Chevrolet Blazers, which only came with two doors, like the full-size pickups on which they were based.

The oil-price shocks of the 1970s abruptly forced Detroit to reconsider, and the sudden popularity of small, fuel-sipping Japanese pickup trucks in the late 1970s came as a shock to GM and Ford. The imposition of the chicken tax on the disassembled Japanese pickups in 1980 slowed the onslaught, but by then GM and Ford were racing to put their own small pickups on sale as soon as possible.[7] The results were the Chevrolet S-10 and Ford Ranger pickups.

Since they had gone to the huge expense of designing the frames, suspensions, axles and other underbody components for the new pickups, GM and Ford looked for ways to reuse the underbodies, so as to spread the design costs over more vehicles. They decided to build SUV versions of both vehicles. So they extended the passenger compartments on both vehicles all the way to the back, replacing the pickup trucks' beds with an extra row of seats and an enclosed cargo area, creating the S-10 Blazer and the Bronco II.

The Chevrolet S-10 Blazer was introduced in September 1982, and the Ford Bronco II came out the following March. Smaller than the original Broncos and Blazers of the late 1960s, they were more the result of the oil-price shocks of 1973 and 1979 than any reaction to Jeep's success. (The S-10 Blazer was later renamed simply the Blazer when GM confusingly renamed the original, full-size Blazer as the Tahoe.)

The S-10 Blazer and Bronco II had two doors, like the pickup trucks they replaced. There were no four-door models of either

SUV, because there were no four-door Rangers or S-10 pickups. Ford and GM were unwilling to invest in extra engineering and design work just to offer more doors on the SUV versions. The Bronco II and the S-10 Blazer were also marketed mostly to outdoorsmen. Ford and GM had created them more for financial reasons than because of any grasp of how American tastes in automobiles were starting to change.

American Motors executives watched with trepidation the early preparations for the Bronco II and S-10 Blazer. Indeed, in some cases they literally kept watch—AMC engineers sometimes hiked secretly into the forests of Milford, Michigan, carrying binoculars to a hilltop from which they could see GM's sprawling test-track complex.

Jeep had become such a big business for American Motors that the company decided to design an entirely new, four-door model from the ground up. Worried about rollovers, Meyers hired one of Ford's most brilliant auto engineers, Roy Lunn.

Lunn played a central role in designing the last American cars to win at the 24-hour endurance race at LeMans, Ford GT's that prevailed in 1967, 1968, and 1969. His racing experience gave him an extremely detailed understanding of how to craft a vehicle that would remain stable at any speed. He had an extraordinary grasp of how all the parts in an automobile underbody interacted.

Fuel economy was also a priority. The Iranian Revolution in 1979 sent oil prices skyward while the American economy swooned, and auto sales with it. Meyers sold the first in a series of stakes in AMC to Renault, which had a lot of expertise in fuel-efficient small cars and sent one of its best engineers from France, Francois Castaing. He embraced American life to the point that he even organized sock hop parties in the basement of his home in Bloomfield Hills, a prosperous Detroit suburb.

Castaing, a man of average height with curly hair, grew up in France in the years after World War II. His family had a little Deux Chevaux car, and when his parents became more prosperous they bought a second Deux Chevaux instead of moving up to a larger car. "Having a car was a blessing, gasoline was expensive," Castaing said. "I was raised with this view of the world that gasoline was rare and to be conserved, and that small cars were great."

Joining Lunn on the four-door SUV project, Castaing scrutinized every component for ways to save weight. He and Lunn chose a modest 2.8-liter engine instead of the much larger volume engines found in other light trucks. When they were done, the vehicle still burned considerably more gasoline than a small car, because it was bigger and had the poor aerodynamics of a taller vehicle. But it was fuel-efficient by light-truck standards, getting 16 miles per gallon in the city and 18 miles per gallon on the highway when equipped with an automatic transmission—and even better with a stick shift.

The new vehicle was named the Jeep Cherokee, and it went on sale in late 1983 as a 1984 model. The timing could scarcely have been better. Incomes were rising again after two deep, back-to-back recessions from 1979 to 1982. Gasoline prices had plummeted in 1981 and would stay low through most of the 1980s, especially after adjusting for inflation. People wanted bigger vehicles again. But they could no longer find them, at least among cars.

When gas-mileage rules were set back in 1975, the nation had been terrified of gasoline shortages, forcing big changes in car design. Each automaker was required to raise the average gas mileage of its new cars from 13 miles per gallon in 1975 to 18 miles per gallon in the 1978 model year and 27 miles per gallon by the 1984 model year in which the Cherokee was introduced.

Japanese automakers mostly made small cars then, so Detroit automakers bore the brunt of the new rules. There was little time to design more fuel-efficient engines and redesign every auto part to minimize weight, so the domestic automakers had to sell many more small cars while cutting back on sales of large cars. The few large cars that could still be sold were marketed through luxury divisions like Cadillac and Lincoln, which commanded high profit margins. The lightweight, fuel-efficient small cars were also less safe at first, because automakers had simply shrunk the front and back ends and taken out a lot of the structure to reduce weight. (Later fuel-economy gains tended to be made by replacing steel parts with parts made from high-strength aluminum or steel alloys, allowing cars to be large, lightweight and fuel-efficient with less effect on safety.)

Cars also became less tall, so as to improve their aerodynamics. But this made it harder for older people to climb in and out. Seats were mounted so low in the passenger compartments that drivers felt as though they were sitting on a cushion on the floor, with their legs out in front of them to push the pedals, instead of sitting in a comfortable, upright chair.

Some car engines were hastily redesigned, but became more prone to stalling and other reliability problems, worsening Detroit's increasingly poor reputation for quality. General Motors rushed out diesel engines, which were inherently more fuel-efficient but had been so quickly and shoddily designed that they were smoky and noisy.

Middle-class families were starved for the big, roomy, reliable, sturdy cars they remembered from the last time gasoline prices were low, and the Cherokee became an immediate hit—and not just in towns and cities in the West and South with easy access to the great outdoors. Even AMC executives were stunned when large cities in the Northeast turned out to be the biggest market. AMC had planned to paint most Cherokees in light shades popular in the southern and southwestern states, but ended up painting a much higher percentage in the darker hues popular in places like New York City.

American Motors was not alone in introducing a light truck for family use in late 1983. The other struggling Detroit automaker, Chrysler, tried the same gambit by introducing the first modern, front-wheel-drive minivan. Minivans were an even bigger success than Jeep Cherokees. Minivans swiftly replaced large station wagons, which Detroit could no longer produce anyway if it also wanted to build large luxury cars and still meet the gas-mileage standards.

To certify a van as a light truck instead of a car, the Transportation Department only required that there be a flat floor extending from behind the front seat to the back of the vehicle, with seats that could be removed with simple tools. The rule had been written in the mid-1970s to make sure that about 12,000 full-size vans being sold each year then qualified as light trucks. The first minivans were carefully designed to meet this test, and while most of the minivans built since then have essentially been modified car designs, they all have the flat floor to qualify for light-truck status.

The EPA did not have a separate rule for vans. To certify any vehicle as a light truck so as to qualify for more lenient air-pollution rules, EPA required that it be "designed primarily for transportation of property or is a derivation of such a vehicle." So Chrysler engineers cagily built the first minivans with not just a passenger version but also a cargo version, with no windows on the sides behind the front seats. They then insisted to regulators that the passenger version was derived from the cargo version and persuaded EPA that it was a light truck—even though less than 3 percent of the sales of Chrysler minivans were actually cargo versions.

Chrysler's request to have minivans certified as light trucks was not without controversy. The UAW objected to Chrysler that the minivan certification violated the spirit of the fuel-economy and emissions laws, and told the automaker that the minivan should be classified as a car. "I remember arguing that a vehicle that hauls goods is a truck, and a vehicle that hauls passengers is a car," said Fraser, who was the UAW's president at the time.

But such positions were already becoming more difficult for the union, because of the harm that fuel-economy rules had caused to the large-car market. The union did not try to turn the minivan certification into a national issue. "We obviously didn't want to go overboard because, frankly, of jobs," Fraser said.

The Reagan Administration, which was seeking to lighten the

burden of government regulations on business, accepted Chrysler's argument that minivans qualified as trucks under the fuel-economy and emissions rules. Roughly 10 million minivans have been driven through this loophole since 1983.

Getting minivans and SUVs certified as light trucks allowed Chrysler and American Motors to crank out huge numbers of them without fear of violating fuel-economy, safety, or pollution rules. Passenger and cargo versions of early minivans did not even have headrests to prevent whiplash during crashes, because headrests were required then for cars but not for light trucks.

The minivan was the creation of Harold K. Sperlich, a Chrysler president. Asked many years later whether he had known the many advantages from certifying minivans as light trucks, he responded with a big grin, "We were aware of that—you take any advantage you can get."

Robert Casey, the transportation curator at the Henry Ford Museum, contends persuasively that the Cherokee was the first true sport utility vehicle in the modern understanding of the vehicle. It was a little smaller than the Wagoneer, making it a manageable size for urban families. It had four-wheel drive. It had a plush interior that resembled a station wagon in many ways. It was marketed to urban families who bought it as a substitute for a car. It was not based on a traditional pickup truck underbody, but it was not based on a car chassis either, so this distinction can be overlooked.

Three years later, in late 1986, AMC introduced the more luxurious but technologically similar Cherokee Limited. Painted black with gold-colored trim on the outside, it had a much more powerful 4-liter engine that was an immediate hit because of the steep fall in gasoline prices. With the Limited, Cherokee sales zoomed even higher. The term "sport utility vehicle" began to be used in the national press for the first time. Workers in Toledo labored around the clock and still could not build enough of them.

But it was the 1984 Cherokee that really started the SUV boom, because it spawned some very important imitators. Its innovative appearance and growing sales through 1984 and 1985, combined with the success of the Chrysler minivans, finally forced the insular world of top auto executives to take a long look at SUVs and start seeing them as possible replacements for cars. Showing the herd-like mentality for which Detroit is famous, Ford and GM both responded to the Cherokee's early success by laying plans to build huge numbers of midsized, family-oriented SUVs. In 1987, Chrysler bought American Motors for $1.5 billion, largely because of the success of the Jeep division. Lee Iacocca, now the chairman of Chrysler, valued Jeep much more highly as an established consumer brand than he had two decades earlier, when he was still at Ford and Jeeps were still for a few outdoorsmen.

Sales of models now classified as SUVs rose to 6.49 percent of the American automobile market in 1989 from 1.79 percent in 1980. The most stunning growth occurred as families began buying midsize SUVs, which tended to be models like the Jeep Cherokee that had four doors and two rows of seats, like a midsize car. Sales of midsize SUVs soared more than thirtyfold in the 1980s, from just one-tenth of 1 percent of the auto market in 1980 to 3.55 percent in 1989.[8] At the same time, larger, full-size models like the Chevrolet Suburban were still being sold to funeral homes and other businesses, while small models like the Jeep Wrangler and Suzuki Samurai were still being purchased by adventurous young people.

This new market segment drew virtually no criticism from environmentalists, even though the gas mileage of midsize SUVs was worse than even the largest cars. Indeed, the off-road capabilities of SUVs meant that they were marketed heavily at first to baby boomers who thought they might someday want to explore the great outdoors. Baby boomers had propelled the environmental movement in the 1970s, condemning their parents' large cars as gas-guzzlers. But they were already beginning to embrace SUVs that were even worse for the environment.

Castaing and many other auto executives attribute the rise of SUVs to the federal government's insistence on preserving strict gas-mileage standards for cars while not raising gasoline taxes. The combination of cheap gasoline and stringent curbs on gasoline consumption by cars forced automakers to transform the family vehicle of choice from a car into an SUV, they contend, with considerable accuracy. "We could not sell big cars, so we turned it into a truck," Castaing said. "The culprits are not frankly the trucks themselves—they are the American customers who don't want to drive small cars with four-cylinder engines."

Like many auto executives, Castaing also defends the shift to SUVs as showing that Detroit became more responsive to its customers, after being heavily criticized in the early 1980s for ignoring them. "All the media were banging on the Big Three, saying that you don't produce what the country wants," he said. "We never had a Machiavellian plan, but we offered something people wanted to buy."

CREATING THE FORD EXPLORER

Bob Lutz was slightly bored, sitting at a folding table at the edge of the Detroit auto show and enduring his umpteenth media interview while waiting for an aide to deliver a cup of coffee. When the coffee arrived, Lutz dug a big Swiss Army knife out of his pocket, carefully opened the largest blade and dipped it in the cup, stirring the coffee a few times. Then he removed the knife and licked the length of the sharp blade once down each side. He folded the knife and put it back in his pocket.

No blood dribbled from his mouth, so he had not cut himself. It was vintage Lutz, emblematic of an executive who defined machismo even in a very macho industry.

Lutz cultivates an image as a car guy, someone who loves to drive fast cars and pore over their engines. He is a powerfully built man with a square jaw and hair that, although white now, he still keeps almost as closely cropped as when he was a pilot in the Marines in the early 1960s. Everyone in Detroit has a Lutz story, like the time a top auto-parts executive, a burly man who had played linebacker on a full football scholarship in college, became so angry that he threatened Lutz during a confrontation in Lutz's office.

"He said, 'I'll whip your ass, I'll take you out,'" Lutz recalls. "I told him that I had been in the Marines for nine years and been a combat infantryman, and I'd been trained in hand-to-hand combat. I told him I only knew one way to fight, and that's to kill.

"Like most bullies, he couldn't take that. His eyes just went wide and he got quiet."

Lutz bought his own Soviet-era military trainer jet, an L-39 Albatross from the former Czechoslovakia, and still flies it on weekends at an airfield near his house. His aides love to talk about the time when a local pilot of a light plane panicked and was unable to land; Lutz, who happened to be flying nearby, talked him down to a safe landing. He and his aides are much less forthcoming about an incident in which Lutz touched down with his landing gear still up, so that his jet slid in a shower of sparks down the runway. The aircraft left behind a residue of slightly radioactive hydraulic fluid that had to be cleaned up at considerable expense, but Lutz was unhurt.

Lutz's penchant for taking risks often made fellow executives nervous. Auto companies ban their executives from racing cars and motorcycles for safety reasons, but Lutz did both. He sneaked into a race in southern France under the pseudonym "Big One," which the announcer pronounced with an Italian accent, "Bi-GO-nay," and Lutz was soon nicknamed Umberto Bigone.[1]

He used to fly his own 1986 model Robinson R-22 helicopter, sometimes taking it for the short hop from his 10-acre wooded estate near Ann Arbor, Michigan, to the local airfield. On one such trip, the engine suddenly went silent at an altitude of 50 feet during the final approach to the runway. The official version afterwards was that the carburetor froze; the unofficial version was that it froze because the engine was not fully warmed up. Whatever the reason, the helicopter plummeted to the pavement below, taking several high bounces and shattering into many pieces. Incredibly,

Lutz walked away from the knee-high wreckage with nothing more than a cut on his hand that required five stitches to close.[2]

But for all his tough-guy image, Lutz is actually a cosmopolitan man of sophisticated tastes. It is hard not to wonder at times if he overemphasizes the machismo to avoid being viewed as too urbane for the auto industry. Overseeing the development of a new Pontiac car after recently becoming vice chairman of GM, Lutz initially wanted to name it the Antibes, after a favorite resort town on the French Riviera. Marketers at Pontiac, a brand catering to young, often blue-collar families, persuaded him that it should be the Pontiac Solstice instead.

Born in Zurich, Switzerland, on February 12, 1932, Lutz was the eldest son of a wealthy Swiss investment banker. His father and wealthy uncle collected Aston Martins and other very expensive sports cars, and he adored them. He claims that at the age of three, he could identify anything on the road by make and year. "I was a tiny idiot savant, saying '1929 Ford Model A,'" he recalled.[3]

Growing up, Lutz bounced back and forth between prep schools in Switzerland and the suburbs of New York City as his family kept switching sides of the Atlantic. He came to speak fluent German and French as well as English. But he also kept being held back a grade each time the family moved from the United States back to Switzerland, where the schools were more demanding. When his family finally settled down in Zurich after World War II, he was more interested in girls than books. Citing "my misspent youth in Europe," Lutz once told me that sex in the back seat of cars was overrated: the front seat was better for that purpose. "You can get that front passenger seat all the way flat," he said, adding that "if there's a chance of discovery, at least you're in the front seat."

As he later recalled in *Guts*, his book of management tips, Lutz ended up being thrown out of high school for showing too little interest in academic pursuits and too much interest in the daughter of the city's biggest industrialist.[4] After six months of manual labor in a leather warehouse, he went to a public high school in Lausanne, Switzerland, and finally graduated at 22. At his father's insistence, he then entered the United States Marines and became a fighter pilot. He reached the rank of captain, although he was never in combat because he completed his training near the end of the Korean War.

Switching to the Marine Reserves, he earned both a bachelor's degree in production science and a master's degree in business administration at the University of California at Berkeley in just five years, graduating in 1962. He returned to Europe and soared through the management ranks of General Motors and BMW. He has spent the last quarter of a century as one of the top executives at Ford, Chrysler and finally back at GM. He is the only executive in recent years to play such a prominent role at all three Detroit automakers. He has succeeded in almost every job because he is an extremely gifted marketer who understands consumers from all walks of life.

Lutz began to put his stamp on the SUV market as a top executive at Ford in the mid-1980s. It was then that he played a little-known but central role in launching what became the best-selling family vehicle of the 1990s, the Ford Explorer. The Explorer would become the foundation of Ford's profits for the next decade, and the start of an evolution of ever-larger SUVs that continued through the Ford Expedition in 1996 and the immense Ford Excursion in 1999. Yet Lutz's creation of the Explorer was something of an historical accident, the result of one of the few setbacks in his glittering career.

As president and then chairman of Ford of Europe in the late 1970s and early 1980s, he had produced enough profits to keep the automaker from being bankrupted by its losses in the American market. He was brought home to Ford's headquarters in Dearborn and made executive vice president for international operations. He also became a member of the Ford board, a rare privilege for an executive vice president, and reserved for stars being groomed to become chief executive and run the entire company.

Board membership gave him tremendous clout with rival executives. The Ford board plays a more active role in overseeing the company than many boards. The Ford family, which still controls 41 percent of the company's voting stock, uses its three seats on the board to guide the company and make the final call on big investments and other decisions. As a board member, Lutz had a seat at the table for these decisions.

But having come so close to reaching the pinnacle of Ford, Lutz faltered. GM had begun investing more in its European operations, and began reaping sales and profits there at Ford's expense. Lutz moved back to Europe in 1984 but was unable to fix the problem quickly. A rival executive, Donald E. Petersen, was named chief executive instead in 1985. Lutz lost his responsibility for international operations at the beginning of 1986 and was banished to the humiliating assignment of overseeing Ford's light-truck operations.

In early 1986, cars were still king and light trucks, mostly pickups, were an afterthought. The light-truck executives at Ford constantly had to borrow engineers from the car divisions because they did not have enough of their own. They routinely reused in pickup trucks a wide range of heaters, radios and other parts originally designed for cars. Thomas J. Feaheny recalls that when he retired as Ford's vice president for car engineering in 1983, he had 12,000 engineers working for him; there were only 400 light-truck engineers then. The light-truck division of Ford was a cliquish place that still saw its market as the same farmers, ranchers, small businessmen and outdoorsmen who had been buying the division's vehicles since before World War II.

This was a grimy, gritty assignment for an executive who had been the toast of the auto shows in Paris, Geneva and Frankfurt during his years in Europe. But Ford's board took pity on Lutz, one of its most colorful and engaging members. Despite his reduced portfolio, he was allowed to keep his title of executive vice president, and he was even allowed to remain on the Ford board. No light-truck executive had ever been exalted enough to sit on the

Ford board before, nor has any done so since. Lutz was a managerial superstar, a master of consumer marketing, who had been
stuck in a tiny corporate backwater. But he had the clout to expand
his little fiefdom, and he set out to do so.

While running Ford's international operations, Lutz noticed with
alarm the early success of the Jeep Cherokee in the United States.
With four doors and a plush interior, it had gained sales at the
expense of the spartan, two-door Ford Bronco II. Built for hunters
and fishermen who wanted something that could get muddy, it was
no match for the plush Cherokee in the family market.

At the start of 1986, the Cherokee problem suddenly became
Lutz's responsibility. He decided that his division needed to start
pursuing family buyers by replacing the Bronco II with a four-door
sport utility vehicle, and quickly. As it turned out, this was not a
new idea. Edsel Ford 2d, the son of Henry Ford 2d,[5] had repeatedly
urged the company in the 1970s to build a four-door SUV. Edsel
had been driving around the wealthy Grosse Pointe suburb of
Detroit in those days with his wife in a four-door Range Rover
imported specially from Britain. But finance executives at Ford had
rejected Edsel's advice, contending that there were not enough
buyers for a four-door SUV to offset the costs of adding two more
doors to the two-door Bronco II.

Three things had changed by the time Lutz revived the idea.
First, the Cherokee had shown that there was a large, untapped
market for four-door SUVs among baby boomers, whom every
automaker coveted because they were moving into their prime
buying years.

Second, the decade-long doubling of cars' gas mileage that Congress had dictated in 1975 had driven the federal fuel-economy
standard for cars all the way up to 27.5 miles per gallon. This made
it extremely difficult for automakers to keep building large cars,
including station wagons, for families. But the required gas mileage
for light trucks was stuck down at 20.5 miles per gallon.

Finally, the safety regulations of the 1970s had largely missed the

SUV market. Turning a two-door coupe into a four-door sedan had become a very expensive proposition, requiring the design of additional door beams for the rear doors and many other details. Turning a two-door SUV into a four-door SUV did not require meeting the same stringent regulations, reducing the design costs considerably.

"If you could save 30 percent off the cost by not meeting the safety standards, it could make a project a whole lot more attractive," said William Chapin, the former Jeep executive.

The economics of producing a four-door SUV at Ford had become too compelling for Lutz to ignore. Right after taking over the truck operations, he summoned one of Ford's best and brightest young engineers, a 31-year-old named Stephen Ross. Lutz made Ross the chief product planner for the new vehicle, the very first person assigned to the project that would produce the Explorer.

Ross is a man of average height, average build and dark hair, the kind of man who could disappear in a crowd were it not for his eyes. You could talk to him for a minute or an hour and he would maintain excellent eye contact, never missing a word.

Lutz's selection of Ross also conferred a special visibility on the Explorer project within Ford. Ross was the son of Louis R. Ross, another of Ford's five executive vice presidents. Lou Ross was the head of all of Ford's North American automotive operations. Like Lutz, he was a member of the Ford board. Lou Ross was riding high within Ford in 1986, having just overseen the wildly successful introduction of the first Ford Taurus sedan, which had revolutionized the midsized car market with its aerodynamic, teardrop-shaped look.

Most auto engineers are obsessed with how vehicles work and how they are assembled. Stephen Ross shared Lutz's genius for the marketing of a vehicle as well as the engineering. Stephen Ross understood as well as anyone that selling an automobile was not just about building a reliable machine, but about designing something that struck an emotional chord in buyers.

Yet when Lutz called in Ross and gave him his assignment, it was anything but certain that Ford's top management would approve mass production of the Explorer. Ford had nearly gone bankrupt during the back-to-back recessions from late 1979 to 1982, and Petersen and his executive vice presidents were still wary of investing a lot of money in the design and engineering of new models. It didn't help that Stephen Ross was trying to design a light truck, entering a market for four-door SUVs that, in the eyes of Ford's car executives, remained unproven.

"It was easier to get money for the car business than for the truck business—it was where the volume was, it wasn't as risky, you didn't need a whole lot of faith," he recalled. So Ross set out to design a vehicle too profitable for the board to resist.

Ross gathered some other young engineers for his project in early 1986. They started by trying to take the cultural pulse of the time, paying special attention to the evolving values of the baby boomer generation. They watched some of the most popular movies at the time: *Rambo First Blood Part II, Rocky IV* and *Top Gun*. They clipped photographs from magazines and arranged them into a series of large collages, each for a different period of a few years, and were struck by how many people were wearing cowboy hats and other Western attire in their collage of contemporary photos. They took note of the wide media attention give to the two Jeeps that Reagan kept at his ranch near Santa Barbara, California.

Several themes emerged from all this work. Station wagons were clearly going out of style. Young baby boomers wanted to express their individuality with a new kind of vehicle. And Americans of all ages wanted to feel a bond with the great outdoors and the American frontier.

Ross and his young team were baby boomers themselves and had grown up driving their parents' station wagons. Ross himself had particularly unpleasant memories of driving his parents' big County Squire station wagon when he was a teenager. "It wasn't impressing the girls," he recalled.

Chrysler had introduced the first modern minivans in late 1983,

and the success had been even greater than AMC's with the introduction of the Jeep Cherokee at the same time. But minivans had
become quickly stereotyped as "mom-mobiles" that older children
would not want to be caught dead in, and that formerly rebellious
boomers saw as an acknowledgment of domestic responsibilities.
Ross and his colleagues interviewed owners of Cherokees and
other off-road vehicles and found that they would not even consider a minivan.

"An SUV buyer is almost anti-minivan—this is a buyer who has
a family but doesn't want to broadcast a docile family message,"
Stephen Ross said.

Since the Explorer was going to be marketed mostly to urban
families, Ford had to decide whether the vehicle really needed
four-wheel drive. The company's surveys showed that buyers
rarely used the capability yet absolutely wanted it. Buyers said
they thought they would be more safe and secure with four-wheel
drive.

Especially interesting to Ford researchers was that buyers liked
four-wheel drive because it offered the promise of unfettered free-
dom to drive anywhere during vacations. These customers might
have given up their childhood dreams of becoming firefighters,
police officers or superheroes, and had instead become parents
with desk jobs and oversized mortgages. But they told Ford
researchers that SUVs made them feel like they were still carefree,
adventurous spirits who could drop everything and head for the
great outdoors at a moment's notice if they really wanted to do so.

These buyers knew that most people going to national parks
and other wilderness areas had no need for four-wheel drive, and
that park rangers discouraged off-road driving in most places anyway. The buyers knew perfectly well that they probably had only
two or three weeks of vacation a year, and would spend all but a
week of it visiting relatives. None of that mattered to buyers, Ross
said. What counted was the fantasy of what they might want to do
during a vacation, and the ability to show their friends and other

motorists that they really were the bold people that they still liked to see themselves as.

"That one week of the year, which may be a small percentage of the year, is the most important week of the year," Ross said. Buying an SUV, he added, "is all about recreation, and they may only use it a day or a week but it's what they're all about as a person."

Customers wanted four-wheel drive even though it meant that the vehicle would be less comfortable and less practical for everyday use. When an SUV goes off-road, the wheels tend to bounce up and down a lot. So an SUV has tall, wide wheel wells, which cut into the usable space inside the vehicle. For off-road driving, the underbody of an SUV also has to be high enough not to scrape on boulders that the driver may straddle. This means that the floor of the passenger compartment has to be quite high, which makes it harder to climb in or out of an SUV than a minivan, and further reduces the usable space available inside.

"They're not as functional as a minivan—they have a higher floor, they're not as wide," Ross said. Yet customers were happy to make these sacrifices to have four-wheel drive, Ford found.

Ross and his colleagues analyzed their prospects before Ford's top management and decided that one of the biggest threats to the Explorer project was internal. Senior management was only likely to approve one risky new project in 1986. The top car executives at Ford did not want to spend a lot of money on a sport utility vehicle—they wanted to build a luxury sports car that would compete with the Chevrolet Corvette and add luster to the Ford brand, although not a lot of sales.

But the sports car project had a vulnerability: It would not be cheap. The car executives could not simply reuse parts from other cars, but would have to design them from scratch at considerable cost. Worst of all, Ford did not have engines or transmissions that were suitable for such a high-performance vehicle. Ford would have to buy them from another company, probably one of the European luxury car makers.

Stephen Ross began drafting a business case for why the Explorer would cost less money to design than the sports car while producing considerably greater profit. The first step was figuring out how many Explorers could be sold each year. Ford had sold 97,000 two-door Bronco IIs in 1985 and would stop selling the Bronco II when the Explorer was rolled out. Ross said he and his colleagues thought they were being optimistic in forecasting that they could sell 160,000 two-door and four-door Explorers a year, and at only slightly higher prices than the Bronco II had commanded.

Part of the 60,000-plus increase in vehicles beyond the Bronco's sales would inevitably come at the expense of other Ford models, like the Taurus sedan and the Ranger small pickup truck, as people entering Ford dealerships would choose Explorers instead. This loss of sales from other models cut further into the projected profit.

With this cautious forecast in hand, Ross's team began figuring out the cheapest possible way to design an Explorer so as to show the board that it would be profitable. They scrambled to find ways to reuse parts that other Ford engineers had already designed. While Lunn and Castaing had been able to design the Cherokee from the ground up as a sport utility vehicle, Ross and his colleagues took the existing underbody of the two-door Ranger pickup truck and Bronco II and made some modifications. They made the passenger compartment a little longer than the Bronco II's, and added two extra doors. They saved even more money because the Explorer could be built on the same assembly line in Louisville, Kentucky, as the Ranger, using mostly the same robots and other equipment. The whole project would cost several hundred million dollars, a pittance by auto-industry standards.

"It always makes business sense to reuse from your parts bin as much as you can—all successful companies do that, business schools teach that," Ross said. Reusing parts can improve quality and reliability, too, because the same parts that worked without cracking, bending or otherwise failing on a previous model are unlikely to prove defective on a new model.

With considerable apprehension, Stephen Ross and his colleagues waited in the late spring of 1986 for the outcome of senior management's review. When the verdict came, they were elated. The company's leadership had told them to proceed with the Explorer, and to put it on sale in early 1990, a quick timetable by Detroit standards then. The luxury sports car would never be built.

Right after the Explorer program was approved, Lutz left Ford to become an executive vice president and board member at Chrysler, with responsibility for both international operations and truck operations. Ford took this desertion the way Detroit automakers always do: It pretended he never existed. When the Explorer was introduced, Lutz received no credit. But a few Ford officials still remember and confirm Lutz's role, including Ross, who has risen through the ranks at Ford and now oversees the development of all new vehicles at its Land Rover subsidiary in Britain.

"He paved the way, got the funding secured," Ross said.

The Explorer and the Chevrolet Blazer both came on the market in the spring of 1990, and both were instant hits. Affluent baby boomers, the kinds of people who were increasingly passing up Detroit's offerings in favor of Honda Accords and Toyota Camrys, flocked to Ford and Chevrolet dealerships. The Louisville factory worked day and night to manufacture Explorers and still could not keep up with demand. Sales did not suffer even after Iraq invaded Kuwait on August 2, 1990, sending oil prices briefly above $40 a barrel and pushing the United States economy into a short recession.

Practically every other automaker ended up taking the same approach as Ford as they raced to redesign pickup trucks in response to the success of the Cherokee, Explorer, and Blazer. They also began looking at the possibilities for even bigger models. Automakers have long taken the approach that if a model is successful, something a little bigger will be even more successful, and even more profitable. This is how the Ford Thunderbird and Mercury Cougar cars went from being svelte coupes in the 1960s to soft-riding large cars with love handles by 1997, when Ford stopped making both cars in order to put them on a radical diet and completely redesign them.

SUVs have had even worse weight-gain problems than many cars. Midsize SUVs began getting heavier and larger, bulging with leather seats, sound insulation and other amenities. Even more important, automakers began looking for ways to up the ante by building full-size SUVs on the underbodies of full-size pickup trucks.

But a big potential obstacle still stood in their way as the Explorer went on the market in 1990: government investigations and regulations, particularly involving the Explorer's predecessor, the Bronco II.

As SUVs became increasingly popular during the 1980s, safety advocates and their allies, personal-injury lawyers, called attention to a disquieting fact: Occupants of early SUVs had an appalling death rate because their vehicles were flipping over with alarming frequency. The Insurance Institute for Highway Safety calculated that in 1980, the driver death rate in all crashes per million SUVs (mostly Jeeps then) was almost exactly double the car death rate in crashes. The huge discrepancy partly reflected differences in who drove cars and SUVs. Sport utilities were still being driven mostly by adventurous young men, a category of people who had a lot of crashes no matter what they drove. But while SUV occupants died in frontal, side and rear impacts much like car occupants, they also died in large numbers in rollovers, a kind of crash that was much less of a problem for car occupants.

Through the 1970s, small Jeeps in particular had acquired a reputation for flipping over and they became the subject of many lawsuits against American Motors. Working with personal-injury lawyers, CBS's "60 Minutes" broadcast an award-winning documentary in 1980 showing that Jeeps could roll over even on a dry, open road if the steering wheel were jerked around hard. A motorist might make such a maneuver to avoid an unexpected hazard, like a child rolling into the street on a tricycle.

Hastily cobbled together SUVs like the S-10 Blazer and especially the Bronco II, which had been bolted on the underbodies of pickups that had also been hastily designed, developed lethal rollover records through the 1980s that were nearly as bad as those of the early Jeeps. The automakers blamed the problem on the reckless drivers attracted to tall, two-door models. But insurers, with their money on the line and statistical evidence that the same young men did not flip other models as often, were not convinced, nor were the personal-injury lawyers. Insurers, lawyers and non-profit safety groups in Washington all pushed in 1986 for NHTSA to issue minimum vehicle stability standards.

The agency studied the issue in great detail. A statistical analysis by the agency's staff showed that SUVs were rolling over much more often than cars. The analysis also showed that the higher a vehicle's center of gravity, the more likely it was to roll over unless it was especially wide to compensate. A simple, common-sense formula, first proposed by researchers working for personal-injury lawyers but later confirmed by government statisticians, fit the data very well: Divide the distance from side to side between the wheels by twice the height of a vehicle's center of gravity. In plain English, this meant that the wider the vehicle, the more stable it would be—while making a vehicle taller was absolute poison for its stability.

The problem came in turning this strong statistical correlation into an actual rule that could be used to ban some models as unstable and allow others. Most models fit the pattern, but a few did not. Chevrolet Corvettes had very low centers of gravity and were fairly wide, but had very high rates of rollover deaths because they were driven by reckless young men. What NHTSA wanted was some way to test each new model by driving it through a set pattern of turns on a road, and then bar the sale of any model that tipped over while running this route.

NHTSA engineers tried to come up with such a test but failed, for several reasons. The biggest problem was that test drivers were unable to swing the steering wheel back and forth with precisely the same timing and force each time; even subtle, unintentional variations by the driver could make a big difference in the test's outcome. Automakers also sold the same model with slight differences in the suspension depending on how many heavy options it carried, like air conditioning, and those slight suspension differences had unpredictable effects on whether a vehicle rolled over during a test. Automakers also certified several different tires for each model, and vehicles performed differently in rollover tests depending on which tires were used, again with no clear pattern that would suggest ways to improve tire design. NHTSA looked at the difficulties of coming up with rollover evaluations for every combination of tires and suspensions on every model and was overwhelmed.

"You could never get repeatability" in the tests, said Kennerly Digges, the NHTSA researcher who was the chairman of the NHTSA-industry rollover committee in the 1980s that tried to address the problem, and who has since become an outspoken critic of SUVs.

In the absence of a reliable test, however, NHTSA decided to do absolutely nothing. It ignored the statistical evidence that vehicles with higher centers of gravity were less stable and left vehicle stability completely unregulated. It was a sharp defeat for the safety advocates and a huge victory for the auto industry, heading off what could have been a major roadblock to the expansion of SUV sales.

Regulatory standards are NHTSA's strongest weapon in requiring safer vehicles, but they are not the agency's only weapon. The agency also has an Office of Defect Investigations that can examine the performance of specific models and, if unacceptable, demand that the vehicles be recalled and fixed. But through most of the 1980s, that office showed little interest in rollovers.

At Ford, the design of the Explorer went smoothly through the late 1980s. But just eight months before its scheduled introduction, a serious threat emerged. *Consumer Reports* conducted a series of rollover tests on the Bronco II and warned its readers in the summer of 1989 that the SUV could be dangerously unstable in certain situations. Safety groups, trial lawyers and insurers persuaded NHTSA to open a formal investigation into whether the Bronco II was so unstable that it should be considered a defective vehicle and recalled. Trial lawyers provided the safety agency with extensive Ford documents showing that the company had been wrestling with how to improve the Bronco II's stability.

Ford engineers disliked the *Consumer Reports* test because its results were not always repeatable, and contended that the investigation was unnecessary. But since the Explorer had much the same design as the Bronco II, there was a clear risk that the new model would be tarred by the influential magazine or a government investigation as well. The result was a hurried effort to improve the Explorer's stability.

Internal memos later obtained by lawyers suing Ford show that the engineers considered three options. They could redesign the suspension to use shorter suspension springs, which would lower the front end by half an inch and the back by an inch. They could recommend a fairly low tire pressure, which would give the Explorer a more stable ride (except when a tire failed), as well as the softer, less bouncy ride favored by people accustomed to cars. Or they could redesign much of the vehicle's underbody to mount the wheels two inches farther apart.

They chose the first two options, but hesitated on the third. Mounting the wheels farther apart would help but still would not solve the problem of rollovers. Based on the government's analyses of how weight and height affected vehicle stability, the widening would have reduced the frequency of rollovers by perhaps 2 or 3 percent. The bigger problem was the Explorer's height, which could not really be addressed without turning it into a lower-riding car.

Mounting the wheels farther apart would also have meant practically scrapping the Ranger underbody and coming up with another underbody, which would probably not fit on the same assembly line as the Ranger—a slow and exorbitantly expensive process. When prototypes passed Ford's stability tests with only the first two changes, Ford engineers decided not to widen the space between the wheels. "Utilize as many of the chassis revisions as possible without delaying Job 1," said a Ford memorandum, using industry jargon for beginning mass production of a new model.

As Ford design engineers raced to improve the Explorer, NHTSA was facing a dilemma on what to do about the Bronco II. The work by Consumer Reports, together with pressure from trial lawyers, had forced NHTSA to conduct an investigation. But very little can be done to improve a vehicle's stability once it has been built. So a recall would have likely amounted to requiring Ford to pull every Bronco II off the road and scrapping them—a costly proposition.

In August 1990, NHTSA made a controversial decision in its investigation of the Bronco II's stability. The Bronco II was not as stable as a car but it was not much worse than many other SUVs, the agency declared. Federal law explicitly bars the agency from setting any rule that would ban an entire class of vehicles. The agency concluded that it would be hard to ban the Bronco II without ordering all SUVs off the road, so the agency closed its investigation without a formal ruling that the Bronco II was safe or unsafe. When some of the agency's officials subsequently left NHTSA, Ford retained them as expert witnesses and used them to defeat Bronco II rollover cases around the country.

A clique of trial lawyers specializing in rollovers had invested millions of dollars of their own money in preparing the cases in hopes of winning a percentage of any verdicts or settlements, and they were livid. They took their huge libraries of internal Ford documents on the Bronco II and began studying the new Explorer for cases. Some reached an unfortunate conclusion from the debacle: Alerting the government to safety problems was not in their best interests or the interests of their clients, because an investigation would prove to be a whitewash that would not produce a recall but would halt litigation.

As the 1990s began, the other threat to SUVs involved gas-mileage regulations. The window stickers on the first Explorers showed that they got 15 miles to the gallon in the city and 20 on the highway for models equipped with an automatic transmission and four-wheel drive, which were most of the Explorers. Later models would get even worse mileage, after Ford started offering V-8 engines in addition to V-6 engines.

Complying with fuel-economy laws was not easy for automakers building SUVs even with the standard at 20.5 miles per gallon for light trucks. But in 1990, Congress was considering big increases in car and light-truck standards alike. Before SUVs could become even bigger and even more numerous, the auto industry would have to win some pitched battles in Washington.

4

PAVING THE ROAD
TO EVER BIGGER SUVS

Most lawmakers know better than to lead a charge against the auto industry. This is not because of political contributions, the bête noire of government reformers in recent years. The auto industry gives money of course, and in recent elections has donated three times as much to Republicans, who tend to favor deregulation in principle, as to Democrats. But other industries give far more, with pharmaceutical companies, commercial banks and oil companies each giving 8 to 15 times as much money in recent presidential election years as automakers.[1]

The real secret to the auto industry's political power lies instead in its vast and well-organized workforce. Representing 800,000 members and 1.7 million retirees and spouses, the UAW is one of the nation's largest unions, and easily the wealthiest, with nearly $1 billion in its strike fund. The bulk of these UAW workers and retirees and their families live in a region of unusual political influ-ence, the Upper Midwest, especially Michigan and Ohio—battle-grounds in every presidential election for the last four decades. The interests of the Upper Midwest receive more attention in national races, for example, than the interests of the Northeast, which Democratic candidates can usually take for granted, or the Plains states, which Republican candidates can usually count on. Because auto factories are also sprinkled across the rest of the Midwest and the South, the UAW has broader influence as well.

The UAW is the 800-pound gorilla when political disputes involve the auto industry. It is a sleepy gorilla that only throws its weight around when genuinely alarmed. The union has suffered a few defeats, notably when it failed to block Congressional approval of the North American Free Trade Agreement in 1993. But the union can defeat practically any legislation specific to the auto industry if it decides to do so.

Environmental issues in the auto industry tend to be especially difficult for union leaders, who rub shoulders with environmental activists as part of various liberal coalitions but must also look out for their workers' interests. The hardest issue of all for the union involves fuel economy. Higher gas-mileage standards for cars contributed to the loss of thousands of jobs in the early 1980s. Today gas-mileage standards for light trucks are the most sensitive political issue for the union, because light trucks are much more likely to be built by union members than cars. The Johnson Administration tariff in the chicken trade war severely limited foreign automakers' role in the American light-truck market for decades, making SUVs an almost exclusive product of Detroit's Big Three until the late 1990s, even as foreign automakers without UAW labor contracts came to dominate the domestic car market.

Gas-mileage standards faded somewhat as an issue in the 1980s. The car standard had stalled at 27.5 miles per gallon, a level reached in the 1985 model year, while the light-truck standard had hit 20.5 m.p.g. in the 1987 model year and also stopped rising. The Reagan Administration had even granted waivers to the auto industry, lowering the standards by 1 or 2 m.p.g. for a year or two at a time.

Senator Richard Bryan, a Democrat representing Nevada,

started to pursue the issue energetically in 1989. Nevada was one of the very few states in the country with no auto-assembly plants and virtually no auto-parts factories. His constituents drove huge distances in the sparsely populated state and sometimes complained about the poor gas mileage of their cars. He was concerned about the nation's reliance on imported oil. He and Al Gore, then a Democratic senator from Tennessee, were also concerned about global warming, which many scientists had begun to link to the burning of fossil fuels. Bryan started drafting a bill in 1989 to require higher corporate average fuel economy (known by the acronym CAFE, which has nothing to do with coffee) for each automaker's sales of new cars and new light trucks.

Dick Warden, the top lobbyist in Washington for the UAW, and Robert Liberatore, a former staff director of the Democratic Policy Committee who had become Chrysler's chief lobbyist, met with Bryan repeatedly. Warden and Liberatore had two concerns: keep any increase small and gradual and change the way it would be calculated.

An increase of several miles per gallon in either standard would have little effect on Japanese automakers because they dominated the small-car market and sold very few light trucks. Honda and Toyota each sold cars with an average gas mileage of 30.8 miles per gallon in the 1990 model year, meeting the car standard with 3.3 m.p.g. to spare.[2] Toyota sold only a few light trucks and Honda sold none. But an increase in the car or light-truck standards would be a huge burden on Detroit automakers, which barely met either the car or light-truck standards.

So Warden and Liberatore proposed that Bryan call for requiring each automaker to raise its existing gas mileage by a small, fixed percentage. (Liberatore recalls suggesting an increase of 10 or 15 percent; Warden and Bryan do not recall discussions of specific numbers.) New engine technologies and advances in the use of lightweight aluminum and high-strength steel alloys had made it possible for automakers to improve gas mileage without simply shrinking the cars. Choosing a percentage increase would force Japanese automakers to improve fuel economy too. The task would actually be slightly harder for the Japanese automakers than for Detroit. Toyota, Honda and Nissan already made a lot of small cars, and in some cases they used slightly more sophisticated engines too. So some of the easy gains had already been made.

Bryan took the two men's advice and went for a percentage increase. But he chose a very large increase: a 40 percent increase over 10 years in each automaker's average car mileage and each automaker's average light-truck mileage. That would have put the car standard at 38.5 miles per gallon and the light-truck standard at 28.7 miles per gallon for Ford and GM, which were barely meeting the government regulations. (Chrysler was slightly higher.) For Toyota and Honda, increasing the mileage of their already fuel-efficient fleets would have translated into a new car standard of 43 miles per gallon.

Environmentalists were delighted, saying that automakers could meet the target by making their vehicles smaller and less powerful. Gore, a rising star in the Democratic Party, strongly backed the bill. Japanese automakers were furious, however, and so were the Big Three in Detroit and the UAW.

The Bryan bill faced fairly long odds against passage in the Senate, even longer odds in the House and the likelihood of a Presidential veto. But the automakers nonetheless set out to defeat the bill and discredit Bryan, while the UAW watched and waited to see if it would have to weigh in.

The Japanese automakers relied on their extensive Washington network, dozens of influential former lawmakers and other federal officials who had joined the lobbying firms of K Street. The Big Three used the clumsier, more ham-handed approach of trying to set up what looked like grassroots groups to oppose higher mileage standards.

Led by GM, the Detroit automakers hired two Washington lobbying firms, FMR and Bonner and Associates. FMR set up a group called Nevadans for Fair Fuel Economy Standards, complete with a Las Vegas address. The firm contacted taxicab owners, outdoorsmen and vendors of outdoor recreation equipment in Nevada and persuaded them to join the group by telling them that higher mileage standards would hurt the cost, affordability and availability of automobiles, including four-wheel-drive vehicles. The group created a letterhead with a list of these citizens and their affiliations and began writing to large numbers of Nevadans, asking them to write short letters to their senators or simply to sign an enclosed sample letter and send it. Bryan began receiving the mail in February 1990, warning him against support for higher mileage standards.

Bryan had never heard of the group, however, so he grew suspicious and called a few people on the letterhead whom he knew. He learned the auto industry was behind the effort, and talked a few of his friends out of supporting it. He obtained copies of the group's mailings, some of which turned out to have used FMR's address in Washington. He dismissed the whole effort as not being a serious threat and pressed on with his bill.

The next month brought another assault. Bonner and Associates had been gathering a coalition of groups who needed large vehicles, and had warned them that higher fuel-economy standards could jeopardize the availability of such vehicles. The lobbying firm flew representatives of these groups on two-day trips to Washington, all expenses paid, to appear at a press conference in a Senate office building with Senator Donald W. Riegle of Michigan, a Democrat. An Alabama sheriff wanted a large, fast car for responding to emergencies. A silver-haired Florida state legislator wanted large vans for carrying disabled senior citizens. An Easter Seal Society official wanted big vehicles to carry the handicapped in wheelchairs. A Nebraska farmer, Bryce Neidig, asked, "Can you imagine pulling a livestock trailer or hauling grain and feed with a Honda Civic?"

The press conference drew public attention to a fairly small but appealing segment of society who could make some claim to need big vehicles. This success was an eye-opener for Detroit automakers, which responded by swiftly creating the Coalition for Vehicle Choice. GM's Johnston led a group of auto lobbyists in hiring Diane Steed, the administrator of the National Highway Traffic Safety Administration under President Reagan, to run the new group. Although bankrolled almost entirely by the auto industry, the coalition styled itself as a consumer group. It enlisted as members more than 200 trade associations representing groups like horse trainers, who needed big pickup trucks to pull trailers, and then rallied these groups to oppose any increase in fuel-economy standards. The coalition also began recruiting thousands of nonpaying individual members across the country, sending them newsletters and encouraging them to send letters or postcards to their members of Congress, opposing higher fuel-economy standards.

The momentum of the Bryan bill slowed over the summer. Then Saddam Hussein of Iraq sent his tanks into Kuwait and energy independence became an issue again. The Iraqi invasion produced a chorus of support in Congress for tougher gas-mileage rules as a way to reduce American dependence on imported oil. Despite heavy lobbying by the auto industry, Bryan nearly got the votes to pass the bill. A month after the Iraqi invasion, Bryan prevailed easily, 68 to 28, on a vote to bring the bill up for consideration.

Senator Riegle of Michigan began a desperate attempt to stop the Senate from considering the Bryan bill by filibustering it. To stop the filibuster, Bryan would need 60 votes in the 100-member Senate, eight fewer than he had received in the first vote.

As the Bryan bill gathered momentum through the autumn, the auto industry made a Herculean effort to stop it. The automakers enlisted three important allies: car dealers, the Bush Administration and auto workers.

Car dealers have even more influence on Capitol Hill than automakers. Dealers tend to be pillars of their communities, joining charity boards and donating to Little League teams, all the while networking with potential car buyers. There are dealers in every state and in almost every House district, and they give to political campaigns more generously than the automakers. Large gas-guzzlers were generating the fattest profit margins for dealers because with low gas prices, demand for big vehicles was so strong that they could be sold with little or no discounting. To fight the Bryan bill, car dealers began flocking to Washington to tell their lawmakers in person that the bill would hurt sales of big vehicles.

The Bush Administration was another powerful ally. Despite legal restrictions on lobbying by federal agencies, NHTSA created a voiceover for a crash-test film, warning that tighter fuel-economy rules could lead to more deaths on the road. The film, which showed a large car demolishing a subcompact, was then leaked to the Coalition for Vehicle Choice. The coalition used the film in an extensive and effective advertising campaign that linked higher fuel-economy standards with extra traffic deaths. (Only much later did it emerge that crash dummies in the small car had actually fared surprisingly well; the small car's crumple zones had crumpled as designed, absorbing much of the force of impact instead of transferring it to the small car's passenger compartments.)

The third force brought to bear was the most powerful of all: auto workers and their union, the UAW.

As the days ticked down to the final vote, GM in particular frantically warned that passage of the bill would force the auto industry to dismiss tens of thousands of workers. Automakers gave extra coffee breaks to factory workers so that they could call their lawmakers on company phone lines. Prodded by all this activity, the UAW finally weighed in, with Owen Bieber, the president of the UAW, personally flying from Detroit to Washington to lobby against the bill. On the evening of September 25 when the Senate was to vote on ending the filibuster, Bieber went to the lobby of the Senate's chambers in the Capitol building and, with Jim Johnston of General Motors, buttonholed senators one by one as they went in.

Senior Bush Administration officials also went to the Senate to warn of a likely veto. When the votes were tallied, 11 senators had switched sides and Bryan had 57: a majority, but not the 60 votes needed to end the filibuster. The actual tally was even closer than it looked, because two senators had agreed to vote for the Bryan bill if it had 58 votes without them, so as to make 60. But neither senator was willing to brave the industry's wrath to vote for a bill that would fail. So for lack of a single vote, the bill died.

"It was one of the proudest days of my life, standing there shoulder to shoulder with Owen and lobbying against that CAFE standard and winning," Johnston said. "On that particular vote, we would not have won without the UAW."

If automakers had been forced in 1990 to raise their light-truck CAFE by even 15 percent, as Chrysler's Liberatore says he proposed then, they would have needed to produce light trucks with an average gas mileage of 23.6 miles per gallon by 2000 (that is to say, 15 percent more than the bare minimum of 20.5 miles per gallon in 1990). Reaching that level would have greatly slowed the rise of SUVs, especially the full-size models.

But the fight in the Senate in 1990 proved to be the last serious attempt for many years to raise mileage standards. Senator Bryan reintroduced his bill in 1991. But it was scuppered by the environmentalists, of all people. The environmental movement was fighting to prevent oil companies from drilling in the Arctic National Wildlife Refuge and enlisted automakers to oppose the drilling, in exchange for which the environmental community dropped its support for the Bryan bill.[3]

The next big threat to SUVs could have been the election of Bill Clinton and Al Gore in November 1992. While seeking the Democratic Presidential nomination that spring, Bill Clinton had proposed on Earth Day to "accelerate our progress toward more fuel-efficient cars and seek to raise the average goal for auto makers to 45 miles per gallon."[4] Like the environmental movement at the time, Clinton did not mention light trucks. But his speech was widely interpreted as a call for raising fuel-economy standards across the board, an impression that the Clinton campaign did not discourage. When Clinton won the nomination and chose Al Gore as his running mate, environmentalists were thrilled.

Gore had just published a book, *Earth in the Balance*, that strongly criticized the effect of automobiles on the global environment. Average temperatures around the world had been gradually increasing over the previous 50 years, and most scientists had come to believe that humanity was at least partly responsible for contributing to this "greenhouse effect." The main gas linked to global warming is carbon dioxide. Automobiles of all types emit carbon dioxide in lockstep with the amount of gasoline they burn, so that the biggest gas-guzzlers emit the most carbon dioxide.

Gore called in his book for the elimination of the internal-combustion engine—that is to say, all gasoline and diesel engines. He was especially critical of automobiles, writing that "we now know that their cumulative impact on the global environment is posing a mortal threat to the security of every nation that is more deadly than that of any military enemy we are ever again likely to confront."

The automakers were horrified. Worse, they barely knew Clinton, the governor of Arkansas, a state with no auto-assembly plants. "We did not have much access to Clinton," recalled Peter Pestillo, a top Ford Motor executive at the time.

But auto executives knew some people whom Clinton would have to heed: the UAW's leaders. Bieber and his top political strategist at the time, Yokich, met repeatedly with Clinton's campaign managers through the summer while Bieber spoke to Clinton himself by phone. The showdown finally came on August 21, when Clinton was to address the Detroit Economic Club, a large group that includes the city's most influential business leaders, many of whom happen to be auto executives.

The Bush-Quayle campaign welcomed Clinton to Detroit that morning with half-page attack ads in both the city's daily newspapers, lambasting Clinton's fuel-economy proposal. "If Bill Clinton has his way 40,000 Michigan autoworkers will go from the assembly line to the unemployment line," the ads warned.[5]

Before speaking to the hostile crowd in the convention center, Clinton attended an elegant reception, where he spoke informally with auto executives and with Bieber and John Dingell, the powerful Michigan Democrat who chaired the House Commerce Committee. When Clinton delivered his speech to the assembled crowd, his position on fuel economy had softened. Higher fuel-economy standards might not be possible, he said, until the feasibility of such higher-mileage vehicles had been proven. "I strongly believe we have to raise the mileage standard, but I never said there was only one way to do it," Clinton told the gathering. "We don't want to put American car makers at a disadvantage just because they make larger cars than their competitors."[6]

After taking office, Clinton did create a new research subsidy program, the Partnership for a New Generation of Vehicles, which provided $200 million to $300 million a year in subsidies, mainly to national laboratories and auto-parts companies. The utopian goal of the program was to create by 2000 a prototype of a midsized car that would get 80 miles to the gallon, and to begin mass production of very high mileage cars by 2004.

But while pursuing the partnership, the Clinton Administration did nothing to raise fuel-economy standards, which remained at 27.5 miles per gallon for cars and inched up by a meager two-tenths of a mile per gallon for light trucks, to 20.7 m.p.g., an increase that had already been authorized by the outgoing Bush Administration. After the Republicans took control of the House and Senate following the midterm elections of November 1994, they began writing each year's Transportation Department budget to ban the spending of any money on fuel-economy issues, either to research them or to raise standards, a ban that would be renewed annually for the rest of Clinton's term in office. Instead of rising, the average fuel economy of new vehicles sold during the Clinton Administration actually sank steadily, as automakers switched production away from cars and toward light trucks, especially SUVs.

Auto lobbyists were delighted with the partnership because it effectively paralyzed any action on fuel-economy standards. "A bad law was not made worse for eight years," said Johnston, the longtime GM lobbyist.

The failure to raise fuel-economy standards in the early 1990s had two very important consequences. It gave Detroit automakers a free hand to increase the size of light trucks without regard to fuel economy, furthering a trend that had begun in the late 1980s. And Bryan's attempt to impose percentage increases in fuel-economy standards helped scare Japanese automakers into producing larger models. By pushing their fuel economy down slowly through the 1990s, Japanese automakers, especially Toyota, became less vulnerable if a later Congress decided to adopt the same percentage-increase approach as in the Bryan bill.

While fuel-economy fights received wide attention, several other developments shortly before and after the introduction of the Explorer received less notice but also helped clear the way for SUVs to take over the nation's roads. All of the changes reflected heavy lobbying by the auto industry, at a time when no one else was really paying attention to light trucks. All of them would help clear the way for a boom in full-size, four-door SUVs.

For starters, there was a strenuous struggle over trade policies pitting Detroit against Japanese automakers. During the 1980s, the Japanese government had limited the number of cars that could be shipped to the United States each year under so-called "voluntary restraint agreements." These restraints successfully headed off pressures in the United States to impose even more stringent limits on imports, even though doing so would have violated international trade laws. But the Japanese government did not impose any restraints on exports of light trucks to the United States.

Japanese automakers began shipping small numbers of SUVs and minivans to the United States and classifying them as light trucks. They paid the 25 percent "chicken tax" for them instead of the 2.5 percent tax on imported cars, because if they had classified them as cars, they would not have been able to ship them at all. Companies like Toyota and Nissan had such an enormous cost advantage that they could make money even while paying the steep chicken tax.

But by the late 1980s, Japanese automakers had begun opening car factories in the United States and the value of the yen was climbing swiftly in currency markets, making it more expensive to export vehicles from Japan. Car shipments from Japan dropped, so that automakers were no longer using their full quotas. So the Japanese manufacturers began declaring that their minivans and SUVs were really passenger vehicles rather than cargo vehicles, and demanded that they be included in the car quotas and charged the much lower car-import tax instead. The Customs Service initially refused, but was then overruled after Treasury Department lawyers studied international trade agreements and decided the Japanese automakers were right and that SUVs and minivans should be treated as cars.

This decision had no effect on American fuel-economy and air-pollution laws, which continue classifying SUVs and minivans as light trucks to this day. But Detroit was furious nonetheless, and a bitter lobbying and legal battle over the import taxes followed, lasting until 1993. Chrysler produced a glossy brochure entitled "Is this a truck?" Each page showed a picture of a minivan, and discussed whether it was classified as a car or a light truck. The emissions page said that it was a truck, the fuel-economy page said that it was a truck and so forth, but the Customs page said it was a car. But in the end, a series of court decisions said that SUVs and minivans were cars for import-tax purposes.

Even so, foreign automakers would still be hampered as they tried to enter the American SUV market. While they made small pickups for Asian markets like Thailand, they made very few large pickups. So while they had pickup truck underbodies they could use to build small and midsized SUVs, they did not have the under-bodies available to make full-sized SUVs (with the exception of Toyota, which had a clunky underbody already used for the Land Cruiser). As Japanese automakers stepped up sales of midsize SUVs like the Toyota 4Runner and the Nissan Pathfinder, Detroit had a natural incentive to shift toward bigger models for which there would be no competition.

As it happened, auto-industry lobbyists also opened loopholes in the tax laws that were big enough to drive a truck through. Light trucks were already exempt from the gas-guzzler tax created in 1978. But the instant success of the minivan and the Jeep Cherokee prompted industry lobbyists to start paying special attention for the first time to gaining special breaks for light trucks so that they could be used as substitutes for cars, even luxury cars.

In 1984, Congress cracked down on abusive tax deductions by realtors, sales representatives, consultants and other owners of small businesses and self-employed businesspeople who used their vehicles partly or entirely for business. These businesspeople had been able to deduct the entire purchase price of their vehicles from their taxable income over just three years, reducing their taxes considerably. This rule had given realtors and the like an incentive to buy the biggest, most expensive Cadillac or Lincoln sedan they could find, since in effect they did not have to pay for the whole cost of the car. Inevitably, they drove these luxury cars for personal use as well.

The 1984 depreciation law severely crimped this game. It essentially limited deductions to just $17,500, no matter how expensive the car, and required that the deductions be spread fairly evenly over five years, not three. The law limited the deductions even further for people who acknowledged practically any personal use of the car at all. This crimped luxury car sales, since many customers could no longer afford to buy as expensive a model, nor could they replace their cars as often.

But special treatment was given to light trucks with a gross vehicle weight over 6,000 pounds, a category that encompassed almost anything built on the sturdy underbody of a full-size pickup. Buyers of these light trucks could still write off the entire purchase price, with as much as half of the price being deducted in the first year and the rest spread over four more years. There were few restrictions on personal use, too, so that farmers could drive their pickups to take their kids to school or go to the movies or a restaurant.

Drawing the line at a fully loaded weight of just 6,000 pounds was a clear victory for Detroit. Previous rules had allowed accelerated depreciation only for trucks weighing 13,000 pounds or more when empty, a stipulation that applied only to very large freight trucks. The new special treatment for large light trucks was initially used mainly by buyers of full-size pickup trucks, which remained Detroit's exclusive turf because of the chicken tax. But once Americans became accustomed to the idea of driving midsized SUVs instead of cars, the depreciation rules buried in the tax code would later prove a huge incentive for people to trade up into very large, luxury SUVs.

Another tax appeared in 1990, when Congress imposed a 10 percent luxury tax on cars costing more than $30,000. But Congress again exempted light trucks with a gross vehicle weight over 6,000 pounds from the luxury tax. The auto industry was very subtle in its lobbying, leaving the issue to farm-state lawmakers who argued passionately that farmers should not pay luxury taxes on large pickups.

"Nobody anticipated the move to make these types of sport utilities into limousines," at least not the members of Congress or their staffs, said Albert Buckberg, the economist handling automotive taxes at the Joint Tax Committee of Congress. "There were no such things as the Lincoln Continentals of sport utility vehicles then."

At the time, very few minivans or SUVs had a gross vehicle weight as high as 6,000 pounds, and almost none of them cost more than $30,000. Chevrolet Suburbans, for example, were big enough to meet the weight requirement but were still spartan, trucklike vehicles with a base price for a four-wheel-drive version of just $16,645.[7] Yet the luxury tax rules had created another huge incentive for automakers to begin selling full-size SUVs luxurious enough to be accepted by affluent Americans as substitutes for luxury cars.

The combination of the depreciation rule, the luxury tax and lenient fuel-economy standards for light trucks all created incentives for consumers to look for company cars that were really large light trucks, and for Detroit automakers to build such vehicles. The final piece of the puzzle lay in air-quality restrictions.

Light trucks had big, gas-hungry engines that also tended to be dirty engines. Automakers invested billions of dollars in new car engines in the late 1970s and through the 1980s, coming up with new designs that were more fuel-efficient and also happened to be less polluting. Light-truck engines were less of a priority and many of them continued to have designs dating to the 1960s and even to the 1950s. They still had two valves per cylinder, for example, instead of using four-valve designs that were more complicated and more expensive to build but improved fuel-efficiency and reduced pollution. No SUVs had four-valve engines until 1994, by which time two-fifths of the cars being sold had them.

Congress addressed air pollution in 1990, producing the first significant update to clean-air laws in 13 years after many previous efforts had been stalled in Congressional committees. The environmental movement fought hard in 1990 to limit emissions of smog-causing gases by cars, and was fairly successful. The Clean Air Act required that, beginning in the 1994 model year, cars were allowed to emit only 0.4 grams of nitrogen oxides per mile.

But the legislation was much kinder to light trucks, a category that attracted virtually no attention from environmentalists. Most light trucks were allowed to emit 0.7 grams per mile of nitrogen oxides, and many full-size SUVs and pickups, like Suburbans, were permitted to emit 1.1 grams per mile.

Auto executives responded to later criticisms of SUV pollution by pointing out that cars and light trucks emitted 3 or 4 grams per mile of nitrogen oxides in the late 1950s, before catalytic converters were required by the government. But the number of vehicles on the nation's roads has tripled since 1960.[8] The total number of miles driven on the nation's roads has actually quadrupled since 1960, as each vehicle tends to be driven farther too, mainly because of urban sprawl.[9] It is now possible to see the mountains most days from downtown Los Angeles, because the purple haze of the 1960s and 1970s has faded. Keeping it that way, even as Americans drive ever more miles, requires steady improvements in emissions of smog-causing gases.

The air-quality rules were the final step that would allow automakers to build larger and larger SUVs with bigger and bigger engines. Plush versions of the Chevrolet Suburban, Chevrolet Tahoe and GMC Yukon became available in late 1994, the Ford Expedition and Lexus LX-450 in 1996, the Lincoln Navigator in 1997, the Cadillac Escalade in 1998, the Ford Excursion in 1999 and the Toyota Sequoia in 2000, to name a few. The highway arms race had begun in earnest.

All of these models competed directly in the marketplace with the big, safe, luxury cars that used to be the vehicles of choice for upscale American families. While the rise of SUVs was brisk after 1990 in the overall auto market, rising to 14.2 percent by 1996, it was nothing short of breathtaking in the luxury auto market.

Data services like Ward's Auto Info Bank, which supplies the United States Commerce Department, define the luxury market as covering all models for which the cheapest, most stripped-down version available costs at least $26,000 or so. (The precise threshold rises with inflation each year and is periodically revised to reflect market shifts.) Cars made up 95 percent of the luxury market in 1990, while a handful of expensive minivans and SUVs made up the rest. But the cars' share of sales had plummeted to just 44 percent by 1996, as the introduction of new models transformed SUVs from bit players into half the luxury market. In an industry in which new models take four to six years to plan and bring to market, enormous changes were coming in the blink of an eye, especially in the luxury market.

With hindsight, one huge question stands out about the many loopholes created for SUVs over the course of several decades: Where was the environmental movement? With millions of members who vote and many wealthy donors to pay for lobbyists, the environmental movement has long been the counterweight in Washington to the influence of the automakers and the UAW. Yet as a slow but steady transformation began taking place on the American road, the environmental movement stayed silent on SUVs all the way into the mid-1990s, and did not campaign in earnest for changes to SUV regulations until 1999.

Environmentalists have a history of not taking notice of tax legislation, and paid no attention whatsoever to the depreciation and luxury tax provisions for large light trucks. More egregiously, environmental groups ignored SUVs in the 1990 battle over the Bryan bill, and even disregarded the air-pollution loopholes for light trucks in the 1990 clean air legislation.

The Sierra Club did criticize minivans once in the early 1990s for having lower gas mileage than the cars they were replacing, but did not mention SUVs then. Air pollution activists paid little attention to vehicular emissions after the 1990 clean air legislation because it barred the federal government from imposing stricter standards until the 2004 model year, although some state governments continued studying the issue.

Part of the problem was that for decades, automakers had heavily marketed SUVs as vehicles suitable for outdoorsy people to explore nature. Affluent baby boomer families who loved nature were the core of the environmental movement, and they were also the main market for SUVs. "Some groups felt that to vilify SUVs was to alienate your members," said Kevin Mills, the director of pollution prevention at Environmental Defense. "It feels like you are blaming them instead of the companies."

Many environmental activists in Washington, including specialists in gasoline consumption and the associated problem of global warming, bought SUVs for their own use. Adam C. Markham, the director of the World Wildlife Fund's climate change program, drove a Jeep Cherokee "because I live up a half-mile track in the country."

John DeCicco, the fuel-economy expert at American Council for an Energy-Efficient Economy, had purchased a 1966 International Harvester Scout in 1977. "I wanted a four-wheel-drive truck to go camping," he said. "That kind of mentality and mindset was very common in our generation."

The environmental movement also had a huge blind spot when it came to noticing new trends in automobiles. Incredibly, no environmental group kept even a one-person office in Detroit dedicated to keeping an eye on the nation's biggest industry through the 1990s, nor does such an office exist even today. Activists tend to be young, single people from fairly affluent backgrounds, and the biggest environmental groups employ hundreds of them in big cities with vibrant downtown areas on the East and West Coasts. The largest offices are in Washington, D.C., an exciting city with plenty of politicians and regulators to lobby. Metropolitan Detroit, by contrast, is the nation's eighth-largest metropolitan area with more than five million people, but remains a fairly insular Midwestern community that has been hemorrhaging young people for decades. Downtown Detroit is only beginning to revive after several very difficult decades.

Mechanical engineering has appealed less to environmentalists than paddling around among endangered whales and coral reefs, or planting trees in deforested regions of the Himalayas. There are fewer than a dozen real experts on automotive issues in the environmental movement, and almost all of them live in or near Washington, D.C.; the rest are in Berkeley, California, where the Union of Concerned Scientists has its automotive office. While Michigan has some homegrown environmental groups, they have traditionally avoided vehicle issues, although they have criticized air and water pollution from local auto factories.

When the environmental movement did pay attention to automobiles, it was easily seduced by hopes that new technologies would provide painless ways to improve gas mileage without compromising vehicle safety or comfort. "If you look at how the environmental movement preoccupied itself in the '90s, there was a huge fascination with technological solutions, and a rallying around the electric car," DeCicco said.

Electric cars fizzled in the market. GM spent hundreds of millions of dollars to develop the EV-1, an entirely electric car with a tiny passenger compartment and limited range that came on the market in 1997, and found fewer than 1,000 customers despite heavy subsidies. Hybrid gasoline-electric cars like the Honda Insight and Toyota Prius have since caused a sensation among environmentalists, with the Insight getting 61 m.p.g. in the city and 70 m.p.g. on the highway, but they also have shortcomings that will likely limit their sales.[10]

The auto industry noticed the environmental movement's fascination with technological fixes, and exploited it. The industry frequently sent its advanced research engineers to Washington with prototypes of futuristic electric or fuel-cell cars to show politicians, regulators and environmentalists. Auto marketers, vehicle designers and manufacturing managers stayed in Detroit and were scornful of regulators, politicians and environmentalists alike for making their jobs more difficult.

As the Clinton Administration drew to a close, Big Three executives showed their prototypes for 80-m.p.g. midsize cars to Vice President Al Gore, environmentalists and reporters in Washington, while cagily avoiding any commitments on mass production. The same day, GM executives held a press conference for auto writers in Detroit to announce plans to introduce 20 more versions of full-sized, gas-guzzling SUVs and pickups by 2003. As research engineers in Washington burbled about hybrid engines, vehicle designers in Detroit were showing us monstrosities like the Chevrolet Avalanche, which is part full-size SUV and part pickup, and a Suburban with three doors on each side instead of two. As GM showed off responsible cars in Washington, it was displaying SUVs in Detroit with designs that practically radiated menace. But the menacing SUVs were likely to be far more profitable, cementing the financial recovery of the auto industry and the economic recovery of Michigan.

5

THE SUV ECONOMY

To understand the economic importance of the auto industry, consider this: if the Microsoft Corporation were selling $22 billion a year worth of auto parts instead of $22 billion a year worth of computer software, Bill Gates would probably be an obscure GM vice president that nobody had ever heard of.

Even in 2002, GM remains seven times the size of Microsoft in terms of sales. As SUV sales rose through the 1990s, the auto industry remained the linchpin of the American economy. GM and Ford each had greater sales than IBM, AT&T and Microsoft combined, and their domestic operations alone each had greater annual revenues than the entire American airline industry. GM's and Ford's combined annual revenues were considerably greater than the American defense budget, although the armed forces were still able to employ far more people because soldiers earn much less than auto workers. Chrysler was the runt of Detroit, yet it was still the nation's seventh-largest company, nearly the size of IBM. After Daimler-Benz bought Chrysler in November 1998, *Fortune* magazine ranked GM, Ford and DaimlerChrysler as the world's three largest companies in terms of sales.[1]

In the high-tech mania that persisted through much of the 1990s, culminating in the stock market bubble for Internet stocks, the economic importance of the auto industry was widely missed. Publications like *Business Week* and *The Wall Street Journal* began ranking the size of companies based on the value of their outstanding stock. But a country's economic output is based not on stock prices but on total sales of goods and services to consumers (plus exports and minus imports). GM and Ford were the only two companies in the 1990s that each accounted for more than a full percentage point of the entire economic output of the United States.

The Detroit automakers achieved wealth in the 1990s on a scale not seen since the 1960s. Their stock prices soared, executives pocketed multimillion-dollar bonuses and workers earned six-digit paychecks from the abundant overtime. Housing prices in the Detroit metropolitan area rocketed up 120.7 percent in the decade, nearly triple the rate at which housing prices rose in the rest of the nation.[2] The arts flourished, as GM bankrolled Neeme Jarvi's Detroit Symphony Orchestra, DaimlerChrysler brought world-class art exhibitions to the Detroit Institute of Arts and the Ford Motor Company helped turn the Michigan Opera Theater into one of the nation's finest regional opera companies, with a magnificent opera complex. The inner city of Detroit began to revive, unemployment nearly disappeared and crime rates tumbled.

This flush of prosperity was built to a great extent on SUV profits, as can best be seen by looking at one factory, the vast Michigan Truck Plant in Wayne, a western suburb of Detroit.

The factory was a ghostly place in the spring of 1996. Engineers, robot repairmen, electricians and plumbers were still preparing a few sections of the assembly line to start production, and large pools of light from the 50-foot-high steel ceiling illuminated them.

But elsewhere the lights had been turned off to conserve electricity. Some daylight came through the few windows that pierced the walls of the 32-year-old factory, so that miles of conveyor belts and hulking robots in steel safety cages could be dimly seen, lurking in the gloom.[3]

The Ford executives leading a group of auto writers through the factory were enthusiastic about the new, full-sized SUVs that would soon be built there. Just as the Ford Explorer had successfully replaced the Bronco II six years earlier, the new Ford Expedition was to finally replace the aging Ford Bronco. The Bronco had been a big, crude, two-door SUV for outdoorsmen ever since its introduction in 1965 and was best known as the vehicle in which O. J. Simpson fled police in a nationally televised, low-speed chase in 1994.

The new Expedition would be little like the Bronco. It would have four doors, three rows of seats and all the interior comforts of a car, while still offering the go-anywhere advantages of a four-wheel-drive vehicle. Standard equipment would include chrome bumpers, power windows, power locks and a rear window equipped with a wiper, washer and defroster. There were even eight cup holders.

Yet the executives also made clear that they were not betting the company on the new Expedition. The entire front third of the Expedition, from the windshield forward, was identical to the front end of the F-150 pickup truck, and the back two-thirds of the Expedition used many of the same parts as the pickup too. The F-150 had just been redesigned the year before with a taller, more aggressive look, so this meant the Expedition would also have a tall, macho front end.

Ford's initial plan was to make 130,000 Expeditions and 100,000 F-150s each year at the factory. The pickups would be interspersed with SUVs going down the same assembly line. Since Ford had only been selling 32,000 Broncos a year, the production plans for the Expedition seemed bold. But if the Expedition were not a success, the extra factory equipment installed in the spring of

1996 would work just fine to make all pickup trucks, for which the market was well established.

Wall Street analysts thought the forecast was on target, however, and predicted that the Expedition would be the most profitable model ever made. The Expedition would sell for an average of $36,000 apiece. Since it was basically a pickup truck with a couple of extra doors and two extra rows of seats, it cost around $24,000 to make, including administrative overhead and modest design costs. The profit on each vehicle would be a lush $12,000.

Those numbers made Wall Street pay attention to Ford shares, which had been terrible performers for years. "I haven't been a huge, rah-rah supporter of Ford stock, but this could make a difference," said David Bradley, an analyst at J. P. Morgan Securities Inc., several months before the Expedition went on sale.

As it turned out, Ford's sales forecast for the Expedition was wildly wrong: it was not nearly optimistic enough. No matter how many Expeditions the factory produced, it could not come close to meeting demand. Ford stopped all production of F-150s at the factory—the pickups were being produced at four other North American factories anyway—and made nothing but Expeditions. The factory still could not ship Expeditions fast enough to satisfy customers. The workers put in 60- and 70-hour weeks and the orders still kept piling up. Ford hired a third shift to operate the factory through the middle of the night and began running the assembly line around the clock, six days a week. The unionized assembly line workers earned as much as $100,000 a year by putting in many hours of overtime. Skilled electricians, plumbers and robot repair specialists, also represented by the UAW, earned $150,000 to $200,000 a year by working nights and coming in practically every weekend to keep the factory equipment properly calibrated and in repair. And still the dealerships could not clear their waiting lists.

Even before the Expedition went on sale, Ford engineers began coming up with a Lincoln version, which would be named the Navigator. In just 13 weeks, the blink of an eye in terms of automotive design cycles that often last four or five years, they went from a few sketches on computers to having a full prototype. Designing the Navigator was easy: they just changed a few of the Expedition's body panels and added a huge chrome grille. The engineers also figured out a way to stuff another 200 pounds of sound-deadening foam into the doors and the rest of the body, so that the interior would be as quiet as a sedan instead of sounding like the pickup truck it really was. The prototype was swiftly approved by the board of directors and went on sale a year after the Expedition. The Navigator was also assembled in the Michigan Truck Plant, but making 40,000 Navigators a year instead of Expeditions was an easy decision for Ford. The Navigator had a much higher sticker price, at $45,000. And the profits on it were breathtaking, with financial analysts estimating them at $15,000 for each vehicle sold.

The fat profits mainly reflected enormous demand for a vehicle that was in short supply. But the profits also resulted from the inexpensive manufacturing process that produced the vehicle. It was a process very different from the way cars were built.

Since the late 1970s, most cars have had what is known as a unit body. The underbody, sides and roof form what amounts to a steel lattice, a single unit in which the steel side panels are part of the vehicle's basic structure. This approach has two advantages. It is fairly light, which improves fuel economy. And it allows for ample crumple zones. The steel exterior panels can be designed to crush in predictable ways in a crash. This absorbs energy that might otherwise be imparted either to the car's occupants or to the occupants of any other vehicle that the car might hit.

The process used inside the Michigan Truck Plant is very different. Known as body-on-frame architecture, it dates back to the days of Henry Ford, and was used for cars as well as light trucks until the 1970s.

The process in the Michigan Truck Plant basically starts with what look like two 16-foot-long sections of steel rail that might have been stolen from railroad tracks at night. Viewed in cross section, each rail is a nearly square, hollow box, 3.5 inches high and 3.2 inches wide and made of specially hardened steel between a tenth and an eighth of an inch thick. These are the frame rails, and they run the length of the underbody of an SUV or pickup. The rails are not actually straight like railroad tracks, but curve up and down somewhat and from side to side down the length of the vehicle to carry the weight better and allow for easy attachment of various parts of the underbody.

These two thick rails are placed almost a yard apart and seven steel beams are welded across them every 24 to 32 inches, forming what resembles a very large ladder lying on the floor. This is the light truck's frame, its foundation. As the frame moves down a yellow conveyor belt, more parts are attached above and below the rails, including the suspension, wheels, fuel tank, fuel lines and engine.

In another part of the factory, vehicle bodies are built. Jets of sparks fly as 10-foot-tall robot welders resembling huge vultures crane their long mechanical necks at various angles to weld together the gray steel panels of each vehicle's sides, hood and roof. The conveyor belt carries the bodies through a nearly airtight room where robot spray guns paint them. Then the belt carries the bodies farther down the assembly line as dozens of crews of workers install everything from headlights and steering wheels to seats, dashboards, windshields, windows, carpeting and taillights.

The conveyor belt carrying the underbodies and the conveyor belt carrying the passenger compartments finally meet near the end of the assembly plant. The belt with the passenger compartments clanks up to a point above the underbodies and then a powerful crane seizes each passenger compartment and lowers it toward a waiting underbody. A dozen thick steel screws jut up from the frame, and fit precisely through a dozen holes in the bottom of the passenger compartment. Strong bolts are tightly attached to hold the top and bottom halves of each vehicle together, and the new vehicle lurches forward for the wiring, brakes and so forth to be coupled together, the headlights aimed, the gas tank filled and a long list of quality checks.

Practically the same process is used at every other assembly plant producing SUVs based on pickup-truck designs. The disadvantages are that the underbody is extremely heavy, which hurts fuel economy, and very stiff, so that it does not crumple well in a crash. The biggest advantage of body-on-frame architecture is that it produces a vehicle that can carry or tow a lot of weight.

Jim Queen, GM's vice president of engineering, is fond of pointing out another distinction between unit-body cars and body-on-frame light trucks. Redesigning the body or the mechanical underpinnings of a car is fairly expensive because any significant changes can affect the entire structure of the vehicle. The economics of redesigning a body-on-frame vehicle are very different. Redesigning the body is inexpensive because the body panels are not part of the vehicle's structure. So it is easy to design lots of different variants, pickups and SUVs, that can all be bolted on top of the same frames, providing consumers with a constant stream of fresh-looking vehicles at modest cost. By contrast, changes to the heavy underbody of a light truck are extremely expensive. The result is that while cars tend to be redesigned every four to six years, light-truck underbodies may go a decade or longer between big redesigns, but there can be lots of changes in the intervening years to offer different bodies on top of the underbodies.

The ease of lowering a new vehicle body onto a previously designed frame is what allowed Ford Motor to begin manufacturing the Navigator so soon after the board approved it. GM uses essentially the same underbodies to offer a plethora of versions of its full-sized trucks, including not just the Chevrolet Silverado and GMC Sierra pickups but also a bevy of SUVs—the Chevrolet Tahoe and Suburban, the GMC Yukon and Yukon XL and the Cadillac Escalade. GM has even begun reusing the underbody for two vehicles that combine pickup and SUV features, the Chevrolet Avalanche and Cadillac Escalade EXT.

To keep earning the huge profits provided by full-sized SUVs, automakers have sometimes gone to extraordinary lengths. They keep the factories open even in dangerous conditions, such as during a blizzard that hit metropolitan Detroit late on Saturday night, January 2, 1999. Driven by a hard prairie wind, the thick flakes seemed to fly horizontally across the earth instead of falling. Yet they quickly piled up, a foot in less than a day, with drifts several feet deep. Hundreds of vehicles were abandoned on the freeways and major roads, making it hard for the snow plows to get through. The Michigan State Police went on the radio to warn everyone without a personal emergency to stay home all day.

Detroit's airport was paralyzed. Dozens of planes had landed, but few of the ground personnel had been able to make it to work and much of their equipment had frozen. More than 4,000 passengers aboard these planes waited up to seven hours before they were allowed to deplane. The airport manager drove out to assess the situation and became disoriented on the grounds of his own airport, unable to see more than a few feet in the blinding snow.

Three miles northwest of the airport, however, skilled workers were already in the Michigan Truck Plant, preparing the factory equipment. More than 1,000 assembly line workers drove through the snow late Sunday afternoon, showing up punctually for the first shift of the week. When trucks carrying engines and axles became stuck in the snow and failed to reach the factory, Ford officials radioed the drivers of trucks bound for other Ford factories. The shipments were swiftly diverted before the Michigan Truck Plant assembly line could run out of vehicles to assemble. Not a single hour of production was lost.

Making such efforts was worthwhile because the Michigan Truck Plant had become the single most profitable factory in any industry anywhere in the world. It was cranking out 1,040 full-sized sport utilities every workday, 245,000 Expeditions and 48,000 Navigators a year. The factory's annual production was worth almost $11 billion—greater than the global sales in 1998 for Fortune 500 companies like Northwest Airlines, CBS, Texas Instruments, Honeywell and Nike, and nearly equal to the sales of McDonald's, Abbott Laboratories or Lufthansa.

The factory's profits from those sales were even more spectacular: about $3.7 billion in pretax profits, a profit margin approaching that of the Microsoft Corporation. Even after Ford had forked out roughly $1.3 billion in taxes—an immense windfall for the federal government and the state of Michigan—it still was left with about $2.4 billion in after-tax profits in 1998 from sales of the Expedition and Navigator.[4]

While Ford had 53 assembly plants worldwide, the Michigan Truck Plant accounted for a third of the company's entire profits. There were fewer than a hundred companies in the world that earned more than this single factory did in 1998. Many of these companies, like State Farm Insurance and Wal-Mart, did not have factories. The rest, like Intel and the General Electric Company, earned more modest profits from each of many different factories and other businesses.

The wealth spread far beyond the Michigan Truck Plant and Wayne. Ford's profits from running the factory for three years were enough for it to buy all of Volvo Cars, in 1999; an automaker with a global reputation and extensive factories and research labs in Sweden. Ford was earning so much money from SUVs by the late 1990s that it accumulated one of the largest cash hoards ever held by a corporation, $24 billion. Ford bought Land Rover in 2000 and considered buying BMW, which declared that it was not for sale.

SUV profits, combined with a strong American economy that lifted auto sales generally, did wonders for Ford's stock price. From the Expedition's introduction through early 1999, the stock produced a total return on investment of 215 percent, including reinvested dividends. That compared with an 85 percent return for the Standard & Poor's index of 500 large stocks. Ford employees owned a fifth of the company's stock, mainly through retirement plans, so they benefited from the run-up as well as lots of overtime for those lucky enough to be working at factories producing SUVs. Early each year, Ford issued profit-sharing checks of as much as $8,000 apiece to its more than 100,000 U.A.W.-represented workers, whether they worked in an SUV factory or not.

Workers at other automakers benefited too. The SUV boom

enriched communities from Janesville, Wisconsin, where the Suburban was made, to Tuscaloosa, Alabama, where workers in one of the poorest states in the nation suddenly were earning so much money that they were able to buy some of the Mercedes M-class SUVs they were building. Automakers now manufacture in-house fewer than half the parts they use in assembling a new vehicle, so workers and managers at independent auto-parts companies also prospered from the boom.

SUV profits helped all three Detroit automakers afford the gold-plated health care benefits that the UAW successfully demanded. Workers, retirees and their families at all three Detroit automakers could choose their own doctors without restrictions or copayments, and could fill prescriptions at virtually no cost and without limit on the number of pills. The Big Three automakers' medical plans covered 2.55 million Americans by 1999, or almost 1 percent of the nation's population. Costs were soaring, because each automaker had as many retired workers as active workers, and the average age even of the active workers was 46. Including the cost of covering retirees and their spouses, Ford's costs for pharmaceuticals alone had reached nearly $2,800 annually for each active hourly worker, six times the national average for corporations that bothered to offer any prescription-drug benefits at all.

By the late 1990s, metropolitan Detroit had some of the best hospitals in the nation. Institutions of higher learning benefited too. The University of Michigan raised $1 billion of its $3 billion budget each year from its top-notch hospital and clinics, which offered premium care to automaker employees at premium prices.

The auto industry's new wealth was especially evident at Chrysler, which probably would have gone bust in the 1991 recession had it not been for its Jeep profits. By the mid-1990s, it was so rich that it had bought a fleet of Gulfstream jets for its executives to use. Top bosses like Bob Lutz were on top of the world, literally and figuratively.

The low manufacturing costs and huge profits of SUVs gave

Detroit's top executives a powerful financial incentive to build ever more of the off-road vehicles. But they had another incentive too: The global market for cars was glutted and quickly becoming a very difficult marketplace in which to make any profits at all. By the late 1990s, the world's automakers had enough factory capacity to build three cars for every two that they could actually sell. Recently industrialized nations like South Korea and then China provided billions of dollars in subsidies for the construction of auto factories, usually in the form of government loans to unprofitable automakers with little hope of ever repaying the money. Automakers in Japan were able at least until the late 1990s to keep attracting domestic investors and building factories despite tiny profit margins. Detroit's Big Three contributed to the glut of capacity, with GM alone building factories in Argentina, Brazil, China, Poland and Thailand in the late 1990s.

Yet powerful unions made it extremely difficult to close factories in the industrialized world even as new factories were built elsewhere. European auto unions used to have the reputation of being the toughest in fighting factory closings, but American, Canadian and even Brazilian auto unions became challengers for that title. Consider the remarkable language in the four-year labor contracts that the UAW signed with each of Detroit's Big Three in the autumn of 1999. The companies agreed that they would "not close, nor partially or wholly sell, spin off, split off, consolidate, or otherwise dispose of in any form, any plant, asset, or business unit of any type, constituting a bargaining unit under the Agreement."[5] Other provisions barred the automakers from permanently laying off workers even if the companies were the victims of acts of God.

The smaller the car, the greater the glut of capacity that developed. Small, cheap cars were the simplest to manufacture, and the first choice of countries that saw having an auto industry as a prerequisite for entering the ranks of industrialized nations. The frightening reality for Detroit automakers was that with each passing decade, they were becoming unable to compete in the market for successively larger cars. Compact cars like the Ford Escort were profitable in the 1980s, but became money-losers by the early 1990s. Midsized cars like the Ford Taurus stayed profitable for Detroit until the late 1990s, when Honda Accords and Toyota Camrys came to dominate that market too. While Honda sells practically all of its well-built and attractive Accords to families in the profitable retail market, Ford now dumps half the Tauruses it makes into rental fleets at rock-bottom prices that are barely high enough to justify keeping the company's two Taurus assembly plants open.

Washington's policy for the last decade of favoring a strong dollar in currency markets has also hurt Detroit. Japanese automakers have loudly trumpeted the fact that they now assemble in the United States more than half the cars they sell in the American market. But financial analysts estimate that even for the cars that are assembled in places like Georgetown, Kentucky, and Smyrna, Tennessee, at least half the costs are still incurred in Japan. Much of the initial design and engineering work still takes place in Japan, and some high-value parts like transmissions still tend to be made there; all of these costs are incurred in inexpensive yen.

As the 1990s progressed, auto executives in Detroit became more and more convinced that their futures lay in selling SUVs. The manufacturing executives knew how to build SUVs in huge numbers at very modest cost. Foreign competition was negligible because American import taxes had prevented foreign automakers from developing much expertise in building light-truck underbodies. Fortunes were waiting to be made with each new SUV model that would be a little bigger and a little more luxurious than what was already on the market. All that was needed was an aggressive marketing effort to persuade affluent Americans that SUVs, for all their flaws, were as good as cars or better. And with the world's largest advertising budgets and a century of marketing experience, nobody was better equipped to mold public opinion than the automakers.[6]

6

REPTILE DREAMS

Automakers employ thousands of people to figure out which models will be popular next with American buyers, and thousands more to figure out how to promote their latest models. A French medical anthropologist by training, Clotaire Rapaille seems an unlikely person to have reshaped American automotive market research and marketing.

Tall and muscular at 60, with sandy blonde hair, Rapaille speaks with a strong French accent, having only moved to the United States at the age of 38. His background makes him an oddity in an industry dominated by the flat Midwestern accents of men (seldom women) who grew up in Midwestern cities like Cleveland, Toledo or Flint. Yet his psychological analysis of how sport utility vehicles appeal to people's most primitive instincts has helped to legitimize the cynical marketing of SUVs.

During the 1990s, Rapaille worked on more than 20 projects with David Bostwick, Chrysler's market research director; Francois Castaing, Chrysler's chief of vehicle engineering; and Bob Lutz. Castaing says that he and Lutz believed in gut instinct more than market research in designing new models, and that they showed prototypes to Rapaille only after the initial design work, so as to double-check that their instincts were right. But providing the reality check on possible future models is a considerable responsibility. Because Chrysler was the unquestioned design and marketing leader in Detroit during this period, Rapaille's work also influenced other automakers, with Ford and GM eventually retaining him for projects as well.

Clotaire Rapaille was born in Paris on August 10, 1941, less than two months after Hitler's troops occupied the city. His father was an army officer who had just been captured by the Germans and would spend the entire war in a forced labor camp; he would emerge from the camp a broken man. His mother, fearful of the dangers of occupied Paris, sent her baby son out of the city to be raised by his grandmother in Vallée de Chevreuse, a small town halfway between Paris and the Normandy coastline.

Rapaille's earliest memory is of playing outdoors under his grandmother's watchful eye when he was three, and unexpectedly seeing some German soldiers running away. "I said, 'How come the Germans are running away, the Germans never run away,' and then I saw a monster coming out of the forest, an American tank," he recalls. "A big American with a net on his helmet and flowers took me on the tank and gave me chocolates and gave me a ride."

That experience made an indelible impression. It convinced him at that early age that he wanted to become an American, because the French were losers in war while the Germans had been mean to everyone during the occupation.

Rapaille's parents and grandparents were nearly wiped out financially by the war. Rapaille put himself through college and graduate school in Paris by driving a beer delivery truck at night, then began consulting for Renault and Citroën, two big French automakers, in the early 1970s.

As he studied and then applied principles of psychological research, Rapaille became convinced that a person's first encounter with an object or idea shaped his or her emotional relationship with it for life. He would apply that conviction after moving in 1979 to America, where he became a prominent market researcher who specialized in psychoanalytic techniques.

Relying on the work of Carl Jung, the Swiss psychologist who founded analytic psychology, Rapaille divides people's reactions to a commercial product into three levels of brain activity. There is the cortex, for intellectual assessments of a product. There is the limbic, for emotional responses. And there is the reptilian, which he defines as reactions based on "survival and reproduction."

Rapaille focuses his attention on the deepest, most reptilian instincts that people have about consumer products. He seeks to identify people's archetype of a product, the deepest emotional identity that the product holds for them based on their earliest encounter with it. His research has led him to some disturbing conclusions about how to sell sport utility vehicles, which he sees as the most reptilian vehicles of all because their imposing, even menacing appearance appeals to people's deep-seated desires for "survival and reproduction."

With the detachment of a foreigner, Rapaille sees Americans as increasingly fearful of crime. He acknowledges that this fear is irrational and completely ignores statistics showing that crime rates have declined considerably. He attributes the pervasive fear of crime mainly to violent television shows, violent video games and lurid discussions and images on the Internet, which make young and middle-aged Americans more focused on threats to their physical safety than they need to be. At the same time, he argues, the aging of the population means that there are more older Americans, who may pay less attention to violence in the media but are more cautious than young people about personal safety in general.

The fear is most intense among today's teenagers, Rapaille has found, attributing the trend to the addition of video games and increasingly menacing toy action figures on top of the steady diet of murders on television that baby boomers had. "There is so much emphasis on violence—the war is every day, everywhere," he said in an interview two weeks before the terrorist attacks of September 11, 2001. The response of teens, he added, is that "They want to give the message, 'I want to be able to destroy, I want to be able to fight back, don't mess with me.'" While teens do not buy many SUVs, youth culture nonetheless tends to shape the attitudes of broad segments of American society.

For Rapaille, the archetype of a sport utility vehicle reflects the reptilian desire for survival. People buy SUVs, he tells auto executives, because they are trying to look as menacing as possible to allay their fears of crime and other violence. The Jeep has always had this image around the world because of its heavy use in war movies and frequent appearances in newsreels from the 1940s and 1950s, and newer SUVs share the image. "I usually say, 'If you put a machine gun on the top of them, you will sell them better,'" he said. "Even going to the supermarket, you have to be ready to fight."

To reach such conclusions, Rapaille has run dozens of consumer focus groups, or "discoveries," as he prefers to call them. First, he asks a group of 30 people to sit in a windowless room and take turns speaking for an hour about their rational, reasoned responses to a vehicle. "They tell me things I don't really care about, and I don't listen," he said.

Then he tells the group to spend another hour pretending to be five-year-old boys from another planet. He asks them to tell him little stories about the vehicle, to get at their emotional responses to the vehicle. But he later discards the notes on these stories as well.

What really interests him is the third stage of research. He asks the consumers to lie down on mats and he turns the lights way down in the room. Then he asks each consumer lying in the near darkness to tell him about his or her earliest associations with vehicles, in an attempt to get at their "reptilian" responses to various designs.

The answers in these consumer groups have persuaded Rapaille that American culture is becoming frighteningly atavistic and obsessed with crime. He cites as further proof the spread of gated communities and office buildings protected by private security guards, together with the tiny but growing market in the United States for luxury vehicles with bulletproof armor. "I think we're going back to medieval times, and you can see that in that we live in ghettos with gates and private armies," he said. "SUVs are exactly that, they are armored cars for the battlefield."

Even Rapaille says that a few of his ideas are too extreme to be practical. SUV buyers want to be able to take on street gangs with their vehicles and run them down, he said, while hastening that television commercials showing this would be inappropriate. He has unsuccessfully tried to persuade ad agency executives working for Chrysler to buy the television commercial rights to *Mad Max*, the 1979 film that launched Mel Gibson's career. The film shows heavily armed thugs in leather on motorcycles, driving around a post-Apocalyptic Australia and killing people so as to steal their gasoline. Rapaille wanted Chrysler to use computers to insert its SUVs into scenes from the movie, with the vehicle rescuing the hero or heroine from the clutches of one of the movie's nefarious villains in hockey masks. But the idea was dismissed as too controversial. And when I checked with someone in Hollywood, I learned that the rights to *Mad Max* are caught in a legal tangle that would make it nearly impossible to use the film for a commercial.

Yet the idea of being civil on the roads has disappeared and SUV design needs to reflect this, Rapaille says. "This is over, people don't care, and for some people, the message is it's *Mad Max* out there, it's a jungle out there and you're not going to kill me, if you attack me I will fight."

As a milder alternative, Rapaille admires SUV television ads like the one that showed a Jeep climbing home over a pile of rocks at the bottom of a house's driveway. "Your house has become a castle," he said.

When Rapaille came to work for Chrysler, one of his first projects was to define what consumers really saw in the company's

Jeeps. His cynical, even brutal view of the world fit perfectly with the "gut" of Bob Lutz, who oversaw Chrysler's light-truck operations in the United States upon his arrival from Ford in 1986. Lutz's corporate empire had grown a lot bigger in 1987, when Chrysler bought American Motors, including its profitable Jeep brand.

Lutz insisted on ever more powerful engines mounted in ever taller SUVs and pickup trucks with ever more menacing-looking front ends—an approach enthusiastically recommended by Rapaille. Lutz's instructions were consistent, said David C. McKinnon, Chrysler's director of vehicle exterior design: "Get them up in the air and make them husky." Lutz gave this advice even for two-wheel-drive versions of SUVs that were unlikely ever to go off-road and therefore did not need a lot of height and ground clearance, McKinnon said. Because Chrysler was Detroit's design leader during this period, and Lutz the most influential car guy in town, Lutz's decisions shaped the way SUVs were designed around the world.

The Jeep Grand Cherokee's debut at the Detroit auto show in 1992 was a vintage Lutz moment. With a large crowd of journalists gathered, he drove a Grand Cherokee up the steps of Detroit's convention center and smashed through a plate-glass window to enter the building. A special window had been installed in advance to make this a little less dangerous than it sounds. The television footage was nonetheless great, and established the Grand Cherokee's credentials as a rough-and-tough vehicle.

The Dodge Ram full-sized pickup truck came out two years later with a front end that was designed to look as big and menacing as a Mack truck; *USA Today* described it admiringly as the kind of vehicle that would make other motorists want to get out of your way.

In his book, *Guts*, Lutz wrote that the Ram's in-your-face styling was carefully chosen even though consumer focus groups showed that most Americans would loathe it. "A whopping 80 percent of the respondents disliked the bold new drop-fendered design. A lot even hated it!" he wrote. However, he explained, "the remaining 20 percent of the clinic participants were saying that they were truly, madly, deeply in love with the design! And since the old Ram had only about 4 percent of the market at the time, we figured, what the hell, even if only half of those positive respondents actually buy, we'll more than double our share! The result? Our share of the pickup market shot up to 20 percent on the radical new design, and Ford and Chevy owners gawked in envy!"[1]

Ford and GM did not take the loss of sales lightly. They responded by making the Ford F-series pickups and the Chevrolet Silverado and GMC Sierra pickups more menacing, too. The Ford and GM pickups were then modified to make seven full-sized SUVs: the Ford Excursion, Ford Expedition, Lincoln Navigator, Chevrolet Tahoe, GMC Yukon, Chevrolet Suburban and GMC Yukon XL. Since all of these SUVs shared a lot of the same front-end parts with the pickup trucks on which they were based, the shift led by Dodge Ram toward more menacing front ends caused the entire full-sized SUV market to become more menacing. Close to 90 percent of the parts for a Ford Excursion are the same as for the Ford Super Duty pickup on which it is based, according to Ford. By turning the Ram into a brute, Lutz indirectly fed the highway arms race among SUVs.

When it comes to specific vehicles, the Dodge Durango comes closest to fitting Rapaille's Hobbesian view of life as being nasty, brutish and short. The Durango's front end is intended to resemble the face of a savage jungle cat, said Rapaille. The vertical bars across the grille represent teeth, and the vehicle has bulging fenders over the wheels that look like clenched muscles in a savage jaw.

"A strong animal has a big jaw, that's why we put big fenders," Rapaille says.

Minivans, by contrast, evoke feelings of being in the womb, and of caring for others, he says. Stand a minivan on its rear bumper and it has the silhouette of a pregnant woman in a floor-length dress. Not surprisingly, minivans are being crowded out of the market by SUVs. Rapaille even dislikes SUVs like the Mercedes M-Class that look a little like minivans.

Convertibles are suffering in the marketplace because women worry that they might be assaulted by an intruder who climbs inside, Rapaille contends. "Women were telling me, if you drive a convertible with the top down, the message is 'Rape me.'"

The reptilian instinct for survival does not just involve crime fears, Rapaille says. It also shows up in the extent to which people are willing to put other drivers at risk in order to diminish the odds that they will be injured themselves in a crash. In other words, people in touch with their inner reptile are most likely to choose vehicles that look especially likely to demolish other people's cars in collisions.

"My theory is the reptilian always wins," he said. "The reptilian says, 'If there's a crash, I want the other guy to die.' Of course, I can't say that aloud."

But SUVs cannot just look macho and menacing on the outside, Rapaille believes. Inside, they must be as gentle, feminine and luxurious as possible. Rapaille's argument for this is based on the reptilian instinct for reproduction.

"Men are for outside and women are for inside, that's just life; to reproduce men have to take something outside and the women take something inside," Rapaille said. "The inside of an SUV should be the Ritz-Carlton, with a minibar. I'm going to be on the battlefield a long time, so on the outside I want to be menacing but inside I want to be warm, with food and hot coffee and communications."

Listen to other auto-market researchers try to define an SUV and you often hear an almost literal echo of Rapaille's advice. "It's aggressive on the outside and it's the Ritz-Carlton on the inside, that's part of the formula," Chrysler's Bostwick said.

Rapaille's emphasis on reptilian instincts reflects not only his early encounter with the tank, he says, but also his subsequent, difficult upbringing. Rapaille says that his father never recovered from the psychological damage of his imprisonment, and his parents were divorced after the war. He was then sent off to a Jesuit school in Laval, France, and grew up there. "I had to stay there all year long because no one wanted to take care of me from my family, but I was alive, the reptilian was survival," he says.

Rapaille has loved automobiles since boyhood. But while he can now afford to buy an SUV, he doesn't own one. Instead, he owns a Rolls Royce and a Porsche 911. Sport utilities are too tall, he says, and he has a terror of rolling over. He likes the Rolls Royce but loves the Porsche, because it allows him to retain control of his destiny with its nimbleness, excellent brakes and tremendous stability. Compared to an SUV, he says, "A Porsche is safer." He may have emigrated to America, but in this respect he remains a European.

Rapaille's work helped automakers begin to understand who buys SUVs and why. But their research has gone far beyond archetypes. Lavishing huge sums, the auto industry has developed year by year an ever more detailed knowledge of what SUV buyers want, and then tapped into these desires with multibillion dollar advertising campaigns that are slick but extremely cynical.

Who has been buying SUVs since automakers turned them into family vehicles? They tend to be people who are insecure and vain. They are frequently nervous about their marriages and uncomfortable about parenthood. They often lack confidence in their driving skills. Above all, they are apt to be self-centered and self-absorbed, with little interest in their neighbors or communities.

No, that's not a cynic talking—that's the auto industry's own market researchers and executives.

Several market research companies conduct big annual customer surveys for automakers, producing an extremely detailed view of who buys SUVs and why. Each of these detailed surveys are filled out by 35,000 to 115,000 people who have bought new vehicles in the last several months. These surveys, backed up by many interviews with consumers in focus groups, dwarf anything done by politicians and journalists, who have far less money and usually form conclusions about public opinion based on polls of 400 to 1,200 people.

Political polling tends to be done by telephone, partly to produce results quickly. The auto industry, in less of a hurry, relies on mailing surveys to randomly selected samples of buyers of each model. The industry's pollsters say the initial response rate to surveys is 30 to 40 percent, somewhat higher than the response rate to random telephone polling. Many Americans would rather give their opinions about their new cars on a questionnaire than discuss their political views on the phone with a stranger, it seems.

Market research companies like Strategic Vision, J. D. Power and AutoPacific need to survey so many people because automakers frequently want to know a lot about buyers of a specific model. If Ford wants to know all about Explorer buyers or Toyota wants to know all about 4Runner buyers, for example, they will go to a market research company that has interviewed so many people that its database already includes plenty of Explorer or 4Runner buyers. A side effect of this thoroughness is that the data available for an entire market segment, like sport utility vehicles, is extremely detailed, with sample sizes running to 10,000 people or more.

The picture that various automakers have formed of why people buy SUVs has been pretty consistent, and it isn't pretty. Some of these SUV buyers might be beautiful people on the outside—SUVs have taken over Hollywood, and are especially popular with people who care about appearances, the research shows. But many SUV buyers seem somewhat less attractive on the inside.

SUV buyers are frequently married with children, but are often uncomfortable with both. "We have a basic resistance in our society to admitting that we are parents, and no longer able to go out and find another mate," said David Bostwick, the market research director at Chrysler. "If you have a sport utility, you can have the smoked windows, put the children in the back and pretend you're still single."

SUV buyers, unlike minivan buyers, frequently care little about anyone's kids but their own. "Sport utility people say, 'I already have two kids, I don't need 20,'" Bostwick said. "Then we talk to the people who have minivans and they say, 'I don't have two kids, I have 20—all the kids in the neighborhood.'"

Honda's research has identified SUV buyers as being very concerned with how other people see them, rather than worrying about what is practical. "The people who buy SUVs are in many cases buying the outside first and then the inside," said Thomas Elliott, Honda's executive vice president for North American auto operations. "They are buying the image of the SUV first, and then the functionality."

For automakers, this raises the tough challenge of designing vehicles that will sell based on their fashion appeal, but which are supposed to look as though fashion was the last thing on the designer's mind. Auto designers say this requires a delicate balance of features that are rugged yet trendy, durable yet chic, intimidating yet modish. "It's an image vehicle, an SUV, it says something about your lifestyle," said Ed Golden, the design director for Ford brand vehicles, and previously the design director for Ford SUVs like the Explorer and Expedition. "That's the key to SUVs, they look like they were not created for fashion, they look like they'll be here tomorrow."

Ford engineers have been impressed to see fashionably dressed women wearing hiking boots or even work boots while walking through expensive malls, Golden said. Nobody needs such boots for such a stroll. Yet the women choose them anyway because the appearance of industrial strength and simplicity is currently in style, Golden said. "The SUV is almost like a utility boot," he added.

GM executives have reached similar conclusions about the paramount importance of fashion in the marketing of SUVs. "With the sport utility buyers, it's more of an image thing," said Fred J. Schaafsma, GM's top engineer for the initial planning stages of new vehicles. "Sport utility owners tend to be more like, 'I wonder how people view me,' and are more willing to trade off flexibility or functionality to get that."

During interviews with consumers, GM officials have noticed that SUV and minivan buyers differ markedly in how they express their desire for control while driving. "Minivan people want to be in control in terms of safety, being able to park and maneuver in traffic, being able to get elderly people in and out—SUV owners want to be more like, 'I'm in control of the people around me,'" Schaafsma said. "The words are identical but the meanings are completely different, and that has implications for how you design a vehicle."

Providing that feeling of control is why automakers mount the seats in sport utilities higher than the seats in minivans, Schaafsma said. Until recently, market researchers did not even ask customers how high they wanted to sit in a vehicle. Now, surveys by companies like AutoPacific show that visibility from the driver's seat ranks even with a vehicle's driving performance and interior comfort as the most important attributes that buyers seek. Not surprisingly, the taller sport utilities do best on this score, like the towering Ford Excursion. Six feet eight inches tall, it allows tall drivers to look over the roofs of Chevrolet Suburbans and into the windows of school buses. Excursion drivers must scale two tall stairs and a short one just to reach the floor of the passenger compartment.

Yet tall vehicles, including high-mounted seats, pose significant drawbacks, and not just in making it more difficult to climb into the vehicle. The higher seats of SUVs also mean that occupants are often sitting above the center of gravity of the vehicle, which is (as we will see later) a recipe for a rollover, because the vehicle becomes a little more top-heavy with every additional pound above the center of gravity. By contrast, people and baggage inside a car tend to be located at the same height from the ground as the car's center of gravity, so a heavily loaded car tends to be just as stable as a lightly loaded car.

The height of SUVs is also making it harder for the people still driving cars to see where they are going. Safety experts advise motorists to be looking for hazards at least a quarter of a mile ahead while driving at highway speeds, but that is hard to do through a mishmash of vehicles of various heights. Many car drivers find this disconcerting. Mary Cumberland, 76, who drives a big 1997 Chrysler New Yorker and lives in Southfield, Michigan, has always driven large cars but is not sure that she wants another because she is tired of having other vehicles block her view of the road. "A lot of people are considering sport utilities just out of self-defense," she said. "I'm trying to get my husband to consider a van, to be up higher."

Women are now the main decision-makers in slightly over half of all auto purchases, a shift from a generation ago, when men played a greater role in automobile shopping even for their spouses. This has also influenced SUV design. Jeep's research showed as early as the 1970s that many women are much more likely than men to prefer vehicles that allow them to sit high off the road. Extensive recent research by other automakers has confirmed this trend.

The result of this gender gap is visible in vehicles like the new Jeep Liberty, which is aimed at women buyers to a much greater extent than earlier Jeeps. The Liberty is supposed to look a lot like a World War II Jeep—it is marketed as "an American hero." But the Liberty is nearly a foot taller than the original wartime Jeeps. "The real key for women was to sit high," said William Chapin, the former Jeep marketing executive. "The new Jeep Liberty feels like I'm driving around on stilts, and there's a very important marketing reason for that."

Just as there is a gender gap in preferences on seating height, there is also a generation gap in automotive buying preferences: the younger a person is, the more likely he or she will prefer an SUV to a car. Americans born before the end of World War II buy extremely few SUVs, even as they completely dominate the market for large cars and account for a big chunk of the midsized car market as well. Americans in their teens and early 20s are practically obsessed with SUVs and will likely dominate the market in the decades ahead, but are only beginning to have enough money to buy new automobiles. The core market for SUVs lies instead among baby boomers—people born from 1946 through 1964, who are currently at the peak of their automobile-buying years.

In studying baby boomers, automakers have been increasingly using so-called generational market research. Generational research is based on the theory that people form their preferences for certain brands and vehicle types based on values that develop during their early teens, and keep those preferences for life. Automaker market researchers like Jim Bulin, an influential Ford vehicle strategist for many years, have paid special attention to baby boomers' predilection for over-engineered products. When affluent men and women in big, warm cities like Atlanta walk around in hiking boots suitable for Mount Everest and buy parkas designed for use at the North Pole, they are subscribing to what Bulin defines as "preparedness chic." So SUVs, with their ability to drive across rough terrain, are likely to remain popular, Bulin concludes.

"The whole four-wheel drive thing is be prepared for everything, the weather is not going to get in my way, the curbs are not going to get in my way, other vehicles that ride lower to the road are not going to get in my way," said Bulin, who recently set up a consulting firm specializing in generational research. "It's about not letting anything get in your way and, at the extreme, about intimidating others to get out of your way."

Owning an SUV also provides reassurance for baby boomers that while they may have office jobs and mortgages now, they have not really changed that much from the days of their youth. "It says, 'I'm adventurous'; it says, 'I'm still virile,'" Bulin said.

The massive surveys by market research companies show that people who buy SUVs tend to be very "self oriented," the automakers' euphemism for self-centered. SUV buyers are people who tend to be more restless, more sybaritic and less social than most Americans are. They tend to like fine restaurants a lot more than off-road driving, seldom go to church and have limited interest in doing volunteer work to help others. They are "less giving, less oriented toward others," says Daniel A. Gorrell, a longtime Ford marketer who is now a vice president of Strategic Vision, a San Diego powerhouse in automotive market research.

This weakness of community spirit is part of a broader social trend in America, as many people spend so much time watching television or working in two-career families that they no longer have time for friends, volunteer work or social groups. The most famous examples of this phenomenon in sociological research are the declining popularity of bowling leagues in the United States and pubs in England.

The self-centered lifestyle of SUV buyers comes through in their approach to traffic safety, especially their willingness to endanger other motorists so as to achieve small improvements in their personal safety, some auto executives say. GM and Nissan executives say that the public perception that SUVs provide considerable protection in a crash has been an important factor in their sales for many years, although they also say that being chic has been very important as well. Other manufacturers, particularly Ford, see traffic safety issues as much less important to buyers than a vehicle's basic sex appeal.

Nissan has found that drivers in Europe and Asia typically have very different attitudes toward vehicle safety from American drivers. Europeans and Asians tend to associate safety with a nimble vehicle with excellent brakes that can swerve or stop quickly so as to avoid an accident entirely, said Jerry P. Hirshberg, Nissan's recently retired president of North American design. Americans tend to have less confidence in their driving skills and assume that crashes are inevitable, so they have gravitated instead to tanklike vehicles that will protect occupants even if they plow into another vehicle. Buyers of sport utilities seem to be especially American in this regard, Hirshberg added.

"When Europeans think about safety, they think about a light, agile car," he said. "The American image of safety is put a tank around me, get as much mass around as possible and let Isaac Newton work his magic."

Chrysler executives have been split on the role of safety in SUV sales. James Holden, who recently retired as president of Chrysler after rising through the company's management ranks, says that the perception that SUVs provide greater protection in crashes has long been an important selling point for them. But Bostwick, the company's market research director, contends that people buy SUVs not so much to protect themselves as to gain a feeling of control of people and situations around them, including the ability to drive over any obstacle they may encounter.

"It's not safety as the issue, it's aggressiveness, it's the ability to go off the road," he said.

It is hard to do reliable research on how much thought Americans give to the people they might hit during collisions. The questions are difficult to pose to consumers: Would you be willing to triple or quadruple other motorists' chances of dying in a crash in order to cut your own chance of dying by 5 or 10 percent? If your answer is yes, how would you feel if tens of millions of other motorists made the same calculation? Drawing honest answers for questions with such profound moral implications is very difficult, marketers say.[2]

As with most social trends, there are exceptions to the decline of community spirit in the United States. Americans do a lot of volunteer work, as the elder President Bush tried to emphasize with his "Thousand Points of Light" initiative. Americans also remain one of the most church-going nations in the world. What the automakers' research says is simply that people who drive SUVs are less likely to be doing these things than people who drive other kinds of family vehicles. Minivan owners, by comparison, tend to be people who are very giving, and are the most likely category of vehicle owners to go to church and engage in volunteer work.

Many SUV owners claim that they need big SUVs because they have large families and simply cannot fit in traditional sedans. But automakers' research has found that even though they rarely, if ever, use the vehicles' four-wheel drive, people shopping for an

SUV almost never consider minivans, which get better gas mileage, emit less pollution, seldom roll over and are far less dangerous to other motorists. Even the most fashionable and sought-after minivan right now, the Honda Odyssey, still does not draw people addicted to SUVs. "My wife, she will drive an SUV, she won't drive an Odyssey—she won't let the Odyssey or minivan label be attached to her," said Thomas Elliott, the executive vice president at Honda. This antipathy to minivans shows precisely how the SUV boom reflects fashion rather than any real need for the big vehicles.

Rising sales of SUVs represent a triumph of image and marketing over practicality. The gradual decline in sales of safe, practical minivans over the last few years represents another sign that Americans care more about image than anything else. A big part of the problem is that when Chrysler introduced the first modern minivan in 1983, the company marketed it with a loving, family-oriented image that is simply not in style these days. "Someone put the 'soccer mom' title on it," said Ralph A. Sarotte, the general manager of Chrysler's minivan operations. "We could sell twice as many minivans in this market if it were not for the image thing."

Automakers have tried to shake minivans loose from the soccer mom image, but with limited success. Pontiac introduced a Montana version of its Trans Sport minivan, with ads in 1996 that featured a minivan driving cross-country surrounded by cowboys. Never mind that the vehicle only had two-wheel drive and that minivans virtually never go off-road—the Montana version became sufficiently popular that Pontiac turned all of its minivans into Montanas and dropped the Trans Sport name entirely. But even the Montana has not sold enough to be considered a real success, probably because it still looks like a minivan.

Yet there are some people who embrace the family image of minivans. They tend to be extremely nice people. Many of them do not fit the image of soccer moms—a quarter of sales are to senior citizens with no children in the home, and half the buyers are men, not women. Chrysler has actually had researchers count people behind the wheels of minivans on roads, and found that as many men drive them as women, notwithstanding all the stereotypes.

Strategic Vision's Gorrell says that the minivan market is neglected by many hard-driving auto executives because the executives simply cannot relate to such good people. He particularly likes to talk about a long interview he did with a woman in Charlotte, North Carolina, about why she chose a minivan.

"She could haul older people around and do good deeds, and I thought, 'How totally different from the auto industry, where they don't go to church on Sunday and are more likely to be on a flight to the West Coast'" for Monday morning business meetings, Gorrell said. "It's something that's lost, it's something that's noble, and yet they get short shrift."

The advertising and other marketing of minivans and SUVs reflect the differences in customers. Minivan ads tend to emphasize themes like protection, togetherness and helping others. One television ad for the Ford Windstar minivan showed a 10-year-old girl named Claire who dreams of becoming a superhero who protects the world. Another ad showed 14 mothers who were Ford engineers, sitting together with their children and discussing ways to make the next Windstar even better.

"The point there is to humanize," said Jim Townsend, the marketing manager for the Windstar. "These are people who are foregoing individual hobbies in favor of more family events."

SUV ads celebrate a more individualistic, sybaritic and even sometimes epicurean vision of life. A television ad soon after the Explorer's introduction in 1990 showed a prosperous couple who sipped from gold-rimmed coffee cups in an expensive restaurant, and were next seen sipping from mugs on a mountaintop. "We only went to four-star restaurants until we went to one with four billion stars," the narrator intoned.

In marketing SUVs, automakers also try to capitalize on motorists' fears of crime or violence. In the process, the manufacturers have subtly raised the stakes in the highway arms race by making it appear unsafe to drive anything but an SUV. This has been one of the "network externalities" that have helped build demand for SUVs despite their poor suitability for service as family vehicles.

Lexus tapped into the menace of SUVs with a series of magazine ads for its huge LX 470 full-sized sport utility. One showed a black LX 470 driving through a dark and ominous forest. The dark shapes of the trees had bent back from the sport utility vehicle, as though in fear. The trees looked a little like people cringing in fear at the sight of the big vehicle. "Introducing the V8 LX 470. Now with added intimidation," the ad said in large white letters.

Another magazine ad showed an LX 470 splashing past crocodiles in a jungle. Not one of the crocodiles showed any interest in going anywhere near the SUV. The slogan: "Introducing the V8 LX 470. Let nature worry about you for a change." (Actually, other motorists and pedestrians should be afraid of the LX 470. Not only is it much harder to control and maneuver than a car, but the bottom edges of its side windows are so high that they obscure traffic in the lane to the right. Anyone driving a full-sized SUV should be adept at checking frequently the side mirror on the passenger side of the vehicle.)

Many television ads have emphasized the physical size of SUVs, using the same theme of intimidation. The ads never mention, of course, that government gas-mileage regulations have limited car size while allowing SUVs to grow to such bloated proportions. One ad showed a silver Isuzu Trooper SUV being driven along an arid, red canyon wall. The narrator concluded his sales pitch by warning, "The world is big and cars just aren't."

Chevrolet took out an unsettling magazine ad to promote its Avalanche, which is a cross between a Chevrolet Suburban SUV and a Chevrolet Sierra pickup truck. The ad showed a black Avalanche towering over the reader and hurtling forwards. The background was a night sky criss-crossed by barren branches. In large white letters at the top of the page was this message: "We didn't intend to make other trucks feel pathetic and inadequate, it just sort of happened."

Of course, even the best ads are not very effective unless a lot of customers see them. In the case of SUV advertising, automakers have spent immense sums to make sure that practically every American gets the message. In fact, SUV advertising soared much faster than SUV sales over the last decade, rising nearly ninefold from $172.5 million in 1990 to $1.51 billion in 2000. Automakers and their dealers spent $9 billion advertising SUVs from 1990 through September 30, 2001, the most recent data available.[3]

This spending has made SUVs among the most heavily advertised products in the nation. The entire American advertising market is about $90 billion a year, but this is broken up into many different categories. The auto industry spends more on advertising than the next three largest industries, financial services, telecommunications and national restaurant chains, combined. Each of these three vast and diverse industries spends a total of $3 billion to $4 billion a year on advertising, but this money is divvied up into many small categories, from banking to mutual funds to cell phones to burger joints.

One of the central tenets of marketing, drummed into future executives at business schools around the world, is that advertising cannot make consumers desire a product that really has no appeal for them. But SUVs did appeal to millions of Americans, providing an image of outdoor adventure and personal security that meshed beautifully with what baby boomers in particular thought they needed.

With all the emphasis on fashion and image that goes into the design of SUVs, does anybody actually need the power and off-road capability built into these high-riding vehicles with big engines? Yes. Auto-industry surveys show that one in six SUV owners use their vehicles at least once a year for towing, especially towing boats. Some owners, no more than one in 10 and perhaps fewer than one in 100, also use their SUVs for off-road driving.

But in moments of candor, auto executives in Detroit dismiss these buyers, especially the off-road enthusiasts, as being too few to really matter in the overall SUV market. "SUVs are about image, it's about who that customer is and who that customer wants to be," said J. C. Collins, Ford's top marketing manager for SUVs and mini-vans. "The only time those SUVs are going to be off-road is when they miss the driveway at 3 a.m."

Virtually no SUV buyers choose the vehicles for the serious off-road driving for which the vehicles are designed. Most SUV buyers live in the most affluent suburbs of very large cities, with particu-larly high concentrations around New York, Los Angeles and Miami.[4] The percentage of SUV owners who say they use their vehi-cles for actual off-road driving varies from 1 to 13 percent, depend-ing on how the question is asked, executives at the big automotive marketing firms say. When market researchers press these people, most of them admit that their idea of off-road driving is to travel on any dirt or gravel road, even if that road is smoothly graded.

Steven Sturm, Toyota's top marketing executive in the United States, likes to tell the story of doing a focus group with wealthy baby boomers in Los Angeles. An elegant woman in the group said that she needed her full-sized Lexus LX 470 to drive up over the curb and onto lawns to park at large parties in Beverly Hills.

Automakers used to pay close attention to how often their SUVs were driven off-road. Now they make little effort to monitor it, having concluded that people are more interested in the fantasy that they could go off-road than the reality. "You don't ask how often because it doesn't matter—you get to be Superman for a day" by driving an SUV even on paved roads, Chrysler's Bostwick said.

One reason why most SUV buyers do not engage in off-road driving is that they have no place to do it. Off-road driving is illegal in many of the most popular areas of federal parks, and completely illegal in pristine wilderness areas. Poorly maintained dirt roads in western states provide an opportunity for bouncy travel, while pri-vate landowners can pretty much do what they want. But many urban SUV owners do not know how to find the right places on public lands and do not know an obliging landowner. The automakers' market research nonetheless shows consistently that consumers want four-wheel drive or all-wheel drive.

So SUV advertising stresses off-road capabilities. Ford has tried to advertise all of its SUVs together under the "No Boundaries" logo, while trying to portray its dealers as "Ford Outfitters." Showrooms now feature kayaks, camping tents and other outdoor gear—dealers actually choose what package of sports equipment they want from a small catalog offered by Ford that makes suggestions based on the size of the showroom.

Yet Ford executives are well aware that very few SUV customers will actually go anywhere that would require an outfitter. "It's more figurative, because most people don't really go off-road in their sport utilities," said James G. O'Connor, the president of Ford Motors' huge Ford division, at the end of the press conference announcing the No Boundaries ad campaign.

The No Boundaries campaign partly recognized this truth with a mixture of ads. Some ads showed remote locations that buyers could visit in their SUVs. Others showed people going to golf courses. "Golf is a huge interest for people who buy sport utilities," admitted Jan Klug, the Ford division's marketing manager.

Automakers have also gone to great lengths to foment demand for four-wheel-drive systems by creating opportunities for customers to use them. Many Land Rover dealerships have little, fake mounds with boulders for customers to drive over. Land Rover and Hummer maintain larger, permanent off-road courses near their headquarters where buyers can bring their vehicles to learn what they can do in the woods, paying fees of as much as $5,000. Ford and Chrysler have traveling shows that set up fake hills at fairgrounds and other big venues around the country, with local dealers inviting potential SUV customers to come try the vehicles.

Chrysler held one such event near its corporate headquarters in Auburn Hills, Michigan, on a beautiful late summer afternoon in 1999. Actually, there were two events practically side by side: a marketing event for Chrysler and Dodge cars and minivans on a very large parking lot and, across a two-lane road, a Jeep promotion in an open field.

The car and minivan event was well presented. There were several long truck trailers with interesting exhibits, like a driving simulator that allowed the visitor to experience the difference between stopping a car with antilock brakes and stopping with regular brakes. There were several airy white tents where Chrysler engineers were making presentations about the vehicles. Parked under and between the tents were some of Chrysler's most attractive models, like a bright-red Dodge Viper sports car, low, sleek and extremely powerful. To entertain children, there was even a fenced area with radio-controlled model cars zipping around the pavement.

The only problem? There were literally no children there to play with the model cars. Two young Chrysler employees in khakis and white polo shirts were using the controls for two of the model cars themselves. The rest of the model cars were sitting idle at the side of the enclosure. Practically everyone under the tents was balding or had gray hair—the Greatest Generation, still buying large cars. Some of them were complaining about the many SUVs obscuring their view of the road.

But there were plenty of parents and children across the street at the Jeep event, which had been promoted in ads as "Jeep 101." Instead of airy white tents, there were green, military-looking tents giving out T-shirts, mugs and other gear with the Jeep logo on it. Most popular of all was an off-road driving course that allowed city dwellers to wrestle Wranglers for a couple hundred yards up and down dirt tracks. Since southeastern Michigan was scraped fairly flat by glaciers during the last Ice Age, Chrysler had to use earth-moving equipment to build the hills for the event.

The kids seemed to enjoy the spectacle most of all. Milo Perreault, an 11-year-old from Shelby Township, Michigan, ogled the sport utilities and spoke wistfully of the long wait until he would be old enough to drive. "I'd actually like a Jeep," he said. "Some of the sports cars, like the Viper, are low to the ground, and in a Jeep I like the height."

Egregious SUV ads are legion, including the Cadillac Escalade ad described in the introduction, which carried the word "yield" in giant letters. A series of magazine ads for the Lincoln Navigator explicitly caters to the selfishness of SUV buyers. One shows the Navigator on a mountain top under the slogan, "Ditch the Joneses." Another shows a huge black Navigator barreling around a corner at sunset near the Golden Gate bridge under the words, "Damn the tuxedos, full speed ahead."

The mention of tuxedos was anything but accidental. The popularity of SUVs is not just about automakers' catering to people's sense of adventure, but about automakers' response to two huge changes in the American auto market: the growing concentration of income among the nation's most prosperous families and the growing availability and reliability of used cars. Taken together, the two trends have given automakers a big incentive to design ever larger, more expensive vehicles and pay little attention to fuel economy.

Through most of the twentieth century, auto manufacturers took pride in presenting themselves as building cars for everyday American families. Henry Ford's Model T was a spartan vehicle built for farmers. It was available only in black for many years because quick-drying automotive paint could only be formulated in black. The faster drying times greatly reduced the time and cost of building a new car. When Henry Ford doubled his workers' wages to $5 a day in early 1914, he made it possible for the workers to pay just five months' wages to buy one of the cars they were building.

Alfred Sloan, who dominated General Motors from 1920 until his death in 1966, offered a "ladder" of models, from simple Chevrolets to elegant Cadillacs, with the slogan, "a car for every purse and purpose." Through the 1970s, buying a new automobile remained a symbol that a family had become comfortably ensconced in the American middle class. Automakers devoted most of their energy to designing and manufacturing cars for the millions of families who were filling up the ever-sprawling suburbs around American cities, and auto executives thought of themselves as selling the quintessential middle-class product. Luxury brands like Cadillac, Lincoln, BMW, Mercedes and others operated in small volumes compared to Goliaths like Chevrolet and Ford.

Income inequality has widened considerably since then, as average incomes have risen briskly for prosperous families while stagnating for the rest of the population. Sales of luxury models have more than tripled since 1980, even as the overall auto market has only expanded about 25 percent. Adjusted for inflation, Census Bureau figures show that between 1973 and 1998, the most recent year available, the household income of a family at the 50th percentile in income only crept up from $36,302 to $38,885. By contrast, household income at the 80th percentile rose from $62,109 to exactly $75,000, and income at the 95th percentile leaped from $98,453 to $132,199.

Mention income concentration at all and it is easy to be accused of being a liberal. Conservatives contend that there is a lot of turnover in the top 20 percent of the income distribution, as some high-earners lose their jobs while the lesser-paid receive raises. To some extent, this is true. But from the automakers' standpoint, it does not matter whether the same families are at the top of the heap every year or whether the faces are constantly changing. What counts is that higher-income families are increasingly the ones with the money to buy new automobiles. This has an ever greater influence on how automobiles are designed and marketed.

The most prosperous 20 percent of the population accounted for 45 percent of the spending on new automobiles as recently as 1990. They now account for 60 percent of the spending and the proportion is rising, according to General Motors. "It's probably the biggest trend ever affecting the auto industry—we continue to shift toward higher-income, better-educated customers," said Paul Ballew, GM's market research director.

A surprisingly large segment of Explorer buyers are extremely affluent indeed and able to purchase even some of the most expensive luxury cars, but choose the unpretentious image of an Explorer instead. "They can afford to buy almost anything," said Ed Molchany, the Ford brand manager for Explorers. "They want to buy a vehicle that's down to earth, isn't flashy."

Automakers still sell roughly five million vehicles a year—or nearly a third of all vehicles—to households with annual incomes of less than $50,000. But auto executives and economists say that figure does not tell the whole story, as these buyers are often not middle-class families. Instead, as many as two-thirds of these buyers are young people whose prosperous parents and grandparents help them with the purchase, or retirees who have considerable assets even though they do not have large incomes, said W. Van Bussmann, the corporate economist until recently for the Chrysler side of DaimlerChrysler.

If middle-income families are no longer buying as many new automobiles, what are they buying instead? Used cars and, in smaller numbers, used SUVs. Used cars are becoming more popular now because they are much more reliable, more available and easier to finance than they were even a decade ago.

Used cars are more reliable because of the disappearance of planned obsolescence, the old Detroit practice of poor quality and frequent model changes that forced people to buy a new car every few years because the old one was wearing out. Foreign automakers showed that it was possible to design more reliable cars in the 1970s and 1980s, and Americans bought them. During every economic boom from World War II through the 1980s, there was a drop in the average age of vehicles in use as people scrapped a lot of old cars and bought new ones. During the 1990s, however, the average age of cars and light trucks rose during the longest economic boom ever, as people held onto the older vehicles even as they were buying new ones. (This trend helped obscure just how fast SUV sales were rising in the 1990s. For a long time, it did not look like there were that many more SUVs on the roads. So many cars were being kept on the road longer that the total number of vehicles in use was rising briskly. Between 1998 and 2000, however, there was finally an uptick in the scrappage rate of older cars, perhaps because the stock market was soaring and people decided they could afford better vehicles. The percentage of registered vehicles in the United States that are SUVs began jumping nearly a full percentage point a year.)

Finding a reliable used car has become a lot easier too. The rise of the leasing market has flooded the used-car market with cars—and lately, SUVs—that are only two or three years old and still in great condition. To resell these vehicles when customers turn them in at the end of leases, automakers have had to offer extensive warranties for used vehicles. State governments have also helped by enacting lemon laws that require sellers to disclose defects in used cars, although these laws remain far less stringent than consumer advocates would like.

Finally, it has become much easier to buy a used vehicle without putting up a lot of cash. Used-car loans and even used-car leases were hard to find as recently as the 1980s but are now quite common. More than 80 percent of new-car buyers finance their purchases with loans or leases. While some of these new-car purchasers may be choosing loans or leases to take advantage of a low-interest-rate promotional campaign, or for tax reasons, the bulk of these buyers simply don't have the cash, say executives in the finance units of automakers. As loans and leases become available for used vehicles, these become an increasingly attractive option for these customers.

The combination of rising income inequality and the expansion of the used-vehicle market is transforming what automakers sell. With middle-income families buying fewer new cars and light trucks, for example, the market for small, fuel-efficient sedans has withered. One, the Ford Escort, the most popular car sold in the 1980s, has faded away without much notice; Ford replaced it in 1999 with the taller, fancier Focus. "If you're going to sell more vehicles, and the first-time buyers are disappearing, you've got to sell more larger, more expensive vehicles," Mr. Bussmann says.

More and more vehicles in showrooms these days—with the exception of a few tiny imports from Korea—come loaded with expensive equipment like power-adjustable leather seats, compact-disc changers and even computer navigation systems. Very few buyers want vehicles with only an AM/FM radio. Alan Helfman, a Chrysler and Jeep dealer in Houston, said his mechanics had to replace so many factory-installed car radios with fancier systems that he eventually ran out of room to store all the discarded radios. Other dealers did not want the radios either.

"We had to throw all those radios out," he said.

Because high-income families care little about gasoline prices, vehicles are getting bigger. Subject to less stringent federal fuel-economy standards than cars, sport utilities in particular are growing so big that the largest models no longer fit in many garages. These larger vehicles burn plenty of gasoline, getting as little as 10 miles to the gallon in the city in the case of the Ford Excursion. Sales of these leviathans suffered remarkably little when springtime jumps in the price of gasoline occurred in 2000 and 2001. This partly reflected the popularity of SUVs among affluent Americans, whose driving habits are not affected greatly by the cost of gasoline.

Detroit's reliance on the mass market really hurt it during the gasoline shortages and quadrupling of oil prices in 1973 and 1974. Sales of big, mass-market station wagons, sedans and coupes plunged and never fully recovered. Middle-class customers, conscious of the pocketbook impact of continued high gas prices, chose smaller cars instead, and bought many of these smaller cars from Japanese automakers.

What is most interesting is that the luxury market, which

included some of the largest gas-guzzlers, behaved very differently then. Sales of Cadillacs, for example, briefly plunged in 1973 along with sales of other models as long as there were long lines at gasoline stations and political leaders were talking about gasoline shortages. But as soon as gasoline became widely available again, Cadillac sales rebounded to their previous levels—even though gasoline remained far more expensive than it had been previously, and even though Cadillacs were especially large gas-guzzlers.

In other words, affluent families cared about the availability of gasoline but were not very concerned about the price of gasoline or the fuel economy of the vehicles they drove. This lesson has become increasingly important as the auto market, and especially the market for sport utility vehicles, has become ever more skewed toward affluent families.

Gas prices peaked at $1.35 a gallon in 1981.[5] Adjusted only for inflation, gasoline would have had to be $2.62 a gallon in late 2001 to match that price. But adjusted for the increase in annual income of the top 20 percent of the population, the price of gasoline would have needed to rise to $3.76 a gallon to have had the same effect on affluent families' pocketbooks as it did in 1981. And adjusted for the increase in income of the top 5 percent of the nation's households, the price of a gallon of gas would need to have climbed to $4.59 to have the same effect as in 1981. These are the households that now buy 11 percent of new family vehicles.[6] Since gasoline prices have stayed far below these levels, fuel economy has not been one of the main concerns of well-heeled SUV buyers.

Cheap gasoline, rising income inequality and the insecurities of many affluent baby boomers have all helped make SUVs so popular. But there is one last factor: the way politicians and Hollywood celebrities have embraced SUVs, giving them lots of free media exposure.

For prominent politicians, driving or being chauffeured in an

SUV is a no-brainer. For starters, mayors, governors and members of Congress tend to have household incomes well over $100,000, which puts them easily into the market for expensive vehicles. SUVs have come to dominate the luxury market, and especially for any politician who feels the need to drive an American-built luxury vehicle. By contrast, Mercedes, BMW and Lexus have routed Lincoln and Cadillac in the market for luxury cars, as Town Cars and DeVilles have lost their cachet compared with Mercedes E-Class and BMW 5-Series sedans. Despite their hefty price tags, SUVs also project an unpretentious image of the sort that most American politicians constantly strive to cultivate.

Mayor Rudolph Giuliani used to rush around New York City in a dark green Suburban, providing GM with free media exposure for the big vehicle, which was so heavy that it violated the weight limit on the Brooklyn Bridge. Governor Jesse Ventura of Minnesota plays on his reputation as a former pro wrestler and general-purpose tough guy by going everywhere in a Lincoln Navigator. On Capitol Hill in Washington, midsize SUVs have been steadily replacing large cars in the most prestigious indoor parking places, the ones reserved for members. "When you go in the garage there's quite a few of them, it's noticeable," said Representative Robert Matsui, a California Democrat who has owned a Jeep Grand Cherokee and a Ford Explorer, although he recently switched to a BMW sedan.

SUVs have also become especially popular with movie stars, directors, singers and other popular entertainment idols. The street outside the Oscars ceremony each year now looks like a gathering for a black-tie off-road derby. Cadillac has developed an impressive roster of celebrities who have purchased its $50,000 Escalade full-size SUVs: singers like Whitney Houston and Natalie Cole, actors like Bruce Willis and Calista Flockhart, basketball stars like Shaquille O'Neal and Gary Payton and extreme sports successes like Tara Dakides, the 26-year-old snowboarder.[7]

The embrace of SUVs by entertainment and athletic stars underlines how far these once-utilitarian vehicles have come. Since the days when Roy Chapin of American Motors used to go duck hunting in the Ontario marshes with his Kaiser Jeep buddy, Stephen Girard, off-road vehicles have captivated America's elite while becoming mainstays of the broader American automobile market and cornerstones of the economic health of the auto industry and the upper Midwest. The glitter of Hollywood stars and the power of celebrity politicians has rubbed off on vehicles originally designed for outdoorsmen. But the glamour and popularity of sport utility vehicles have disguised several basic problems. SUVs remain little more than modified pickup trucks. Their rollover and other safety problems have not been solved. Their environmental record is appalling, from inefficient engines that guzzle gasoline to inadequate catalytic converters that allow too much smog to foul the air. The SUV is displacing the family car even though it is still, mechanically, a very poor substitute indeed.

PART TWO

THE DARK SIDE
OF THE SUV

THE MYTH OF
FOUR-WHEEL-DRIVE SAFETY

The full-page newspaper advertisement seems at first glance to suggest that the Jeep Grand Cherokee is an especially safe vehicle. The top half of the page is occupied by five aging insurance policies. "Earthquake Insurance Certificate" says one policy with a brown border and elaborate calligraphy. "Avalanche Insurance Policy" says another policy with an ornate blue border. Floods, mud slides and tornadoes are covered by the other policies.

Across the middle of the page is a simple message printed in large, black letters: "Jeep Grand Cherokee. Still the best insurance policy out there."

Below the slogan is a Jeep balanced on four boulders. Underneath the vehicle, in somewhat smaller type, is a brief paragraph extolling its safety, which begins: "It's your classic man vs. nature struggle. Man goes out in 4x4—nature gets nasty. So we engineered Jeep Grand Cherokee to be one of the safest 4x4s out there. Its legendary four-wheel drive shows no fear in the face of a blizzard. Its braking system helps you stop even when the rain or sleet or snow hasn't."[1]

Detroit has long been subtly suggesting that SUVs are safer than cars. But the ad writers cagily avoid making explicit claims, with good reason. The truth is that for a wide range of real-world hazards, driving an SUV is a safety liability, not an asset.

If a potential crash looms, an SUV's brakes will stop you no faster than a car's brakes and may take longer, especially in slippery conditions. An SUV will not allow you to swerve around a hazard as handily as a car. If you hit another vehicle or a solid object, you will be less protected from injury in an SUV than in a car of the same weight. And if an icy patch sends you sliding to the edge of the road, or if another vehicle delivers a glancing blow that pushes you into a curb or guardrail, an SUV is far more likely than a car to kill you or paralyze you by rolling over.

The Grand Cherokee is actually one of the less dangerous SUVs on the market because it was designed with rare care to reduce the risk of rollovers. The ad for it is nonetheless a masterpiece in the dark art of hinting at SUV safety benefits that do not exist. How would four-wheel drive, a collection of mechanical components in a vehicle underbody, ever possibly show "fear in the face of a blizzard"? Don't every vehicle's brakes help you "stop even when the rain or sleet or snow hasn't"? The ad exemplifies how automakers tout the safety of SUVs without actually making any promises for fear of being held accountable in court.

What is four-wheel drive? While ad agencies have surrounded four-wheel drive with an almost magical aura of safety, it actually is a fairly modest technology of little use to the average motorist—and downright dangerous to motorists who overestimate what four-wheel drive can do for them.

There are several different mechanical approaches to four-wheel drive systems, but all perform the same basic function: they use power from the engine to turn all four wheels. By contrast, the engine turns only the front wheels in a front-wheel-drive car, or the rear wheels in a rear-wheel-drive vehicle.

Marketers also like to use the term "all-wheel drive." Since all family automobiles have four wheels, this might seem like the same thing as four-wheel-drive. In practice, "all-wheel drive" is used to describe four-wheel drive systems that do not have an extra-low gear ("below" first gear) for ascending or descending extremely steep slopes during off-road driving. For the purposes of this discussion, however, the terms "all-wheel drive" and "four-wheel drive" are effectively synonymous.

Four-wheel drive provides no benefit whatsoever when the driver hits the brakes, because the engine automatically stops providing power to the wheels then. Indeed, SUVs actually tend to have longer stopping distances than cars for a slew of reasons ranging from their considerable weight to the design of their tires to loopholes in federal regulations. SUVs tend to be especially hard to stop on surfaces that are wet, snowy, icy or otherwise slippery. Yet these are precisely the driving conditions in which an SUV driver might be tempted to go faster than a car driver because the four-wheel drive helps the SUV driver accelerate without slipping.

Four-wheel drive also does not help a driver to turn while driving across a slippery surface. What matters in such a turn is how much friction the tires retain against the surface, which reflects tire design, and not the number of wheels that receive power. Once the tires start sliding sideways, it makes little difference whether the engine is driving four wheels or only two. Drivers who go faster in slippery conditions because they are trusting their four-wheel drive systems to keep them on the road are making a potentially lethal mistake— and a common mistake, as even auto-industry engineers concede.

"When you're going around a corner or braking, you have the same four wheels whether you're in a four-wheel-drive vehicle or a two-wheel-drive vehicle," said Timothy J. Dougherty, a traction performance engineer at Michelin.

Four-wheel drive is useful in four situations, all of them uncommon:

- *Driving through deep snow that has not been plowed or through deep mud.* People who live in rural areas, especially the small number of Americans who live far from paved roads, may occasionally need to do this. Jim O'Connor, the president of the Ford brand division at Ford Motor Company, likes to say that his company's four-wheel-drive systems allow bass fishermen to drive across mud and grass to reach the edges of partly dried-up lakes and pull their boats out. Farmers also need four-wheel drive to pull equipment in and out of muddy fields. But urban and suburban families who live in places with snowplows will seldom if ever need to traverse deep snow or mud. On the rare occasions when this does happen and you get stuck, try rocking the vehicle back and forth, using first gear and reverse. If that doesn't work, dig some snow or mud out of the way of the tires, or put some cardboard, leaves or sand in front of the tires.

- *Using the engine to slow down the vehicle if the brakes fail entirely.* Yet brakes almost never fail entirely. More common is for the power to the brakes to fail, so that it takes a far greater effort to depress the brake pedal. The first thing to do then is to mash the brake pedal with all the strength you can muster, and to keep the brake pedal mashed to the floor as long as necessary. There is seldom time in an emergency to put the vehicle in the lowest available gear.

- *Using the engine to descend a steep, unpaved surface very slowly without applying the brakes.* Four-wheel drive is valuable for serious off-road driving, such as traversing boulder fields or scaling hills and mountains. It can be dangerous to apply the brakes while descending a muddy hillside, because the wheels may lock up and the vehicle may simply start sliding.

Putting the vehicle in the lowest possible gear and keeping the foot off the brake is the best way down such surfaces, crawling down at 2 or 3 miles an hour. But outside of special off-road driving clinics bankrolled by automakers, the number of people who actually do this is tiny. So-called all-wheel-drive systems commonly lack the extra, very low gear of traditional four-wheel drive systems and are of little use in descending such trails because their first gears allow the vehicles to roll too fast down the slope.

- *Accelerating on icy, snowy or rainy roads without slipping.* This is the main benefit of four-wheel drive for most motorists.

All four of these situations fall into the category of what some auto engineers call "tracking," the ability of a vehicle to keep moving forward despite slippery conditions. But they are not really safety issues, as some engineers candidly acknowledge. "I don't consider four-wheel drive as a safety feature or a safety-beneficial technology—it's first and foremost a question of tracking," said Christer Gustafsson, Volvo's senior safety engineer.

Many safety experts say that the ability to accelerate without slipping actually hurts safety rather than helping it. The car driver whose wheels spin once or twice while backing out of the driveway knows that the road is slippery. The SUV driver who navigates the driveway and street without difficulty until she tries to brake may not find out that the road is slippery until it is too late. A top engineering executive at a big automaker puts it bluntly, after insisting on anonymity for fear of being called as a witness in a lawsuit someday: "Many end up in the ditch because they don't realize the deceleration is not enhanced."

The myth that four-wheel drive helps braking is widespread and completely wrong, but it is perpetuated by ads like Chrysler's ad for the Jeep Grand Cherokee. Four-wheel drive simply means that the driving force of the engine is being used to turn all four wheels. As soon as you touch the brakes, the engine is no longer sending power to the wheels so the four-wheel drive provides no benefit.

Every automobile, whether a car, SUV, minivan or pickup truck, has brakes for all four wheels. Another top engineer, Thomas Davis, GM's group vice president for light trucks, expressed the reality clearly in 1999: four-wheel drive means you have four-wheel go, but every vehicle has four-wheel stop.

As it happens, not all automobiles have exactly the same "four-wheel stop." If anything, SUVs tend to have slightly longer stopping distances than cars, although how much longer is the subject of some debate. The reasons are well known to engineers at automakers, brake companies and tire manufacturers, who have struggled with them for years.

Start with the extra weight of SUVs. They typically weigh half a ton more than a car of similar seating, which by itself makes them harder to stop. The weight in an SUV also tends to be higher off the road because of the vehicle's greater ground clearance for off-road driving. That means the weight of an SUV "leans" forward more during sudden braking, so the front brakes have to do most of the work. Brakes lose most of their effectiveness once a tire stops turning and starts simply sliding across the road, so relying mostly on the front brakes means relying on the friction generated by the front tires against the road.

Each tire on an SUV or car typically has just five square inches of rubber in contact with the road at a time. So during panic braking, an SUV driver is relying heavily on the traction of the mere 10 square inches of rubber that the two front tires have in contact with the road. Cars also lean forward during panic braking but not quite so much, so they make somewhat greater use of all 20 square inches of rubber in contact with the road by all four wheels.

Auto engineers use a simple mathematical formula to calculate the extent of the problem of vehicles that lean forward during sharp braking. Forward weight transfer is equal to the height of a vehicle's center of gravity divided by the length of its wheelbase (the distance from the front wheels to the back wheels) and then multiplied by the vehicle's weight and then by how quickly the deceleration takes place. This means that forward weight transfer is greatest in tall, fairly heavy SUVs that are not very long and are subject to sudden braking. Unfortunately, this means that forward weight transfer can be a particular problem in a panic stop in a small, heavy, pickup-based SUV of the sort increasingly marketed to teenagers and people in their early 20s.[2]

The "macho" tires on many SUVs only make matters worse. Many SUVs are sold with tires that have fairly wide, deep grooves and are promoted as providing good traction during off-road driving. The grooves allow mud and snow to squirt out the back as the tire moves across the mud or snow, allowing the tire to dig in deeper for traction. But the grooves actually hurt traction on a paved road, because they reduce the surface area of rubber in contact with the pavement, tire manufacturers say. Even worse are the extra-macho replacement tires sold for SUVs, which may have even wider grooves than the automakers tolerate as original equipment on their vehicles.

"It has been a compromise—do you want better wet and dry stopping distances or do you want better off-road traction," Michelin's Dougherty said.

Automakers strike a different compromise in choosing the tires for each SUV, in the hope of providing adequate braking performance while still offering enough off-road capability to impress influential automobile reviewers at major newspapers, magazines and television networks. Reviewers tend to like to be able to drive up and down muddy hillsides in vehicles borrowed from the manufacturers, and off-road performance plays a big part in many SUV evaluations by the media. Yet it is a safe bet that hardly any SUV buyers, especially those living in urban and suburban areas, know that their vehicles' stopping distances have been compromised so as to provide off-road traction that virtually no drivers really need.

The rubber compounds in SUV tires also tend to be not very

good. High-performance sports cars have wide, expensive tires with special rubber compounds that provide extra grip on the road. But automakers are reluctant to install such tires on the front of SUVs for fear of making another problem worse during sudden stops: rollovers.

"The higher center of gravity puts more weight on the front tires, so the front tires have to have more grip, but when the front tires have more grip, they have more propensity to roll over," said Gregory P. Stevens, a vehicle dynamics supervisor at Ford, in an interview in 1999.

Many SUVs have antilock brakes, and these systems also tend to be a little less effective in SUVs than in cars. Antilock systems work by applying more and more braking pressure to the wheels until the wheels stop turning and start skidding. Then the systems almost instantly reduce the brake pressure back to the last level at which the wheels still turned, so that the brakes retain their effectiveness and the driver retains some ability to maneuver. Brake engineers say that when the wheels start slipping, the antilock systems on SUVs are programmed to back off even farther than car brakes. When an SUV starts sliding, it is more likely to roll over, so the brake engineers take extra pains to prevent this from happening by having the antilock brakes let off the pressure a little more. But less vigorous application of the antilock brakes means slightly longer stopping distances, especially on slippery surfaces like icy roads or gravel roads.

Until the late 1990s, the brakes on SUVs suffered from one additional problem: They tended to be the cheapest, simplest brakes that money could buy. Until very recently, automakers continued to equip most SUVs with cheap drum brakes, which are prone to overheating during repeated use on long downhill stretches. By contrast, most cars have been equipped for years with more sophisticated disc brakes. Automakers have long equipped pickup trucks with drum brakes because many pickups are sold to corporate fleets whose purchasing managers demand absolute rock-bottom prices.

Since brakes are part of the underbodies that most SUVs share with pickup trucks, SUVs inherited the same cheap brakes installed on pickup trucks. Lucas Varity, the world's largest manufacturer of SUV brakes and the world's second largest brake company overall, tried in vain for years to interest the automakers in better brakes for SUVs, said John H. Sapp, the company's senior brake systems manager, in an interview in 1997.

Automakers can address these brake problems if they try hard enough. They are belatedly moving toward disc brakes for all SUVs. For some of the more expensive models, they are also linking rear wheels to the underbody of an SUV using coiled springs instead of a system of long steel strips, known as a leaf-spring suspension, that flex up and down as the vehicle passes over bumps. The coiled suspension springs essentially push the rear wheels down against the ground at all times, which improves their traction even when the weight of the vehicle is mostly on the front wheels during sudden braking.

Ford used the more primitive suspensions on its Explorers through the 2001 model year, then introduced rear suspensions using coiled springs on four-door Explorers (but not the Explorer Sport or Sport Trac) for the 2002 model year. Together with other improvements, the effect on braking performance was dramatic. Dale Claudepierre, Ford's top SUV engineer, says that the stopping distance in a fully loaded 2002 model at 60 miles an hour is just 135 feet. That is roughly what you would expect in a family sedan, although sports cars, with their pavement-gripping tires and low bodies, can stop in less than 120 feet. By contrast, the stopping distance in Explorers for the 2001 model year and earlier was 164 feet, according to Ford. That is a frighteningly long distance, especially because most of the slowing of a vehicle occurs near the end of the stopping distance.[3] Put another way, the 2001 Explorer would still be traveling roughly 20 miles an hour at the point where the 2002 Explorer had come to a full stop.

An impact at 20 miles per hour might not sound serious, but it

is. Being stopped cold at that speed, by hitting an unyielding surface like a bridge abutment or a vehicle of equal weight moving the
opposite direction, is like dropping a vehicle on its nose from a
height of 13 feet. This can cause serious injuries for the occupants,
especially if they are not wearing seat belts.

According to Claudepierre, most of the improvement in stopping distance came from the change in rear suspensions. Yet while
virtually all cars use rear suspensions with coiled springs these
days, most SUVs still do not. Upgrading the rear suspension on an
SUV is expensive, adding as much as $1,500 to the cost of a vehicle.
Putting coiled-spring suspensions on an SUV that is based on a
pickup-truck design involves a lot of engineering work and extra
space at the assembly plant, all of which costs money. The coiled-
spring suspensions are less suitable for carrying heavy cargo and so
are seldom used on pickup trucks.

Ford decided to upgrade the Explorer's suspension only after
noticing that Mercedes had chosen an expensive rear suspension
for its M-Class SUVs. Inexpensive two-door SUVs marketed to
younger buyers with less money still have old-fashioned suspensions, including the Explorer Sport and Explorer Sport Trac.

Recent tests by *Car and Driver* and *Consumer Reports* have found
smaller gaps between cars and SUVs in braking performance than
the Explorer's record might suggest, indicating that the latest SUVs
have mostly caught up with cars. *Consumer Reports* calculated in
December 2001 that the average stopping distance at 60 miles per
hour was only 4 feet longer than for cars on dry surfaces, and 5.5
feet longer on wet surfaces—a small difference.[4]

Car and Driver found a somewhat wider discrepancy in 2000 and
2001, running tests on dry surfaces at 70 miles an hour. The magazine's tests found that large SUVs took an extra 8 feet to stop compared to low-priced family sedans. Luxury midsized SUVs needed
11 feet longer to stop than comparably priced luxury sedans.

Is it legal to equip SUVs with less effective brakes than cars?
Absolutely. In brakes, as in so many other areas, light trucks have

been subject to more lenient regulation than cars since the 1960s, and SUVs have been categorized as light trucks. Light trucks have been allowed longer stopping distances and fewer safeguards against partial brake failure. This will finally change in the 2003 model year, when light trucks will become subject to the same brake regulations as cars for the first time. But as usual with auto regulations, nothing new will be required of the 20 million SUVs already on the road, since very little can be done to improve a vehicle's design once it has been built.

The old regulations and even the new ones represent a fairly low standard—the barest minimum performance needed for a vehicle to be allowed on the road. The old standard, for example, was that when traveling 55 miles an hour, a car should be able to stop in 181 feet and a light truck should be able to stop in 204 feet. When I wrote a front-page article challenging the adequacy of SUV brakes in December 1997 after Lucas Varity's Sapp gave a speech on the problem at a closed-door engineering conference in Dearborn, Michigan, Ford in particular bitterly denied that there was a problem. Ford engineers spent several months retesting their SUVs using the different procedures for car brake tests, and the company issued a press release the following spring announcing that their SUVs had met the car standards. But Ford engineers also acknowledged then that some of their SUV models had only barely met some of the car standards, although they declined to identify specific models. By contrast, cars tend to beat all the standards by a significant margin.

Problems with SUV brakes continued to spread in subsequent months. The UAW's top leaders urged GM to improve the performance of its SUV brakes after a spate of crashes involving UAW officials who insisted that their brakes had been inadequate. The need to improve SUV brakes became more clear to Ford in the autumn of 1998, when the U.S. Army conducted braking tests on 10 vehicles at its vast vehicle testing area in Aberdeen, Maryland, at the request of federal safety regulators. Drivers in five passenger cars, two minivans, a full-size cargo van, a full-size pickup truck and a full-size SUV, the Ford Expedition, accelerated to 62 miles an hour (100 kilometers an hour, a speed picked to be consistent with European tests) and then slammed on the brakes. Each vehicle was tested with 40 stops: 10 stops on dry pavement with just a driver inside, 10 stops fully loaded on dry pavement, 10 stops on wet pavement with just a driver inside and 10 stops fully loaded on wet pavement.

Regulators were wise to have had the tests done at the Army facility, which has long straightaways. With just a driver inside, the cars stopped in 148 to 160 feet on dry pavement while the Expedition needed an average of 170.4 feet to stop. The cars did a little worse when fully loaded on dry pavement while the Expedition actually did slightly better when fully loaded, probably because putting a lot of well-restrained cargo in the back of an SUV helps hold down the back of the vehicle and makes the rear brakes more effective.

But when the Army wetted down the pavement, the Expedition sailed far down the track, especially when fully loaded. The fully loaded cars all stopped between 164 feet (a Cadillac DeVille, a good, roomy alternative to the Expedition for not much more money) and 174 feet (a Toyota Camry, a model that fared poorly overall in the tests). But the fully loaded Expedition rolled an average of 220 feet down the track.[5]

After three years of denial, Ford changed its stance in January 2001, when it announced at the Detroit auto show that it would upgrade all of the brakes in its SUVs to make them as effective as car brakes. "The stopping distance of light trucks has traditionally been more than cars—we're trying to make them have the same," said Gurminder Bedi, Ford's vice president for North American SUVs and pickup trucks, in an interview before the announcement. "They meet the minimum standards, the question is whether they can do better than that—the answer is yes."

Yet other automakers have not made comparable pledges. They

say instead that they feel confident that all their vehicles will meet the new brake standards for the 2003 model year—a less ambitious goal. After more than three years of research, regulators have not yet begun a rating system for automobile brakes. The auto industry wants more research done before any such system is adopted—the industry's standard stalling response to ideas it dislikes.

A ratings system would be valuable to consumers by alerting them to one of the many dangers of SUVs. Federal ratings would be particularly valuable because private lawsuits, often a powerful incentive for automakers to improve safety, have not been an issue in terms of stopping distance. While there has been a lot of litigation over the years involving brakes that malfunction, it is virtually impossible to sue an automaker for selling vehicles with stopping distances that are long but still comply with regulations. So while lawsuits have been valuable in improving the reliability and quality of brakes, they have played little role in setting everyday brake performance.

How many people have been killed or injured because of excessively long stopping distances in SUVs? Remarkably, no one has any idea. Statisticians have never even been able to demonstrate conclusively that shorter stopping distances make a vehicle safer. Sports cars have the shortest stopping distances but their drivers have some of the highest death rates. Does this mean that having a short stopping distance is hazardous to your health? No, it means that sports car drivers tend to be young men who take a lot of risks. Indeed, a recurrent problem in assessing the value of good brakes lies in driver behavior. If drivers think they can stop on a dime, they may be more willing to tailgate other motorists and take other risks. Antilock brakes have produced virtually no improvement in traffic deaths even though they reduce stopping distances on most road surfaces. One popular explanation for this surprising pattern is that drivers may simply drive more aggressively if they feel they can stop quickly.

But safety experts still say that shorter stopping distances are better than long stopping distances. And what is clear is that the worst case of all is when drivers think they can stop quickly when they cannot.

Some automakers' safety executives are starting to become concerned that too many people mistakenly think that four-wheel drive helps braking. These executives say that while other safety issues may be more important—like wearing seat belts and looking far down the road to see hazardous situations early—motorists should be more aware that four-wheel drive does not improve braking distance.

Helen Petrauskas is a lawyer who defended Ford on safety and environmental issues for three decades, becoming the company's vice president for safety and environmental issues. After fighting countless lawsuits for Ford, she was extremely careful about what she said. But shortly before her retirement in the spring of 2001, even she acknowledged in her carefully hedged way that more should be done to tell consumers that four-wheel drive does not help braking. "Is that the most important thing we can tell them about how to drive? Probably not. Should we tell them? Yes."

The owner's manuals of four-wheel-drive SUVs and pickups do contain disclaimers about braking. But many customers do not read the manuals, which are full of warnings that lawyers like Petrauskas put there to help them in litigation. What is needed is more restraint in advertising, plus better training for SUV drivers.

The restraint in advertising simply does not exist yet. The Grand Cherokee ad cited at the start of this chapter ran in August 2001. The Grand Cherokee actually has fairly new, effective brakes, especially by the standards of SUVs. But it is unwise to tout braking performance and four-wheel drive in the same ad, and especially to suggest that this makes an SUV any safer in rain, sleet or snow. It would be much more accurate for the Jeep ad to say something like: "The braking systems of all vehicles, including the Grand Cherokee, help you stop even when the rain or sleet or snow hasn't." But this would make very poor advertising copy.

Training drivers on the differences between SUVs and cars might help. But insurance industry studies have found that the only driver education courses that make much of a difference are those taken when someone first learns to drive. Nobody learning to drive for the first time should be anywhere near the driver's seat of an SUV. Yet by the time a driver is old enough and mature enough to be at the wheel of an SUV, his or her driving habits are probably set and unlikely to change much.

Ford nonetheless began working in late 2000 on a free, voluntary course for its customers on how to drive SUVs. Ford started the project after buying a stake in Top Driver Inc., the nation's largest operator of for-profit driving schools. Preparations for the course have moved at a glacial pace as Ford lawyers have gone over every word of it. Bill Waslick, who is Top Driver's vice president for health and safety and is overseeing the preparation of the course work, said that the instruction would emphasize the importance of looking well down the road for possible hazards, and would cover the difficulties of stopping an SUV.

"Most people think it brakes faster," he said. "It does not."

Ever notice that while many car ads show cars roaring up narrow, twisting roads in the mountains, SUV ads virtually never show this? SUV ads tend to show the vehicles plowing ahead in a straight line, whether on a road or off it. There is an excellent reason for this: automakers do not want to encourage people to start hurtling around sharp corners in SUVs. The vehicles are not nearly as well designed for this as cars, and are considerably more likely to suffer a horrific crash if they encounter a guardrail.

Sports cars are low-slung vehicles with road-gripping tires because the lower the center of gravity and the better the tires, the easier it is to go around a corner at high speed. SUVs, with their high centers of gravity and off-road tires, lumber around curves with much greater difficulty. That is at least an inconvenience on curvy roads, but can be deadly when a motorist must swerve to avoid another vehicle, a pedestrian or some other hazard.

The ability to swerve quickly is an important safety feature because changing lanes requires much less distance than braking. If a sleepy drunk starts drifting across the center line toward you or a heedless pedestrian steps off the curb in front of you, and there's not enough time to stop, the best bet is to try to swerve out of the way. But doing that in an SUV is difficult.

Some of the best experts on vehicle handling characteristics are found at automotive specialty magazines that test hundreds of vehicles each year. *Car and Driver* is the most authoritative and objective of the car magazines, and the only one that has had the courage to question, albeit gently, the automakers' wisdom in building so many SUVs instead of cars. One of the magazine's routine tests involves determining the maximum speed at which a vehicle can safely change lanes to the left and then quickly change lanes back to the right again, all within 160 feet of road. A driver might perform this maneuver in trying to pass another vehicle or in swerving around a pedestrian, deer or other hazard on a two-lane road. Family sedans could accomplish the maneuver at a top average speed of 57.7 miles per hour before they started sliding down the road and knocking down the safety cones that the magazine's writers set up. Luxury midsize SUVs could only manage the lane changes at a top average speed of 52.6 miles per hour. For large SUVs, the top average speed was just 50.9 miles per hour.

Automakers acknowledge that SUVs are less agile. "Trucks are not as nimble, they're not as light, and if you don't have the need for the load-carrying capability or the three rows of seats, the passenger cars are a great value and a lot of fun to drive," said Ronald Boltz, a senior vice president at Chrysler.

Maneuverability can be a real asset if a drunk driver, falling asleep at the wheel, starts drifting across the centerline toward you. Dodging an oncoming drunk may be impossible on a crowded road or if the drunk runs a red light or crosses the centerline abruptly when the road turns and the drunk does not. But dodging is worth a try on a less crowded, straight road with a drunk driver who moves across the centerline more slowly.

"The bottom line is that in every measurement of dynamic ability on pavement, cars outperform trucks," Csaba Csere, the magazine's editor in chief, concluded in one of his monthly columns in 1998. "Those advantages may mean little to drivers who feel that traffic accidents are as random and uncontrollable as lightning strikes. Such drivers are behaving rationally when they select trucks primarily for their crash-survival characteristics. But if you are a capable, alert driver who believes that accidents can often be avoided by decisive action behind the wheel, you'll find a car to be a much more capable partner than any truck."[6]

More recent data suggests that Csere was wrong in 1998 in suggesting even that motorists with no confidence in their ability to avoid crashes should rationally choose light trucks. Even when a crash becomes inevitable, a car provides better protection than an SUV in many kinds of crashes.

Standing a shade over 6 foot 2 and weighing 5,800 pounds, the Cadillac Escalade would probably have an imposing reputation even if it were not promoted with menacing ads telling other drivers to "YIELD" when they see it coming. The nearly $50,000 Escalade is also evocative of an earlier era in American automotive luxury, a huge, poor-handling barge of a vehicle loaded with amenities. It has an 11-speaker Bose Acoustimass audio system, a six-disc CD changer, heated leather seats and enough chrome on the outside to be blinding on a sunny day.

But for all that size and luxury, does the 2002 Escalade provide any more protection in an actual crash than a minivan or large car? That depends to some extent on the impact, but for the most part the answer is no.

Start with federal crash tests. Regulators have slammed hundreds of vehicles into concrete barriers at 35 miles an hour. Sitting in the vehicles are dummies wired for all kinds of measurements of the kinds of forces that a person would experience in such a crash.

Of course, very few people in the real world hit concrete surfaces in head-on collisions. But the test basically shows what happens in a crash that stops a vehicle dead in its tracks. So the test resembles what happens in a head-on collision with another vehicle of the same weight moving the opposite direction at the same speed.

The 2002 Escalade's federal scores for a frontal crash are so-so at best: three stars (out of five) for the driver and four stars for the front passenger. But the regulators' system of assigning stars is an antiseptic approach. Raw test scores are more revealing. Based on the federal crash-test results, an Escalade driver hitting an unyielding surface at 35 miles an hour would have a 16 percent chance of a life-threatening head injury and a 20 percent chance of a life-threatening chest injury. The driver's left leg would stand a 2 percent chance of a fractured femur. The femur of the right leg would have an unusually high 35 percent chance of snapping.[7]

Compare the eight-seat Escalade to the humble Ford Windstar minivan, which is less than half the price ($23,000) and seats almost as many people (seven). In the same collision at 35 miles an hour, the Windstar driver would have a 2 percent chance of a life-threatening head injury, a 4 percent chance of a life-threatening chest injury and less than a 1 percent chance of breaking either leg.

There are SUVs that score better than the Escalade, but none that come close to matching the test scores of the Windstar or a half-dozen other minivans and large cars. Indeed, no SUV won a five-star rating for driver protection in a frontal crash at all until the 2001 model year, when the pickup-based Ford Expedition and Lincoln Navigator and the car-based Ford Escape and Mazda Tribute managed the feat by slender margins. Throughout the 1990s, SUVs lagged behind cars and minivans considerably in safety improvements, and more than 10 million SUVs from the decade will be in the used-vehicle market for years to come.

Designing an SUV to fare well in crash tests is difficult. Scoring well requires using the front end of the vehicle to absorb as much as possible of the force of the crash, so that the dummies are not tossed forward too violently by the impact. The front ends of vehicles absorb energy in a crash by crumpling sheet metal. Race cars fly apart spectacularly when they hit walls at speeds in excess of 100 miles an hour. But the drivers frequently survive because the cars are, in effect, sacrificing themselves for the driver. (It also helps that most racing circuit crashes occur when cars strike glancing blows against walls, instead of hitting them head-on.)

An insurance industry test of an F-150 pickup truck showed that the passenger compartment almost completely collapsed in a crash at 40 miles per hour into a concrete barrier. The front end of the truck could not absorb all the crash forces created by the vehicle's considerable weight. The front ends of the Ford Expedition and Lincoln Navigator SUVs are very similiar to the pickup truck's, although the insurers have not tested these costly models in 40 miles per hour impacts into walls. Cars' passenger compartments seldom collapse when they are flung into concrete barriers in tests at this speed.

SUVs typically outweigh cars and minivans by at least a quarter-ton and sometimes as much as a full ton, and outweigh race cars by as much as two tons. But SUVs have little more sheet metal than a car or minivan to absorb the force of all this extra weight in a crash. The front ends of SUVs, measured from the windshield to the front bumper, are not much longer than the front ends of cars or minivans. SUVs typically have much larger engines than cars or minivans, but engines are so stiff that they barely crumple in a crash and absorb little energy.

The stiff steel rails in the underbodies of most SUVs, a legacy of their pickup-truck ancestry, are another hindrance in crashes. These rails have traditionally had very little give, partly because they need to be stiff to support heavy loads during bumpy off-road travel. Automakers are now cutting notches near the front of the rails so that they will crumple somewhat in a crash. But the rails still tend to be stiffer and less yielding than the steel panels that make up the body of a car or minivan.

Into the late 1990s, some of the crash-test scores for SUVs were horrific. The 1997 Chevrolet Blazer, GMC Jimmy and Oldsmobile Bravada, which are all essentially the same vehicle, carried a single star, the worst possible rating, for protecting the occupant of the front passenger seat in a frontal crash. In a test, the dummy suffered head injuries that, in a real person, would have meant more than a 50 percent chance of a life-threatening injury.

The lousy score probably reflected the fact that these models did not have air bags for the front passenger seat until the 1998 model year. While cars were required to have air bags for the driver and the front passenger by the 1995 model year, light trucks were given three extra years to install air bags for both front seats. When the government tested the Blazer again after the air bags were added, the chance of a life-threatening head injury plunged to less than 5 percent.

Even with air bags for both the front seats, the 1999 Dodge Durango was another loser. When the government tested it in a frontal crash in December 1998, the dummy in the driver's seat received scores indicating an 18 percent chance of a life-threatening head injury and a 20 percent chance of a life-threatening chest injury. The result particularly dismayed regulators because it was the second time they had tested the Durango; DaimlerChrysler had made a few small safety improvements to the vehicle after it scored just as badly a year earlier.

"If I look at the truck, it's beautiful, but my gosh, it does let tremendous forces go into the dummy," said Richard Morgan, the group leader of the government's New Car Assessment Program, which conducted the tests. The answer, he said, would be a longer, less stiff front end for the Durango. But a longer front end would make the Durango harder to maneuver and less nimble for going off-road, which could hurt sales.

The government runs a similar test at 30 miles an hour before allowing any vehicle onto the market. If the Durango had recorded the same head- or chest-injury scores on the slower, less violent test, it would have flunked and been barred from sale. But the Durango was not subjected to this test before going on sale, because regulators accepted DaimlerChrysler's assertion that the Durango was virtually identical to the Dodge Dakota pickup, which had previously passed with good scores. Indeed, the Durango and the Dakota use the same parts from the windshield forward to the bumper. DaimlerChrysler says the Durango is completely safe. The company kept tweaking the Durango's design, which finally did better on a crash test of a 2001 Durango.

Automakers have had several responses to the overall lackluster crash-test scores of their SUVs. One response is to question the tests themselves. The regulators typically conduct a single test of a vehicle, because crashing vehicles into walls is an expensive exercise, incurring the cost of the vehicle plus up to $10,000 more for the test equipment. Bad luck can play a role in a poor crash-test score—if a dummy's head happens to strike a hard edge in the passenger compartment, the score for that test can be pretty miserable. But safety-conscious automakers can address this by using softer materials and more curving surfaces in the passenger compartments.

The main argument made by automakers is that the frontal crash tests are too severe for SUVs because the majority of the vehicles that an SUV might hit are going to be lighter than the SUV. The test only simulates a crash with an unyielding object; if an SUV hits a car head-on and both are traveling at similar speeds, the car is likely to be pushed back. That makes for a less violent collision for the SUV's occupants—and a much more violent impact for the car's occupants. In other words, SUVs fare badly when hitting another vehicle their own size but do better picking on smaller vehicles.

SUVs perform somewhat better than cars in side-impact crash tests. For these tests, regulators use a 3,015-pound barrier shaped somewhat like the front end of a Ford Taurus. The barrier is towed at 38.5 miles per hour into the side of a parked vehicle. SUVs commonly receive five stars, the top rating, on these tests because they weigh more than the barrier and because the barrier hits them fairly low. Side impacts are deadly, but they are not quite as common as frontal impacts. The National Highway Traffic Safety Administration estimates that 4.6 million frontal impacts are reported to the police nationwide each year—most of which just do minor property damage—and 2.5 million side impacts.

SUV occupants do have below-average death rates in collisions with other vehicles, and SUVs are especially effective at protecting the people inside when hit from the side, according to federal and insurance industry crash data. Yet SUV occupants still have as high a death rate as car occupants or higher. The reason lies in the nemesis of high-riding vehicles: rollovers.

8

ROLLOVERS

As sales of SUVs boomed through the early 1990s, especially Explorer sales, Ford executives began wondering why customers were not more concerned about the stability of the new vehicles. Rollovers had been a staple of television documentaries since 1980, and *Consumer Reports* had begun campaigning on the issue in 1988, demanding that the federal government establish rollover standards for SUVs. Basic physics dictated that taller vehicles were more vulnerable, which was one reason why sporty cars like Chevrolet Camaros rode low to the ground. Auto engineers had been aware of vehicle stability issues for decades, and knew that the higher a vehicle's center of gravity was, the more likely it was to flip over in a crash.

Jim Siegel became Ford's manager of advanced product research in 1993, and was in charge of market research into how customers would respond to future models still being designed. Siegel's staff held focus groups in which they would bring groups of consumers into a room, show them some prototypes and then ask their opinions.

Many of the customers had said that they wanted something bigger than an Explorer, and Ford was responding by starting to design a full-sized model that would become the Expedition. Many buyers, especially women, also said that they wanted to ride high off the road, so that they could see farther. When asked why they gravitated toward models with considerable ground clearance, customers frequently surprised Siegel with an unexpected answer, telling him that, "If the vehicle is up high, it's easier to see if someone is hiding underneath or lurking behind it."

With such frequent requests for high-riding vehicles, Siegel and his staff kept expecting customers to ask about rollovers. It seldom happened, and customers instead said that they thought the sturdy appearance of the SUVs made them look safer overall in traffic. "There was very little concern about stuff like rollovers, and if people didn't bring it up themselves, our moderator led them," Siegel said. "They would say, 'If you drive them right, they're not going to roll over.'"

The researchers passed on the customers' eagerness for taller vehicles to senior management, hoping for the best in terms of safety. "At the time, we thought if people were intelligent about driving these vehicles and respected them as trucks and not as cars, and understood they didn't corner as well, everything would be okay," Siegel said.

No problem associated with SUVs is so widely known, and yet so widely misunderstood, as rollovers. Rollovers have been the bane of sport utilities ever since the Jeeps of World War II. But numerous surveys by automakers and federal regulators alike have shown that most people still underestimate the real risks.

The consequences of a rollover are extremely serious. Rollovers account for less than 1 percent of the crashes in the United States, but are the cause of a quarter of the traffic deaths—10,000 deaths a year, more than from side and rear impacts combined. SUVs roll over with particular frequency: 5 times per 100 crashes, compared to 3.8 times per 100 crashes for pickups, 2 per 100 crashes for minivans and 1.7 times per 100 crashes for cars, according to federal crash statistics.

Flipping over in a vehicle puts extraordinary strains on the neck and spine, strains that are seldom found in crashes when all four wheels of a vehicle stay on the ground. The resulting neck and spine injuries can easily paralyze occupants lucky enough not to be killed. No national data exists on paralysis in crashes, but when the Utah Department of Health conducted a review of every paralysis case reported to hospitals in the state, it found that even though rollovers were rare, they accounted for three-quarters of all traffic-related cases of paralysis in the state. Traffic accidents, in turn, accounted for half of all cases of paralysis by any cause, including illness, falls and shootings, the 1991 study found. Researchers in Arkansas have found nearly the same rate of rollover-related paralysis.[1]

Part of the problem is that drivers routinely overestimate their own driving skills and underestimate the skills of other people. A large-scale survey in Oregon found that the average driver believed that he or she was more skilled than 80 percent of the other drivers on the road—a mathematical impossibility. This collective arrogance has meant that drivers routinely discount the risks of single-vehicle crashes, even though these account for almost half of all traffic deaths.

Another problem involves a big misunderstanding of how rollovers occur. Most rollovers do not occur because someone veers back and forth on a road, as drivers do during frequently televised vehicle tests by *Consumer Reports*, or during reenactments staged by personal-injury lawyers and their consultants for television shows. Federal research has found that more than 90 percent of rollovers occur instead when a vehicle is "tripped." Tripping occurs when a vehicle strikes a curb, guardrail, lower-riding car or other low obstacle and then flips over. Tripping can also take place when one side of the vehicle starts traveling on a high-friction surface, like a gravel road shoulder, while the other side of the vehicle is on a low-friction surface, like pavement. The mediocre brakes and poor handling of SUVs makes them harder to keep on the road than a car, while their high centers of gravity make them more prone to flipping over if they start straying from the road. It is a lethal combination.

Tripping can occur if a mechanical problem, like a defective tire, causes the vehicle to start sliding sideways. SUV occupants have long had nearly double the death rate of car occupants in tire-related crashes: regaining control of a vehicle with only three tires in good condition is especially difficult in a vehicle with a high center of gravity.

Tripped rollovers are the kinds of mishaps that can happen to anyone who makes a mistake while driving—especially someone who misjudges his or her speed on a curve and winds up at the edge of the road. Even changes in the friction provided by a paved surface, such as when a road switches from blacktop to concrete, can be hazardous if a driver tries to turn sharply at the same time. When a driver for *AutoWeek* magazine flipped a Jeep Liberty during a slalom test at 40 miles per hour in October 2001, DaimlerChrysler itself later attributed the mishap partly to a 10 percent change in pavement friction where the crash occurred.[2]

While there are many kinds of tripped rollovers, some of the most alarming are those caused by guardrails—roadside features that are actually supposed to save lives, not end them. Hitting a roadside guardrail probably ranks way down the list of most people's traffic fears, even after rollovers, to the extent that people think about guardrails at all. But guardrails suddenly become very important if you start sliding on an unsuspected patch of ice, or if you carom off another vehicle in a glancing collision and start hurtling toward a steep embankment at the side of the road.

If that happens, hope that you are driving a car and not an SUV. Hundreds of thousands of miles of guardrails in the United States are not designed to keep SUVs upright and on the road. And millions of SUVs are not designed to bounce off guardrails and return safely to their lanes of traffic.

Over the last few years, a series of increasingly alarming studies have been done on how SUVs and pickup trucks can tear through the rails, drive over them or ricochet back onto the road and flip over. The problem involves the way the guardrails are made and the way SUVs are made.

Most roadside guardrails have a top edge that is designed to be 27 inches above the road surface—barely higher than the top of the bumper on many SUVs, and well below hood height. More frightening still is that many guardrails actually end up lower. Highway workers may drive the supporting pillars too deep in the ground, the road surface may be raised by repeated resurfacing and patching, or the road surface may be temporarily raised, in effect, by a coating of snow or ice.

Federally funded tests have found that SUV drivers can face disaster if they strike a glancing blow at high speed against a guardrail with a top edge at 26 inches or lower. The rail can either "trip" the vehicle, causing it to roll over, or may even fail to keep the SUV on the road at all. State and local governments only go to the expense of putting up guardrails when there is an especially deadly hazard on the other side, such as a bridge abutment or a steep slope that might cause a vehicle to roll over.

Concrete bridge pillars in the middle of a divided highway are especially dangerous to hit, which is why they are typically surrounded by guardrails. Tests at the Midwest Roadside Safety Facility at the University of Nebraska in Lincoln have found that when a pickup truck or SUV hits a 27-inch-tall guardrail head-on, the light truck can vault right over it and into the pillar.

Even when guardrails are high enough to prevent vehicles from going over the top, their design poses special risks for SUVs. The problem, once again, is that SUVs are designed for off-road driving and have the wheels placed differently from car wheels.

If you drive a car along a flat road and then turn up into a steeply inclined driveway, you will probably scrape the driveway with the lower edge of the bumper, or with some of the components below and behind the bumper. An SUV driver does not have this problem. The SUV's front wheels are close to the front of the vehicle with very little of the vehicle's structure in front of them so that they can climb up and over large rocks, or handle the transition from flat ground to a steep incline.

The problem, according to researchers at the Texas Transportation Institute, is that guardrails work best when they interact with a vehicle's metal structure. Problems arise when one of a vehicle's wheels gets far enough under the guardrail to snag the pillar holding up the rail. Since the pillars are virtually unbreakable, a snagged wheel either rips off or, if it stays on, anchors that corner of the vehicle to the pillar while the rest of the vehicle swings around. In both cases, a rollover is likely.

Four-wheel-drive vehicles pose an even more serious hazard. When researchers finally got around to testing four-wheel-drive SUVs against guardrails in 1999 and 2000, they found that the wheels ripped off especially easily because they were less solidly attached to the vehicle. When the wheels came off, they exposed especially sharp suspension components that sliced a hole in the guardrail. The most common kinds of rails are like taut ribbons of steel, prone to disintegrating if even partially torn.

"If you put just a minor cut in it, it'll break," says Dean Sicking, the director of the Midwest Roadside Safety Facility. "Then you're done."

Crashes involving guardrails tend to be especially deadly, mainly because these crashes commonly involve rollovers. In the vast majority of crashes that do not involve guardrail interactions, it is quite rare for more than one person to die in a crash; this is usually the person closest to the point of impact, although other vehicle occupants may be seriously injured. But tumbling down an embankment, slamming into a concrete pillar or hurtling into oncoming traffic after hitting a guardrail can wipe out a whole family. Fatal crashes that start with guardrail impacts kill an average of two people, a remarkably high average given that the majority of the vehicles on the road have only one person inside.

Federal crash data shows that of the 36,161 vehicle occupants who died in crashes in 2000, 2,120 of them, or almost 6 percent, perished in crashes that began with an impact with a guardrail. SUVs were involved in fatal crashes with guardrails at a rate 20 percent higher than the typical vehicle. That is a surprisingly high number, because heavier vehicles usually protect their occupants better in guardrail crashes and SUVs outweigh cars by nearly half a ton. Dean Sicking estimates that SUV occupants are as much as 50 percent more likely to die in a guardrail crash than occupants of cars of similar weight.

In other words, this is a fairly sizable category of crash deaths in which SUV occupants are more likely to perish than car occupants. It is one of many seemingly obscure categories of traffic deaths in which SUVs fare poorly, offsetting the extra protection they may provide their occupants in collisions with lower-riding cars.

A group of midlevel state and federal highway officials decided in 1993 to study how to improve guardrails and bridge rails to accommodate the shift in the vehicle fleet toward more light trucks. After a series of tests using mainly two-wheel-drive pick-ups—SUVs and even four-wheel-drive pickups were deemed too expensive—researchers concluded that roadside guardrails could be improved by changing the way they are attached to the pillars. The most common kind of guardrails, which look like a foot-tall sheet of steel bent to look like the letter "W" lying on its side, needs to be attached differently to the support pillars. The guardrails are commonly attached now to a 6-inch-thick steel block, which in turn is attached to the pillar. But the blocks crumple too easily when hit hard, and are not thick enough to keep SUV and pickup tires from reaching the pillars. The Federal Highway Administration ended up requiring that beginning on October 1, 1998, all road construction projects receiving federal money would have to install thicker blocks made of wood for the so-called W-beam guardrails.

But huge holes remain in these regulations. There is still no federal standard to require taller guardrails around concrete pillars and other objects that might be hit head-on by SUVs, although a half-dozen states, led by Nebraska, did raise their own standards in 2001. The 1998 federal standards are also still based on research using two-wheel-drive vehicles that are less prone to tear the guardrails open with their suspensions. The federal rules also assume that vehicles will not weigh more than 4,400 pounds, at a time when many full-sized SUVs are approaching 6,000 pounds even when empty.

SUV design is also changing in ways that may make this problem worse, not better. To reduce the risk of rollovers during everyday driving and improve overall vehicle stability, automakers have been mounting SUV wheels wider on new models. On some of the best-selling new models, like the 2002 Ford Explorer and Chevrolet Trailblazer, the wheels almost stick out from under the sides of the vehicle, with very little metal in front of them. I mentioned the latest roadside hazard research to many SUV engineers in 2000 and 2001 as I noticed the trend toward the wider mounting of wheels, and never found an engineer who had ever heard about the problem that tires might go under guardrails and snag the pillars. Even the automakers' safety engineers professed to be unaware of the roadside safety research when I asked them about it. The roadside safety community exists almost independently of the vehicle safety community, with separate conferences and journals and even separate regulators—the Federal Highway Administration oversees roadsides while the National Highway Traffic Safety Administration oversees vehicle safety.

The two communities mostly talk past each other. A few auto-safety engineers gripe that guardrails should be taller, although they have not looked at the details. Rudolph M. Umbs, the chief of the safety designs and operations division of the Federal Highway Administration, sees the problem the other way around, complaining that automakers should design vehicles to fit the roads, since vehicle designs can change a lot more quickly than road designs. In the meantime, he advises that drivers "should know their vehicle and the capabilities of their vehicles and drive accordingly."

Like mediocre brakes and poor maneuverability, guardrail problems are an excellent reason for SUV drivers to be more cautious on slippery roads, especially on older roads, even if their vehicles' four-wheel-drive systems give them the illusion of control. Fortunately, federal crash statistics do suggest that bridge rails do not pose the same risk for SUVs as guardrails. Bridge rails are commonly made of concrete and are required by separate federal standards to be tall enough to keep commercial trucks from going over the side. But bridge rail accidents are very rare compared to guardrail accidents, probably because there are a lot more guardrails than bridge rails.

As with many SUV issues, the biggest problem lies in the years ahead, as SUVs are likely to spread faster than guardrails can be replaced or improved. The new state and federal standards call for upgrading guardrails only when a new road is built or an existing road has substantial repairs or reconstruction. Even the most heavily traveled highways are only redone on this scale every 10 to 20 years, while less heavily traveled routes may not be rebuilt for 30 or more years. Nobody has seriously proposed replacing all existing guardrails to improve the safety of SUV occupants, because this would cost billions of dollars.

"There are hundreds of thousands of miles of this stuff out there and state departments of transportation budgets don't go up," said Malcolm Ray, a civil engineer at Worchester Polytechnic Institute. "That's not going to make you feel better if you hit that barrier, but it's kind of the reality."

Once begun, a rollover is a terrifying thing. The physics of vehicle occupants in rollovers were described in considerable detail by the auto industry's own safety consultants at a closed-door auto-engineering conference in Dearborn in December 1997. A computer simulation showed that when a vehicle rolls over sideways (they virtually never flip end over end except in the movies), the driver is hurled at the side window in the direction of the roll. Unlike windshields, side windows do not have shatter-proof glazing because the glazing would make the windows too heavy to be rolled up (although new and lighter glazings are starting to become available). So even if the window is rolled up, the driver's head and shoulders punch right through.

Wearing a seat belt is the best protection against rollovers. If the driver is not wearing a seat belt, he or she is thrown headfirst against the pavement and then the vehicle often rolls over the driver, inflicting crushing injuries. Federal statistics show that while three-quarters of motorists wear seat belts these days, four-fifths of the deaths in rollovers are motorists who were not wearing their seat belts.

Even if the driver is wearing a seat belt, the driver's head and neck can still go through the side window, where it may be crushed against the pavement by the door of the tumbling vehicle. There have been some reported cases of even belted occupants being ejected from a vehicle during a rollover—belts are not required to restrain occupants from being thrown sideways, and most are not designed to do so. Only in the last two years have automakers, especially Ford, begun designing seat belts with "pre-tensioners" that automatically yank the belt tight against the occupant as the vehicle starts to roll, reducing the risk of ejection from the vehicle.

Frontal air bags do little good in a rollover, nor do side air bags that deploy from the sides of the front seats to protect an occupant's chest during a side impact. Curtain side air bags that extend down from the vehicle's roof are very effective in keeping occupants' heads and necks inside the vehicle during a rollover, but few vehicles are yet equipped with them. And even these devices do little good if the roof caves in excessively, crushing the space occupied by the motorist's head and neck.

GM in particular has opposed proposals over the years that roofs be strengthened, contending that stiffer roofs would be more dangerous to occupants. "You actually increase accelerations, because if the roof doesn't deform at all then you can end up transferring more energy to the occupants," said Harry Pearce in an interview at the Detroit auto show in January 2001, when he was still vice chairman of GM.

Yet there is growing evidence that federal regulations on roof strength, which took effect in 1973 for cars and in 1991 for the smaller light trucks, set standards that are too weak. Moreover, light trucks with a gross vehicle weight of more than 6,000 pounds—anything bigger than an Explorer—are exempt from any federal roof-strength standards at all. The roofs of cars, minivans and small and midsize SUVs and pickup trucks are required to cave in by no more than 5 inches while supporting up to 1.5 times the unloaded weight of the vehicle. But even 5 inches of roof crush could be a problem for a tall driver whose head is already near the roof. The government test also uses a methodology that makes it easy for vehicles to pass the test. A very large steel plate is carefully and gradually pressed against the top of the roof above the windshield. The gentle application of pressure in the government test leaves the windshield in place, where it bears as much as 30 percent of the weight applied during the test. But windshields almost always pop out of their frames during real rollovers, when the force of impact is likely to be neither gradual nor evenly distributed. When automobiles roll over, they almost always strike a corner of the roof against the ground first, bending the windshield frame and popping out the windshield, instead of neatly turning 180 degrees in the air and landing precisely upside down, which is what the federal test simulates. With the windshield gone, the roofs of some current models cannot even support the weight of the vehicle when it is empty, to say nothing of what the vehicle might weigh if it has several adults strapped inside.[3] Add in that vehicles do not roll over gradually but turn over with some force, so that the roof is subjected to a considerably greater force than that produced just by the vehicle's weight at rest, and the federal standard seems weak indeed.

NHTSA has moved glacially to address the problem. For many years roof strength did not seem that important because few people wore seat belts and were therefore hurled through side windows against the pavement before the roof could cave in. But as seat-belt usage improved, a 1992 study by the agency found that roof intrusion had emerged as a leading cause of injury for belted rollover occupants.[4] NHTSA then acknowledged in a 1998 study that pressing steel plates against roofs was an unrealistic way to measure roof strength in a rollover.[5] Finally, in November 2001, the agency formally asked the public for ideas on what to do about the problem, a preliminary step toward a possible proposal of new rules. The request for ideas included a calculation that between 1988 and 1999, 14 percent of the people killed or seriously injured in rollovers were belted occupants who made contact with a roof that had intruded.[6]

Since seat-belt use is rising, roof intrusion is almost certainly an even bigger problem now. The problem will grow in the years ahead, moreover, as used SUVs come to be owned and driven by inexperienced drivers and drunks, who are more likely to make the mistakes that lead to rollovers. Any new standards that NHTSA devises, if it takes any action at all in the face of what is likely to be strenuous industry lobbying, are unlikely to take effect until at least the 2006 model year. Little can be done to strengthen the roofs of the 20 million SUVs on the road already, or the 10 million more that will go into service before any new standards would take effect. So for years to come, even SUV occupants who scrupulously wear their seat belts will simply have to take their chances in rollovers.

Intriguingly, the Jeep Cherokee and Jeep Grand Cherokee have low rates of rollovers. They also happen to have fairly unusual underbodies. Both Jeeps have very thick frame rails like a traditional SUV, but neither is built on a pickup-truck underbody.

Indeed, neither vehicle is assembled with a body-on-frame approach at all; both have unit bodies, with the roof, sides and underbody all welded together into a unit. Chrysler calls this approach a "uniframe," to suggest that it is a unit-body vehicle like a car but with a sturdy underbody frame. Whatever you call the design, the Cherokee and Grand Cherokee each have very low rollover death rates by SUV standards.

The rollover death rate for a Jeep Cherokee is barely higher than for a car, and the Jeep Grand Cherokee's rate is almost as low. Even now, nearly two decades after the Cherokee went on sale, no automaker has been able to design a small or midsize SUV with anywhere near as low a rollover death rate as the Cherokee. Only the largest SUVs, like the Suburban, have similar rollover rates to the Cherokee simply because they are so big and heavy. It is possible to roll over in a Cherokee, just as it is possible to roll over in any vehicle under the wrong circumstances, like sliding sideways at high speed into a curb. But it is not easy.

The strangest part of all, however, is that to this day, nobody has figured out for sure why the Cherokee is so stable—not the insurers, not the safety researchers and not the auto industry. The Cherokee's center of gravity is only slightly lower than in other SUVs, and it is not especially wide. Yet it stays on all four wheels practically like a car.

In 1999, the most recent year available for insurance industry data on specific models, drivers of four-wheel-drive Cherokees died in rollovers at a rate of just 15 per million registered Cherokees, according to insurance-industry calculations from federal crash data. The Cherokee death rate is still not as good as the figures for large cars (9 deaths per million registered large cars) or the bigger midsized cars (14). But by SUV standards, the Cherokee is superb. Drivers of the bigger midsized SUVs with four-wheel drive, like the Ford Explorer, have an average rollover death rate of 39 per million registered vehicles.

Two-wheel-drive SUVs are less common, and typically purchased by younger drivers who cannot afford four-wheel drive and are more prone to making mistakes that can lead to a rollover. Two-wheel-drive Cherokees still have a respectable rollover death rate of 21 per million registered vehicles. Bigger midsize models of other SUVs with two-wheel drive have an appalling driver death rate of 69 per million registered vehicles. The exception is the Jeep Grand Cherokee, which has a driver rollover death rate per million registered vehicles of just 36 for the two-wheel-drive model, and 23 for the four-wheel-drive model.[7] But the Grand Cherokee is bigger and more expensive than the Cherokee, and is marketed to an older buyer, so its performance is not as impressive as the Cherokee's.

Roy Lunn, who retired after designing the Cherokee and now lives in Florida, insists that the uniframe is responsible for the Cherokee's stability. When a passenger compartment is bolted onto a truck underbody, as is done for traditional SUVs, the compartment can move very slightly with respect to the underbody, and this makes it hard to tune the suspension and other components with great precision for maximum stability, Lunn maintains. To make a pickup-based sport utility as rigid as a unit-body vehicle, Lunn adds, "you would have yourself such a heavy chassis that it wouldn't be practical, so you just live with it."

Many engineers do not accept this argument, however. The motion of a passenger compartment relative to an underbody is so tiny that it cannot possibly be relevant, they argue. Francois Castaing himself contends that all three kinds of vehicle architectures—body on frame, unitized body and uniframe—can be equally stable, and that the art lies in how the whole system fits together.

The Cherokee and Grand Cherokee went through unusually stringent stability tests before American Motors and Chrysler, respectively, put them on the market. American Motors was haunted in the early 1980s by the costs of Jeep rollover litigation, and Castaing subjected the Cherokee to the extremely demanding tests that Renault used in Europe. Manufacturers in Europe have traditionally had tougher tests because their models may be used on the German autobahn, where there are no speed limits and drivers often go over 100 miles an hour. But American automakers have beefed up their stability tests in recent years and still nobody has matched the performance of the Cherokee.

The obvious way to test whether uniframe designs are superior would be for automakers to build more of them. Yet only one more has come on the market, the Jeep Liberty. It was only introduced in 2001, to replace the Cherokee. Not enough Liberties are on the road yet for there to be reliable statistics on their crash rates. But *AutoWeek* and Germany's *Auto Bild* have each flipped Liberties in driving tests, so the mystery of the Cherokee's and Grand Cherokee's stability remains.

Uniframe designs do have two serious drawbacks that have discouraged their use. One is that engineering them is a very slow and expensive process, because every part of the vehicle depends on everything else. It is not a good design to choose for rushing a new model to market with a modest investment in case the model is a flop.

The other drawback to uniframes is that they are fairly noisy inside. When automakers attach passenger compartments to pickup-truck underbodies, they thread big steel bolts from the underbody up through a thick rubber doughnut and into the passenger compartment. The passenger compartment essentially rides on the rubber doughnut, which does an excellent job of insulating the passenger compartment from the noise of the underbody and the wheels against the road. The lightweight underbodies of cars, with only vestigial rails, also do not conduct sound very well. But uniframes, which have the thick steel rails and do not have the rubber doughnuts, allow considerable road noise into the passenger compartment. Since SUVs are mainly sold to families, and family buyers tend to put a premium on being able to hear each other when talking inside a vehicle, automakers have been very wary of investing in uniframe SUVs.

SUV rollovers killed 12,000 Americans in the 1990s, plus

another 2,049 in 2000 alone, according to NHTSA. Recent statistical studies, most notably by the Insurance Institute for Highway Safety, have found that the rollover death rate per million registered SUVs is at least double the rate for cars.[8] This is true even if you adjust for such variables as the fact that SUVs are slightly more likely than cars to be driven on rural roads (which tend to be more dangerous than urban roads). To put it another way, roughly 1,000 Americans died needlessly in rollovers in 2000 because they were in SUVs instead of cars, and another 6,000 died needlessly in the 1990s. While paralysis cases are hard to estimate with any precision on a national basis, it appears that thousands of them could have been avoided if Americans had not begun treating SUVs as substitutes for family cars.

Yet despite the carnage of rollovers, the safety record of SUVs actually improved through the 1990s, to the point that SUVs became practically as safe as cars. For every million registered SUVs on the road in 2000, there were 134 occupants killed in crashes of all types, including those not involving rollovers, according to the Insurance Institute for Highway Safety.[9] The occupant death rate was barely lower for cars, at 126 per million.

For large SUVs, the death rate was even lower, at 104 per million. That was respectable, although still higher than the average for upper-midsize cars like the Ford Taurus and Pontiac Grand Prix and minivans like the Dodge Caravan, for which the combined occupant death rate was 96 per million registered cars.[10]

The sad part was how SUVs reached such a low death rate, after having a much higher death rate than cars for decades. The short answer is that they got so big and heavy that they could push around practically any other vehicle on the road in a crash. The SUV occupant still had a high risk of perishing in a rollover. But by making sure that it was the other guy who usually died in a multiple-vehicle collision rather than the SUV owner, automakers reduced the overall death rate for SUVs to the point that it was in line with other models.

Looking at overall traffic safety, however, the worst possible situation is a shift toward vehicles that perform badly in single-vehicle crashes but compensate by obliterating other automobiles in multiple-vehicle crashes. Yet this is exactly what the shift toward SUVs has done.

As SUV sales rose through the 1990s, there was a huge bill in blood to be paid for the fashion tastes of the nation's more affluent families. But for the most part, they would not be paying that bill themselves. Their own death rates would be little higher than if they had bought large cars. Instead, they would have the nation's car drivers pick up the tab.

9

KILL RATES

Diana de Veer, a slim, petite, 35-year-old physical therapist with shoulder-length black hair, climbed into her Saab 900S sedan on a bright, sunny Sunday morning in May 1997 for what should have been a short drive to church. She ended up instead at the hospital where she treated patients during the week, and she arrived in an ambulance.

She was driving south on Maple Street in Pasadena, a leafy, prosperous suburb northeast of Los Angeles. She was wearing her seat belt. Her life was permanently changed when she passed through the intersection with Walnut Street at 8:25 A.M.

A 1988 Range Rover was heading west on Walnut Street then at about 35 miles an hour, the same speed de Veer was traveling south on Maple.

The black Range Rover, driven by a local real estate developer, weighed 4,455 pounds; de Veer's black Saab weighed 2,770 pounds. The Range Rover was equipped with a grille guard in front of the bumper and headlights. The bumper itself was 23 inches off the ground, 3 inches higher than is legal for a car bumper. Looming a foot over the bumper was the Range Rover's tall, rectangular grille. Behind the bumper, just inside the front end of the vehicle, were the front ends of the two thick steel rails that ran the length of the vehicle and gave it the strength and rigidity to carry heavy cargo up muddy mountain tracks.

The sides of the Saab, including the steel safety beams inside de Veer's door, were fine for passing the federal side-impact crash test, which uses a 3,015-pound barrier that roughly resembles the front end of a Ford Taurus. The barrier has a fairly soft aluminum bumper with a lower edge 13 inches off the ground and an upper edge that is 21 inches off the ground. Behind the barrier's bumper is a 15-inch-thick aluminum honeycomb, designed to simulate the soft front end of a car, with ample crumple zones composed of sheet metal. But the top of the aluminum honeycomb is only 33 inches off the ground, half a foot shorter than the Range Rover's hood, and the honeycomb is much softer than the front end of a Range Rover.

There was a traffic light at the intersection. One of the two drivers must have run a red light, but there were no witnesses to tell later who might have been at fault. What happened is not in dispute, however: the tall front end of the Range Rover slammed into de Veer's door.

A subsequent police report chronicled the extraordinary damage to the Saab: "The driver's door and front area of the left rear quarter panel were impacted more than a foot. The driver's seat was pushed and bent towards the center console. The driver's window and rear compartment window were both completely shattered. The steering wheel and left portion of the dash were forced to the right and the roof was buckled and raised in the area above the driver's seat."

The impact fractured De Veer's pelvis, but her legs, arms and the rest of her torso survived this maelstrom largely unscathed as the Saab mostly protected her from the lower part of the impact. But behind the shattered driver's window and just below the buckled roof was de Veer's head. Subsequent investigation never settled whether the Range Rover hit de Veer's head or whether she was struck by her own car's door or side pillar, but something struck her head so hard that while her skull was not fractured, her brain suffered massive injuries.

She gradually awoke from a coma nearly four weeks later at Huntington Memorial Hospital. Soon after she regained full consciousness, she was transferred to a brain injury treatment center in Pomona, where she spent the summer.

Visits to physical therapists were particularly difficult because she noticed that she seldom saw the same therapist twice, and guessed the reason why: "As a therapist, people like me are people I would sometimes see and I'd say, 'This is way too much, I've got to get another patient load.'"

Four months after the crash, she was able to walk around and speak haltingly. She was discharged to the care of her husband, Glenn, a successful architect who runs his business from home. But Diana de Veer has never completely recovered from that single, shattering moment in 1997.

De Veer took English classes at Pasadena City College, the same place where she had started studying to be a physical therapist 16 years earlier. But she still speaks somewhat slowly, pronouncing each word separately and distinctly. She often forgets things within a minute of hearing or doing them. If she tries to boil water, she has to put a sticky note on her arm or a wall to remind her to take the water off the stove when it is hot. She took a course to relearn CPR, but was unable to comprehend fully the material she had once mastered and failed to win recertification. She has not returned to work as a physical therapist and spends her days as a volunteer at a local museum and helping handicapped teenagers. She and her husband count themselves lucky now that they never had children.

"It's a life-changing accident," Glenn said. "Diana will never be the same, that's just part of brain injury, you just pick up the pieces and go on. I'm very fortunate to have my own business at home so I can give the care."

Men and women like Diana de Veer are being needlessly maimed and killed every day by stiff, high-riding SUVs that slide over cars' bumpers and sturdy door sills, slamming into the passenger compartments. What makes these deaths especially disgraceful is that many researchers pointed out in the 1970s and early 1980s that it would be lethal ever to design vehicles that were especially stiff and had high front ends. Yet automakers ignored this research until the late 1990s, helping millions of Americans switch from low-riding cars with fairly soft front ends to tall, stiff SUVs.

While automakers are taking a few steps now to make SUVs less dangerous to other motorists, these steps remain grossly inadequate. The automakers are acting in response to public pressure, because regulators are years away from issuing any rules to address the problem.

The best estimate of federal regulators is that the height and stiffness of light trucks, as opposed to their considerable weight, were causing an extra 2,000 deaths a year in 1998 in cars that they struck, and rising. SUVs account for almost half of these extra deaths. Pickup trucks account for most of the rest. The SUVs are the more serious problem because the proportion of vehicles on the road that are SUVs will likely double in the coming decade, while the share of pickup trucks and minivans on the road will probably rise little if at all.

Compounding the problem is that the height and stiffness do not provide any extra protection for SUV occupants to offset the harm they inflict to car occupants. The extra height makes them more prone to rollovers, while the extra stiffness causes them to transfer the force of impacts to their occupants during crashes, instead of crumpling. While a few buyers need tall, stiff vehicles that can go off-road or tow heavy loads, most SUVs are tall and stiff to attract desk-bound buyers who want to give the illusion that they lead adventurous lives. SUV buyers who do not need to go off-road are literally putting their neighbors at mortal risk for the sake of fashion.

The actual toll for car occupants from the rise of SUVs is considerably higher than 1,000 lives a year, because the weight of SUVs kills, as well as their design. SUVs tend to be the heaviest family vehicles on the road, typically outweighing cars by half a ton and sometimes by a ton or more. SUVs are allowed to be much heavier than cars because they are subject to much lower fuel-economy standards than cars. In a crash, the heavier vehicle tends to transfer the violence of impact, as well as the injuries and deaths, to the lighter vehicle.

The extra weight of SUVs rearranges where the deaths occur in crashes, transferring deaths from the SUVs to the cars. Requiring SUVs to be lighter would save lives in cars but cost lives in SUVs. Safety experts agree that the death rate in SUVs would be considerably higher than in cars if the SUVs were not able to use their weight advantage in multivehicle collisions to offset their high death rate in rollovers.

Auto executives never tire of pointing out that mismatches between vehicles are nothing new. If a fast-moving, fully loaded freight truck hits a family vehicle of any size, whether a car, SUV, minivan or pickup, the results are likely to be catastrophic for the people in the family vehicle. Indeed, the earliest traffic safety research in the 1950s and 1960s showed that weight is by far the most important factor in collisions between two cars. If a 4,000-pound car traveling 30 miles an hour runs into a 2,000-pound subcompact going the same speed in the opposite direction, the large car literally pushes the small car backward. The large car decelerates to 10 miles an hour in the impact, meaning that its velocity has dropped by 20 miles an hour. But the small car is now going backwards at 10 miles an hour, so its velocity has changed by 40 miles an hour.

Changes in velocity are important because they affect not only the damage to the vehicles but also what happens to the occupants. Until seat-belt usage and air bags started to become common in the mid-1990s, most of the deaths and injuries in crashes occurred during the so-called second impact: after a crash has stopped the motion of the vehicle, the unrestrained occupants keep going, flying against the steering wheel, dashboard and other features of the passenger compartment.

But by focusing on weight discrepancies, researchers developed a serious blind spot—they looked only at collisions involving cars, while ignoring light trucks. The reason is simple: It is hard to figure out from government crash records how much a light truck weighs. A four-door Ford Explorer with four-wheel drive outweighs a two-door, two-wheel-drive Explorer by nearly 500 pounds, or 13 percent. Yet both vehicles show up in government crash records simply as Explorers. Figuring out the weight of an Explorer in a crash requires checking its vehicle identification number against factory records of that particular vehicle's manufacture. Only in the last few years have computer programs become available that can do this—and these programs sell for $5,000 apiece, limiting their use to the most serious, well-funded researchers. By contrast, cars are much more standardized, as automakers use different names to sell two-door and four-door versions of essentially the same car. It is therefore easy to estimate the weight of cars that show up in crash databases, simply using the name of the model. So for decades, safety researchers focused on car crashes.

Until the late 1990s, automakers contended that the aggressiveness of vehicles in crashes depended solely on their weight, and that design decisions played essentially no role. In an interview in August 1997, Alex Trotman, then the chairman and chief executive of Ford, dismissed questions about crashes between cars and SUVs by saying that these collisions simply reflected laws of physics going back to the Greeks. If you hit a small rock with a large rock, the large rock wins, he said, adding that what counted for Ford was

SUVs' acceptance by the general public: "It's a good formula for the customer, and that's what we're providing."

If weight is the only factor in vehicle safety, then manufacturers can always resist changing their models, by contending that lighter models would provide less protection for their occupants. Some vehicles also need to be larger than others because some families are larger or have more belongings to haul, and larger vehicles weigh more. But if the designs of SUVs are at fault, as well as their weight, then safety improvements can more readily be made. For many years, virtually no research was done on the design of SUVs. A flood of research since 1997 has shown, however, that the designs are even more lethal than the weight.

During the 1970s—the heyday of automotive-safety research— safety experts made a few tentative efforts to assess a vehicle's "aggressiveness" or "compatibility" with other vehicles in crashes. Most of these efforts were devoted to predicting what would happen when the large, heavy cars of the 1950s and 1960s hit the smaller, more fuel-efficient models that were starting to come on the market. But a few researchers looked at whether more than just weight was involved.

In 1971, the French transportation ministry issued a research paper strongly arguing that too much attention was being given to protecting vehicle occupants. The paper contended that vehicles' aggressiveness should receive equal attention. The paper dealt particularly with side impacts, and stated prophetically that the front ends of automobiles should be kept low so that they would strike cars' sturdy door sills, instead of punching through the much weaker doors above. "We believe that it is useful to reinforce the lower part of the front under the bumpers in order for it to push the base of a car struck more effectively," the paper said.[1] But this prescient advice, which could have saved thousands of lives if followed from the beginning of the SUV boom in the mid-1980s, was totally ignored by automakers until the late 1990s.

A lucid paper in 1972 by Phillippe Ventre, a safety engineer at

Renault, followed a similar line of inquiry, identifying three basic contributors to an automobile's "aggressiveness": weight, stiffness and design. Ventre said that while the relative weights and stiffnesses of vehicles were important, automakers should also pay attention to the arrangement of auto parts inside the front ends of cars. Ventre's main concern was that automakers not place very stiff components inside the very front of a car. He warned that placing stiff components like the engine too far forward under the hood would allow them to punch quickly into another vehicle during the first milliseconds of a crash, before much sheet metal could crumple and absorb some of the impact. But he did not worry about the height of these stiff parts—everybody was driving cars in those days, especially in France, where pickup trucks were never as popular as in the United States, and cars all rode at fairly similar heights.[2]

Ventre was not alone in 1972 in calling for car designs to be more compatible in crashes. Enzo Franchini, the director of the safety center at Fiat, an Italian automaker that mostly made small cars, started giving presentations on the subject at international conferences that year. He called for an especially broad interpretation of crash compatibility, warning that automakers should make sure that their vehicles were also compatible with roadside features like guardrails—an admonition sadly forgotten by SUV designers.

Responding to the French and Italian research, an American government researcher, Jerome M. Kossar, issued a paper at a subsequent international conference of safety regulators, held in London in 1974. "We must give attention not only to the safety of the occupants of our vehicles but also to the safety of the human cargo aboard the vehicle with which we may collide," he wrote. He called for requiring heavier cars to be equipped with elaborate bumpers that would limit the damage they would inflict on lighter cars during collisions. The bumpers would conceal hydraulic fluid in pistons that would be pushed in during a crash, absorbing much of the forces generated by the heavier vehicle's weight.[3]

This utopian idea went nowhere, however. Indeed, today's SUVs are in many ways worse than heavy cars. The front ends of SUVs are actually less capable of crumpling and slowing down the vehicle in an impact than the front ends of cars, which is why SUVs have mediocre performance in crash tests.

The American Automobile Association (AAA) became interested in 1979 in collisions between freight trucks and cars, and commissioned a study by researchers at the University of Michigan. The resulting analysis, finished in 1982, covered trucks of all sizes, including pickup trucks and vans. The study accurately warned that because pickups and vans were gradually gaining in popularity while more heavily regulated cars were getting smaller, collisions between light trucks and cars were becoming more frequent and more deadly. But the study had two drawbacks: It assumed with little analysis that mismatches occurred mainly because of weight differences, and it ignored utility vehicles, which were still too rare to show up much in traffic statistics.[4]

The Motor Vehicle Manufacturers Association, the lobbying arm of the Detroit automakers, responded to AAA by commissioning a statistical study of federal crash data to determine if light trucks were especially deadly because they weighed more than cars or whether other factors were also responsible. Completed in 1984, the study found that vehicle weight remained the dominant factor in injury rates as unrestrained occupants continued to be thrown about most violently when the velocity of their vehicles changed abruptly during collisions with heavier vehicles.[5]

But the study had another conclusion which, with hindsight, should have attracted more attention. Pickup trucks and vans were punching deeper into car bodies during collisions than weight differences alone would have predicted. "In summary, the vehicle damage analysis generally supported the hypothesis that something other than vehicle weight is involved in light truck aggressiveness," the report said. "That 'something else' presumably includes structural factors such as frontal stiffness."

The final sentence in the study was a prescient recommendation that more be done to understand the extra damage: "While there is a possibility that structural factors can effect injury through occupant compartment intrusion, this bears further investigation."

The National Highway Traffic Safety Administration issued another report in January 1986 that should have been a wake-up call for automakers. The agency crashed a dozen 3,000-pound barriers into the sides of Volkswagen Rabbits. The barriers were variations of the standard barriers that the government would later use in side-impact tests before allowing cars like Diana de Veer's Saab on the market. Four of the barriers had bumpers that were lowered to 12 inches instead of the usual 17 inches for car bumpers. Four had hoods that were 25 inches high at the front instead of the usual 30 inches or so for a car hood. And four of the barriers were unusually soft, so that they would crush more easily than the typical front end of a car. Half the barriers in each category were crashed into everyday Rabbits, and half were crashed into Rabbits in which extra side padding had been installed.

Side padding in the Rabbit and softening the front end of the striking barrier helped a little, while lowering the bumper on the barrier reduced the risk of pelvic injuries in the Rabbit. But what really made a difference was lowering the hood height—this cut the risk of serious chest injuries to a mere 11 percent, compared with 97 percent for the standard car hood. This was an extraordinary accomplishment, as safety engineers go to huge lengths in vehicle design to achieve much smaller improvements than this.

The 1986 report concluded that "there appeared to be more potential benefit in altering the front end characteristics of the striking vehicle than in modifying the side of the struck vehicle." If anybody had been paying attention, the reports should have been a clear warning of the dangers of making vehicles with even taller bumpers and hoods than typical cars.[6]

But no one was paying attention. Bumpers and hoods were getting higher, not lower. The industry was ramping up production of

SUVs with 23-inch bumpers and hoods that were a towering 40 inches or more off the ground. Instead of looking at vehicles' aggressiveness, automakers and regulators mainly focused through the 1980s and 1990s on protecting occupants from harm when they bounced around the interior of passenger compartments after impacts. After decades of resistance, automakers finally embraced the use of air bags in the late 1980s, and regulators responded by making them mandatory in the 1990s. Usage of seat belts, the most important safety equipment in any vehicle, also finally improved during this time, rising from 14 percent in 1984 to 73 percent in 2001 and saving thousands of lives a year. Seat belts and air bags also reduced the severity of hundreds of thousands of injuries each year, mainly by preventing occupants from being hurled about the passenger compartment during crashes. But seat belts and air bags offer far less protection when auto parts are literally shoved into belted occupants with great force.

One of the many sad aspects of the SUV boom is that even as most motorists have finally become properly restrained, consumer tastes have been shifting to those vehicles that are most likely to pierce passenger compartments and injure even restrained occupants. Yet for many years, this problem of incompatibility in crashes received little attention from regulators. The issue finally began to be revived in the mid-1990s by one man who never forgot the early research in the 1970s: Tom Hollowell.

Tom Hollowell is a tall, lean man with thinning, dirty blonde hair who is fairly shy and dislikes public attention. He received his bachelor's degree in aerospace engineering at the University of Virginia in 1971, and then worked for a NASA contractor for four years in Huntsville, Alabama, using punch cards to create early computer models for the stability of spacecraft. He came to NHTSA in June 1975 to work on computer models and has worked for the regulatory agency practically ever since.

The safety agency hired Hollowell to oversee a contract that the agency had just signed with Ford. Following the publication of the Kossar paper in 1974 on compatibility between large and small cars, NHTSA paid Ford to develop a basic computer model of what happens when two different vehicles collide. Hollowell's first job at the safety agency was to work with Ford computer specialists and safety experts to do this, while separately creating the agency's own computer model for simulating crashes.

When President Reagan took office in 1981 and halted a lot of safety research, Hollowell, unlike many of his colleagues, did not leave in disgust, nor was he forced out. Instead, he took the opportunity to start earning a doctorate in engineering at the University of Virginia in his spare time. His dissertation would be on how to create accurate computer models from crash-test results. Hollowell continued to work for NHTSA while doing the doctorate, except for a one-year leave of absence. The University of Virginia won a contract from NHTSA to improve the computer model that Ford had created, partly by combining it with Hollowell's own model, and Hollowell oversaw this contract. The university, in turn, hired as a consultant one of its recent graduates, a young nuclear engineer named Clay Gabler.

Gabler looked a little like Hollowell, and was also somewhat shy. Gabler had a stutter, sometimes struggling to get a word out, which would make later public presentations a challenge. But he was also an excellent computer programmer who saw the future of the nuclear power industry fading after the Three Mile Island disaster, and quickly became fascinated by the dynamics of traffic crashes instead.

Hollowell and Gabler spent countless hours tweaking the new, combined computer model. But they did not have the budget to do actual crash tests, which would allow them to test whether the model reflected reality. Gabler ended up leaving in 1992 to pursue a doctorate in engineering at Princeton, focusing on vehicle crashes, while Hollowell was promoted to become one of the nine research division chiefs at NHTSA, overseeing a range of research into auto-safety systems, like padding and air bags.

The computer model languished, but neither man forgot about it. NHTSA has dozens of panels to coordinate research with the automakers, and Hollowell organized a working group that held meetings in 1991 and 1992 to discuss computer modeling of crash compatibility. Two events in 1993 renewed Hollowell's hopes of winning the funding and bureaucratic support to resume studying crash compatibility. First, President Clinton took office, calling for the development of a new generation of fuel-efficient cars that would be up to 40 percent lighter than existing cars. Hollowell worried that these cars would have to be made of very high-strength composites first developed in the space industry. These composites tend to be extremely stiff and do not crumple easily, so Hollowell wondered whether they might pierce deeply into other vehicles during crashes.

Second, there was a growing controversy over the insurance industry's use of so-called offset crash tests, in which the front left corner of a car is smashed into a concrete barrier instead of the car's entire front end. Insurers praise the test as more realistic than the government's tests, which use the whole front end, because people usually try to swerve before an impact. But automakers were already saying that to pass the offset tests, they would have to make the corners of their cars stiffer. Hollowell thought that might increase the threat to other motorists.

He had little luck at first in persuading his bosses at NHTSA. "Quite frankly, early on the agency didn't think compatibility was a problem, because they thought it was a weight issue," he said. If heavy SUVs were no more deadly to other motorists than the heavy full-sized station wagons of an earlier generation, regulators were not interested.

Hollowell's biggest need was to raise money for grants to statisticians at universities and for crash tests. Like many other federal agencies, such as the National Institutes of Health, NHTSA does some research in-house but relies mostly on grants to outside experts to do statistical analyses and perform crash tests.

With the Clinton Administration preparing to give Detroit more than $200 million a year to develop more fuel-efficient cars, Hollowell began lobbying for some of the money to be dedicated to safety. He sought $2.5 million a year for six years to refine the old Ford computer models saying that it was needed to analyze how very stiff, lightweight vehicles would interact in crashes.

Hollowell persuaded NHTSA's senior management to include the money in its budget proposals for fiscal 1995 and for fiscal 1996. But House and Senate staffers, particularly from the Republican side, wanted to trim Clinton's costly plan and asked the auto industry how to do it. Auto lobbyists had a ready answer: give Detroit the lavish research subsidies but eliminate the safety analysis by regulators. "We told the staff if they were looking for a place to cut, that was a place," Michael Stanton, one of the auto industry's top lobbyists then and now, recalled. "We didn't want to be against it, but the question is, is that a good place to cut." Stanton said that the auto industry's concern had been that it was premature to be developing computer models for the safety of cars that would not even exist as prototypes until the 2004 model year. He insisted that he had no idea that the computer models could be used to look at crash-compatibility issues in vehicles already on the road.

After this setback, Hollowell persisted and decided in late 1995 to put aside the computer model and take a fresh look at the national database on fatal crashes. Gabler helped him, working part time for NHTSA while continuing to pursue his doctorate. The two men decided to put together a ranking of the models that posed the greatest danger to other motorists. The two men calculated that a ranking would be so provocative and controversial within the traffic safety community that Detroit and top regulators would have to pay attention, Gabler later recalled.

The two men analyzed the kill rate for different models: How many people in other vehicles were killed annually in crashes per million registered vehicles of a given model. They calculated, for example, that Honda Accords killed 21 other motorists each year per million Accords on the road, while Ford Tauruses killed 38.

From the very first data runs, Hollowell and Gabler noticed that large cars were no longer the biggest hazard. Light trucks had become a far greater problem. While large cars had a kill rate 8 percent above that of midsized cars, SUVs had a kill rate that was 85 percent higher. The kill rate for SUVs was considerably higher than for the compact pickup trucks on which most of them were based.

More ominously still, full-sized pickup trucks had an even higher kill rate than the SUVs, and automakers were just starting to build a lot of full-sized SUVs then. The full-sized Chevrolet Blazer, which has since been renamed the Chevrolet Tahoe, led a list of "top 20 aggressors," killing 122 other motorists annually per million full-sized Blazers. The Hollowell and Gabler paper warned that the weight and stiffness of light trucks were hazardous to other motorists, and said that the height of light trucks' front ends should be studied.[7]

The deadliness of light trucks was a surprise to both men. Like most safety researchers, they had not been keeping track of the slowly growing percentage of vehicles on the road that were light trucks. Their computer model, now two decades old, only permitted the simulation of crashes between cars.

"In our model, we had planned to put in light trucks, but we had no idea that was where the real problem was until we did the accident analysis," Hollowell said.

The paper set out research priorities that Hollowell and Gabler hoped to pursue. But their rankings had a serious drawback that helped automakers to ignore them initially. By calculating kills per million registered vehicles, their results were slightly skewed. The deadliest models were not just those that crushed other vehicles but also models that happened to be in lots and lots of crashes because they were typically driven by young men. The calculations showed, for example, that the Chevrolet Camaro, with a kill rate of 86, was far more deadly to other motorists than any other car on the road, and deadlier than many SUVs, pickups and vans too. Since the Camaro is a low-riding, not especially heavy car, its high ranking had to reflect the way it was driven, not its design.

The paper was among hundreds presented in various seminars at the Fifteenth International Conference on Enhanced Safety of Vehicles in Melbourne, Australia, in May 1996. Top regulators agreed at the Melbourne conference to try to coordinate their research in five areas, and one of them was vehicle compatibility. The interest in vehicle compatibility came to a large extent from European regulators, however, and reflected concern in Europe about the damage that large cars were inflicting on small cars as falling gasoline prices made large cars more affordable to operate again and more common on the roads.

The paper and the international research goal helped Hollowell finally win Congressional approval in the autumn of 1996 for the first $2.5 million needed to resume work on the Ford computer model, which was two decades old by then. Another $800,000 a year of Hollowell's own budget for research into automobile safety systems was also earmarked for compatibility research, including crash tests and statistical analyses by university experts. Even within NHTSA, however, the paper and the research received little attention. Auto-industry lobbyists had decided that a six-year computer modeling exercise posed little if any threat.

Because the whole Melbourne conference was literally at the other end of the Earth from the United States and Europe, it attracted practically no media coverage. American journalists and regulators were captivated by dozens of tragic cases in which children and short women sitting in the front seat had been killed by air bags that had been designed to inflate with enough force to restrain a 180-pound man not wearing his seat belt. SUVs had rekindled the American love affair with automobiles and revitalized the upper Midwest, and compatibility concerns were far from the minds of most motorists and automakers.

*

In August 1997, Ford's board approved plans to introduce the biggest SUV yet. The behemoth, eventually named the Excursion, would weigh more than three tons, be taller than Michael Jordan and be typically sold with a V-10 engine that got just 10 miles to the gallon in the city. It was so big that a tall driver could look in the windows of school buses. It shared the front end of an F-250 Super Duty pickup truck, with a hood that was 49 inches off the ground, almost as high as the roof of a Ford Taurus. But when the Ford board gave its approval for mass production of the Excursion, no tests had been done on the dangers the vehicle would pose to other motorists.

Meanwhile, Hollowell and Gabler were continuing to work on their computer model. At a routine quarterly public presentation by NHTSA of its research plans on September 23, 1997, Gabler described the pair's Melbourne paper and plans for further research. The audience, composed almost entirely of auto-industry officials, was very skeptical that a compatibility problem existed at all. "They were furious, they were so angry—there was a guy there, I think from Ford, the pickup division, who stood up and said, 'If this is such a problem, why isn't this in the newspapers?'" Gabler said.

Purely by coincidence, the next day *The New York Times* published a long article I had written on crash compatibility. Illustrating the story was a large, front-page photo from a recent British crash test showing the front end of a Range Rover passing clean over the door sill of a Ford Escort in a side-impact collision and punching deep into the passenger compartment. The damage was serious even though the test was conducted at just 18.6 miles an hour.

A review of an inch-thick printout of the government's thousands of crash tests over the years showed that there had never been a test pitting a sport utility vehicle against a car. The $800,000 a year earmarked for crash tests and outside statistical experts on crash compatibility was being spent instead by NHTSA on air bag research, the big issue of the day.

New British research was pointing to the height of vehicles' front ends as being more important than weight in side-impact collisions. Yet American automakers had no procedures to analyze the effects of their vehicles in crashes.

"We first of all worry in most cases about the occupants of the vehicle we're selling," acknowledged Chris Magee, Ford's director of vehicle systems engineering, who had worked with Hollowell in the 1970s on the crash-compatibility computer program. "As far as vehicle mix aspects, we might look at them, but there's not really any processes or procedures for doing anything."

The auto industry's top lobbyist on safety issues, who had just stepped down from being one of the industry's top safety regulators, admitted that the designs of SUVs and pickups posed a particular hazard when they hit cars in the side. "You're more likely to be hit in the parts of the body that are more prone to injury, like the chest or the head," said Barry Felrice, the safety director at the American Automobile Manufacturers Association.

Yet most Detroit auto executives dismissed crash incompatibility as an inevitable fact of life. "Even if you're driving a tank down the road, you could always get hit by a locomotive," said Robert Purcell, GM's director of advanced technology.

More embarrassing for Detroit was that Mercedes in Germany had begun studying crash incompatibilities and was trying to do something about it. Just as the company was designing its first sport utility vehicle in 1993, the German equivalent of the American Automobile Association had performed a head-on crash test pitting a large Nissan SUV against a Volkswagen Golf. The Nissan rode up over the VW's hood, nearly to the base of the Golf's windshield; the crash dummy in the Golf suffered head injuries that measured 3,177 on a scale for which readings above 1,000 are considered life-threatening. Traveling under the Nissan, the front end of the Golf had struck the base of the SUV's steering column, hammering it up into the dummy in the SUV's driver's seat with enough force to impale and probably kill a real person.

Partly in response to that test, Mercedes carefully crafted the front end of its new M-class SUV. Below and behind the bumper, Mercedes installed a hollow, horizontal tube that amounts to a second bumper at the same height as a car underbody. Mercedes even did a crash test pitting an M-class against a Mercedes so small that it is not sold in the United States; a crash dummy in the car "survived."

Bumper heights seemed fairly important. Cars are required by federal regulations to have bumpers that could resist an impact between 16 and 20 inches off the ground. SUVs and other light trucks are exempt from this rule, and automakers have mounted the bumpers considerably higher, ostensibly to reduce the risk of their snagging on boulders during off-road driving but mainly for the macho look this gives the vehicles. Charles R. Baker, a top Honda engineer, said that, "If you get a frontal collision, the sport utility vehicle bumper will tend to go over the hood of the car—that's bad."

Subsequent research has found that the height of an SUV's frame rails, engine and hood are much more important than the height of the bumper. Bumpers are only designed to protect a vehicle from damage in collisions at up to 2.5 miles an hour, and are little more than tin foil in crashes at speeds exceeding 10 miles an hour. But the light truck exemption from the bumper-height rule has still had a pernicious effect on safety. Auto designers have had to keep the front ends of cars fairly low to mount the bumpers, and have lined up their crumple zones behind the bumpers. Freed of any such constraint, designers of SUVs and pickup trucks have been able to create ever taller front ends.

Fear of litigation sometimes constrains auto designers, but the automakers correctly concluded that it would be hard to sue them for the harm their vehicles inflicted on other motorists. The first SUV compatibility case was filed a few weeks after my September 24 article in *The New York Times*, and it was filed by the de Veers against Land Rover, which makes the Range Rover. It was the first lawsuit citing incompatibility between cars and SUVs as a basis for liability. The de Veers accused the company of negligently designing an unsafe product on the grounds that the Range Rover had caused so much harm in the crash. The allegation was that the Range Rover's bumper was too high and that Land Rover should have anticipated that customers might buy grille guards and install them on Range Rovers. The de Veers' lawyer, Arnold Schwartz, filed the case in a local California court in November 1997 and asked for a jury trial.

Land Rover responded that it was not liable, partly because the Range Rover's bumper needed to be high for off-road driving and partly because the company could never hope to anticipate the design of all the other vehicles that a Range Rover might hit. By the de Veers' reasoning, Land Rover's lawyers contended in a court filing, "Busses would be defective unless they were identical to mobile homes; both would be defective unless identical to ambulances; all three would be defective unless identical to pickup trucks; all four would be defective unless identical to vans; all five would be defective unless identical to family cars."

Judge Jan A. Plum of the Superior Court of California in Los Angeles read the arguments from both sides, spoke with the lawyers and decided that Land Rover was right. Land Rover could not possibly be expected to anticipate all the other kinds of automobiles that its products might hit, she ruled, as she threw the case out of court on January 26, 2000, without even allowing it to go to a jury; a state appellate court subsequently upheld her dismissal of the case. Only one case similar to the de Veers' case has been filed, a lawsuit against Nissan in Connecticut on behalf of a Pontiac station wagon driver who died in a collision with a Nissan Pathfinder SUV. The case against Nissan was swiftly withdrawn when the automaker, citing Judge Plum's verdict in Los Angeles, threatened to countersue on the grounds that it was frivolous even to argue in court that an SUV's manufacturer could be held liable. And with that, the legal profession lost interest in the dangers of SUVs to other motorists. Because neither case ever made it to trial, there has never been any legal discovery of automakers' internal documents on crash compatibility.

As the issue of crash compatibility grew in prominence, the automakers began to marshal their own studies. Priya Prasad, who had worked with Tom Hollowell on Ford's crash-compatibility model in the 1970s and was now Ford's top safety researcher, did a computer analysis in 1997 of the federal crash database to calculate that collisions between cars and SUVs accounted for an average of 4 percent of all traffic deaths a year during the early and mid-1990s. On this basis, he contended that the problem was overblown. The percentage was small, he argued, partly because nearly half of all traffic deaths occur in single-vehicle crashes, and partly because SUVs still accounted for well under 5 percent of all vehicles on the road during the period he reviewed. He pointed out that the overall number of crash deaths on the nation's roads had leveled off at about 42,000 a year in the 1990s, and was still falling gradually when measured as a death rate per 100 million miles traveled.

The problem with Prasad's argument was that it did not assess whether collisions between cars and SUVs were unusually deadly. If that 4 percent was twice what it should be, that would still be more than 800 unnecessary deaths each year—the equivalent of a fully loaded Boeing 747 passenger jet crashing every six months. More important, even as seat belt use was becoming widespread, drunk driving was declining and air bags were becoming common, the overall number of traffic deaths had rather abruptly stopped falling in the 1990s. One culprit seemed to be SUVs, especially given that deaths in collisions between cars and light trucks were rising, even as most other categories of crash deaths were declining. And with SUVs amounting to 17 percent of new vehicle sales and rising, it seemed only a matter of time before they would account for a much larger proportion of all vehicles in use, and therefore a growing share of all crashes with cars.

Another group becoming interested in SUVs was the Society of Automotive Engineers (SAE). Founded in 1905, SAE set common technical standards for automakers, including some safety standards, for decades until the creation of the National Highway Safety Bureau in 1966, which then became NHTSA in 1970. Supported by dues-paying members and the automakers, the SAE still sets industry guidelines and standards for obscure details like the height at which headlights are mounted. The oil thickness numbers on the side of a can of oil come from an SAE rating system.

SAE held a two-day, closed-door conference on the dangers of SUVs at a Hyatt Hotel in Dearborn on December 10 and 11, 1997. Top safety researchers and auto engineers from around the country were invited to present technical papers. The media was not invited, but I heard about it anyway because I had gone on the SAE mailing list after buying copies of old technical papers from its library. I identified myself as a reporter when I registered, with *The New York Times* paying the conference fee, and was told that while I would not be allowed to tape the proceedings in any way, everything said would be on the record and could be quoted in print.

The meeting proved a gold mine of information. John Sapp, the brake manager at Lucas Varity, warned that SUV brakes were not as good as car brakes and needed improvement. NHTSA's Charles Kahane said that large sport utility vehicles and pickups accounted for an unusually high proportion of pedestrian deaths, and suggested that this might be because of their weaker brakes and lack of maneuverability.

Hollowell and Gabler had updated their Melbourne analysis to look not at kill rates per million registered vehicles but per 1,000 crashes reported to the police nationwide. This allowed them to examine whether specific models were more likely to cause deaths in crashes. The new approach did not entirely exclude the reckless driving factor that had put the Chevy Camaro so high on their previous list of deadly vehicles, because models driven by heedless young men might be going faster on average in crashes than models driven by middle-aged families. But the analysis did reduce the effect of driver demographics.[8]

The new calculations showed that SUVs were nearly three times as likely as cars to kill the other driver in a crash. Full-size pickup trucks and full-size vans were even deadlier, but the small pickups on which most SUVs were based were less deadly. Hollowell and Gabler also calculated that when a car strikes another car in the side, the driver of the struck car is 6.6 times as likely to die as the driver of the striking car. But when an SUV hits a car in the side, the death ratio rises to 30 to 1.

Looking for a cause for this disparity, Hollowell and Gabler zeroed in on height mismatches. They looked at the height of the bottom exterior panel below the doors of each vehicle. SUVs had the highest average height, 15.4 inches, while subcompact cars had the lowest, 6.9 inches. "SUVs ride almost 200 mm (8 inches) higher than mid-sized cars—a geometric incompatibility that would readily permit the SUV to override any side structure in a car and directly strike the car occupant," the two men concluded in a subsequent paper summarizing data presented by Hollowell at the Dearborn conference.

Hollowell and Gabler also reviewed the relative stiffness of various models, and concluded that SUVs were much stiffer than cars. They calculated this from the forces exerted against a concrete barrier during routine crash tests of various models. For example, they compared a Ford Taurus sedan and a Ford Ranger pickup (which shares the same underbody as a Ford Explorer). The Taurus and Ranger weigh about the same, so differences in the forces against the barrier would reflect differences in the stiffness of the two vehicles. Sure enough, pressure sensors on the concrete barrier detected that the Ranger smacked the barrier with more than twice the peak force of the Taurus, which had a front end that crumpled more, absorbing energy. Crash dummies in the Taurus also suffered less harm in their crash test than dummies in the Ranger.

Little of this seemed to have registered on the leading auto executives at the Detroit auto show in January 1998, who were planning to build SUVs even taller. Automobile shoppers, particularly women, perceived tall vehicles as safer, said Ross H. Roberts, the general manager of Ford cars and trucks. "We can sit them lower if we want, but the height has been an advantage" for marketing, he said.

Dr. Ricardo Martinez, the administrator of NHTSA and a Clinton appointee, became publicly involved in the compatibility debate for the first time on January 12, 1998, when he mentioned in a couple of sentences near the end of a speech in Detroit that automakers should address the problem. His remarks infuriated Detroit auto executives, who were incensed that a senior regulator publicly mentioned the issue. "The industry was so upset, you would have thought we shot their dog," Martinez later recalled.

The day after the speech, Martinez had a meeting with the chief executive of one of the Detroit automakers. Martinez refused to identify the CEO, but said that the Detroit industry leader had greeted him by saying half-seriously, "My God, don't touch my cash cow."

Chrysler in particular went on a public-relations offensive in January and February. Chrysler chairman Bob Eaton gave a speech to the car dealers' convention on January 31 calling for them to flex their lobbying muscle in defending SUVs from regulation and predicting that the American people would not stand for any restrictions on SUVs. "When the government comes to take away the customer's sport utility vehicle because it supposedly poses an environmental threat, or supposedly poses a threat to small cars, we may suddenly find we have the strongest possible ally," Eaton said.

Chrysler officials also began contending that it was a bad idea even to discuss compatibility issues in public because it might prompt survival-conscious consumers to choose the most lethal-looking models. As evidence, they cited rising SUV sales over the preceding year. They carefully omitted mentioning that SUV sales had been rising for a decade, and that growth in the market share of SUVs had actually slowed over the preceding year.

Officials at Chrysler and other automakers also suggested, without statistical evidence, that SUVs might be saving at least as many lives as they destroyed. As long as SUVs are merely rearranging in which vehicles the deaths occur in a crash, the auto executives argued, regulators should not intervene.

The only problem with this argument was that it was not true. The Insurance Institute for Highway Safety, which is bankrolled by insurers seeking to reduce the cost of crash claims, jumped into the fray on February 9 with a report stating that while compatibility was not the only traffic safety issue pending, it did need to be addressed. The institute's statisticians came up with new evidence that SUVs were actually increasing the overall death rate on the nation's roads, and not just rearranging the deaths among various vehicles.

To do this, the statisticians added together all the deaths that occurred in each class of vehicle—SUVs, pickups, cars and mini-vans. Then they added to each category's total the number of deaths they inflicted on other road users, including pedestrians as well as other motorists whom they hit. The study found that the death rate in crashes involving sport utility vehicles, for people inside and outside the vehicle, was 17 percent higher per million registered vehicles than the rate for cars, and 47 percent higher for pickups than for cars. By contrast, large cars actually reduced the overall death rate in crashes, by providing lots of protection for their occupants while only moderately increasing the risk for other drivers that they hit.

The pickups looked even worse than the SUVs because pickups are more likely to be driven by reckless young men and because the bulk of the pickups on the road are full-sized models while the bulk of the SUVs on the road are midsized models. But with sales of full-sized SUVs rising, and with SUVs beginning to find their way into the hands of more young men, the SUV statistics are likely to move toward the pickup truck number.

The institute concluded with a statement that SUVs and pickup trucks posed fundamentally different and more serious crash-compatibility issues than the longtime disparity between large cars and small cars. "These analyses show the major concerns that have been raised about crash incompatibility between light and heavy cars are overstated for the U.S. vehicle fleet," Brian O'Neill, the institute's president, said in a statement. "Automakers should design their cars so occupants are as safe as possible, without worrying about incompatibility among cars in crashes. The principal focus for incompatibility improvements needs to be on pickups and utility vehicles and the sides of passenger cars."

The crash-compatibility issue came to a boil at the SAE's annual convention in Detroit in late February 1998. The SAE convention included a seminar on crash compatibility for the first time, and researchers from automakers and universities around the world presented papers. A throng of journalists showed up, including television crews, to hear Hollowell and Gabler present the information I had heard in Dearborn, but the SAE barred television cameras from seminars and banned journalists from quoting anyone by name or by corporate affiliation. Frustrated by the SAE's strict rules, the journalists waited for Hollowell and Gabler to finish their remarks. When the two men came outside and declined to give a press conference, they ended up being literally chased through the hallways of Detroit's convention center by reporters eager for quotes.

Meanwhile, a pronounced hostility continued to build in Detroit toward anyone raising crash-compatibility issues. "In all the years I've covered the business, I've probably never heard as negative a reaction by the industry to anything, except possibly the fuel-economy debate, as the SUV safety debate," said Paul Eisenstein, a reporter who has written about automakers for various publications since 1979.

When my wife and I went to a dinner party around this time, a woman whom I did not even know told me, "Suburbans are great cars, you should die." (I lacked the presence of mind to respond that Suburbans are not cars at all, but modified pickup trucks.)

While the rest of the national media still largely ignored SUV issues, Detroit newspapers and magazines ran front-page stories about automakers' absurd suspicions that a shadowy conspiracy of environmentalists, consumer activists and journalists wanted to take Americans' SUVs away. "We seem to have a back-room group plotting against a product that is extremely popular and serves the people who buy it very well," Land Rover's top executive in North America told *AutoWeek*.[9]

But at an SAE conference for auto lobbyists and regulators in Washington in April, the auto industry's stance began to change slightly. Ford's Priya Prasad said in a speech that the design of light trucks, as opposed to their weight, was causing about 1,000 unnecessary deaths a year in other vehicles that they struck, mainly cars. Almost all of these deaths were caused by SUVs and pickups, he said, because minivans were based on car designs. Some of the deaths were inevitable, he said, because some SUVs and pickups need strong frames or high underbodies for towing and off-road travel. Reducing the 1,000 deaths a year would take a long time because it takes more than a decade for a significant proportion of the nation's vehicles to be scrapped and replaced, Prasad noted. His comments nonetheless represented an acknowledgment that a problem existed.

The biannual international conference on traffic safety was held in early June across the river from Detroit at a convention center in Windsor, Ontario. An entire day was added to the four-day event so as to allow time for a thorough discussion of light-truck incompatibility with cars. NHTSA officials presented the results of a first round of crash tests in which they had hurled a series of vehicles at 33 miles an hour into the sides of Honda Accords. The tests showed that a Ford Explorer, a midsize sport utility vehicle, was twice as likely as a midsize car, minivan or pickup truck to inflict a critical or severe injury to a car driver's chest and somewhat more likely to hurt a car driver's head and neck. Not one of the crashes produced enough harm to the dummies to kill a real person, a fact that auto officials gleefully seized upon; NHTSA officials countered that they had not chosen a fast enough speed to "kill" the dummies.

At the same Windsor conference, Dr. Martinez of NHTSA estimated that the design of light trucks was causing 2,000 unnecessary deaths a year, twice as many as Prasad had mentioned. NHTSA
had hired one of the top American traffic safety analysts since the
1960s, Hans Joksch of the University of Michigan, to begin conducting a series of statistical analyses of crash compatibility. To help
Joksch, regulators culled from their records an exceptionally
detailed and comprehensive database of SUV crashes. Joksch came
up with the figure of 2,000 lives by looking at death rates in crashes
involving light trucks and death rates in crashes involving cars, and
calculating how many fewer deaths would have occurred if the
light-truck death rate had matched the car death rate. Automakers
said that Joksch must have miscalculated somehow, but did not
provide any detailed criticism of his methodology.

After the Windsor conference, the compatibility issue quieted
down considerably. Most of the issues had been publicly aired, and
the regulators and automakers seemed to have staked out their
respective positions. But a few research studies continued to trickle
out.

The most interesting paper was presented by the Insurance Institute for Highway Safety at a conference in San Diego in October
1999. The institute had crashed six vehicles into the driver's side
doors of six Mercury Grand Marquis sedans: a big Lincoln Town Car
sedan, four Ford F-150 two-wheel-drive pickup trucks and a Ford F-
150 four-wheel-drive pickup truck. The goal was to figure out the
relative roles of weight, stiffness and height in crashes.

Most of the results were unsurprising. The Town Car inflicted
the least harm, while the stiffer pickups all inflicted more damage
to crash dummies in the sedans. When the institute put extra
weight in a two-wheel-drive pickup it did a little extra damage, and
when another two-wheel-drive pickup had its suspension raised, it
did considerably more damage.

The institute expected the four-wheel-drive pickup to inflict
devastating injuries on the dummy because it was the tallest,
stiffest, heaviest model of all. But the four-wheel-drive model actu-

ally caused the least harm to the dummy in the Grand Marquis of any of the pickup trucks, although still more than the Town Car. The institute's researchers were mystified at first by this outcome, and studied the pickup truck and freeze-frame pictures of the crash at length before they realized what had happened. The four-wheel-drive pickup had hooks below the bumper so that the vehicle could be towed, while the two-wheel-drive pickups did not. In the crash, the tow hooks had caught the door sill of the Grand Marquis and shoved the vehicle sideways even as the grille and hood punched inwards. The two-wheel-drive pickups had gone clear over the door sill, with disastrous results. It was as clear an illustration of the importance of design in crash compatibility, as opposed to weight, as anyone could ask.[10]

The institute's conclusion was not, however, that the front ends of SUVs and pickups should be immediately redesigned. Instead, the institute called for automakers to install side air bags on many more vehicles. These air bags come in various designs, deploying from the side of the seat or the side of the vehicle, and typically protect the occupant's head, neck and chest when the side of the vehicle caves in. Many luxury cars have side air bags, but they are seldom found on less expensive models. Wider installation of side air bags is the best approach because they protect occupants not only during crashes with light trucks but also when a car slides sideways into a utility pole, tree or other solid object.

That same autumn, the institute also quietly overhauled its statistics on occupant death rates for different classes of vehicles. It turned out that the occupant death rates for large cars and very large cars had been inflated by the inclusion of police cars, which have tragically high death rates. Occupants of police cars—mainly police officers—have high death rates in crashes partly because of their participation in high-speed chases.[11] Taking out the police cars, plus a couple of technical adjustments, showed that cars (and minivans—the institute lumped them together) had a lower death rate overall than SUVs per million registered vehicles. Large cars and minivans had the lowest death rate of all, even lower than the largest SUVs, which outweighed them by a full ton.

The crash-compatibility issue seemed a stalemate on the surface, with automakers implacably opposed to recognizing a problem. But this was just an illusion. Inside the vast research laboratories of the automakers, a lot of work was starting to take place to address the compatibility problem. The results of this effort only began to leak out in 1999 and 2000, but turned out to have started earlier.

Ford appears to have been the first to take seriously the problem of SUV crash compatibility. Priya Prasad, the safety researcher whose public studies initially concluded that SUVs were not a problem, was also meeting with senior executives all over Ford in late 1997, arguing that something had to be done to make SUVs less dangerous to cars. "That was the time we were beginning to talk about all safety standards being the same in SUVs as in cars," he said.

His campaign bore fruit, as Ford's leadership ordered an immediate and extensive series of crash tests and computer analyses, to be conducted in such secrecy that the details did not seep out until many years later. Not until June 2001 did Prasad and two of his aides reveal in a little-noticed technical paper at a conference in Amsterdam just how extensive their crash tests had been and how ghastly the results.[12] When the technical paper did come out, it was like finding a blood-stained KGB document after the fall of the Berlin Wall. As Tom Hollowell observed, everything in the paper read more like something that he might have written, rather than the product of research by the automaker that did more than any other to create the SUV boom of the 1990s.

With a huge supply of vehicles to crash, unlike federal regulators, Ford researchers had crashed many different models into Ford Tauruses at a variety of angles, destroying $50,000 to $80,000 worth of vehicles with each crash. The Explorer proved far more dangerous than a minivan, pickup truck or car of similar or marginally lower weight.

One series of crash tests, for example, involved crashing each of these vehicles at 35 miles an hour into the front, driver's side corner of Ford Tauruses also traveling at 35 miles an hour. Head injuries to the driver dummy in the Taurus were 34 to 192 percent more severe when the Explorer was the striking vehicle than the minivan, pickup or car. Chest injuries inflicted by the Explorer were triple to quadruple the severity of injuries inflicted by the other vehicles. And the Explorer totally destroyed the left leg of the driver dummy in the Taurus, causing 7.5 to 8.2 times as much damage as the other three vehicles. The car, which was not identified, did the least damage to the Taurus.

While the Explorer was causing terrible carnage in the Taurus, it also was doing only a so-so job of protecting its own driver dummy. Head and leg injuries in the Explorer were slightly worse than for the minivan and somewhat better than for the pickup or car. Chest injuries in the Explorer were considerably worse than in the minivan and a little worse than in the car, but were better than in the pickup truck. In other words, the minivan provided the best protection, the Explorer and then the car were runners-up and the pickup truck was the worst. But when it came to occupant protection, the figures showed nothing like the huge disparity between the Explorer and every other vehicle in causing injuries.

An obvious question facing Ford researchers was whether an even larger SUV would do even more damage. So they also crashed several Lincoln Navigators and Ford Explorers into Tauruses at a couple of different angles. Surprisingly, the Navigator did little more harm than the Explorer even though it weighed 1,236 pounds more.

Poring through all this information, Prasad and his staff decided that the height of the frame rails was crucial in frontal collisions. The Explorer's frame rails were three inches higher than the vestigial rails in the underbody of a Ford Taurus. During frontal crash tests, the Explorer frame rails slid up and over the front ends of the Taurus, allowing Explorers to hurtle up to the base of the windshield. The Navigator had slightly lower frame rails and shoved in less of the Taurus's passenger compartment. This nearly balanced the effect of the Navigator's greater weight, so that the Navigator overall did little more damage than the Explorer.

The conclusion of the Ford research was clinically written but stark: "Preliminary results indicated that geometric incompatibility was the dominating factor in the studied vehicle design characteristics." In other words, the way SUVs were built, and not just their weight, was killing other motorists. Ford had done a total reversal of its position in 1997, when Ford's chairman compared vehicle crashes to hitting a small rock with a larger rock, simple masses governed by laws of physics known since the Greeks.

The terrible consequences that Ford researchers found in crash tests of Explorers are being confirmed daily on the nation's roads, as Explorers have been killing a remarkable number of other motorists. The Explorer has been the nation's best-selling SUV every year since 1991, to the point that one in seven SUVs on the nation's roads now is an Explorer. Tens of thousands of Explorers have been involved in crashes over the years, and more than 1,000 have been in fatal crashes. This is such a large number that statisticians have been able to study the Explorer's real-world deadliness in detail, something that is not possible for most models.

Hans Joksch of the University of Michigan has looked at how Explorers behave in crashes compared to large cars of the same weight. Such cars include the Ford Crown Victoria, Mercury Grand Marquis, Lincoln Town Car, Cadillac DeVille, Mercedes E320 wagon and the now discontinued Chevrolet Caprice.

Large cars are good for comparison because they represent excellent alternatives to Explorers. Large cars provide more space for passengers. They offer capacious trunks for luggage and other gear. They are less capable for off-road driving and towing, but few SUV buyers use these features. And while a Cadillac, Lincoln or Mercedes may cost more than an Explorer, a Crown Victoria or Grand Marquis costs less.

So what do the safety numbers show? The results of Joksch's

research are frightening. Explorer drivers die slightly less often in two-vehicle crashes as large car drivers, but take many more drivers of other vehicles to the grave with them. For each Explorer driver whose life is saved in a two-vehicle collision by choosing an Explorer instead of a large car, an extra five drivers are killed in vehicles struck by Explorers.[13]

The extra person who survived in the Explorer would certainly be relieved to be living after the collision. But it is probably not in society's interest to be killing five people in vehicle-to-vehicle collisions for each extra survivor in an Explorer. Indeed, some ethicists contend that making such lopsided tradeoffs in human lives is immoral.

What makes matters worse is that the apparent safety of the Explorer is an illusion. The Explorer drivers are sacrificing the lives of the five car drivers largely in vain—or for vanity, if the Explorer owners bought their SUVs because they were stylish. Explorers roll over less often than most other midsized SUVs, but they still roll over often enough to wipe out any safety advantage in overall safety compared to large cars.

When you take into account that there are more than three million Explorers on the road, the deaths add up in a hurry. Joksch estimates that Explorers alone are killing at least an extra 100 people a year compared to how many people would die if Explorer owners had purchased large cars instead.

Faced with appalling crash-test results, Ford and other automakers began to change the designs of their SUVs. The changes were made quietly and with considerable secrecy, partly because no automaker wanted to tip off its rivals about the design of future models and partly for fear that design changes would seem like an acknowledgment of a problem and stir up further controversy.

After crash test compatibility became a national issue in September 1997, the first model to be reviewed for design changes appears to have been the Ford Excursion, since it had just been approved by the Ford board for mass production in August 1997 and would be the largest SUV on the market. Ford's initial tests were horrifying: The Excursion turned out to have such a high front end that it vaulted right over the front end of a Ford Taurus in a head-on collision and slammed into the base of the windshield. Being hit by three tons of flying steel that passes over the crumple zones would be a lethal experience for car occupants.

By December 1997, Prasad and his staff had already come up with a partial solution, an answer that the French transportation ministry's researchers would have liked back in 1971. They decided to mount a 50-pound hollow, impact-absorbing steel bar below the front bumper of every Excursion. They dubbed it the Blocker Beam, even patenting the design and obtaining a trademark on the name. They also lowered the horizontal steel beam that supports the trailer hitch in the back of the vehicle, so as to prevent cars from sliding under the back of the Excursion.

The engineers also had to tweak the Excursion's suspension, lowering the vehicle by an inch. This was done partly to prevent the Blocker Beam's extra weight in front of the front wheels from affecting the vehicle's balance and handling and partly to lower the front end even more, said Paul Mayer, an engineering supervisor for the Excursion. Ford's senior management was wary at first of the expense of adding a large and completely new auto part to its designs, but ended up relenting as Prasad took his presentation to meeting after meeting.

When Ford finally unveiled the Excursion at a press briefing on February 26, 1999, engineers even showed two videos of computer simulations. The Excursion without the Blocker Beam hurtled over the hood of a Taurus, while an Excursion with the Blocker Beam engaged the front end of the Taurus and crushed it back to the front wheels, but did not penetrate the passenger compartment.

The Excursion had the same front end and underbody as a F-250 Super Duty pickup truck, which had gone on sale a year before the

Excursion and had no Blocker Beam. I once accompanied a *Times* photographer to a nearby school parking lot and carefully parked a borrowed Super Duty with its grille an inch or two from the side of a Mercury Sable midsize sedan. The hood came up to the top of the driver's window on the car. The photographer shot a bunch of pictures, a couple of which we used in the newspaper. When he was almost done, a woman came running out of the school, very upset. She assumed I had clobbered the side of her car with the pickup, since the pickup's front end was nearly touching the car and the photographer was clicking away. When we told her what we were doing, however, she was reassured and let us proceed. Ford did not get around to installing Blocker Beams on Super Duty pickups until late 2000, two years after they had gone on sale. Heaven help anyone in a car hit by a 1999 or 2000 Super Duty pickup, as Ford has not recalled them to add Blocker Beams because the safety devices require accompanying changes in suspension design.

Ford had more time to work on the next generation of Explorers, which did not go on sale until April 2001. A team of engineers led by Dale Claudepierre studied the front end of the Explorer and noticed that the frame rails curved up at the front to a point behind the bumper, a little like the runners on a sleigh. An unintentional side effect of this design is that the curve makes it easier for the frame rails to slide up and over the front of objects they strike, just as the runners of a sleigh run up and over bumps outdoors.

Claudepierre and his team examined the rails and realized that they could simply invert the front segment of each rail, so that the front 18 inches of each rail curved down slightly, instead of up. The front ends of the rail would then match up almost perfectly with the front ends of the strongest steel beams in the underbody of a Ford Taurus. The same factory machine could even make the same welds in connecting the front segment of the Explorer frame rails to the rest of the frame rail; the gently curving segments simply had to be mounted upside down in the machine so that they would curve down instead of up. So Ford was able to make the change at very little cost, Claudepierre said. Ford also drilled holes near the front of each frame rail so that it would crumple more in a crash, softening impacts for Explorer owners and for those whom they hit.

"More so than in the past, we are concerned about the impact our vehicles have on other vehicles," he said.

The change also did not hurt the Explorer's ground clearance, because the frame rails were far from being the lowest elements of the SUV's underbody. Indeed, by rearranging key parts of the new Explorer's underbody, Ford was actually able to raise the vehicle's ground clearance by an inch even while making it less deadly to other motorists.

Ford officials declined to say how many lives would be saved by these changes, however. The Explorer's hood remained as high as ever, and at two tons, the SUV still weighed a half-ton more than the typical midsized car. But it was at least a move in the right direction.

Other automakers also started to take action. In 1997 Toyota began conducting its own secret series of crash tests pitting cars against SUVs. Toyota was preparing to offer a full-sized pickup truck, the Tundra, in 1999 and a full-sized SUV based on the same design, the Sequoia, in 2000. Toyota engineers independently reached the same conclusion as the Ford engineers, and tweaked their designs to add hollow, impact-absorbing steel bars below the bumpers.

General Motors lowered the frame rails on its midsized SUVs—the Chevrolet Trailblazer, GMC Envoy and Oldsmobile Bravada—by nearly two inches when it redesigned them for the 2002 model year. Unlike Ford, GM did not put out technical papers on its crash-compatibility research. I only learned about the company's efforts when I met Yih-Charng Deng, the GM computer programmer running the research, at the introduction of some new models in the summer of 2001. GM never would have allowed me to schedule an interview with him, but with a spokeswoman standing next to him who did not understand the significance of the conversation, Deng candidly described the company's extensive efforts, which GM had never shared before even with regulators.

When crash compatibility became controversial in late 1997 and early 1998, GM did an extensive series of crash tests and used them to develop an extremely powerful computer model for how vehicles interact. The problem facing previous computer modeling attempts, including Hollowell's attempts, was the presence of thousands of auto parts in the front of each vehicle that can bend in different directions. Auto parts also tend not to bend at all when first subjected to pressure, and then give way all at once, much as an aluminum soda can will briefly support the weight of a person before suddenly caving in on one side and flying off to one side. It is the difficulty in predicting the pressures at which parts suddenly give way that has given fits to computer modeling attempts.

GM largely overcame this problem in 2000 and 2001 by developing an immense computer model that dwarfed anything Hollowell had attempted. GM then ran the model using some of the world's fastest supercomputers—the whole effort would have been impossible before 1999 because the computers and software tools were not yet powerful enough, Deng said.

The GM computer model creates a three-dimensional map of the front end of an automobile and keeps track of 500,000 different points in this map. The program includes not only the material located at each of these 500,000 points—plastic, steel and so forth—but also the pressures at which each material will bend and how it will bend.

Deng was a little cagey about the results of the models. But when I asked him whether vehicle weight, stiffness or shape turned out to be the dominant variable in crashes, he replied that "geometric incompatibility" had proven to be the most important consideration for many crashes. If GM ever shares this work with regulators—and by early 2002 GM had not even told regulators that the computer model existed—then it could be a powerful tool for assessing the crash-compatibility problem.

Chrysler was especially late in paying attention to crash compatibility. Daimler-Benz, the parent of Mercedes, bought Chrysler in November 1998. Bob Lutz retired (and later joined GM) even before the deal was consummated, while Eaton quickly lost influence to German executives after the merger and ended up taking early retirement. Mercedes engineers stepped in to begin advising Chrysler engineers on ways to make their SUVs less dangerous. For the 2002 model year, they reconfigured the front end of the Dodge Durango, lowering the bumper and moving down some of the stiffest parts inside the front end so as to make it less dangerous to cars in crashes.

When Frank Klegon, DaimlerChrysler's vice president for pickup truck engineering, unveiled the new Dodge Ram full-sized pickup truck to the media at its headquarters on January 29, 2001, he said that the two-wheel-drive version already rode low enough not to override cars. But the four-wheel-drive Ram pickup, one of Chrysler's best-selling models, still rode higher than cars because the design process had been "pretty far along" before the company decided to address crash compatibility, he said. "We're very focused on that, a lot of development work," Klegon remarked, adding that the company planned to modify the design of the four-wheel-drive Ram after it went into production.

Fixing a safety problem after the assembly line starts running is a more expensive and usually less effective approach than designing such features from the beginning. But it is better than nothing, and a big change from Chrysler's intransigent position when Eaton and Lutz were in charge.

Yet even with all these steps, SUVs will remain deadlier than cars. Even when SUVs' frame rails are lower, they are still heavier and stiffer than cars. They still have minimal crumple zones. And they still have hoods that are too tall. Joksch estimates that the steps announced by automakers so far will eliminate no more than a third of the extra deaths caused by SUVs. Indeed, the number of unnecessary deaths is still likely to rise rather than fall each year, as the proportion of vehicles on the road that are SUVs surges to catch up with their share of new vehicle sales, and as more used SUVs fall into the hands of bad drivers.

The threat of regulation—combined with some auto executives' sense of personal duty to improve safety—has prompted the auto industry to begin addressing crash compatibility. Hollowell's research could someday produce a proposal for actual regulations. Any government rules would likely be based on requiring each new model to be crashed into a barrier resembling a vehicle. If a new model either inflicted too much damage or suffered too much damage itself in the test, it would be banned from going on the market.[14]

But Hollowell and many other researchers concede that there is no consensus on what the barrier should look like, how fast it should be moving and so forth. Make the barrier too big and heavy and it would be impossible for small cars to pass because they would suffer too much damage. Make the barrier too small and flimsy and it would be impossible for large SUVs and pickup trucks to pass because they would destroy it.

A few auto executives, mainly European and Japanese, nonetheless contend that international regulation is needed to improve compatibility. Louis Schweitzer, Renault's director general and top executive, said in 2001 that free markets would not address the crash-compatibility problem because light-truck buyers will not be willing to foot the extra cost of features that only improve the safety of others. "You cannot sell to the buyer of a light truck the fact that he is less dangerous to a car," Schweitzer warned. "He is not willing to pay a single dollar for that—it must be addressed by regulation."

General Motors, Ford and DaimlerChrysler say that some coordination of design is needed but that this can be done by forming industry partnerships, although GM and DaimlerChrysler say that there may someday be a role for government regulation, too. If automakers start sharing information about the height, stiffness and shape of future models, without actually sharing the vehicles' design and appearance, more progress can be made in improving vehicle safety, said Terry Connolly, GM's director for North American vehicle safety. "Some sort of long-term guidance is going to be necessary," either from an industry group or from governments, he said, adding that GM had shared some computer model information and crash-test data with other automakers.

In the absence of regulations, there are two other possible pressures on automakers to address compatibility: market forces and litigation. Automakers say that their market research shows that few vehicle buyers specifically consider the safety of other motorists in deciding what model to buy. But I have certainly met some people socially who say that they would never dream of buying an SUV because they think it would be immoral to put other people's lives at risk, and a handful of newspaper columns have made this point, too. If the deadliness of SUVs ever becomes a broad, high-priority issue for buyers, sales would falter and automakers would have to redesign them in a hurry.

Free-market pressures on automakers to improve crash compatibility would increase somewhat if all insurers updated the way they calculated liability premiums. As will be discussed in the next chapter, if all drivers had to pay premiums based on their actual likelihood of killing or maiming somebody else, some drivers might choose the less deadly models on the market.

Litigation could also become a risk for automakers if public sentiment changes. Liability law tends to respond more quickly to changes in the public's mood than any other area of the law, because a lot of it depends on how judges and juries interpret the responsibilities of a company to innocent bystanders as well as to customers.

The legal question for every SUV manufacturer on crash compatibility lies in what did they know and when did they know it, personal-injury lawyers say. If public sentiment ever changes significantly in the United States, such lawyers will do legal discovery in an effort to locate internal memos discussing the crash-compatibility problem before it became a public issue in 1997. If lawyers do find incriminating memos, they could wave them before juries and contend that the manufacturers knew of a lethal problem and chose not to address it for years—a legal argument that could help them win cases involving any of the millions of SUVs built before 1997.

My suspicion is that automakers knew early on that SUVs might be a problem for other road users, but underestimated the scope of the problem and then simply chose not to do research that might produce uncomfortable conclusions. The closest I ever came to confirming this suspicion occurred during an interview with an engineer who had recently retired from one of Detroit's Big Three automakers. He continued to work for the automaker as a safety consultant during his retirement and never testified against the automaker for personal-injury lawyers as a highly paid expert witness, so he had no financial incentive to tell me what he did. But after insisting on anonymity, he told me that the safety staff at his company had raised early concerns, but that the marketing staff had ignored them.

"Voices were heard," he said. "They just weren't listened to."

10

THE SUV INSURANCE SUBSIDY

The underlying principle of auto insurance is pretty simple. In theory, an insurance company adds up all of the money it has paid out for claims, adds some more money to the pot to cover its administrative costs and then tops it off with yet more money for profits. Then the insurer roughly divides this amount by the number of policyholders to calculate what the average premium should be for each policyholder. The riskiest people, such as drunk drivers, are then required to pay above-average premiums—they must pony up a larger share of the overall pot than less risky people, who pay below-average premiums.

That is the theory of insurance, as it is presented in textbooks and endlessly promoted by insurance executives and their lobbying groups. The reality is much messier. Some policyholders are more profitable than others. Insurers make most of their profits from affluent people who buy many different kinds of insurance and keep doing business with the same insurer year after year. Insurers are reluctant to adjust their rates in ways that will raise rates for these customers. As it happens, SUV buyers tend to be prosperous, middle-aged families who buy lots of insurance policies and stay with a single insurer—precisely the people the industry is least willing to offend.

Insurance is also a heavily regulated industry. This is especially true in the United States, where each state sets its own rules and the state insurance commissioner is often an elected official. As a result, insurers are discouraged or banned from adjusting their rates based on some factors. This is often good, as insurers are discouraged from setting rates based on a person's zip code, and banned from setting rates based on race. The bad side is that insurers are sometimes discouraged from adjusting rates in ways that will raise premiums for politically powerful groups in American society. The upper-middle class buyers of SUVs are the people most likely to vote and make political contributions—a constituency that any state insurance commissioner can only antagonize at considerable peril.

The affluence of SUV owners and their political clout form a powerful combination that has made insurers loath to raise rates for them. Instead, the insurance industry has quietly pursued practices that have gouged car owners to the tune of hundreds of millions of dollars in order to keep rates low for SUV owners. In the process, since the 1970s the insurance industry has been quietly feeding the shift toward ever more menacing vehicles that pose ever greater dangers to other motorists.

The calculation of insurance premiums was pretty crude until the late 1960s. That changed when computers started becoming powerful enough for insurers to calculate exactly what they were paying out in claims for every model of vehicle.

The insurers quickly made the unsurprising discovery that sports cars like Porsches and "muscle cars" like the Chevrolet Camaro ended up in a lot of expensive wrecks and were frequently stolen. This was partly because these cars were coveted and driven by young men. But the insurers also found that drivers of the same age, driving record and so forth were more likely to get into crashes when at the wheel of a sports car or muscle car than when tooling around in a more sedate model. So some insurers began raising their rates on sports cars and muscle cars for collision insurance in the early 1970s. They did the same thing for comprehensive insurance, which covers policyholders against theft and fire. As drivers of sports cars and muscle cars began paying for more of the "pot" of claims costs, administrative costs and profits, insurers raised rates less, despite inflation, for other models that produced fewer claims.

State Farm, the nation's largest insurer, resisted this trend. Its executives reasoned that as long as they could continue collecting enough premiums to cover the entire pot of claims costs, administrative costs and profits then they did not need to infuriate drivers of sports cars and muscle cars by raising their rates. But State Farm gradually ran into trouble. As other insurers sharply and repeatedly raised rates for high-risk cars, more than doubling them over several years, the owners of these cars began switching in large numbers to State Farm. As the bills for wrecks and thefts came flooding in for these cars, State Farm's claims costs began rising faster than premiums. State Farm finally capitulated, and began adjusting its own collision and comprehensive insurance rates by model in the late 1970s, after an internal study showed that it was insuring every single Porsche in Southern California.

Rising insurance rates hurt the sports car market, but rich, middle-aged men who could afford the higher premiums continued to buy sports cars. The real effect of higher insurance premiums, combined with rising gasoline prices, was felt in the market for muscle cars, which was devastated.

Muscle cars were likely to be driven by young men who were struggling to make ends meet. The way insurance companies adjust rates hit them especially hard. This is because insurers make adjustments by multiplying the average premium by an adjustment factor, instead of just adding on an extra charge. A middle-aged man with a clean driving record and living in a rural area might qualify for an average premium of $100 a year for collision and comprehensive insurance. This could be increased by an extra 50 percent, for an extra $50 a year, if the man chose a high-performance Pontiac Firebird instead of a similarly priced luxury sedan.

A 22-year-old man with a couple of tickets for running red lights and other traffic infractions could face an average premium of $1,000 a year for collision and comprehensive insurance. Mark up the premium by 50 percent for choosing a muscle car and the young man would have to pay $1,500 a year—enough to persuade some young men to choose a safer model.

Sales of GTOs and other muscle cars had boomed in the 1950s and 1960s but collapsed in the 1970s and early 1980s under the burden of higher insurance rates and higher gasoline prices. Auto enthusiasts still lament the insurers' decision to adjust rates by model. But the effect of the policy change was to discourage the most dangerous drivers on the road from choosing muscle cars in which they would tend to get in more crashes—a plus in terms of safety.

Collision and comprehensive insurance are only part of the cost of auto insurance, however, and some motorists choose not to buy these policies at all. More important is liability insurance, which pays for injuries and property damage inflicted on others during a crash. Every state except Nebraska requires liability insurance.

The same computers that calculated in the 1970s how various car models affected claims on collision and comprehensive insurance also told insurers how much money they were paying in liability claims for various models. Not surprisingly, the very large cars made in the 1950s and 1960s were inflicting a lot of damage in collisions. Less damage was caused by the smaller cars that Detroit and foreign automakers were selling in ever-greater numbers in the 1970s in response to higher gas prices and regulations from Washington. Even Cadillacs were becoming smaller than the Chevys of the 1960s.

Before and after the 1970s, Americans have driven the biggest cars they could afford, with the rich driving the largest cars and lower-middle-class families choosing smaller models. But during the 1970s, the smaller cars were often driven by families affluent enough to have just purchased a new car, while the older land barges of the used-car market were being driven by the less affluent. Adjusting liability rates in the 1970s would have meant raising premiums for the less affluent and lowering them for the affluent.

The 1970s also represented a peak for American populism and especially for the consumer movement. State insurance commissioners and state legislatures tended to be Democratic, and sympathetic to the interests of the less affluent.

So while many insurers talked about adjusting liability insurance by model, they actually did fairly little about it, for fear of appearing to penalize poor people still stuck with large, old cars. Allstate, for instance, began giving a 10 percent discount on liability rates for the handful of truly tiny subcompact cars weighing less than 2,100 pounds, but did not charge anything extra even for the heaviest cars.

The Insurance Services Office, which calculates adjustment factors used by the hundreds of the nation's smaller insurers, came up with five broad categories based on the ratio of a vehicle's weight to horsepower. This system raised liability rates somewhat for sports cars that were lightweight but very powerful. But the system had an obvious shortcoming: If you made an extremely heavy vehicle, it would qualify for the lowest liability rates even if you put in a very powerful engine.

Throughout the 1980s and well into the 1990s, most insurers paid virtually no attention to how drivers' choice of vehicles affected their rate of liability insurance claims. They simply added up their claims costs, administrative costs and profits and divided them among all the drivers. As long as no mainstream insurer started raising rates for the most dangerous models, no other insurer was under any pressure to do so. No insurer was at risk of ending up like State Farm in the late 1970s—stuck with all the high-risk vehicles—unless a rival broke ranks. And nobody broke ranks.

But while the stodgy insurance industry slept, some big changes were taking place. Liability insurance costs were soaring and became the biggest part of insurance premiums, as the United States became more litigious. Comprehensive insurance was becoming less important as a share of overall insurance bills as auto-theft claims declined. At the same time, SUVs were also coming on the nation's roads in ever-greater numbers.

SUVs were almost perfectly designed to take advantage of the peculiarities in how insurers calculated premiums. Their stiff, tall bodies suffered little damage during collisions, so collision insurance costs were very low. Indeed, the virtual absence of crumple zones in the front ends of SUVs meant that there was little to fix after a crash.

By contrast, their stiff bodies did tremendous extra damage to cars that they hit. But insurers did not charge SUV owners extra for this—indeed, SUVs were often assessed lower premiums. SUVs were extremely heavy compared to cars, so even with powerful engines, they routinely qualified for the lowest possible liability rates calculated by the Insurance Services Office, for example.

By the mid-1990s, the economics of liability insurance had been completely changed from the 1970s. Prosperous families were driving large SUVs that inflicted massive damage during collisions, while paying no higher liability premiums than less affluent people driving 10-year-old family cars that were a full ton lighter. Add in the higher collision insurance paid by owners of cars with ample crumple zones to protect their occupants and other motorists in a collision and the total insurance bill was often higher for car owners than for SUV owners.[1]

The Highway Loss Data Institute, a research group in Arlington, Virginia, that is bankrolled by the insurance industry, did a study in 1994 that documented the growing damage inflicted by SUVs. The study found that property damage liability costs for insurers from accidents involving large sport utility vehicles were 72 percent higher than for the average car, even after excluding all other variables, like driving record and the driver's age. By contrast, property damage caused by large luxury cars was 19 percent below the average, as the extensive crumple zones in the long front ends of luxury cars absorbed the forces of impacts. The disparity in liability costs was a clear sign that the design of SUVs, and not just their weight, was posing a problem.

The study did not cover liability insurance claims for bodily injury to others, however. Insurers have been slow to share this data even with their trade groups, because the data involves a lot of proprietary calculations about how much the insurers really pay to settle lawsuits involving paralysis, serious burns and other injuries. But while there is still no publicly available data on bodily injury liability claims, crashes that produce more physical damage are almost certain to produce more serious injuries.

The property damage study received little attention in the American insurance industry, said Kim Hazelbaker, the institute's senior vice president, who oversaw the study. Insurers overseas, where SUVs were less popular, paid more attention. Insurers in Germany, for example, began adjusting liability rates by model on a wide scale in 1995, particularly increasing rates for large sport utility vehicles.

One American insurer that was paying attention, however, was Progressive. Based in Mayfield Village, a suburb of Cleveland, Progressive had long been active in the tiny, virtually unregulated market for insuring motorists with truly terrible driving records whom mainstream insurers would not cover. Operating with little oversight from state insurance commissioners, Progressive started modestly adjusting liability rates in 1987 based on what models its customers chose, with slightly higher rates for SUV owners and marginally lower rates for car owners.

During the 1990s, Progressive began growing briskly in the far larger, regulated market for insuring most motorists. Progressive continued to adjust rates by model as it entered the broader market. Regulators had discouraged such adjustments a generation earlier but with a couple of exceptions had never actually banned it, and Progressive's moves attracted little attention. Constantly monitoring liability insurance claims by model and taking note of Hazelbaker's study, Progressive began quietly increasing in 1995 and 1996 the percentages by which it adjusted rates upward for the more dangerous models and downward for the less hazardous models.

Progressive's new adjustments called for liability insurance premiums that were up to 20 percent higher for the bigger and most dangerous sport utility vehicles and pickups. Premiums were roughly 8 percent higher for smaller SUVs and pickups, while Progressive actually subtracted 10 percent from the average premiums for drivers of the least dangerous car models. These adjustments were probably smaller than the actual difference in claims costs, but insurers like to keep rate adjustments fairly small. Rate increases invariably upset customers, while matching rate decreases tend to win insurers little thanks, as customers tend to assume that they were being overcharged in the first place.

The first big mainstream insurer to try to adjust liability premiums by model was Farmers Insurance, the nation's third largest provider of auto insurance. Farmers, which was headquartered in Los Angeles and did business mainly in California and other western states, was wary of upsetting its existing customers with SUVs or pickup trucks by increasing their premiums. But Farmers was also just beginning to move into eastern states. When Farmers began selling auto insurance in Pennsylvania in September 1997, every liability insurance policy was calculated from the beginning using the vehicle model, although Farmers made no announcement of this and there was no immediate media coverage.

Using their extensive experience in other states, Farmers actuaries charged an extra 5 to 16 percent for liability insurance on SUVs and pickups, together with discounts of 5 to 19 percent for cars. "It's pretty obvious the size and weight of these vehicles and the way they're built is contributing to the loss experience," said Jonathan Adkisson, a Farmers actuary. "When an accident occurs, the heavier vehicles are more likely to inflict damage and injuries, and these result in larger claims, so it seems appropriate to charge the drivers of those vehicles higher premiums."

Adjusting for models would be the biggest change in insurance since the advent a quarter-century earlier of no-fault insurance. (No-fault laws, present in 23 states, reduce the cost of liability insurance but do not eliminate the need for it.) Several insurance industry officials even described SUVs as the neutron bombs of the American road—the people inside might be killed or seriously injured in a crash, but the vehicle itself survived, so the collision insurance costs were low.

Allstate, Nationwide, Geico and USAA all began working in 1997 on statistical studies on how to adjust their rates along the same lines as Farmers. Only one insurer, State Farm, long the dinosaur of the insurance business, adamantly took the position that it did not want to adjust liability insurance by model. Dale Nelson, a company actuary, said that the insurer's data did not show much variation in losses by model. The sheer size and height of SUVs might actually save money for insurers by killing other motorists who might otherwise survive if hit by a car, he said, explaining that serious injuries produce larger legal settlements than deaths. This seemed like faint comfort for car drivers.

On October 17, 1997, *The New York Times* published a front-page story of mine on how Farmers and Progressive were adjusting liability rates while other insurers were considering the same step. The headline was "Big Insurers Plan to Increase Rates on Large Vehicles." The first paragraph of my story said that SUV and pickup drivers faced higher rates because such vehicles were "inflicting unusually costly harm to cars and their occupants in collisions." In the third paragraph, I said that car drivers would see a decrease in rates.

Radio and television accounts of my story on the morning that it appeared highlighted only the prospect of higher rates for SUVs and pickups. The result was an outcry against insurers. Farmers and Progressive, in particular, received complaints from policyholders with SUVs and pickup trucks. Some customers of Farmers and Progressive canceled all their policies in protest, not just their auto-insurance policies. Over the next few days, insurance commission-ers in several states with lots of pickup trucks, starting with Texas, denounced the very idea of adjusting liability rates by model.

A North Carolina man called me to say that he had contacted insurers and his state insurance commissioner to tell them what a terrible idea it was to raise liability rates for SUVs and pickups. More people should drive SUVs, he said, noting that his wife had only suffered a shoulder injury three years earlier when a Toyota Tercel car had slid sideways into her Chevrolet Blazer midsized SUV. When I asked what had become of the Tercel driver, there was a pause, followed by, "He died three days later," of injuries received in the accident. His wife had bought an even larger Chevrolet Tahoe SUV after the crash.

One group was conspicuously quiet during all of this: the silent majority of vehicle owners who still drove cars. Insurers heard almost nothing from them. Progressive and Farmers did not notice a sudden influx of car customers, nor were they especially seeking such an influx. Insurers make all their money on customers that they have retained for five or more years, because they develop a very detailed understanding of how often they file claims. Insurers are always wary of new customers, even if they seem to have clean driving records. So insurers give their greatest attention to retain-ing auto-insurance customers, instead of finding new ones.

Advocacy groups like Consumers Union and the Consumer Fed-eration of America declined to endorse the adjustment of liability insurance by model. They worried that insurers might use such adjustments to raise rates for SUVs and pickup trucks without cut-ting them for cars, so as to grab greater profits instead of distribut-ing the costs of liability claims more fairly.

Farmers and Progressive had another problem in explaining their rate increases for SUVs and pickup trucks. There were still more than twice as many cars and minivans as SUVs and pickup trucks on the roads, so even if SUV and pickup owners paid considerably more money into the pot, car and minivan owners would see only a small drop in their share of payments. An increase of 10 or 20 percent in premiums for SUVs and pickup trucks meant less than a 5 or 10 percent cut in premiums for car and minivan owners.

Progressive refused to discuss its rate adjustments after my story ran, but went on using them. Farmers used the system when it began selling auto insurance several months later in Maryland, and tried to defend the need for adjusting liability rates by model. "The regular car drivers are subsidizing SUV and pickup drivers on liability insurance," said Diane S. Tasaka, a Farmers spokeswoman.

But Farmers did not expand the use of adjustments to other states, and then virtually halted the adjustments even in Pennsylvania and Maryland a year later when it was purchased by a Swiss company, the Zurich Financial Services Group. Other insurers looked at adjustments and backed away.

By the middle of 1998, the insurance industry had decided that adjusting by model was just not worth the trouble. "It's a political issue, and in a political year, the soccer moms are everything and they drive SUVs," said Steven Goldstein, the spokesman for the industry's Insurance Information Institute. "No regulator would allow it—no regulator who wanted to be elected to a second term."

Executives like Richard W. Bernstein, the general counsel for auto and home insurance at Metropolitan Property and Casualty Insurance, were skeptical that anything would change unless state legislatures actually set new laws and required regulators to implement them. SUV owners made up such an influential segment of society, he said, that insurers would be reluctant to antagonize them by raising their rates unless ordered to do so by state lawmakers.

"I couldn't imagine that any company would do it on its own volition, because of the regulatory issue and the anger of sport utility owners," he said. "We don't like to be overly regulated, we don't like to be told what to do by state legislators, but there are times when it has advantages, when you have constituents like SUV owners."

From the point of view of public safety, insurers' pricing of liability insurance has been a terrible lost opportunity over the last quarter of a century. Changing the way insurers set premiums is becoming even more important with each passing year, as millions of SUVs age and pour into the used-vehicle market, becoming increasingly affordable for young drivers. The example of muscle cars and collision insurance rates in the 1970s shows that insurance-industry practices can make a difference in what models are chosen by the most dangerous drivers. Adjusting liability rates by make and model would discourage risky drivers with already high insurance rates from selecting vehicles that are especially likely to maim other motorists. Rate adjustments would have less effect on safer drivers, who would pose fewer hazards to other motorists even when they chose SUVs.

The insurance industry's resistance to adjusting rates by model has recently started to weaken. Public sentiment has begun to shift against SUV owners, and consumer groups have begun advocating liability insurance adjustments by model after studying the issue carefully. SUVs are becoming common enough that their effect on insurance has become hard to ignore. Regulators have wisely and belatedly stopped criticizing the idea. A few insurers have finally begun very cautiously to make adjustments by model, although the adjustments tended to be smaller in percentage terms than their claims losses could have justified.

Allstate quietly began adjusting by model in Oregon in late 1999. The company only did so for vehicles for the 2000 model year and subsequent model years. This meant that Allstate did not have to antagonize any policyholders by raising rates on vehicles they already had; it simply quoted them a different rate when they bought or leased their next vehicle. At the same time, Allstate also modified its personal medical policies by model.

Drivers of new Suburbans, for example, received a modest 6

percent cut in personal medical premiums, because a Suburban is so big and heavy that it provides a little extra protection in a crash. But the same Suburban drivers were also assessed 9 percent extra on liability insurance. The net effect was to raise rates for SUVs, since liability insurance is a much bigger part of insurance bills than personal medical insurance—indeed, most drivers do not even buy personal medical insurance because they are covered by employer health plans.

Owners of minivans and of large and midsize cars fared best with the new rates, because these vehicles generally provide excellent protection for their occupants, while their ample crumple zones also limited the harm to other motorists. Allstate granted a 10 percent discount on liability coverage and a 10 percent discount on personal medical coverage to drivers of Chrysler Town & Country minivans, and a similar discount to drivers of Buick LeSabres, the nation's best-selling full-size car.

When the Oregon experiment produced no outcry, Allstate expanded its shrewd approach to a dozen other states, and publicly acknowledged it in December 2000. Nationwide, the nation's sixth-largest insurer, started adjusting by model for liability and personal medical insurance in Arkansas in August 2000 and expanded the practice to Pennsylvania, Virginia, Ohio and Alabama by the end of 2001.

But Nationwide is not doing enough to improve public safety, because its adjustments are simply too small. Nationwide limits its rate adjustments to plus or minus 10 percent, no matter how lethal or how safe any particular SUV or car might be.

Larry Thursby, Nationwide's auto-insurance director, freely admits that if the company were to reflect the actual cost of claims then the adjustments would be larger, especially for liability insurance. "We're fairly conservative with it right now," he said in early 2002. "We're taking less than what is fully indicated." (Allstate allows adjustments of plus or minus 15 percent and insists that this reflects the actual variation in liability claims.)

Most insurers continue to resist making any adjustments at all. State Farm, still the nation's largest auto insurer by a wide margin with a fifth of the market, is hewing to its long tradition of making no adjustments at all unless forced to do so by competitive pressures. State Farm can get away with gouging car owners on automotive-liability insurance to subsidize SUV owners because its core market consists of Americans in rural areas and small towns, who shop other insurers for lower rates less often than urban and suburban Americans.

State Farm and other big insurers that have also refused to adjust liability rates by model—like USAA—are essentially offering low-rate havens for any teenager or other risky driver who wants to drive a large SUV and not have to pay for the extra risk that this imposes on other motorists. This was a bad idea even in the 1990s, when most SUVs on the road were so new and therefore so expensive that they were beyond the reach of young drivers. For insurers to keep these policies in the new century, when more used SUVs will inevitably fall into the hands of less responsible drivers, represents a cowardly and irresponsible reaction to the power of SUV owners.

TROUBLE FOR CITIES

Wearing blue jeans and a New York Rangers jacket that had an American flag on it even before the terrorist attacks on the World Trade Center, Cliff Adler Jr. waves me to hop into his Ford Explorer near the corner of West 41st Street and Ninth Avenue in Manhattan. But this is no ordinary Explorer: it is bright yellow, has a meter in the middle of the dashboard, a taxi light on top and a taxi registration medallion, number 3A96, on the hood.

Adler used to drive Ford Crown Victoria sedans, the model that still dominates the taxi fleet of New York City. But he hated the fairly low seats in the car. He had been spending six or seven days a week since 1975 with his legs out in front of him to drive, and his back ached constantly. He became convinced that the higher, chair-like seating of the Explorer, with the driver sitting well above the brake and acceleration pedals, would relieve his back pain. He began badgering the city's Taxi and Limousine Commission to let him buy a Ford Explorer instead.

The commission approved the use of Explorers in 1996, and Adler was the first of several dozen taxi drivers to buy one. "Within

24 hours of getting the Explorer, my back, which was going out of line, I swear to God, was straight," he said. "I live in it 12 hours a day—somebody's got a problem with me being comfortable?"

Unlike most drivers, Adler chose a two-wheel-drive Explorer. Having four-wheel drive added $3,000 to the price, and would have hurt the fuel economy. Adler has only gone off-road in the Explorer once, and it was a fiasco. An amateur photographer, he pulled off the road onto grass near the runway of John F. Kennedy Airport, only to come back later and discover that the grass had been growing on sand and the wheels of his two-ton vehicle had sunk in deep. A tow truck had to pull him out, using an electric winch. He vowed never to go off-road again.

Because the Explorer does not have four-wheel drive, it gets 14 miles to the gallon. That is only 2 m.p.g. worse than a Crown Victoria gets in taxi service in New York, but 7 or 8 m.p.g. worse than a Honda Odyssey minivan manages as a taxi. If gas prices go up significantly above $2 a gallon and stay there, then Explorers will become uneconomical. But with gasoline at $1.50 a gallon or below, the price difference is not really a problem, Adler says.

The Explorer had a heavy, steel grille guard until it was damaged in a minor accident. The guard was actually several thick bars of specially hardened steel that went across the front of the vehicle and connected with lattices of thinner steel bars that cover the headlights. Grille guards were invented in Australia, where they were designed mainly to protect the front ends of light trucks from impacts with kangaroos, although they also help in barreling through heavy underbrush. Adler has no intention of bludgeoning his way through undergrowth or hitting kangaroos, however, but says he just wants to make sure his Explorer doesn't get any dents or broken headlights. Ford does not sell grille guards, so Adler bought one at a store and attached it.

"I live in the city and I park on the street," he said. "You know how often people back into you?"

I asked whether he had hit any pedestrians with the hardened steel bars. "That's been my major wish—so many pedestrians and so little time—I'm just kidding," Adler replied, adding that he has not hit any. But he later returned to his dislike of jaywalkers who cross the street heedless of oncoming traffic. "As far as pedestrians go, they stick their nose up at everyone, the pedestrian attitude is terrible."

Adler is also unconcerned about what his Explorer, grille guards and all, might do to a car in a collision. "This doesn't sit that high and I can't be responsible for every vehicle on the road, and I have to be a good driver," he said. "I'm out here to earn a living and look out for my truck, I'm not out to play bumper cars."

Adler has insisted on staying parked by the curb while we talk, lest a city inspector see him being interviewed while driving and deem that an unwise distraction. When I run low on questions, he turns on the engine and we go trolling for customers. A few blocks later, near the city's convention center, he pulls over to pick up two young women returning to their offices from lunch. As one of them, a 33-year-old sales manager, slides into the back seat, I ask what she thinks of the use of Explorers as taxis. She is enthusiastic: "It's much better than the cars, it rides more smoothly and they're cleaner because they tend to be newer."

If you can make it in New York City, you can make it anywhere, to paraphrase the song, and SUVs have definitely made it in New York. By the end of the 1990s, they accounted for a quarter of all new vehicle registrations in Manhattan, compared with a little under 17 percent nationwide. Automakers more than doubled their advertising of SUVs in the city between 1995 and 1999, making them one of the most heavily marketed products in the city. "In terms of driving, in New York City a sport utility vehicle makes sense—they're tough, you've got good visibility, you're surrounded by yellow cabs," which are relatively low and easy to see over, contended Mark H. Schirmer, a spokesman for Land Rover, which sells more Range Rovers in the New York area than anywhere else in the country.

The fastest-growing SUV markets in the country in recent years have tended to be the nation's wealthiest cities. Some of the biggest markets for SUVs are now in Houston, affluent Florida communities like West Palm Beach and the prosperous northern suburbs of Los Angeles, all cities better known for sun than deep snow or mud. By contrast, SUVs were a much smaller share of the market in Fairbanks, Alaska, a city so far north that residents might actually need four-wheel drive for deep snow.[1]

Yet SUVs are particularly ill suited for urban use. They make traffic congestion worse. They are hard to see around. They are too big and heavy for some aging roads and bridges. They are lethal to pedestrians. They make parking shortages more acute. And they are magnets for thieves and carjackers.

SUVs exacerbate traffic congestion, an affliction of suburbs as well as cities. Hugh Greechan, the director of road design in New York's Westchester County, puts it best. If he arrives at a red stop light and there are three cars ahead of him, he knows he'll get through on the next green light. If there are two sport utilities ahead of him, he'll also get through the light. But if there are three sport utilities ahead of him, he will not get through the light.

The evidence for this is not just anecdotal. Two civil engineers at the University of Texas used a video camera with a computerized stopwatch to time thousands of vehicles as they traveled through two large intersections with stoplights. They found that motorists tended to follow light trucks—SUVs, pickups and minivans—at a greater distance than cars, a wise decision given the difficulty of seeing through or around a light truck. When SUVs, pickups and minivans were the first in line as the light turned green, they also tended to accelerate more slowly than cars, probably because of their greater weight. Just as Greechan noticed in Westchester County, the presence of light trucks, especially large SUVs, reduced the number of vehicles that could cross an intersection during each green light, contributing to gridlock. The researchers calculated that for traffic traveling straight through an intersection, a large SUV took as much space as 1.41 cars. A minivan took as much space as 1.34 cars, a pickup was equal to 1.14 cars and a small SUV equaled 1.07 cars. SUVs and other light trucks that were turning left or right in the intersections instead of driving straight through had less of an effect on congestion.[2]

The traffic problems are not limited to intersections with stoplights. Federal standards call for stop signs to be mounted seven feet off the ground, so that car drivers can see them over the car in front of them. Spotting a stop sign from behind an SUV that is six or more feet tall is very difficult. In closely spaced traffic, SUVs can also obscure car drivers' view of highway exit signs.

SUVs pose a particular problem on older roads and bridges. Weighing up to three tons, they increase the wear and tear on road surfaces and bridges, although not as much as freight trucks. In a few cases, SUVs even exceed the weight limits for bridges, but are not barred from crossing them because traffic engineers have decided that it is impossible to enforce the rules. Trucks weighing three tons or more with cargo included are banned from the Brooklyn Bridge, which was built for streetcars. Most large SUVs exceed this limit when they have a couple of adults aboard, and a few exceed it when empty. Yet the New York City police are making no effort to enforce the rule. Henry D. Perahia, the city's chief bridge engineer, said the bridge would survive as long as there was never a traffic jam of Chevrolet Tahoe full-size SUVs on it; if that happened, he said, there could be structural damage but not an actual collapse.

Older roads and bridges also tend to have fairly tight curves that are not banked for high-speed travel. Traffic engineers say that they were able to keep raising the speed limits on these roads and bridges over the last several decades anyway because cars were becoming more stable and nimble. But the spread of tall, clumsy SUVs on curvy roads with narrow lane markings is now posing a problem.

Domenico Annese, a retired engineer who helped design several of the parkways in the New York City area, said that he did not anticipate their use by such tall vehicles (New York banned pickups from its parkways until 1999). Now he routinely sees sport utility drivers speeding and unable to stay in their lanes on the Saw Mill River Parkway. "They're straddling the yellow line and fishtailing a little bit and they're putting on the brakes in the middle of the curves, and that's bad," he said. "People have a false sense of security in the bigger vehicles."

Seeing around an SUV is especially difficult on older roads and bridges, which often do not meet federal standards for having lanes at least 12 feet wide. While only a few cars are over 6 feet wide, many SUVs are. The Ford Excursion is exactly 6 feet 8 inches wide, the maximum width allowed before regulators demand that truck warning lights be placed across the top of the vehicle at the front and back. The auto industry's defenders point out that many roads were built in the 1950s, when a few cars were even wider. The 1959 Cadillac Eldorado was 6 feet 9.2 inches wide, in an era before the warning lights were required. But while it was possible to see over an Eldorado, or through it, a big SUV presents a much taller, more imposing wall of sheet metal and tinted glass.

The height of sport utility vehicles' windows is not regulated, and has been getting higher with each passing model year, although nobody has gathered statistics on this. Taking a tape measure to neighborhood dealerships, I have found that the bottom of the rear window of many SUVs tends to be roughly the same height as the top of most car windshields, about four feet.[3] That makes it impossible for a trailing car driver to see through an SUV in order to watch the traffic ahead.

Paul Mercer, a computer software executive in Cupertino, California, encountered this problem firsthand while driving a sporty Mazda Miata compact car in dense traffic on Interstate 880. The traffic slowed suddenly, but Mercer was behind a large sport utility and unable to see through it to observe the high-mounted brake lights come on in the rear windows of vehicles ahead. The sport utility braked and swerved at the last minute to avoid a wheel lying in the road. Mercer, who was going 50 miles an hour and was two car lengths behind the SUV to prevent other motorists from cutting in front of him, had too little time to react. "I ran over the wheel and blew out my tire and had to limp off at the next exit," he said. "I was happy to be alive."

The auto industry's reaction to this kind of misadventure is to blame excessive traffic and aggressive drivers for making it hard for motorists to leave a gap in front of themselves equal to at least one car length for every 10 miles per hour that they are traveling. "It's not the vehicle we can point at, then," said Sonya L. Bultnyck, a Chrysler spokeswoman. "It's the inconsiderate drivers."

Mercer's incident could have been worse. High-mounted center brake lights, usually placed in rear windows, are becoming less effective in preventing multivehicle pileups. The height of light trucks may be one reason, according to a NHTSA report.

In 1987, vehicles with the high-mounted brake lights were 14.6 percent less likely than vehicles without them to be hit from behind in pileups involving three or more vehicles. But in the early 1990s, vehicles with the high-mounted lights were only 2.45 percent less likely to be hit in such crashes.[4] The eroding effectiveness probably reflects a combination of the spread of light trucks and the declining novelty of the high brake lights—people might have been startled into slowing down faster when they first saw them.

A partial answer to the problem of not being able to see the lights through tall vehicles might seem to be for the center lights to be mounted a few inches higher, on top of vehicles instead of at the top of the rear window. But auto engineers say that even a small bump at the rear edge of a vehicle's roof can seriously disrupt the air flow over it, hurting gas mileage.

Headlight glare is another visibility problem that has become increasingly serious as SUVs and pickup trucks have grown taller and taller. The normal headlights of an oncoming full-size sport utility vehicle or pickup truck can create so much glare that they appear to car drivers as bright as high beams. When such a big vehicle follows a car at night, the car's rearview mirror and side mirrors reflect very bright glare.

It is a problem that infuriates some drivers. "It is incredibly distracting when you're on the road," said David Lichtenthal, an accountant in Marlboro, New Jersey, who drives a Mercury Mystique sedan. "Sometimes I wind up pulling over to the right to let the sport ute pass me."

A 1996 study by a panel of the Society of Automotive Engineers found that the level of glare a driver perceives rises as much as 1,000 percent when a headlight bulb is mounted at the same height as a driver's eyes or a car's side mirror.[5] There are no official measurements of SUV headlight height, but by my tape measure, full-size SUVs with four-wheel drive tend to have headlight bulbs that are 36 to 39 inches off the ground.[6] That is the height of the side mirror of a compact car like the Dodge Neon, although below the height of the side mirrors of larger cars. The new Hummer H2 has its headlight bulbs 43 1/2 inches off the ground, as tall as the top edge of the side mirror of a Cadillac DeVille, GM's largest car.

Yet the only regulation on the books is that headlights may not be mounted more than 54 inches off the ground, a rule aimed at intercity freight trucks rather than family vehicles. The brightness of headlights has also increased by 30 percent since the 1970s for conventional headlights through technological improvements, and the latest halogen headlights, which cast a blue light, are even brighter.

Automakers contend that the headlights of SUVs and pickups need to be mounted higher than car headlights. Light-truck drivers sit higher than car drivers, and headlights provide more effective illumination when mounted as close as possible to the height of a driver's eyes. Road signs are designed to reflect light directly back, and might seem less bright for motorists who sit in tall vehicles with low-mounted headlights, the automakers say.

But most minivans, whose drivers sit fairly high, are based on car designs, and their headlights are mounted almost as low as car headlights. The 1996 study, drafted by a panel of auto-industry engineers, concluded that "the argument that a loss of sign legibility will have dramatic negative safety effects does not appear to be substantiated."

The real problem, some auto executives say, is style. A vehicle's headlights are its eyes, and would look silly if mounted down near the bottom of a tall, macho grille, they say. Forcing automakers to mount the headlights lower might improve overall safety, however, by discouraging very tall front ends.

That seems unlikely to happen, however. NHTSA has opened a formal review of headlight-mounting height, and the mounting height for heavy trucks may be lowered from 54 inches. But manufacturers of light trucks seem more likely to be told to tilt their headlights so that they shine at a slight angle downward, something that is already done for heavy trucks. Tilting light-truck headlights will help reduce glare for car drivers who are well ahead of them on a country road, but the glare will still be ferocious for car drivers waiting at a stop light with a light truck just behind the back bumper.

The auto industry urges people who particularly complain of visibility problems in cars to buy taller SUVs instead. This has blunted public criticism of the problem, but is not a long-term solution. As an Internet site once observed, driving a taller vehicle is like bringing a Manhattan phone book to a theater and sitting on it—it helps you see better but irritates the people behind you. And if everybody buys a taller vehicle then almost nobody has a better view. If everybody sits on phonebooks in a theater except the people in the front row, the only people with an improved view are the people in the second row.

Even SUV drivers have trouble seeing through other SUVs because of their tinted windows. Federal regulations bar auto manufacturers from installing dark glass in car windows. But the regulations have long allowed manufacturers to use tinted glass for the rear windows of light trucks. This practice began with cargo vans as a way to make it hard for passersby to see, and perhaps steal, the tools of plumbers, electricians and other craftsmen. It then spread to minivans and SUVs as a way for owners of these vehicles to make their luggage and other belongings less visible because they do not have trunks like cars. Now tinted glass is becoming more common in cars, as motorists ape the fashion-setters in SUVs by paying car dealers and repair garages to install tinted film to cover the untinted glass that automakers must provide for cars. One Volvo dealer in Ann Arbor, Michigan, now installs tinting on two-thirds of the new station wagons he sells because that is what customers want.

Safety studies, some bankrolled by the glass-tinting industry, have not documented a clear pattern of crashes relating to tinted windows. But this may be because car drivers have trouble seeing through high SUV and minivan windows anyway. As more drivers choose tall vehicles and are up at the height of the tinted windows, not being able to see through the darkened glass will likely become more of a problem. Police associations also dislike tinted windows, because they make it difficult for officers to see possibly armed passengers in back seats while talking to drivers during routine traffic stops.

Yet automakers have found the tinted windows so popular that they are installing as many as possible in light trucks sold in the United States. When Ford introduced the 2002 Ford Explorer, the new model was sold in Europe with untinted windows, because the European Union has wisely told automakers not to install tinted windows. But beginning with the 2002 model year, all Explorers sold in the United States are being equipped with tinted windows. So few American SUV buyers want the untinted windows that Ford decided it was not worth the trouble of offering them even as an option.

*

Big cities not only have a lot of traffic but also a lot of pedestrians. One in eight people who die in a motor-vehicle crash in the United States is on foot, not in a vehicle. When these pedestrians are hit by SUVs, they are especially likely to suffer life-threatening injuries.

A recent, little-noticed academic study calculated that large SUVs killed 10.6 percent of the pedestrians they hit in the United States from 1995 through 2000, while midsized and small SUVs killed 6.6 percent. Minivans and cars were much less deadly, each killing about 5 percent of the pedestrians they hit.[7]

In fairness, SUVs hit pedestrians at all at a slightly lower rate than other kinds of vehicles. Nobody is sure why this is the case, but it is likely that the initial owners of SUVs are simply very safe drivers who take care when people are in the street. As more SUVs fall into the hands of inexperienced drivers and drunks, the pedestrian death toll is likely to rise.

Grille guards on the front ends of SUVs, also marketed as bull bars or brush guards, are part of the danger to pedestrians. Tests at the University of Adelaide in Australia have found that putting a solid grille guard on the front of an SUV increases fivefold the force of impact on models of children's heads. The reason is that the impact is concentrated on the hard, leading edge of the grille guard, instead of being spread out across the surface of a flat, softer grille.

Putting a grille guard on the front of an SUV may also make the driver more willing to drive dangerously, in the hope that the grille guard will minimize harm in crashes. A survey of urban drivers in Melbourne, Australia, in 1984 found that they gave three reasons for installing grille guards: to protect against parking collisions, to make their vehicles more attractive and, most interesting, to drive more aggressively when roads are crowded.

As it happens, SUV occupants should not trust in a grille guard for safety either. While grille guards might limit property damage to an SUV, statistical analyses by the Australian government's Traffic Safety Bureau have found no evidence that the grille guards do any good in protecting SUV occupants in a crash.[8] Indeed, some safety experts have warned that they might endanger SUV occupants too. Grille guards are almost never installed as factory equipment, but are purchased later at a store and then installed. SUV front ends do not crumple much to absorb energy in a crash, but they do crumple a little; having stiff bars across the front end of the vehicle can prevent this crumpling. And by preventing the crumpling, grille guards can also confuse the sensors in the front end of a vehicle that tell the air bags when to inflate.

While American regulators have paid little attention to grille guards, some foreign governments have been encouraging a switch from the use of hardened steel grille guards to recently developed molded plastic grille guards that are less dangerous. Britain's Department of the Environment, Transport and the Regions recommended such an approach to the European Union in 1997. Automakers in Europe ended up making a "voluntary" pledge to European Union officials in Brussels not to install any grille guards in their factories. But dealers remain free to buy grille guards from independent auto-parts companies and add them on to vehicles before selling them, and do so.

The front vehicle in the Land Rover area at the Detroit auto show in 2002 was a Freelander with a grille guard on the front. When I pointed it out to Stephen Ross, Land Rover's head of vehicle development, he was appalled. "It's dumb," he said. "I don't release them, I don't know anything about them. It's a free world, of course, [but] we don't engineer them."

SUVs without grille guards are also deadly, because they are not built like cars. Cars typically hit pedestrians low and flip them up onto their hoods, which are designed to be soft enough to minimize serious injuries. Automakers make sure that the hood has plenty of clearance above the engine so that it can give way a little and cushion the impact of a head, almost like a trampoline. They even test the hardness of hoods by striking them with models of human heads. Car bumpers inflict terrible injuries to adult pedestrians' knees, which can cause permanent disabilities, but they seldom kill.

The weight difference between a car and an SUV makes no difference in a collision with a pedestrian, safety experts agree, pointing instead to the shape and stiffness of SUVs to explain their deadliness. Some experts blame the very rectangular front ends of many SUVs, a fashionable legacy of the days when Jeeps were made in a former washing machine factory. "If you're going to be hit and you're a pedestrian, and the crash is in the speed range where you are going to be hurt but not killed, then smoother designs are better than boxy or angular designs," said Brian O'Neill, the president of the Insurance Institute for Highway Safety.

Another possibility is that the tall, stiff front ends of SUVs are more likely to strike children and short adults in the chest or head, instead of scooping them up with the bumper and depositing them on the softer hood. In some cases, especially involving children hit by SUVs traveling at low speeds, the vehicles knock down pedestrians and drive over them. In most crashes, the worst place for a pedestrian to be is under the vehicle.

In rare circumstances, a tall SUV may pass entirely over a small child without any contact between the child and the vehicle's underbody. There was one such case in the suburbs of Washington, D.C., a few years ago. But it is easy to end up with a head, torso or a limb crushed by a tire, or to bounce up against the underside of the vehicle. The underbody of a vehicle is typically made of the hardest metals with no give at all, because they must support the weight of the vehicle. Being hit by an axle or suspension component is like being struck by a fast-moving crowbar.

SUVs do not just hit pedestrians with their front ends—they also back over pedestrians. Drivers in SUVs appear to be particularly likely to run over people while backing up in driveways, especially children who are not tall enough to be seen out the high rear windows of SUVs. Driveway deaths might seem to be rare accidents, but they are not: a fifth of the children killed as pedestrians by motor vehicles perish in driveways in the United States.

Until recently, the evidence for a special problem with SUVs in driveways was largely anecdotal—a handful of deaths involving Suburbans. The first good study of this issue was recently performed in Australia, and lumped together four-wheel-drive vehicles with light commercial vehicles. The study found that these vehicles made up 30.4 percent of the registered vehicles in southeastern Australia but accounted for nearly two-thirds of the children killed in driveway accidents. Almost all the deaths occurred when these vehicles knocked down a child and then crushed the child's head with a tire.[9]

Automakers have started to respond to this problem by installing radarlike proximity sensors that start beeping inside the passenger compartment to warn drivers if they are about to back into something. The devices can detect poles or children, although they tend to miss pets that are either small or very furry—as one Ford official rather bluntly put it to me, Fluffy the Cat might still get run over, but not a boy or girl. Yet millions of SUVs without these systems will continue to circulate through the used-vehicle market for years to come. The authors of the Australian study recommended that parents of very young children who have vehicles lacking proximity sensors should install temporary fences along the sides of their driveways.

My own advice is that SUV buyers should insist on models with backing sensors, especially if they live in a neighborhood with young children. And all parents, regardless of whether they own vehicles, should warn children from an early age about the extra dangers of going anywhere near large SUVs in school parking lots and other public places. The windows are simply too high in SUVs for drivers to see nearby children.

SUVs are not just too big for the world's roads. They are also too big for parking decks, forcing malls to repaint their lots and prompting multideck garages to ban the largest models. While many cities passed ordinances in the 1970s and 1980s requiring builders to set

CARRYALL SUBURBAN
112-inch wheelbase

This all-purpose vehicle combines the advantages of a passenger car and a light delivery unit. There are four seats, providing for eight passengers. By quick, easy removal of seats it becomes a large-capacity unit for loads of merchandise, produce or luggage. Its utility is proved by its wide demand by private estates, country clubs, hotels, bus and transfer companies, airports, as well as operators who use it for business and pleasure. Chrome-plated hub caps and bumpers and full-length running boards are standard, smart appearance features.

Early Chevrolet Suburbans, like this 1936 model, were beautiful vehicles but seldom viewed as substitutes for cars

A generation of Americans rode in Jeeps during World War II, including President Franklin D. Roosevelt.

As chairman of American
Motors, Roy Chapin Jr. bought
the Jeep brand in 1969 and
began transforming Jeeps into
family vehicles.

Jeep Wagoneers of the 1960s and 1970s looked like the sort of tall station
wagons for families that modern SUVs have become, but they were poorly
marketed and never really caught on.

Bob Lutz has brought commercial success to each of Detroit's Big Three automakers by designing SUVs that appeal to Americans' most selfish and even vicious instincts, but prefers passenger cars for his own use, as seen here in the garage on his estate.

Automakers build the bodies of most SUVs separately from the underbodies, bolting them together at the end of the assembly line. At the Michigan Truck Plant, the world's most profitable factory by the late 1990s, extra Ford Expedition and Lincoln Navigator bodies are kept in huge racks so that production can continue day and night.

**JEEP GRAND CHEROKEE.
STILL THE BEST INSURANCE POLICY OUT THERE.**

JEEP GRAND CHEROKEE   It's your classic man vs. nature struggle. Man goes out in 4x4—nature gets nasty. So we engineered Grand Cherokee to be one of the safest 4x4s out there. Its legendary four-wheel drive shows no fear in the face of a blizzard. Its braking system helps you stop even when the rain or sleet or snow hasn't. Its agile suspension can see you through a rock slide. And should the sun come out, Grand Cherokee is ready for that too. Contact us at 1-800-925-JEEP or www.jeep.com for more info.

THERE'S ONLY ONE

Jeep is a registered trademark of DaimlerChrysler.

Automakers subtly suggest in ads like this one that four-wheel drive improves safety, even though it does not.

Ditch the Joneses.

Although there's something to be said for getting ahead, the all-new 1998 Navigator has more to do with getting away. And taking life's luxuries with you. For more information about this full-size luxury sport utility vehicle, call toll-free 1 888 2ANYWHERE (1 888 226-9943), visit www.lincolnvehicles.com or see an authorized Lincoln Navigator dealer.

⊕ LINCOLN   **Navigator from Lincoln. What a luxury [🚙] should be.**

SUV advertising caters to people who are described by the automakers' market researchers as being especially self-centered.

The tall front ends of SUVs like this Lincoln Navigator, left, are prone in crashes to override the bumpers, hoods and crumple zones of sedans like the Honda Accord, right.

When Diana DeVeer's Saab sedan was struck from the side by a Range Rover SUV in May 1997, she ended up in a coma at the same hospital where she had previously worked as a physical therapist. Despite receiving therapy for five years, she still has not fully recovered from her brain injuries and needs help from her husband, Glenn.

William Clay Ford Jr., right, a great-grandson of Henry Ford who became chairman of the Ford Motor Company in 1999, tried to improve the environmental and safety record of SUVs but pulled back when Ford Motor ran into financial difficulties because of mistakes by the company's CEO, Jacques Nasser, left.

In the summer of 2000, when Firestone tires came apart on Ford Explorers, as on this vehicle, the SUVs frequently rolled over, sometimes with deadly consequences for the occupants.

In the decade since its introduction, the Jeep Grand Cherokee has gone through a few minor design changes but remains one of the few SUVs built with a so-called uniframe construction. Like its cousin, the Jeep Cherokee, another uniframe SUV, it has shown unusual stability.

Arnold Schwarzenegger, the actor and body builder, drove into Times Square in Manhattan in the spring of 2001 in this prototype of a Hummer H2 to promote General Motors' decision to mass-market civilian versions of the military vehicle known as the Humvee.

aside up to 50 percent of their parking spaces for compact cars so as to encourage energy conservation, many of these ordinances are now being repealed. Parking lot designers now recommend that even standard-size spaces be arranged to accommodate vehicles that are an average of 6 feet 7 inches wide and 17 feet 1 inch long—4 inches wider and an inch longer than in 1987.[10]

On a sunny morning at a shopping mall in prosperous Costa Mesa, California, it was easy to see why parking spaces are growing wider and compact-car spaces are disappearing. Terry and Amara Crandall sat in a huge, maroon GMC Suburban full-sized SUV, waiting for a white Jeep Grand Cherokee to back out of what was clearly labeled as a space reserved for compact cars. Amara Crandall was upset that the mall had even tried to give preference to small cars.

"It's discrimination against the big car," she fumed. "Most of the time I find parking in the compact spaces. They're useless—most of the time there is one car across two spaces."

A few spaces away, Jack Valley was trying to figure out how to back his tan Cadillac Seville full-sized sedan out of a space between two large SUVs, which completely blocked his view of any other automobiles that might be weaving through the parking lot. "I just hope the guy coming the other way sees me," he said. "I'm sort of a gambler, I guess."

Chrysler now recommends that car drivers back into spaces between two tall light trucks, so that they can see better and avoid fender-benders when they drive out. That is a fine idea in theory, but does not work well in practice. Backing into a space is a nuisance if you're in a hurry, and many parking lots do not allow it because it takes longer. And it is easy for a car driver to park nose-in between two cars, only to return later and discover that the cars have been replaced by massive light trucks.

Marketers like Clotaire Rapaille portray SUVs as menacing battlewagons that provide reassurance for customers with deep-seated fears of crime. Yet buying an SUV may actually be a good way to wind up losing a vehicle to a thief.

New technology has made it almost impossible for joyriders to hotwire the latest vehicles. The thick, black plastic base on most automobile keys these days contains a tiny radio transmitter; the engine will not work unless a sensor in the steering column detects the coded transmissions of the key and relays this information to the engine. Partly because of this innovation, the overall frequency of auto theft declined in the United States throughout the 1990s, although it inched up by 1.2 percent in 2000, to 1.16 million vehicles stolen.

But while casual joyriders are deterred by the systems from stealing unattended cars, professional thieves and violent criminals are not, insurance industry officials say. There are two approaches to stealing an automobile with the latest anti-theft technology. One is to tow the vehicle or put it on a flatbed truck and take it to an unscrupulous repair shop that can either dismantle it for parts or else install a new set of sensors and keys. But the simpler approach is to get the vehicle's keys by beating up the vehicle's owner or threatening him or her with a gun.

Carjackings were extremely rare until automakers began making it very difficult to steal a car without the key. Carjackings still represent a tiny minority of auto thefts, but they have become a problem in many cities. An average of 49,000 carjackings a year took place in the United States in the early 1990s. In half of them, the criminals were successful in stealing the vehicles.[11]

"If it's not going to run without the key, they're going to walk up and put a gun to your head and demand the key," said Edwin P. Sparkman, the senior manager for vehicle theft at the National Insurance Crime Bureau.

There are no good statistics on the models preferred by carjackers. But 97 percent of carjackers are men in urban areas, usually young, so they fit the demographics of people especially interested in SUVs. For all types of auto theft, not just carjackings, SUVs now rival large luxury cars in producing the heaviest losses for insurers.[12]

Up to half the vehicles stolen and never recovered these days are shipped overseas, according to insurers. Seven of the top 10 metropolitan areas for auto theft are ports or communities with easy access to the Mexican or Canadian borders, led by Phoenix and Miami, according to the National Insurance Crime Bureau. The eventual destinations of these vehicles tend to be countries with weak or corrupt systems for tracking vehicle ownership, notably the former Soviet republics and South American nations. As it happens, such countries also tend to have lousy roads, which makes four-wheel-drive vehicles especially popular.

Gangsters in countries like Colombia and Russia actually order the model of their choice, and then criminals go find one in the United States, steal it, put it in a seagoing container and ship it, said Julie Rochman, a spokeswoman for the Insurance Institute for Highway Safety. The United States has tight controls on imports because of concerns about narcotics trafficking, terrorism, and illegal immigration, but few checks are done on exports.

"Some drug lord in Colombia says, 'I want a Mercedes M-class,'" Rochman said. "And *poof*, a Mercedes disappears in San Antonio or San Diego and it shows up in Colombia in a crate."[13]

Most SUVs are sold and driven in affluent cities and their suburbs. The last thing the world's increasingly crowded cities need are more big vehicles that are hard to maneuver, dangerous to pedestrians, difficult to see past and popular with thieves. Yet the problems posed by SUVs are not limited to safety issues or to cities. Just as serious, and possibly even more damaging over the long term, are the harm they cause to the air we breathe, the climate of the earth and perhaps even to international peace.

12

GLOBAL WARMING, GASOLINE MILEAGE, AND A GENTLEMEN'S AGREEMENT

It looked like a political campaign event, and in many ways, it was. When Chrysler converted its factory in Newark, Delaware, to SUV production in September 1997, the company threw a party at the assembly line that looked like an election rally. Two bright red Durangos, built days earlier just a few feet away, drove up to a stage covered with red and white bunting and disgorged several of the state's top politicians along with Bob Eaton, Chrysler's chairman.

Hundreds of auto workers cheered as Eaton and the politicians joined hands and held their arms aloft in a victory wave. The workers then listened politely as a long succession of speakers, including the governor of Delaware and the mayor of Newark, expressed their gratitude to Chrysler for converting the factory instead of closing it as demand withered for the previous model, the Dodge Intrepid full-sized sedan. Governor Tom Carper, a Democrat, pointed out in his speech that Chrysler's $623 million investment to retool the factory was the equivalent of $1,000 for every man, woman and child in the state. Delayed by a vote on the Senate floor, Delaware's two senators, Joseph R. Biden Jr., a Democrat, and William V. Roth Jr., a Republican, arrived by helicopter at the end of the ceremony.

The politicians and executives descended from the stage and into the cheering audience, shaking hands with the workers. When I asked Governor Carper about the environmental issues surrounding SUVs, he immediately volunteered to help Chrysler. "We've not been asked to get involved in other fights," he yelled over the noise of the crowd. "If they need our help, we'll give it to them."

But while the politicians had a large and captive audience, they paid for it afterwards by listening to personal appeals by Chrysler and local union officials. As described by the politicians, the appeals were low-key but clear: Do not do anything to hurt SUV sales.

The speeches and cheering were scarcely over when the politicians, Chrysler officials and a few reporters retreated to a plush conference room in the 6,000-worker factory's administrative wing. As a buffet lunch was served, Chrysler's top lobbyist, Rob Liberatore, took Senator Biden by the left elbow and gently steered him away from me. "Don't worry, it won't be any EPA lobbying," Liberatore said as he led the ranking Democrat on the Senate Foreign Relations Committee over to a corner to have lunch with him and Eaton. Senator Roth, the chairman of the powerful Senate Finance Committee, soon joined them and the four men in dark suits ate sandwiches from clear plastic plates while carrying on a lively conversation.

Asked as they later walked away from the lunch what they had discussed, the senators said the conversation had mainly involved Chrysler's interest in free trade with South America and Eastern Europe. Both senators warily volunteered that they, not Chrysler, had paid for the helicopter trip from Washington. But when pressed, Senator Biden allowed that Eaton had also spoken about the dangers of raising fuel-economy standards: "He said, 'We're building what people are buying.'"

*

Eaton had good reason to be worried about fuel-economy laws. Americans were buying ever larger SUVs, and in such impressive numbers that Chrysler, GM and Ford were once more having trouble meeting fuel-economy standards. By 1997, all three were straining to meet the light-truck average of 20.7 miles per gallon, and their difficulties in meeting the standards would only get worse with each subsequent year. Between 1990 and 1997, annual SUV sales rose from 708,000 to 2,446,000 even as the rest of the auto market showed little growth; by 2001, sales would reach 3,501,000. SUVs went from being slightly iconoclastic fashion statements by some with-it baby boomers to being perceived as a necessity by millions of upscale families.

Midsized SUV sales nearly tripled between 1990 and 2001. But the biggest growth took place because of the introduction of large, four-door SUVs with all the interior comforts of cars and then some, including separate air conditioning for the rear seats, leather seats, compact disc players and more. These also happened to be the vehicles that benefited the most from various government loopholes. Moreover, they appealed to rich and upper-middle-class families whose incomes were soaring through the 1990s while gasoline prices fell. Large SUVs went from 0.6 percent of the auto market in 1990 to 7.1 percent in 2001.[1]

Automakers were designing increasingly fuel-efficient engines in this period. Energy-saving features like port fuel injection, lock-up torque converters and four-valve cylinder designs all became common, at least in cars. The improvements tended to go into car engines first because car engines were tuned for efficiency while SUV engines tended to be tuned for power, especially towing power. But some of the improvements percolated into some SUVs as well, especially those made by Japanese automakers, who placed more importance on fuel economy because of high gasoline taxes in their home market.

But despite these improvements, the average fuel economy of SUVs gradually declined. SUVs were bulking up faster than the engines were improving.

SUVs would fatten up to an average weight of 4,478 pounds in 2001, packing on an extra 638 pounds compared to 1987, the year that fuel economy had peaked. Cars, bound by a more strict fuel-economy standard, only put on half as much weight in the same period, rising to 3,380 pounds.[2]

Getting tubbier did not slow SUVs down. Indeed, the opposite happened. Automakers installed much more powerful, thirstier engines, so that the average horsepower of an SUV climbed to 209, compared to 169 for cars.[3]

The typical SUV needed 13.3 seconds to reach 60 miles an hour from a standing start in 1987. By 2001, the average SUV took just 10.6 seconds, nearly matching the average car, at 10.3 seconds. The average acceleration time for full-sized SUVs like the Lincoln Navigator was just 10.4 seconds because they tended to be luxury models with gigantic engines.[4]

Automakers began marketing SUVs to appeal to the same speed-obsessed drivers who used to buy high-performance sports cars. Chrysler began offering a new engine in the midsized Jeep Grand Cherokee in 1997 that allowed it to go from zero to 60 miles an hour in seven seconds—as fast as a 1978 Chevrolet Corvette. Several subsequent models, like the ML-55 AMG version of the Mercedes M-Class SUV, now go even faster.

I once asked Jürgen Hubbert, the head of Mercedes, whether it was responsible to offer such speed and power in SUVs that lacked the handling of a low-riding sports car. He was scornful and a little contemptuous, in the way many auto executives are when the safety of high-speed driving is questioned, especially German auto executives accustomed to driving on an autobahn with no speed limits. "I drove my M-Class to my winter holidays—I went 230 kilometers per hour (140 miles per hour) and it feels absolutely good," he said. "We once tried to teach customers, and it's a very bad decision. If customers want to have that kind of car, we must build it."

As millions of Americans switched to SUVs, especially big ones, overall gas mileage suffered. After peaking in the 1987 and 1988 model years at 25.9 miles per gallon, the average efficiency of all new cars and light trucks sold in the United States declined steadily. It was 24.5 miles per gallon by the 1997 model year, and would drop to 23.9 miles per gallon by 2001.

The true gas mileage of vehicles coming onto American roads is much lower. This is because the government has long allowed automakers to inflate the mileage of all their vehicles, cars as well as SUVs, for the purpose of meeting the fuel-economy standards.

Consider a 2002 Ford Explorer with a V8 engine and four-wheel drive. The window sticker says that it get 14 miles to the gallon in the city and 19 m.p.g. on the highway. Yet when Ford is calculating whether all of its light trucks have an average fuel economy that meets the current light-truck standard of 20.7 m.p.g., it counts the Explorer as getting 19.5 m.p.g.

How is this possible? Devised in the 1970s, the government test for gas mileage has long been done on rollers in a laboratory, in a test that assumes unrealistically low driving speeds on the highway and little traffic in the city. The lab figures were initially used in window stickers in the 1970s, but drivers complained that they could get nowhere near the mileage on the stickers. The average speed on the highway portion of the government's mileage test is just 48 miles an hour; going 70 instead can cut mileage by 30 percent, mostly because of extra aerodynamic drag. So the government began adjusting the lab figures downward in the late 1970s for the window stickers, reducing gas mileage on the highway by 22 percent and the city mileage by 10 percent.

But the government kept using the lab figures in calculating fuel-economy averages for regulatory purposes. Use window sticker figures instead of the lab figures and the average fuel economy of new vehicles in the United States was not really 23.9 miles per gallon in 2001, but a mere 20.4 m.p.g., according to recent calculations by the EPA.

Even this assumes that drivers can match the current figures on the window stickers—many drivers complain that they cannot do so. The window sticker values still assume that drivers scrupulously obey speed limits, and most drivers do not.

Another peculiarity involves how the city and highway driving are combined to calculate a single average. The mileage standards assume that 55 percent of the driving is in the city and 45 percent on the highway, which was the pattern in the late 1960s. The latest figures, however, show that 62 percent of driving is done in cities and 38 percent on highways. Since city driving produces lower fuel economy than highway driving for most vehicles, this shift toward city driving has shaved another four-tenths of a mile per gallon off average fuel economy. So the best estimate of the EPA is that the true fuel economy of new automobiles sold in 2001 was exactly 20.0 miles per gallon.[5]

That is appalling by international standards. New vehicles in Japan averaged 30.3 miles per gallon in 2000, using rigorous tests comparable to the true fuel economy in the United States. Japanese regulators have already ordered automakers there to improve the average to 35.5 miles a gallon in 2010. Automakers with operations in Europe, including Ford and GM, have reluctantly agreed under pressure from the European Union to increase fuel economy there to 41 miles per gallon in 2008 from 33 miles per gallon in 2000.[6] Of course, the biggest reason why vehicles in Europe and Japan attain such high mileage is that they are much smaller than the vehicles that most Americans choose. But Europe and Japan, much more than the United States, also continue to rely heavily on cars instead of SUVs.

To understand why SUVs get such poor mileage, compare a 2001 Chevrolet Malibu midsized sedan to a 2001 Chevrolet Blazer midsized sport utility vehicle with four-wheel drive. They each seat five people, but the Blazer has a few advantages. The Blazer's tall cargo area in the back has twice the volume of the Malibu's, although the two vehicles have similar floor space in their cargo areas for stowing grocery bags. The Blazer can tow 5,000 pounds, while the Malibu can tow 1,000 pounds. The Blazer can push its way through deep snow or thick mud, while the Malibu is really designed for driving on roads.

But the Blazer gets considerably fewer miles to the gallon than the Malibu all of the time, even when there is no tall cargo to haul or heavy trailer to tow or swamp to traverse. According to GM, the average window-sticker gas mileage for the Blazer is 17.9 m.p.g., compared to 24.0 m.p.g. for the Malibu. In other words, the Malibu goes 6.1 miles farther per gallon, or 34 percent farther.

The Blazer has worse gas mileage for five reasons, GM says. For starters, it is 1,125 pounds heavier, which accounts for 2 m.p.g. of the difference. The Blazer has a heavy steel frame, mainly for towing, while the Malibu does not, and the Blazer has a heavy four-wheel-drive system.

The Blazer has a larger engine, partly for towing and partly for moving its extra bulk, which costs another 0.5 m.p.g. Engines and transmissions can be designed so that they are very efficient during highway driving in a fairly empty vehicle. Or they can be designed to be very powerful when slowly pulling a heavy boat up a steep boat ramp. But it is extremely difficult to design an engine to do both of these tasks well. What has evolved instead is that car engines tend to operate efficiently during everyday driving but have limited power for low-speed pulling, while SUV engines have lots of power for low-speed pulling but are not very efficient for daily use without a trailer.

"Whether you're towing or not, it's less fuel-efficient," says Kelly Brown, Ford's director of vehicle environmental engineering.

The Blazer's four-wheel drive makes the transfer of energy from the engine to the wheels slightly less efficient, for another 1.6 m.p.g. penalty. The Blazer also has bigger tires, partly to carry its extra weight, costing another 0.2 m.p.g.

Finally, the Blazer's poor aerodynamics produce another 1.8 m.p.g. loss compared to a Malibu. The Blazer's height, width and squared-off corners together give it the aerodynamics of a large brick. Its high ground clearance for off-road travel allows eddies of air to form underneath that cause considerably more drag than occurs in a car.

The Blazer's side mirrors are also part of the aerodynamics problem, although many SUVs have even bigger side mirrors. Because many trailers block the view out the rear window, automakers use considerably larger side mirrors on all vehicles that are designed for towing. But side mirrors are a huge problem for a vehicle's aerodynamics, because they break up the smooth flow of wind past the vehicle.

"The drag on a mirror is really big, and trucks tend to have bigger mirrors," Brown says.

Fullsized sport utilities have even worse aerodynamics, partly because they have extremely high roofs. As someone who is tall, and with an especially long back, I used to marvel at how much headroom I had in fullsized SUVs. I wondered who could possibly need so much vertical space. The mystery was explained when I met Tom Baughman, Ford's truck engineering director. He pointed out that the big SUVs shared the same roofs as full-sized pickup trucks, and the roofs in fullsized pickup trucks are tall because they are designed for a peculiarity of the Texas market, which is the country's biggest market for pickups. "In Texas, you have to be able to wear your cowboy hat," he said in total seriousness. "The proportions have sort of stayed the same."

Nobody disputes that fuel economy has been declining in the United States. But that raises two big questions: Does it matter? And if it does matter, are federally mandated fuel-economy averages the best way to address the problem?

Four arguments are commonly given for why fuel economy matters: conserving resources for future generations; reducing dependence on unstable oil producers in the Middle East; saving money for consumers; and slowing global warming. Conservation, reducing imports and saving money were all arguments used for the original fuel-economy law in 1975. Global warming became an issue tied loosely to cars in the late 1980s, faded after the defeat in 1990 of the Bryan bill, which would have forced automakers to improve average fuel economy by 40 percent over a decade, and then returned as an even bigger issue linked to SUVs in 1997.

To understand the connection between global warming and automobiles, a very brief, very simple chemistry lesson is needed on how internal-combustion engines work. Gasoline and diesel fuel consist mainly of carbon atoms, the residue of plants that lived millions of years ago. When an engine burns fuel, it is essentially combining each carbon atom in the fuel with two oxygen atoms from the air coming through the grille and under the vehicle, to form carbon dioxide.

Almost everything that comes out the tailpipe is carbon dioxide. When an automobile engine burns a gallon of gasoline, it typically combines 5.3 pounds of carbon from the gasoline with 14.2 pounds of oxygen from the air.[7] This produces 19.5 pounds of carbon dioxide, a quantity that dwarfs the traces of unburned fuel and nitrogen oxides that cause smog. Diesel is 12 percent denser than gasoline, with more carbon, so burning a gallon of diesel produces about 22 pounds of carbon dioxide, while also providing better mileage per gallon.

Since the days of wood-burning stoves, engineers have struggled to make combustion as efficient as possible by having it convert all of the available fuel into carbon dioxide, with no traces of unburned fuel. So auto engineers are deeply frustrated now at being told that the carbon dioxide is a problem for global warming. "For a thousand years, the holy grail for engineers has been to take combustion and make it so efficient that the only products are water and carbon dioxide," Ford's Petrauskas said. "I don't know of any technology that can take CO_2 and turn it into something that is not CO_2 and is benign in its own right."

Most scientists specializing in the environment, especially climate issues, describe global warming as the biggest environmental danger of our lifetimes. They perceive humanity as upsetting the balance of nature by burning too many fossil fuels, increasing the amount of carbon dioxide and other substances in the air and turning the Earth's atmosphere into a greenhouse that will steadily warm up in the decades ahead. The consequences of such a warming could be dire: rising sea levels as polar ice caps melt; flooding and accelerated erosion of shorelines; chronic droughts in some areas as weather patterns shift; and the spread in temperate-climate countries like the United States of previously tropical diseases like malaria, cholera and the West Nile virus.

But uncertainties remain, including the speed of global warming and the role of natural factors in its progress—such as a possible increase in the sun's warmth, the immense emissions of carbon dioxide that accompany volcanic eruptions and even the methane gas that livestock produce as part of their digestive processes. Through much of the 1990s, the auto industry ranked among the most outspoken critics of the theory that humanity has played a significant role in global warming. The auto industry and oil industry have helped to bankroll groups like the Global Climate Coalition, which has fought international limits on emissions of greenhouse gases like carbon dioxide.

When he was president and then vice chairman of Chrysler, Bob Lutz was among the most vituperative critics of the theory of global warming, and especially of the idea that his industry was a contributor. "Sure, cars and trucks account for a higher percentage of the manmade CO_2," he said in the prepared text of one speech in 1998. "But given that scientists at this point in time have the barest of understandings of the effect of things like oceans and volcanoes and sun spots on our atmosphere—let alone my personal favorite, what is delicately known as bovine flatulence—it seems to me that making cars and trucks the icon of this debate is like blaming the boy who spit in the ocean for every flood that might happen in the future!"[8]

The world's family vehicles, including SUVs, do not cause global warming by themselves, but they are a contributor, accounting for 12 percent of all manmade emissions of greenhouse gases. The United States, with its huge fleet of fairly large vehicles each being driven an average of 12,000 miles a year, is an especially big part of the problem. The United States has 5 percent of the world's population, but produces nearly a third of all greenhouse gases from automobiles.

To put it another way, automobiles in the United States account for 4 percent of the entire world's emissions of manmade greenhouse gases. If American automobiles were a separate country, their emissions would exceed those of every country except the United States, China, Russia and Japan.[9] Since SUVs are still only a tenth of vehicles in use in the United States, they account for a small share of global, manmade emissions of greenhouse gases.[10]

But the focus of international efforts to address global warming has been on reversing the slow, steady growth in manmade emissions. The switch to SUVs is actually pushing emissions up. Cars and light trucks were one of the fastest-growing major category of emissions in the United States by the late 1990s, and gas-guzzling SUVs are likely to double as a share of registered vehicles in the United States in the next few years. The Dodge Durango SUVs that Chrysler executives and Delaware politicians were celebrating in 1997 burned 57 percent more gas per mile and therefore emitted 57 percent more carbon dioxide than the Dodge Intrepid full-sized sedan that the factory used to build.

By contrast, many big corporations have been actually reducing emissions of greenhouse gases from their factories. They have improved energy efficiency and halted the use of obscure but powerful chemicals that also play a role in global warming. Electric power utilities, another focus of controversy over global warming, have also taken significant conservation steps.

Auto executives offer many reasons why gas mileage has always been lower in the United States, and perhaps always will be. Americans like big vehicles partly because they drive long distances. On the East Coast, for example, Washington, D.C., and Miami are farther apart than London and Rome in Europe. Americans also tend to be bigger physically—a polite way of saying that obesity is a national problem.

Most important, gasoline prices are much lower in the United States than in any other large, industrialized nation. Gasoline taxes in Europe and East Asia run as high as $3 a gallon. Yet they do not produce nearly the controversy of federal gas taxes of 18.4 cents a gallon and state gas taxes of 8 to 30.3 cents a gallon in the United States. Most European and East Asian countries began imposing steep taxes on gasoline before World War II. This was done partly because gasoline was seen as a luxury—only the affluent had cars. It was also done for national security reasons—while the United States had huge oil fields in Texas and Southern California, Western Europe had very little oil, at least until large-scale production began in the North Sea in the 1970s. By contrast, the United States and other oil-producing nations had domestic oil industries with the clout to stop such taxes.

As gasoline prices fell to $1 a gallon in the late 1990s, Detroit executives with the thankless task of selling small cars were in despair. "The consumer is acting kind of rationally, and they're moving to larger vehicles," said Mark Hogan, GM's vice president for small cars and an executive with extensive international experience. "It's an aberration, if you look at anywhere in the outside world other than Venezuela or Saudi Arabia."

The favorite remedy of economists would be to raise gasoline taxes, instead of increasing fuel-economy standards. Fuel-economy standards only affect future vehicles and have no effect on the distances that Americans drive. With cars and light trucks now lasting 15 to 20 years, it would take a very long time for more stringent fuel-economy standards to have much effect on gasoline consumption or global warming.

Higher gasoline prices, by contrast, would provide all Americans with an immediate incentive to drive fewer miles. Higher prices would also give motorists an incentive to drive those miles in the most efficient vehicles they own, while leaving the SUV parked at home except when it is really needed.

The problem is that Americans have long paid extraordinarily close attention to gasoline prices, using them as a (poor) indicator of inflation and even of the effectiveness of political leaders. My favorite radio station, an all-news AM station in Detroit, encourages listeners to call in every day on their cell phones with the locations of especially inexpensive gas stations. Presidential candidates like Ross Perot, Paul Tsongas and John B. Anderson have all proposed increases in gasoline taxes over the last two decades, only to be accused of wanting to raise taxes. Significantly, none of them made it to the White House.

Clever economists have come up with proposals to get around public opposition to tax hikes. N. Gregory Mankiw, an economics professor at Harvard, has promoted the idea of coupling an increased gasoline tax with a cut in income taxes. Pietro S. Nivola, an economist at the Brookings Institution, has suggested offsetting an increased gasoline tax with lower payroll taxes.

Such plans face another hurdle, though. Gas taxes penalize people who drive long distances, and that means people in the Plains states and the Rockies. My in-laws live on the outskirts of a town of 300 people in rural Wyoming, and think nothing of driving 140 miles round-trip when they go out for dinner. Used-car dealers from such states prowl auto auctions on the East Coast, buying cars that are spurned as having too many miles on them. The dealers then ship the cars west and resell them at a profit to westerners who are happy to buy a car that has been driven an average of 15,000 or even 18,000 miles a year. (Of course, the dealers' customers may not know that these were punishing miles in bumper-to-bumper traffic in eastern cities, instead of barreling down wide-open highways.)

While the Plains states and Rocky Mountain states have few

votes in the House, they each have two senators, the same as more populous states on the East and West Coasts. When President Clinton sought a sharp increase in gasoline taxes to help reduce the budget deficit in 1993, it was a member of his own party, Senator Max Baucus of Montana, who forced him to whittle it down to a mere 4.3 cents per gallon. Even then, the president's tax package barely passed, and Republicans have called for the repeal of the 4.3 cent tax during every spike in gasoline prices since then.

While higher gasoline taxes should be effective in prompting people to drive fewer miles, they might be less effective now in persuading people to buy fuel-efficient vehicles. The automakers' economists say that gasoline prices have less and less effect on auto sales. The higher-income families who increasingly dominate the new vehicle market spend such a small percentage of their incomes on gasoline that they give little attention to gas prices. The Ford Motor Company calculates that the typical buyer of a full-sized SUV spends a smaller percentage of his or her income on gasoline than the typical buyer of a compact car. The incomes of the two categories of buyers are wider, in percentage terms, than the difference in gas mileage.

A fifth of all vehicles are also being leased now instead of being purchased outright. Since lessees need only consider their gasoline costs for the two to four years that they lease a vehicle, they can assign less weight to gasoline costs than someone who plans to buy a vehicle and keep it longer.[11]

If energy conservation and slowing global warming are serious goals, fuel-economy standards are imperfect substitutes for significant gasoline taxes. But with little political will evident for higher gas taxes, fuel-economy standards have remained the favorite choice of environmentalists. Stringent standards for cars and lax standards for light trucks have had the pernicious effect, however, of encouraging automakers to abandon large cars in favor of SUVs.

The hostility of automakers toward mileage standards has turned into hostility toward doing anything about global warming.

With the considerable influence that automakers wield in Washington, that has helped make the United States a laggard in addressing the problem.

President Clinton and his advisers had worked hard before the big meeting with auto-industry leaders late in the afternoon of October 2, 1997. The day before, the White House had threatened South Korea with trade sanctions unless it removed unfair trade barriers, like auditing the tax returns of anyone who bought an imported car. The Clinton Administration was shoveling more than $200 million a year into research programs to help Detroit build higher-mileage cars.

But when the CEOs of the Big Three automakers and Stephen Yokich, the president of the UAW, came into the White House that afternoon, they had little interest in talking about South Korea or subsidies. They wanted to talk about global warming, and the United Nations conference that was to begin two months later in Kyoto, Japan.

Like many of Clinton's meetings, it ran overtime. It was dark and unseasonably cold by the time the CEOs and Yokich came out into the White House driveway, where a row of television cameras and bright lights had been set up. Alex Trotman, the chairman and CEO of the Ford Motor Company and an outspoken critic of environmental regulations, stepped up to a lectern festooned with microphones, looking grim.

The auto industry was deeply worried, he warned, about the Administration's plans to pursue a global agreement to limit greenhouse-gas emissions. Particularly upsetting for the industry was the Administration's intention for the pact to cover only industrialized countries, which have very high emissions of such gases per person. Developing nations like China, India and even South Korea would be excluded from the pact, as the Europeans wanted, because their emissions per person were low, although rising.

"That would be bad for the auto industry, in terms of jobs and the economic vitality of this country," Trotman scowled, adding a thinly veiled warning to move auto factories to developing countries exempt from the limits. "There will be an incentive to move plants."

Yokich stepped up to the microphones, looking equally unhappy. "We're taking a hard look at it because it is our jobs that are concerned," he said.

Three weeks after the meeting, President Clinton announced his position for the Kyoto talks. The United States would pursue an agreement limiting industrialized countries' emissions of greenhouse gases. But Clinton conspicuously omitted any mention of raising fuel-economy standards or gasoline taxes. The Partnership for a New Generation of Vehicles, the federal program that Clinton had created after taking office instead of increasing mileage standards, would continue to give huge subsidies to the auto industry without requiring any actual progress in the fuel economy of new vehicles going on the road.

In the weeks before the Kyoto meeting, another problem was starting to emerge. John German, a prescient researcher at the EPA's vehicle emissions office in Ann Arbor, Michigan, had been studying the computer models that the Energy Department, the Federal Highway Administration and EPA had been using to forecast gasoline demand and air pollution. It turned out that the models were failing to take into account that a growing proportion of the vehicles on the road were light trucks instead of cars. As a result, the models underestimated how much gasoline would be burned in the coming years, how much carbon dioxide would be emitted and how much smog-causing nitrogen oxides would be produced.

The Energy Department's model, developed jointly with the oil industry, was especially flawed. The model had grown so vast and complicated over the years that even the programmers had trouble figuring out all the relationships. German deduced that while the model included annual light-truck sales, these sales had little effect on the model's estimate of the proportion of vehicles on the road that were light trucks. Indeed, the model forecast that light trucks would remain under 33 percent of all family vehicles on the road through 2015.

German calculated from vehicle registration data that light trucks had already become 34 percent of vehicles in use, and were rising by a percentage point a year, mostly because of soaring SUV sales. He forecast that light-truck sales would reach 50 percent of the market by the 2002 model year, a prediction that would later prove exactly right, and that the proportion of vehicles in use that were light trucks would continue rising by roughly a percentage point a year for the next two decades.[12] Projections for gasoline consumption and carbon dioxide emissions by 2010 should be raised by 8 percent, he wrote. Government forecasts of smog-causing nitrogen oxides pollution from family vehicles in 2020 should be raised by 6 percent to 23 percent.[13]

German presented his brilliant but dry statistical analysis at an obscure technical conference in North Carolina at the end of October 1997. When I spoke to Energy Department officials soon after, they scoffed at the criticism. The oil industry was also dismissive. The profits in the oil business were in finding the oil, shipping it to a refinery and later shipping refined products like gasoline to service stations for sale to the public. But there was little profit in the actual refining. Increasingly stringent environmental rules had forced oil companies to invest billions of dollars in more sophisticated refinery equipment to produce cleaner-burning fuels, but oil companies had trouble passing on the extra costs to consumers. When Shell Oil and Texaco had merged some of their refining operations in March 1997, Wall Street had welcomed the deal as an opportunity for the two companies to cut back capacity further by eliminating similar operations. "Refining is not a place where one earns a lot of money," a leading financial analyst said, echoing the then conventional wisdom in the oil industry. "It's not going to be a place where one earns of lot of money in the next 10 years."[14]

No new refineries had been built in the United States since the 1970s, although existing ones had been expanded somewhat. By 1997, the existing refineries were running at practically full capacity. But nobody wanted to hear about German's forecast that more gasoline would be needed, because that would mean a need to invest in more refinery capacity.

Even a 1 percent increase in gasoline demand beyond available capacity can cause a huge increase in gasoline prices, because few people are willing to cut back their driving unless prices rise considerably. German politely refrained from predicting the consequences if he were right. But his calculations clearly suggested the United States would begin experiencing sharp annual spikes in gasoline prices at the start of each summer driving season, as refineries would be unable to keep up with demand and stockpiles would start running dangerously low. There would also be sharp spikes in heating oil prices each winter, because refineries would have to keep producing mostly gasoline until very late each autumn, leaving them little time to accumulate heating oil reserves before cold weather set in. Several years later, precisely these price spikes would occur.

Six weeks after German presented his paper, the United States and 54 other industrialized countries agreed to the Kyoto Protocol. The pact required them to cut their emissions of greenhouses gases by 2012 to an average of 5 percent below 1990 levels. Because American emissions were rising steadily, the pact effectively required the United States to reduce its consumption of coal and oil by as much as 30 percent from forecasted levels.[15] (The United States has done virtually nothing since 1997 to implement the Kyoto Protocol, and President George W. Bush declared the agreement dead soon after taking office in 2001.)

As it happened, the auto industry was ready in 1997 to give fuel economy another big push—in the wrong direction. As sales continued to increase for Durangos and other, even larger, SUVs, Chrysler, Ford and General Motors found that they could not sell enough relatively fuel-efficient compact pickups and minivans even to bring their light trucks up to a lab average of 20.7 miles per gallon. So they resorted to some clever tricks that actually hurt fuel economy but helped them meet the letter of the law and go on selling larger and larger SUVs.

It was the kind of event that automakers love to hold to improve their environmental image. Ford invited several dozen reporters to its well-guarded test track in Dearborn. Surrounded by a high brick wall to shield prototype cars from the eyes and cameras of engineers from rival automakers, the test track was a sprawling operation. Numerous large, well-equipped garages and warehouses held extensive equipment for preparing and testing new models. There was a 2-mile-long oval track with banked turns for testing new models at speeds of 100 miles per hour or more. Inside the oval was a large area of grass crisscrossed with roads that have curves, some sharp and some wide. A short but very steep manmade hill stood nearby, with a road going precipitously up one side and down the other.

The press conference itself was in a spartan, two-room building near the middle of the oval. A dozen Ford executives and engineers stood at the front of the larger room and took turns giving details of the company's plans to build a quarter of a million alternative-fuel vehicles by 2001, mainly Ford Ranger compact pickup trucks. These would be able to burn either gasoline or "E85," a mixture of 85 percent ethanol and 15 percent gasoline. The ethanol, a type of alcohol, could be made from the nation's abundant supplies of grain, or even from grass, both completely renewable resources. Every engine in these vehicles would be equipped with a special fuel-line sensor, initially costing $200, but Ford would not charge customers anything extra for the sensor. The fuel-line sensor would monitor the proportion of ethanol going to the engine from the fuel tank and modify various computerized engine controls accordingly.

The Rangers would emit smaller quantities of smog-causing gases and even get 5 percent better acceleration when fueled with E85.

Ford officials did briefly acknowledge one problem, however: fewer than 60 of the nation's nearly 200,000 service stations sold E85. "Ford has taken the leadership position here, we're going to provide the vehicles in the hope that the infrastructure will follow," said Phil Novell, Ford's general sales manager. Then the reporters were all given a chance to drive around in the track in vehicles fueled with E85.

It all sounded wonderful, and a few days later Chrysler announced that it would start selling minivans that could burn gasoline or E85 too. As it turned out, it was too good to be true, part of an elaborate plan to take advantage of a loophole in federal fuel-economy regulations.

For starters, the infrastructure did not exist for a reason. Gasoline is mostly shipped by pipeline, and many of the older pipelines allow in moisture where pipe segments are welded together. That is not a problem with gasoline, because oil and water do not mix and the water is readily drained off when the gasoline arrives at the end of the pipeline. But ethanol mixes swiftly with water at the slightest contact, and it is extremely difficult to separate out the water later. So ethanol must be moved in more modern pipelines or else shipped in special tanker trucks or tanker rail cars at extra cost. It is then mixed with the gasoline at the last moment at a gasoline terminal, which sends the fuel in trucks to local service stations.

Big oil companies with billions of dollars tied up in pumping and distributing oil have had especially little interest in selling E85. Six big oil companies now own or franchise 55 percent of the gas stations in the United States and not one of their gas stations sells E85. By the beginning of 2002, there were still only 136 stations selling E85 to the public in the United States, plus another 120 private E85 stations for the fueling of commercial and government fleets, according to the National Ethanol Vehicle Coalition, which is bankrolled by farmers and ethanol distillers. All of these stations were run by independent entrepreneurs, many of whom had accepted offers from the coalition to cover all the installation costs for E85 pumps.

Another problem involves the price of E85. Even the ethanol industry concedes that the retail price per gallon of gasoline is lower than the price per gallon of E85 if the price of oil is below $25, as it has been for most of the last two decades.

Even when E85 costs the same per gallon as gasoline, it still costs slightly more for a motorist to burn E85. That is because a gallon of E85 provides less energy than a gallon of gasoline. So a light truck goes 5 to 12 percent fewer miles on a tank of E85 than on a tank of gasoline.

Finally, there is a tax problem. Federal and state fuel taxes pay for road construction and repairs. But while the federal government collects 18.4 cents in taxes on each gallon of gasoline, it only collects 13.05 cents of taxes on each gallon of E85. State governments also collect much lower taxes on E85.[16] Part of the gap is made up by the fact that vehicles need to burn more E85 per mile than gasoline, but overall, switching from gasoline to E85 erodes the financing of road budgets. Ethanol benefits from lower taxation because of adroit maneuvering by the farm lobby. If ethanol did become subject to the same fuel taxes as gasoline, it would become much too expensive to use unless gasoline prices jumped considerably.

So why did Ford and Chrysler bother building dual-fuel vehicles? What Ford officials barely mentioned in their initial briefing was that selling dual-fuel vehicles does wonders for an automaker's average fuel economy. An obscure regulation, crafted by the corn lobby and the auto industry, allows an automaker to count any vehicle that could run on either gasoline or E85 as getting superb gas mileage. A Ford Ranger that got 27 miles to the gallon in the lab could suddenly be counted as getting 44 miles to the gallon for calculating Ford's fuel-economy average—even if it never actually burned any E85. Building dual-fuel vehicles allowed Ford and Chrysler to sell more full-sized SUVs while still meeting, barely, the government's requirement of an average fuel economy of 20.7 miles per gallon.

GM initially refused to play the same game as Ford and Chrysler. "It doesn't do any good to produce a powertrain that burns ethanol if you don't think people are going to burn ethanol in it," Harry Pearce, GM's vice chairman, told me at the 1998 Detroit auto show. "Without the infrastructure, who are we kidding in terms of the impact you're going to have?"

A few months later, GM had second thoughts and joined Ford and Chrysler in playing the same silly game. By 2001, Ford's original target for a quarter-million dual-fuel vehicles, the Big Three had actually produced 1.9 million of them and the rate of production was still rising swiftly. The National Ethanol Vehicle Coalition estimates that a million dual-fuel vehicles will be manufactured in 2002 alone. This will allow each of the Big Three to add a fictional 1 m.p.g. or so to their light-truck CAFE figures, keeping them in compliance with the letter of the law, if not the spirit.

The final draft of a Transportation Department report leaked to me in June 2001 pointed out that virtually nobody was burning E85 in their dual-fuel vehicles. Not only were there few filling stations, but few owners of dual-fuel vehicles even knew they could use E85, the report said. Automakers only mentioned the capability briefly in owner's manuals, which few people read cover to cover. The report calculated that by making possible the sale of more gas-guzzlers, the dual-fuel vehicles had actually increased American gasoline consumption by 473 million gallons in 2000. Between 2005 and 2009, the report projected that the increase would be 9 billion gallons.

The final draft had received full approval at all levels of the department and even been approved in two reviews by the President's Office of Management and Budget. It had gone to the office of Transportation Secretary Norman Mineta for signature, and was to be forwarded to Congress within a week. Congress had ordered a decade earlier that the report be submitted by the end of September 2000, but the Clinton Administration had been reluctant to tackle the politically touchy issue in an election year, so little had been done. The report was already almost nine months late by the time the final draft reached Mineta's desk.

But Mineta never signed it. With Democrats and Republicans in Congress vying with each other to keep farmers happy, and with the auto industry appalled by the final draft, Mineta's staff opened an unsuccessful investigation into the source of the leak and sent the document back to the bureaucrats for a rewrite. The bureaucrats spent nearly a full year rewriting the report, expunging most of the criticisms of ethanol incentives from the text. Once more, the world had been made safe for big SUVs.

The ethanol loophole was only part of a broader effort by automakers to sell as many large SUVs as possible without paying penalties for violating fuel-economy laws. As the years have gone by, these efforts have become increasingly creative.

One gambit involves imports of used vehicles, which are exempt from fuel-economy standards. Detroit automakers in particular ship large numbers of full-sized SUVs to Canada. But gasoline taxes are 20 cents higher per gallon in Canada, incomes are lower and there is less income inequality on the northern side of the border. The result is that larger models tend to be slower sellers there, with dealers commonly offering deep discounts that are not available in the United States. The weakness of the Canadian dollar has made the disparity with American prices even wider, as automakers have not raised their prices as quickly as the Canadian dollar has fallen. Full-sized SUVs like the Ford Expedition now sell for as much as $5,000 less north of the border.

So entrepreneurs have been buying tens of thousands of new SUVs, pickups and large minivans, as well as some cars, and shipping them back to the United States for resale. The vehicles enter the country legally, under a program originally set up to help immigrants from Canada bring their cars with them. Imports of suppos-edly used vehicles from Canada jumped twelvefold in the two years after September 1, 1997, when Canada adopted American stan-dards for vehicular air pollution. Until Canada adopted the same rules, importers had to engage in the costly task of replacing emis-sions systems to bring vehicles across the border. After the rule change, entrepreneurs simply replaced speedometers and odome-ters that measure distances in kilometers with ones denominated in miles. Shipments climbed to nearly 200,000 vehicles in 2001, or 1.2 percent of the American auto market, and are still rising.

American dealers, who are losing sales, have been demanding since 1998 that automakers crack down on this practice. Detroit automakers say that they oppose the imports. But while Honda took the obvious step in 1999 of severely limiting the availability of replacement odometers and speedometers, Detroit automakers have not done so. The torrent of Canadian vehicles is feeding another dispute too: Canadian regulations require brighter daytime running lights than regulations in the United States, where the use of headlights in the day has caused more controversy, and the entrepreneurs bringing Canadian vehicles across the border seldom replace the headlights.

Yet another way that automakers play the fuel-economy game is simply to violate the standards and pay the modest fines assessed by law. Land Rover did this for years on its SUVs, until Ford acquired the company in 2000 and had to include it in its average. Luxury European car makers like Porsche and BMW have long paid the fines as simply a cost of doing business in the United States. This has given the luxury European automakers a competi-tive advantage over American rivals like Lincoln and Cadillac, by allowing the European companies to offer more powerful cars equipped with rear-wheel drive, which is less fuel-efficient than front-wheel drive but is more popular with driving connoisseurs.

The fines are $5.50 for each tenth of a mile per gallon that an automaker falls below the standard, multiplied by the number of vehicles sold. If an automaker manufactures a million vehicles a year with an average fuel economy that is 1 m.p.g. too low, it would owe $55 million a year. The potential profits to be earned by selling large SUVs with profits of more than $10,000 apiece dwarf the fines.

So why haven't GM, Ford and what is now DaimlerChrysler simply broken the laws and paid the fines? The concern of Detroit automakers has always been that if they pay any fines, they and their boards of directors and top executives could be sued by shareholders for having deliberately violated federal laws. Any environmental group could buy a few shares on the stock market and then file such a lawsuit. "In the litigious U.S., that's always a concern," a GM executive said. "Why open yourself up to that?"

Only companies that are based in the United States are vulnerable to such lawsuits, according to the auto industry's lawyers. But DaimlerChrysler is now incorporated in Germany. While the company insists that it plans to comply with all American laws, it does have the option of flouting the law if Congress ever tries to require significantly higher average fuel economy. The real danger of this strategy for DaimlerChrysler lies in the public relations mess that would follow, and in the possibility that Congress might respond by sharply raising the fines for any manufacturer that flouts the law. Even though the fines are paid now only by European automakers, Detroit automakers have long used their political muscle to block increases in the fines for fear that they might wind up paying the fines themselves someday.

One fuel-economy gambit has backfired for the auto industry. This has been to make SUVs so enormous that their gross vehicle weight exceeds 8,500 pounds, excluding them from all gas-mileage calculations.

By 1996, fully 4 percent of new vehicle sales consisted of light trucks that happened to weigh barely over 8,500 pounds, and so were exempt from inclusion in manufacturers' fuel-economy aver-ages.[17] Almost all of these vehicles were commercial-grade pickup trucks. There were also a few hundred military-style Hummer SUVs and a few thousand Chevrolet Suburbans with extra heavy-duty suspensions that were used by railroad and utility repair crews. These leviathans also qualified for even more lenient air-pollution rules than other full-size SUVs, being allowed to emit roughly 1.5 grams of smog-causing nitrogen oxides per mile, or 7.5 times the pollution of a car.

Not content with producing bruisers like the Lincoln Navigator, Ford decided in 1997 to manufacture a mass-market SUV version of its Brobdingnagian Super Duty pickup truck. Ford could scarcely have chosen a less suitable vehicle for family use. The Super Duty pickup was designed strictly for commercial use. It had an immensely powerful engine and such a strong suspension that the vehicle bounced around queasily unless it had at least a half-ton of cargo in the bed for ballast. Ford advertised this behemoth pickup on television by showing that it had the capacity to pull a freighter as tall as a 10-story building across a harbor.

When it went on sale two years later, the SUV version of the Super Duty would be named the Excursion. It would weigh 6,650 to 7,700 pounds even when empty, depending on whether the cus-tomer chose four-wheel drive and whether it was equipped with a V-8 or V-10 gasoline engine or a giant diesel engine. A well-equipped Excursion would weigh more than two Jeep Grand Cherokees or three Ford Focus compact sedans. Best of all for Ford, nearly 90 percent of the parts of an Excursion would be simply reused at little cost from the Super Duty pickup truck, and the two vehicles would be put together on the same assembly line in Louisville, Kentucky.

But as it turned out, the Excursion was too big. It sold well for a few months after its introduction in 1999 and then sales fell sharply, after the 50,000 families who wanted such a leviathan had purchased theirs. The Excursion never challenged the Suburban for dominance in the SUV market. Worst of all for the auto industry, the Excursion finally helped goad the environmental movement to begin paying close attention to the SUV problem.

The Sierra Club's Dan Becker and a few other staff officials at environmental groups had begun ruminating about how to address SUVs, after noticing the growing number of full-sized models starting to appear on the roads. Indeed, they were kicking themselves for not having noticed the problem sooner, and knew that the auto industry was far ahead of them in molding public opinion of SUVs. "We were stupid, we didn't know where the auto industry was going and we didn't have contacts in the auto industry to tell us," Becker says.

Environmentalists began looking for catchy slogans to attack a difficult target, a popular consumer product widely marketed with scenes of the great outdoors. They faced a big hurdle just in persuading other environmental activists and donors to environmental groups to criticize SUVs, since the off-road vehicles had been so successfully marketed to these groups. The immense Excursion became an easy target for environmental activists. Not only would it be the ultimate gas-guzzler, but it was two years away from mass production. No wealthy donors to environmental groups could possibly own one yet.

After a front-page article of mine appeared in 1997 about Ford's plans to build a monster SUV—one auto-industry source called it "the biggest, baddest vehicle on the block"—Dan Becker immediately started a contest on the Internet to name the vehicle. The frontrunner from the beginning was the "Ford Valdez," a reference to the Exxon Valdez oil tanker spill in 1989, which had fouled Alaska's Prince William Sound. Every television network and major news magazine in the country ran stories describing it as the Ford Valdez and recounting Detroit's rush toward larger SUVs.

"That was the first time we really broke through to large numbers of people who had never thought about the issue before," Becker said. By early 1998, the Sierra Club, Environmental Defense,

Friends of the Earth, the Natural Resources Defense Council, the Union of Concerned Scientists and the Public Interest Research Group had all begun gathering information about SUVs. But it would take another year before the environmental movement would mount its first big push for tougher regulations on SUVs.

While the environmentalists were slowly waking up, the automakers were still wheeling and dealing. Soon after the antipollution legislation in 1990 was approved by Congress, a dozen states from Virginia to Maine had begun protesting that it was not strict enough. The 1990 legislation did not allow the EPA to impose tighter federal standards until the 2004 model year, except if the industry voluntarily agreed to a tightening. But state governments had more discretion in setting rules. They could simply adopt California's standards instead, which were considerably stricter than the federal standards.

General Motors became concerned in the mid-1990s that the 12 states would follow California's example. Catalytic converters had been steadily improving, and reducing emissions would not be that difficult, but it would involve some extra expense that automakers wanted to minimize. So GM lobbyists conceived a cunning plan, and rallied other automakers behind it.

The automakers publicly volunteered to the EPA to reduce emissions nationwide by the 2001 model year to a level well below the federal standard, although still slightly higher than California's. Cars would only be allowed to emit 0.2 grams of nitrogen oxides per mile instead of 0.4 under the federal standard at the time. In exchange, the states had to agree not to tighten their standards down to California levels.

On December 17, 1997, the EPA and auto-industry officials triumphantly announced the deal, which would be phased in during the 1999, 2000 and 2001 model years. They all congratulated each other on having done something about air pollution, and the auto industry issued a blizzard of press releases touting the deal.

Not until the following day did it start to emerge that in putting together the plan, the auto industry had snuck in another loophole. The deal covered all cars, but it only covered light trucks with a gross vehicle weight of up to 6,000 pounds, which were required to reduce pollution to 0.4 grams of nitrogen oxides per mile from the previous federal standard of 0.7 grams. The agreement froze regulations for full-sized SUVs and pickups at the levels already prevailing. This meant that the big vehicles, the fastest-growing segment of the American market, could continue emitting as much as 1.1 grams of smog-causing nitrogen oxides per mile—five and a half times as much as the cars would be allowed.

Robert D. Brenner, the EPA's air policy director, and Samuel A. Leonard, the General Motors Corporation's top expert on air quality, said then that environmental regulators from the dozen states had never mentioned large light trucks, so they had not included them. But Sonia W. Hamel, director of air policy and planning for Massachusetts, strongly disagreed. She said the automakers abruptly announced at a meeting with the state regulators in the summer of 1996 that they wanted to freeze regulations for large light trucks, and had been criticized then by the state regulators. The EPA had nonetheless accepted the auto industry's position. State regulators grumbled a lot about this, but ended up accepting the deal because it would reduce emissions nationwide for smaller vehicles, while they could only act in their own, pollution-conscious states.

The air-pollution reduction plan was just one of several ways that the EPA repeatedly compromised during the Clinton Administration when it came to SUVs. The agency also abruptly stopped issuing in 1996 its detailed annual report on trends in automobile fuel economy. The official reason given by EPA was that the report was unnecessary because the Transportation Department issued raw data three times a year on the average fuel economy of new cars and light trucks. But the EPA report had been far more valuable because it included detailed statistics on why fuel economy was declining: horsepower and vehicle weight were rising and aerodynamics were deteriorating as automakers replaced cars with light trucks. Government officials told me on background that the real reason for discontinuing the report was that the EPA did not want to put a spotlight on how Detroit's popular SUVs were hurting American fuel-efficiency. (The EPA resumed issuing the report annually in 2000, by which time SUVs had become controversial, and many of the fuel-economy figures in this book are drawn from the report.)

The agency's leadership was concerned about SUVs by 1997, but not yet ready to criticize them publicly. I tried repeatedly in the autumn and early winter of 1997 to interview top EPA officials for a lengthy article about SUVs' contribution to smog and global warming, and was rebuffed. Top editors at the *Times* insisted I speak with the agency's leaders. Finally, the EPA press office arranged for me to speak with a top EPA official about the politically risky subject, but only if I refrained from identifying the official by name.

The official assured me that the agency was looking at the issue, but added a comment that neatly summarized Washington's attitudes toward SUVs for more than a generation: "We don't want to kill the goose that lays the golden eggs for the domestic industry."

While Washington dithered, however, Ford was becoming concerned that criticism of SUVs might hurt sales. Its public-policy committee, cochaired by two executive vice presidents, Peter Pestillo and Jacques Nasser, had made the issue a priority after the Excursion became controversial. The committee asked Kelly Brown, Ford's director of vehicle environmental engineering, for help and he had some interesting ideas.

It turned out that Ford vehicles were not only a little safer than those of other manufacturers—earning more five-star crash ratings than the vehicles of every other automaker combined—but tended to be less polluting, too. During the 1980s, Ford had sometimes paid large fines when its vehicles failed to meet EPA standards, particularly when the emissions systems on Ford vehicles had deteriorated too quickly in the first few years of use. Punished for these failures, Ford engineers had responded by overdesigning their catalytic converters through the 1990s, to the point that Ford Expeditions were only emitting a third of the pollution of Chevrolet Suburbans in EPA tests.

Catalytic-converter engineers at GM ridiculed the Ford designs to me on more than one occasion, saying that Ford was wasting money by making its vehicles cleaner than they had to be. The mark of efficient engineering, they said, was to meet a target with as little to spare as possible. But when the top executives on Ford's public-policy committee learned what the Ford engineers had already been doing for years, they decided to turn it into a competitive advantage.

Alex Trotman, Ford's chairman and CEO, announced to a sports arena full of auto writers at the Detroit auto show on January 5, 1998, that the automaker would voluntarily begin building all of its SUVs to emit roughly the same pollution as cars, starting with the 1999 model year. The Ford Expedition and Lincoln Navigator would be included in the plan, even though both had a gross vehicle weight well over 6,000 pounds and were completely exempt from the agreement that GM had crafted for the EPA to reduce emissions in the 2001 model year. "On emissions, anyway, there will be nothing to feel apologetic about in driving a sport utility vehicle," Trotman declared.

Brown and his aides calculated that it would only cost Ford another $100 per SUV to reduce their pollution to roughly the level of cars. The extra cost would be mainly for extra palladium, a precious metal more expensive than gold that makes catalytic converters work. For GM or Chrysler to match the same low emissions would cost them at least $200 per SUV, because their models were dirtier. Even foreign automakers like Toyota and Honda, which traditionally had led the way on clean-air issues, would be making dirtier SUVs than Ford. It would be years before other automakers could redesign their catalytic converters anyway. And the Ford initiative could prompt regulators to force every automaker to reduce pollution, a step that would force other automakers to spend more money than Ford.

Rival auto executives were livid. Bob Eaton of Chrysler called Ford executives in a fury, warning that the pollution initiative would backfire on the entire industry. Rival executives were especially mad because Ford reaped a public relations and lobbying bonanza from the announcement. Some news organizations initially ignored Trotman's announcement—*The Wall Street Journal*, with a dozen reporters at the auto show, did not even mention it the next day. But my editors put the story on the front page, and the *Times* ran an enthusiastic editorial a day later. Environmental groups found themselves in the unaccustomed position of lauding Ford as a good corporate citizen.

Somewhat later, I found myself in a very long, rambling conversation with the head of one of the Detroit automakers, chatting into the evening in his penthouse office. As the setting sun dyed the southeastern Michigan landscape below in beautiful shades of purple and magenta, the conversation turned to why the SUV pollution initiative had been so controversial within the industry. The executive confided that the real anger had been that Ford betrayed the other Detroit automakers by breaking what the executive described as a "gentleman's agreement" not to compete on reducing light-truck pollution. The executive refused to elaborate and told me not to use his name but gave me permission to use the information provided that I would "clean it up, sanitize it."

This was hard to sanitize—indeed, had any corporate lawyers been in the room, they probably would have keeled over on the carpet. Prompted by a young lawyer named Ralph Nader who had not yet become famous on auto-safety issues, the Justice Department had actually investigated the Detroit automakers in the mid-1960s on a very similar issue. The Department ended up filing an antitrust case against the manufacturers in 1968, accusing them of having a gentleman's agreement not to install catalytic converters and other costly emissions-control technology on any cars. The industry had quickly settled the lawsuit after President Nixon took office, not admitting any wrongdoing but agreeing to start installing catalytic converters and not to engage in any future gentleman's agreements to avoid competition on environmental matters. The Reagan Administration later allowed the agreement to expire, so it was not in effect in early 1998. But businesses in any industry are still not supposed to have gentlemen's agreements to avoid competition in any way.

I tried in vain to find executives willing to discuss the gentleman's agreement in detail and with their names attached. Executives from the Big Three denied that they ever shook hands on an agreement. Their occasional public statements that further reductions in tailpipe emissions were not feasible might have had the effect of signaling their positions to each other informally, however. I eventually gave up on finding any executive to go on the record, and only mentioned the existence of a gentleman's agreement briefly at the end of a later article, with vague attribution. Nader happened to read the article and urged Clinton Administration antitrust officials at the Justice Department to investigate. But with the antitrust office consumed by its attempt to break up the Microsoft Corporation, nothing ever happened.

13

SEDUCING THE PRESS

When the Ford Motor Company wanted to introduce the Lincoln
Mark VIII car to the media in the autumn of 1996, it followed a
time-honored script. About two dozen reporters met a dozen public
relations people at one of the entrances to Ford's headquarters in
Dearborn, Michigan, where we drank cups of apple cider, an
appropriately seasonal drink. Then two reporters and a PR person
climbed in each of the dozen Lincolns parked nearby. Inside each
car was a detailed route to follow for a long drive down freeways
and picturesque rural roads to a lovely inn on a bluff overlooking
the deep blue waters of the St. Clair River, about 60 miles away.
We had drinks on the veranda, then went inside for a lengthy dinner, during which a succession of auto engineers stood up and
described why the Mark VIII was an improvement on the Mark VII.
Late in the evening, the group drove back to Ford headquarters,
having been told to pay special attention to the illumination provided by the cars' bright, new halogen headlights.

All in all, it was an informative event, but quiet and not a lot of
fun. Other car introductions have been held in more glamorous

American cities, like San Francisco. European automakers like to introduce their cars in southern France and southern Spain, flying auto writers from the United States to attend. But the car introductions are generally tame, bland events, with a lot of driving on paved roads. The SUV introductions are different.

When the Explorer was redesigned, Ford's travel agency sent free round-trip airline tickets to auto writers around the country for a November jaunt to balmy Phoenix, Arizona. Clean-cut Ford employees in polo shirts met the incoming flights in Phoenix and ferried nearly three dozen arriving journalists in shuttle buses to the parking lot of a local museum. More Ford workers registered us for the event, handed out shirts emblazoned with an Explorer logo, and directed us to what was quickly dubbed the executive port-a-potty—a long trailer with green marble bathrooms inside. We were then pointed to a row of gleaming Ford Explorers of the previous model year.

Pairs of reporters hopped in the SUVs and drove up a highway into the hills, past saguaro cactus with upraised arms, finally turning left onto a dirt road. At the end of the road, near the site of a historic fort, Ford had erected a large, dark-green tent. Inside were a series of exhibits on why the new Explorer would be better than its predecessor, and a cluster of Ford engineers stood near each exhibit to provide extra details. The engineers and auto writers later sat around large tables in the tent for a catered lunch, then broke up into small groups to start driving the new Explorers, most of which had leather seats and every possible option.

For the next drive, I was assigned to an Explorer with Dale Claudepierre, Ford's top SUV engineer and the father of the Ford Expedition, and Jon Harmon, a Ford public relations person specializing in light-truck issues. We took turns driving up twisting, two-lane roads into the mountains.

When Harmon's turn came to drive, Claudepierre soon began needling him for only going a few miles per hour over the speed limit—a clear sign of inadequate virility among auto engineers. "If it says 50, you ought to go 70," Claudepierre said, sitting in the front passenger seat as I took my turn in the back, listening to the vehicle's interior noise level and scribbling notes.

Harmon drove faster, cars whistling past us in the other direction on the public road. Claudepierre was still not satisfied, saying that the rigidity of the new Explorer's passenger compartment could only be fully appreciated by taking corners at speeds far above what traffic engineers recommended on speed-limit signs. He chided Harmon for not making the SUV work harder, saying, "It'll get fat if you don't step on it!"

Harmon did step on it, and when we crested the next rise, the vehicle almost became airborne. On the downhill side of the rise, however, a police officer was just climbing out of his patrol car with a radar gun, preparing to catch speeders making exactly Harmon's mistake. Harmon violently mashed the brake pedal. Had we not all been wearing our seat belts—a requirement on press junkets—we would have been plastered to the inner surface of the windshield. The police officer did not get his radar gun up in time; Harmon narrowly escaped a ticket and drove more cautiously after that, while Claudepierre kept quiet.

A little farther into the woods, we came to a pleasant roadside chalet that Ford had partly leased, and we sipped hot cider. It was time to tackle the off-road driving course that Ford employees had marked in the nearby woods. A selection of expensive four-wheel-drive and all-wheel-drive vehicles waited outside for us to compare to the Explorer, including a Mercedes M-Class, a Dodge Durango and a Lexus RX-300. Like the other reporters, I tried the lengthy course several times in different models, lurching through muddy bogs, grinding up slippery slopes and trying to avoid ripping out the suspension on stumps. But these were not our SUVs, nor were we liable for any damage we might inflict, so the reporters approached the course with the gusto of teenagers at an amusement park with very, very expensive rides that were suddenly free for a day.

That night, Ford didn't send reporters out to tents under the stars—there would be no roughing it after a rough-road day. Instead, with dusk falling, we climbed back into the Explorers for the short drive to the elegant Enchantment Resort, where the suites cost $325 a night even in the off-season. Natural-gas fireplaces lit at the touch of a button in the spacious living room of each suite, which also had a bedroom and a four-chamber marble bathroom. Ford thoughtfully put a box of souvenirs in each reporter's suite, including warm windbreakers for the evening's entertainment.

Snugly dressed, we walked down a short path to a large clearing at the foot of red rock cliffs. A hired cowboy was sitting there by a large campfire and crooning Western songs. A hired astronomer had set up a large, powered telescope to provide views of Jupiter's moons while he talked about the night sky. Waitresses strolled through the group, offering duck pâté and other hors d'oeuvres. As the air grew chillier, we went into a large, heated tent where chefs served a gourmet meal of venison and other local delicacies, accompanied by a selection of excellent wines. We waddled back, stuffed, to our hotel suites, where it was hard to think critical thoughts about SUVs.

For a second shift of Ford employees, however, the work was just beginning. After a lavish breakfast at an outdoor amphitheater, my group of reporters was going to return to Phoenix the next day by test driving the new Mercury Mountaineer, a midsized Ford SUV that was nearly identical to the Explorer. That meant we were done with the Explorers that we had driven into the mountains. As we caroused at the campfires with Ford engineers, more Ford employees drove the mud-spattered Explorers back to Phoenix in the dark, arriving in the wee hours of the morning. Then they assiduously cleaned each Explorer inside and out and checked it out mechanically so that by midmorning it was in mint condition once more. For my group of reporters was just one of three waves of journalists whom Ford was hosting in Arizona that week, more than 100 auto writers altogether.

The Explorer junket reflected two media trends that have fed the SUV boom over the last two decades. Published reviews of new models too often include detailed assessments of off-road driving features that virtually no one needs. At the same time, automakers have warmly and lavishly embraced the media in ways that sometimes make it difficult for reporters to maintain objectivity. Indeed, while film studios take movie critics to fancy hotels to show them the next big releases, and while banks and brokerages sometimes entertain reporters at very expensive restaurants in New York, no other industry comes remotely close to wining and dining reporters to the extent that automakers do.

Even some auto executives and engineers complain that media comparisons of off-road driving capabilities have put pressure on them to design ever taller vehicles with ever more expensive four-wheel-drive systems that almost nobody needs. In an interview with *Automotive News* in 1999, Tom Schramski, a supervisor in Ford's SUV driveline engineering group, publicly acknowledged the influence of auto reviewers and the few other people who fully use four-wheel-drive systems. "Their rating of a vehicle under extreme conditions will influence the opinion of a person who never intends to go off road," he said. "We're going to continue to err on the side of satisfying the extreme user."[1]

Yet even while grousing, automakers compete to offer ever more extravagant junkets for the introduction of new SUVs, with off-road driving in increasingly exotic locations. The Explorer launch was somewhat unusual in that it was held in the United States at all—Canada's Hudson Bay, Mexico's Baja California and the jungles of Belize have all drawn recent junkets. Top honors in the category of adventurous introductions belong to Land Rover, which flew journalists all the way to Mongolia to introduce the Discovery Series II, so that press photographs of the new model would show it in the Gobi Desert.

Automakers pay all the expenses for most reporters on these junkets—indeed, the junkets are so lavish that it is beyond the means of almost all news organizations to cover the cost, and especially for the automotive-specialty magazines that send most of the journalists on these outings. Some national news organizations seldom send reporters because they have policies banning free trips, but corporate standards vary, especially for stringers who sell articles but are not actually drawing salaries.

In any case, paying your own way is often difficult. *The New York Times* sent me on the Explorer junket and paid for my air fare, and I did not take the gifts. But Ford refused even to tell me the cost of the resort suite, food and other amenities, so I made an estimate and wrote a check. Ford was so unaccustomed to reimbursement that it had no procedures for handling my check and never deposited mine, so I ended up insisting six months later that the company take another check, which Ford finally deposited.[2]

The automakers' generosity extends well beyond junkets. I had been on the auto beat in Detroit for less than two weeks in January 1996 when I interviewed Ford's chief financial officer, John Devine. He asked me what I drove and I told him that as a bureau chief for the *Times*, I had a company car, a two-year-old Ford Taurus. When he asked my opinion of it, I couldn't help mentioning that a problem with the starter had stranded me in a parking lot for several hours the previous weekend. Devine, who has since become the vice chairman of GM, immediately offered me a brand new Taurus as a replacement; I declined, citing the *Times*'s ethics policy.

For automakers, the junkets and other freebies are another form of marketing at a time when people around the globe are increasingly inured to advertising, especially the constant flood of automobile ads. Media coverage of the auto industry has a huge influence on which models people buy, an influence that is far greater than for other consumer products, according to Christopher J. Fraleigh, GM's executive director for marketing and advertising, who was recruited from the Pepsi-Cola Company.

"In most other categories—like soft drinks, the one I came from—90 to 95 percent of the messaging that reaches consumers is paid media," Fraleigh said in a speech in January 2002. "But paid

media represents less than 20 percent of the information that a consumer gets about new vehicles. They get the rest from *Consumer
Reports*, the automotive magazines, local newspaper articles, TV and
radio shows, and scores of Internet sites—not to mention their relatives and friends who are car enthusiasts. Running Pepsi and Mountain Dew, I didn't have to factor in what consumers were going to
read in buff books, *Consumer Reports* or their local newspaper."

Despite the limitations of auto advertising, the industry is also
the nation's largest advertiser by an enormous margin, accounting
for one in every seven dollars of all advertising spending. At the
peak of the dot-com boom in 1999, companies spent $3.18 billion
promoting all types of Internet services. But even this heavy spending, which prompted numerous newspaper and magazine articles
and caused many publications to step up their coverage of technology issues, was dwarfed that year by the ad spending of automakers and their dealers, at $13.3 billion.[3] The auto industry spends
more than twice as much money advertising its products as the
next two largest advertisers combined, financial services (from
banks to brokerages) and telecommunications businesses (from
local and long-distance phone service to cell phones and high-
speed data lines).

The auto industry's immense purchases of advertising, especially
for SUVs, can make it tricky for reporters to cover the industry. Top
auto executives hold frequent, off-the-record meetings with the
nation's leading publishers and editors, enjoying a level of access
that most politicians can only dream of. Automakers claim that
they do not use their advertising spending to influence coverage;
the biggest news organizations (especially *The New York Times*) try
to insulate their reporters from business pressures. I was never contacted or pressured in any way whatsoever by the business side of
The New York Times during all my critical coverage of SUVs, nor
were my editors, nor was I involved in efforts by the newspaper to
sell ads, even before I began writing articles that criticized SUVs.
But smaller publications have periodically run into advertising
problems after running stories that the automakers viewed as cre-

ating an unfavorable milieu for promoting their products. When *Sierra* magazine, which is affiliated with the Sierra Club, ran a fairly mild article criticizing the fuel economy of sport utility vehicles in November 1996, all of its SUV advertising disappeared immediately—7 percent of its gross revenues. The magazine's ad representative in Detroit tried unsuccessfully to block publication of the article before it ran, and quit in disgust when it appeared anyway. The magazine had to cut back the number of articles it printed in each issue, but remained willing to criticize the auto industry, said Joan N. Hamilton, the magazine's editor in chief.

The SUV boom has also benefited from the balkanization of automotive coverage at most large news organizations. Reporters in Detroit usually report to their organizations' business-news departments and either review new models or cover company news like profit reports, sales trends, manufacturing trends and management power struggles. Detroit-based reporters have extensive access to executives and engineers at auto shows, engineering conferences and other events, and the automakers' public-relations departments are usually happy to schedule interviews for these reporters.

Environmental issues involving automobiles are often covered by environmental reporters based in Washington, who typically report to their news organizations' national-news departments and stay in close touch with the EPA and environmentalists. Broad safety issues are covered by national-news reporters based in Washington who keep an eye on the Transportation Department. Allegations of safety defects in specific models tend to be covered as national news, rather than business news, by investigative reporters or product-liability reporters in Washington or New York.

Automakers provide environmental, safety, investigative and product-liability reporters with little access to engineers or executives, having them speak instead with public-relations representatives, corporate lawyers, lobbyists or, sometimes, former top regulators whom the automakers have hired as consultants. Environmental reporters, like the environmental movement they covered, largely ignored SUVs until the late 1990s. Safety reporters, especially those who specialized in personal-injury litigation, have heavily covered rollovers and rollover lawsuits for the last two decades, beginning with the "60 Minutes" documentary on Jeep rollovers in 1980. But safety reporters paid little attention until recently to many other SUV safety issues for which lawsuits were not being filed, like the damage inflicted by SUVs that hit cars.

What gives glamour to a story is a gripping tale from a survivor, a multimillion-dollar settlement, a billion-dollar verdict for punitive damages or a monumental struggle pitting corporations against personal-injury lawyers. Lawyers provide reporters with exhaustively reconstructed crashes, access to bereft crash victims or their family members and reams of automaker documents obtained through legal discovery. Media coverage, especially national television coverage, helps lawyers find clients who may have suffered similar fates, and who can be inexpensively and efficiently represented using the same automaker documents already obtained in previous litigation.

Another difficulty hampering the media's coverage of SUV issues has been the revolving door between auto writers in Detroit and the auto industry itself. Automakers hire a steady stream of auto writers, usually as public relations people but occasionally as marketers, too. This sometimes produces the disorienting effect of standing next to a reporter at a press conference one week, and finding the same person the next week on the other side of the room, representing an automaker. During the space of a few months in 2000, Ford hired reporters covering it for *The Wall Street Journal*, *Fortune* and Reuters.

The automakers offer better salaries and much better medical and retirement benefits to their white-collar employees than most news organizations do. This is mainly because the UAW negotiates superb benefits for its workers and the automakers then feel compelled to offer nearly as good benefits to managers. Public relations jobs are much coveted among auto writers as a result. When GM announced on February 20, 1996, that it was combining its Pontiac and GMC divisions, the very first question posed at the press conference involved what this would do to the total number of PR jobs available at the two companies. Automakers also give part-time consulting contracts to reporters with expertise in recently popular areas like towing.

The public relations departments of the automakers are immense, dwarfing those of federal agencies in Washington. GM has 150 press officers worldwide, plus battalions of media assistants who are not authorized to provide comments to the press. Just figuring out which spokesperson to contact on a given issue can sometimes require several phone calls. By comparison, George W. Bush campaigned successfully for the presidency of the United States with four spokespeople who had a dozen assistants.

Steady hiring by automakers for these giant public relations departments is one reason why media organizations have difficulty finding writers to cover the auto beat. An even bigger problem is metropolitan Detroit's reputation as an unattractive place to live and the auto beat's unfortunate reputation as an unglamorous form of newsroom Siberia. The city's winters are dreary, gray, cold and long, and the city's cultural life, although improving, is still hardly a match for New York, Washington, Chicago or Los Angeles. Moreover, the auto industry is widely perceived by reporters as a mature, often stodgy industry. Whereas hundreds of journalists flocked to cover exciting new computer and Internet technologies in California in the 1990s, Detroit attracted no such throngs even as SUVs brought renewed prosperity to the city.

The result is that automotive reporting, unlike the reporting on any other big industry in America, is dominated by a small contingent of reporters who have been covering the industry for decades and often share the industry's hostility to any criticism of automobiles. Many auto executives, in turn, have a limited awareness of safety and environmental concerns because they mainly read coverage of their industry, which is written by reporters who share their point of view.

But in the late 1990s, a well-read, more cosmopolitan executive rose to the top of the insular auto industry, a born leader who did not have the blinders of most managers in the auto industry, especially on environmental issues. The complete backing of Detroit's most powerful family allowed him to undertake experiments that no one else would have tried—indeed, that few auto executives would even have imagined. And no segment of the auto industry would be more shaped by his influence than SUVs.

14

THE GREEN PRINCE

Automakers have traditionally held their annual shareholders' meetings at big, impersonal hotels. Rows of chairs are arranged in the hotel ballroom, and the chairman stands at a lectern on a short, simple stage and tries to persuade the investors that the company is headed for larger and larger profits.

The Ford Motor Company's annual meeting on May 11, 2000, was nothing like that. It was held at the Atlanta Zoo, to which the company had given so much money that the zoo had gone from being ranked as one of the 10 worst zoos in the country to one of the 10 best. Ford Motor and the zoo erected an immense, air-conditioned tent at the back of the zoo and decorated the interior with palm trees and exhibits about electric cars, fuel cells, recycling and other environmentally responsible technologies. Ford Motor's top management spoke from a stage fringed with bamboo.

Stacked at the entrance to the tent were copies not just of Ford Motor's annual financial report but also its first annual "corporate citizenship report." The corporate citizenship report was not what anyone might expect of a giant automaker, especially the world's largest manufacturer of SUVs. William Clay Ford Jr. himself, the company's chairman, said in the front of the report that global warming was "a real issue" and warned that smog and traffic congestion were causing people to hate automobiles. A two-page section on SUVs later in the report bluntly acknowledged public concerns about the vehicles' poor fuel economy, high emissions of smog-causing gases and deadly effects on other motorists during crashes, and said that Ford would pursue technological solutions to these problems. A sidebar quoted at length the Sierra Club's scathing criticism of Ford's biggest SUV: "The nine-passenger Excursion is a suburban supertanker, stretching over 19 feet in length and slurping one gallon of gasoline for every 12 miles it travels. This 'suburban assault vehicle' spews as much global warming pollution into the air as two average cars."

Bill Ford had been the chairman of Ford Motor for 16 months, and had personally overseen the drafting of the report. The front of the report even contained a question-and-answer section in which an environmentalist asked him if he were concerned whether the auto industry might develop the same kind of liabilities as Big Tobacco as a result of manufacturing and promoting SUVs. Bill Ford began his reply with a one-word sentence: "Certainly." He went on to talk about the difficulties of improving fuel economy as long as gasoline was cheaper than bottled water. When I came across him in the tent before the annual meeting, I asked about the Big Tobacco comparison and he made the point again: "The court of public opinion sometimes decides before you're ready for them to decide, and I want to make sure we're ready and ahead of the curve." It was a gutsy stance to take for someone whose company depended on SUV profits.

Ford Motor's corporate citizenship report provoked an uproar. Television networks and most local stations across the country had skipped the annual meeting but covered the story heavily the next day. Environmentalists were surprised and cautiously favorable. But Ford dealers were furious at the company for saying anything about the shortcomings of its best-selling vehicles. GM and Chrysler executives were outraged. Bill Lovejoy, GM's group vice president for sales and marketing, had a typical response: "I for the life of me can't understand the comments he made—he must have been torn inside with that revelation. The sport utilities we produce are in line with government regulations and what consumers want."

The automotive press and Michigan lawmakers were upset too, warning that Bill Ford's position would embolden regulators. In an Op-Ed column for *The Wall Street Journal*, Brock Yates, editor-at-large for *Car and Driver* magazine and an outspoken defender of the auto industry's traditional positions on safety and environmental issues, asked "if the latest Mr. Ford isn't yet another guilt-ridden rich kid, not a proud tycoon like those who preceded him."

Looking just at his bloodlines, William Clay Ford Jr. seemed an unlikely knight to confront the dragons stalking the nation's roads. His father was the youngest of Henry Ford's four grandchildren, an heir to one of the world's great industrial fortunes. His mother was Martha Firestone, a granddaughter of Harvey Firestone, the tire magnate. His parents' lavish wedding on June 17, 1947, in Akron, Ohio, united two of the world's great manufacturing families and was described by breathless journalists at the time as the wedding of the century.

It would have been easy for Bill Ford to keep building SUVs and not worry about the problems, counting instead the billions of dollars pouring into the coffers of Ford Motor and the Ford family. Wall Street would have preferred that he do just that, and Bill Ford had to pay attention to what the financial community thought. Although a special class of stock gave the Ford family 40 percent of the votes on big corporate decisions, the family owned only 6 percent of the company's equity, with pension funds, other big institutions and the retirement accounts of Ford employees holding most of the rest.[1]

But despite being born as the closest thing Detroit has to royalty, despite growing up in the heart of the auto industry and despite spending his entire career at Ford Motor, Bill Ford was determined to make his company more progressive on social issues, especially the environment. It was a determination that came from his upbringing.

Born in Detroit on May 3, 1957, Bill Ford grew up in Grosse Pointe, a conservative, wealthy suburb with lots of trust-fund children of the auto industry's early barons. The Fords had been at the top of the Grosse Pointe social pyramid for three generations, above even the Chapins, and were lionized at the country club and closely followed by gossip columnists. But Billy, as he was known all the way into early adulthood, led a surprisingly normal existence. His parents relied less on nannies than many wealthy families, raising him and his three sisters themselves and encouraging him to play hockey with blue-collar children from outside Grosse Pointe. His father had grown up in the shadow of his elder brother, Henry Ford II, and Billy in turn received less media attention than his first cousin, Edsel Ford II, Henry's son. It was Edsel, not Billy, who was expected to grow up and run Ford Motor someday.

Billy's family also used to take him fly-fishing in northern Michigan. They waded some of the same streams that Ernest Hemingway fished as a boy and later described in stories like "Big Two-Hearted River." Billy was enchanted, and the experiences permanently shaped his view of the world. "I loved to camp and fish and be in the wild as a young boy, and what always struck me was when I went back to a place and saw it degraded," he recalls. "That really was the catalyst for me becoming interested" in the environment.

Young Billy also had an early exposure to liberal politics. While Henry Ford II had been quite conservative, William Clay Ford Sr. was not. He opposed the war in Vietnam. In 1968, when Billy was 11, his father and eldest sister worked hard as volunteers in the unsuccessful presidential campaign of Eugene McCarthy, a liberal Minnesota senator.[2]

Billy picked up trash as part of river cleanup efforts at Hotchkiss, the favorite New England boarding school of the Ford family as well as the Chapins of American Motors. As an undergraduate majoring in history at Princeton, Billy stayed up late into the night with other students discussing how to save the environment. He also met, and later married, a fellow student named Lisa who, like Billy, loved to play tennis. She shared his interest in the environment but thought he could make the biggest difference working within the family business.

Billy joined Ford Motor as a vehicle-planning analyst shortly after his graduation from Princeton in 1979. From the beginning he found it difficult. "Having come straight out of university, and one that had a liberal bent to it, and coming to an old-line automaker where people looked at me like a Bolshevik for even asking the questions—I was really dismayed," he said. He worried whether he was selling his soul by working for a company that produced large quantities of hazardous wastes in its manufacturing processes and assembled a product with substantial tailpipe emissions. "I wrestled nightly as I came up through the ranks," he said. "There were more than a few times that I told my wife I was going to leave to start an environmental group."

Each time, he was talked into remaining at the company. "My friends and my wife always convinced me that the impact I could have would be far greater if I stayed," he said. "And they were right, ultimately, but they were more patient than I was."

Lisa in particular persuaded him every time to stick with the company. When he decided to spend a year at business school, he leaned toward Harvard Business School, where the case study approach appealed to him because his verbal skills tended to be stronger than his math skills. But Lisa talked him into attending the highly quantitative program at the Massachusetts Institute of Technology instead, using a tennis analogy: If your forehand is strong, you should work on your backhand. He was one of only two people in his class who were not engineers by training.

He started working his way steadily up the management ranks at the same time, taking whatever job he was assigned. But he faced considerable hostility from top executives who felt threatened by the presence of a Ford family member. Henry Ford II had been an often tyrannical and moody boss leader, firing even company presidents like Lee Iacocca, whom he dismissed in 1978 with the famous comment, "Well, sometimes you just don't like somebody."[3] When Henry Ford II retired as chairman in 1980, Edsel Ford II was only 32, and Billy Ford was 23, too young to be given control of such a sprawling empire. So Henry turned the running of the company over to non-family managers for the first time in its 77-year history.

Henry declared publicly that there were no "crown princes" at the company, meaning that no one should assume that Edsel or Billy would ever run the company. Henry retained, however, the position of chairman of the Ford board's finance committee. Since the finance committee approved all large investments by the company, this allowed him to keep considerable power.

After working as a vehicle planner, Billy became a sales zone manager in New York and New Jersey. He was a member of the Ford negotiating team with the United Automobile Workers union in 1982, which produced a path-breaking model for cooperation between labor and management. He oversaw the marketing of commercial vehicles in Europe, then became the chairman of Ford Motor's Swiss operations in 1987.

The tour in Switzerland was an eye-opener for Bill Ford, as he started to be known. Environmentalists and business executives worked closely and harmoniously on many issues there, without anything like the mutual animosity he found in the United States, especially in Michigan.

Henry Ford II died on September 29, 1987. Bill Ford's father succeeded him as chairman of the board's powerful finance committee six weeks later. In 1988, while remaining in Switzerland, Bill Ford became a member of Ford Motor's board of directors. Top executives at Ford wanted him to abandon his membership in the Nature Conservancy, a moderate environmental group, as a condition for joining the board. "Somebody close to the board thought it would be a good idea if I stopped associating with crazies, and I assured them that not only was I not doing so, but that the group I was involved with, which was very benign—the Nature Conservancy—was made up of a cross-section of our customers," Ford said.

When he was transferred from Switzerland back to Ford headquarters the following year, he briefly oversaw heavy truck engineering and manufacturing. Then he became director, and later executive director, of business strategy at Ford Motor, giving him his first opportunity to put his environmental ideas into practice.

He circulated a memorandum scheduling a meeting to discuss the company's environmental policy in a conference room in the middle of the 11th floor of Ford Motor's headquarters, at the center of the company's executive suite. The memo drew an immediate response from the company's legal department, which warned him that the memo and any meeting could be used against Ford Motor in court. Bill Ford defiantly held the meeting anyway and began pushing environmental initiatives, starting with the recycling of office paper and moving on to more ambitious projects. Clipped wires were found in his office, and he suspected that his enemies within the company had bugged it, although he was never able to prove this.

Bill Ford began talking regularly to the leaders of environmental groups and to prominent environmental thinkers in the early 1990s. He looked at how companies like Dow Chemical had improved their performance. He read voraciously on how corporations could pursue environmentally sustainable growth. He bought a company in Colorado that produced some of the world's most expensive fly-fishing rods, so as to practice his skills at running a business and pursue his interest in environmentally responsible corporate practices at the same time. He also became a vegetarian and began exploring a wide range of religious practices, including several forms of Buddhism.

He and Lisa had four children, two girls and then two boys, and he took them fishing on the same rivers in northern Michigan that he had enjoyed as a boy. He watched with interest how they were exposed in elementary school to much more environmental education than he had ever received. He concluded that a younger generation of people around the world was increasingly interested in the environment, and would prefer to work for and buy the products of a company that shared their values. "It all helps the corporation, and in the end, I do believe it helps you in the marketplace," he said.

He also found that many young colleagues at Ford Motor shared his ideas. "There was a lot of grassroots desire to do this, but there were a few people in key management positions that didn't want to hear of it," Bill Ford said.

As his children grew up, Bill Ford increasingly saw his role at the company as being a steward or caretaker, someone who would look after the business for his children and grandchildren. He was alarmed when some of his cousins, needing money to support lavish lifestyles or costly divorces, sold some of their special shares to the general public. Although one of the youngest of Henry Ford's great-grandchildren, he took the lead in organizing a family fund that would buy the shares instead from any family member who wanted to sell, so as to keep the shares in the family and preserve family control over the Ford Motor Company.[4] For many years, Bill Ford would talk about his environmentalism in one breath and his desire to preserve the Ford Motor Company in the next, perceiving no conflict whatsoever between his top two priorities.

At the end of 1994, his first big opportunity at the Ford Motor Company came. His father stepped down as chairman of the finance committee and Bill Ford succeeded him. To take the powerful job, he was required to resign from active management at Ford, where he had just become vice president for commercial trucks. But the chairmanship allowed him to work closely with the company's outside directors, who would have the final say on who would eventually succeed Alex Trotman, who had become chairman and chief executive a year earlier.

Bill Ford's cousin, Edsel Ford II, had also been working his way up the management ranks. The cousins had joined the board at the same time in 1988. But Edsel did not have a committee chairmanship, so he had less contact with other board members. Within the company, where he had become president of Ford Credit in 1993, he did not have the same reputation as Bill. Edsel was genial and knew how to work a room—the dealers loved him. But Bill had an incisive intelligence. He had the manners of an investment banker, along with the intensity and a direct, earnest gaze. The outside directors and the rest of the Ford family were impressed with him.

During the mid-1990s, Bill Ford was an enthusiastic supporter of SUVs. He and Lisa sent their children to a Detroit-area prep school, instead of following the family tradition of dispatching them to a New England boarding school, and Bill noticed how many of the other parents were driving SUVs. Like many environmentalists, he was attracted to the vehicles' outdoorsy image and had not particularly focused on the environmental implications of a large-scale shift away from cars. On the board, he supported the decision to produce the Ford Expedition and Lincoln Navigator full-sized SUVs and then the gigantic Ford Excursion. While Bill took pride in driving an electric-powered Ford Ranger compact pickup truck to work, Lisa drove a Navigator after it came on the market in 1997.

Bill Ford did not have a long enough or broad enough track record at the company to become its chief executive officer, nor did he really want that job, with its all-consuming responsibilities for running the day-to-day operations of a giant global enterprise. Like his parents before him, he was devoted to his children, regularly leaving the office to attend their soccer games and other events. He also had his hands full running the Detroit Lions, a professional football team owned by his father, who was in declining health.

But Bill Ford did want to be chairman of the board, overseeing the company without having a lot of daily duties. Alex Trotman, like the many professional managers who had chafed in the days when Henry Ford II summarily hired and fired talented executives like Lee Iacocca, opposed any such resumption of direct family control over the company. Trotman argued that Ed Hagenlocker, the president of Ford automotive operations and the man who had continued building the company's light-truck operations into a powerhouse after Lutz's departure, was the obvious choice among the professional managers to succeed him as chairman and chief executive. Hagenlocker was a superb engineer and an excellent manager who was adored by his subordinates. But he was a weak public speaker who sometimes got his tongue tangled. He once embarrassed the company by accidentally but repeatedly referring in a speech to the Mercury "Mistake," when he meant the Mercury Mystique sedan.

Hagenlocker had an ambitious deputy, however: Jacques Nasser, the company's group vice president for vehicle development. Born in a mountain village in Lebanon, Nasser was four years old when his family moved to Australia. He was the only non-Anglo child in his class, and encountered frequent racism. "My brother and I [went] to school together, and we'd be in a fight almost every day," Nasser told *Fortune* magazine. "And if we weren't, we got to the point where we would start to look for one."[5] He added that the experience "taught me to read people pretty quickly. You're genuine or you're not. You're on my team, or you're not on my team. I'll beat the hell out of you, or you're going to beat the hell out of me."[6] That attitude served Nasser well after he joined Ford Motor as a financial analyst in Australia in 1968 and quickly rose through the ranks, serving in Europe, South America and the United States. He developed the nickname "Jac the Knife" for his ability to cut costs and lay off workers. He also had an eye for noticing details in a car that would not cost much to improve, but for which customers would be willing to pay considerably more.

From 1996 through 1998, Bill Ford steadily gathered support from the board's outside directors for a fairly unusual corporate structure: He would become chairman while Nasser would become CEO. The two men came up with a rough proposal of how they would work together. If made chairman, Bill Ford would handle public policy issues and serve as the liaison between the company and the board and between the company and the Ford family. Nasser would actually run the company, consulting frequently with Bill Ford on major strategy decisions and keeping him sufficiently informed that Bill Ford would be able to answer any questions from the board and the Ford family. But despite repeated requests from the board, the two men never actually put their division of responsibilities in writing, leaving it surprisingly nebulous just how involved Bill Ford would be in running the company.

When the drawbacks of SUVs started to become controversial in 1997, Bill Ford paid attention earlier than most auto-industry leaders. While other auto executives tended to read *The Wall Street Journal* or *USA Today*, which largely ignored the problems of SUVs, he and others in the extended Ford family were avid readers of *The New York Times*. Some cousins lived in New York City, and all 13 cousins, Henry Ford's great-grandchildren, shared the use of a vacation estate on Long Island.

Unlike many boards, the Ford board did not have a public policy committee then, delegating the task to a panel of top managers. Jacques Nasser and Peter Pestillo, an executive vice president who had long been a close ally of Bill Ford and lived a few houses from him in Grosse Pointe, jointly led the panel. In late 1997, the panel approved the plan for Ford to reduce voluntarily the air pollution from all its SUVs to roughly the same level as car emissions, a plan that Alex Trotman grumbled about but announced anyway at the Detroit auto show in January 1998. Executives at rival automakers were furious. Bill Ford was delighted.

Through this period, the Ford board remained wary of whether Nasser and Bill Ford had the seasoning to run the company, so the board extended Trotman's contract as CEO to run until December 31, 1999, more than a year after he would turn 65 and normally be expected to retire. But Bill Ford and Nasser were impatient. In September 1998, Bill Ford finally prevailed over Alex Trotman in a board vote, and Trotman was told by the board to retire at the end of the year, a year earlier than he had planned. According to *Fortune*, Trotman bitterly told Bill at the board meeting, "So now you have your monarchy back, Prince William."[7]

At 41, Bill Ford was now chairman. Nasser, now 50, was CEO. In an interview several months after he took over the top job, Bill Ford promised to pursue an environmental agenda. "I'm not sure, if I were chairman 10 years ago, the world would have been ready for my views," he said. But he maintained that his agenda would maximize profits for shareholders as well, by attracting more customers to the company's vehicles and by attracting better managers to Ford Motor.

Early differences between Nasser and Bill Ford were apparent even in their offices. The two men initially took equal-sized, adjacent offices, each with a 20-mile view across metropolitan Detroit. Bill Ford turned his office into a veritable greenhouse, with most of the vista obscured by potted ficus trees. More plants festooned the desk, coffee table and conference table, while the long shelf behind his desk was covered with peace lilies under special growing lights. "I need a machete," Mr. Ford quipped while walking in the office.

Nasser's office next door was a desert. A single, small plant in a small pot sat incongruously on the floor in front of the immense window. The plant, with coiled leaves resembling spikes, did not look happy. When asked soon after he became CEO how he became interested in the environment, Nasser never mentioned camping or rivers or great books. Instead, he turned the subject to the Internet, which fascinated him, plunging into an 11-minute soliloquy on the importance of brands and how their images were formed in the public mind. In an increasingly global economy, he said, consumers turn to a few brands known the world over, like

Volvo (which Ford Motor bought four weeks into Nasser's tenure). At the same time, the rise of the Internet and other forms of communications made it possible for information about a company's activities in any city to spread quickly all over the world. So to have a popular, global brand that consumers will seek out, a company must be a good corporate citizen everywhere, Nasser concluded. His enthusiasm seemed to wax every time he mentioned the Internet and wane when he came back to the environment.

But under Bill and Jacques, as they liked to be known, Ford Motor steadily pursued a theme of "Cleaner, Safer, Sooner." The goal was to deliver safe, environmentally responsible vehicles before the competition, and SUVs were a cornerstone of this effort. Within weeks, the announcements of safety and environmental advances started coming, each more surprising than the last, and each antagonizing the rest of the auto industry a little more. Through 1999 and the first half of 2000, it seemed like Ford was going to lead the auto industry into a fierce competition to produce the cleanest, safest SUVs possible.

On February 26, 1999, Ford Motor officials unveiled the first Excursion and proudly pointed out that it had a hollow, impact-absorbing steel bar below and just behind the bumper. They also touted the fact that more than 90 percent of the vehicle's parts had been designed for easy recycling. The reuse of resources was one of Bill Ford's pet causes, and Ford Motor also began buying up junk yards in the United States and acquired Europe's largest chain of repair shops, Kwik-Fit. The goal was to make money and do good by salvaging and reselling used auto parts instead of having them end up in landfills.

On May 17, 1999, Nasser himself stood in front of a row of television cameras at Ford headquarters and announced that Ford would voluntarily build all of its pickup trucks to emit as little smog-causing pollution as cars, just like its SUVs. The public relations staff released hundreds of helium-filled balloons, which began floating into the sky. Nasser gave the balloons a sour look—environmentalists have warned that turtles and other sea animals can choke on the remains of balloons—and joked that these were edible balloons. To build so many low-pollution SUVs and pickups, Ford Motor began stockpiling enormous quantities of costly palladium for high-performance catalytic converters.

Through the summer, Ford advertised its low-emissions SUVs and pickup trucks, trying to gain some advantage among consumers from its initiative. Executives at other automakers were deeply skeptical of this as a marketing strategy. "People don't really care—they just presume that we meet the standards and the standards are stringent," said Bernard Robertson, senior vice president for North American engineering at DaimlerChrysler.

Yet public pressure to do something about SUV air pollution was definitely building through the summer of 1999. Environmental groups were mounting their first real challenge to SUVs by urging the EPA to set tougher standards for them in the 2004 model year. The Public Interest Research Group, which is especially strong on university campuses, had young men and women go door to door and buttonhole motorists in parking lots, successfully arranging for more than 100,000 postcards to be sent to the EPA demanding a crackdown. The group also commissioned a 15-foot-tall inflatable red SUV dubbed the Exterminator, and used it as the centerpiece for holding small demonstrations in two dozen American cities to call for tighter rules. Auto lobbyists and public relations people amused themselves at some of the demonstrations by trying to count how many protesters had shown up in SUVs themselves. EPA officials were already moving to crack down on light-truck air pollution by this time, but the protests made it hard for the auto industry's allies in Congress to oppose the environmental agency.

On December 6, 1999, Ford Motor dropped out of the Global Climate Coalition, the industry group committed to blocking action to address global warming. While two junior European members, British Petroleum and Shell, had previously dropped out under pressure from European environmentalists, Ford was the first company on the coalition's board to leave the group, and the first American company to abandon the coalition. Bill Ford was becoming increasingly worried about global warming, remarking in a later speech: "The climate appears to be changing, the changes appear to be outside natural variation, and the likely consequences will be serious. From a business planning point of view, that issue is settled. Anyone who disagrees is, in my view, still in denial."[8]

Yet Ford Motor retained the position that the Kyoto Protocol should be broadened to include developing nations. Connie Holmes, the coalition's chairman, cynically observed that Ford's position did not seem much different from the coalition's. As it happened, Ford's engineers were secretly working on ways to address global warming, but were not yet ready to announce their plans.

Two weeks after Ford Motor left the Global Climate Coalition, President Clinton went to an elementary school in one of the poorest areas of Washington, D.C., and announced that he was imposing much stricter air pollution rules on all family vehicles. The new rules required steep reductions in allowable pollution from cars and light trucks alike manufactured in the 2004 and subsequent model years. Further reductions were required of light trucks in the 2007 and 2009 model years to bring them all the way down to the same level as cars. The choice of the school, Maury Elementary School, was no accident: the school nurse, Gloria Hickman, said that 25 of the school's 315 students suffered from asthma. "They come in frightened, short of breath, scared," she said. "It tugs at my heart."

GM had hired a law firm that prepared a four-inch-thick document for the Environmental Protection Agency on why the new rules were too stringent, laying the groundwork for a legal challenge. But Ford cut the ground out from under GM's arguments by saying that it had no objection to the new rules, that it had already met the 2004 standards with many of its SUVs and pickups, and that it was already working on ways to meet the 2007 and 2009 standards. GM decided not to sue the federal government to block the new rules, and reluctantly said that it would comply with them.

The rules nonetheless had an obvious shortcoming: They did nothing to address the high emissions from light trucks already on the road or from those scheduled to be built before the 2004 model year. Serendipitously, the regional transportation planning council for the greater Washington area realized after Clinton's announcement that it would probably be unable to comply with federal air-quality rules for the region in the years ahead. The main culprit? The council had been assuming that people were still driving mostly cars, and had failed to take into account in its pollution projections the shift toward more heavily polluting SUVs. The council has been struggling ever since to come up with a way to reduce emissions enough to meet the air-quality rules; failure to meet them could result in the region's losing federal transportation subsidies.

The Ford annual meeting in Atlanta five months later marked another milestone. With the presidential campaign in full swing, Bill Ford was asked at the press conference after the meeting what he thought of the famous comment about eliminating internal-combustion engines in *Earth in the Balance*, the book by Al Gore, the Democratic nominee. Bill Ford bravely responded that while he didn't agree with all of Al Gore's positions, Ford Motor had "very good relations" with the Vice President and believed that "the internal combustion engine has contributed to a lot of environmental woes."

Prominent Republicans had been saying that Gore was vulnerable in industrial states like Michigan and Ohio to accusations that he was a menace to auto-industry jobs. Bill Ford's comments were seized upon by Democrats to show that Gore was not an environmental extremist. And in the end, Gore's stance on automobiles did not become a significant issue in the election campaign. Republicans seethed, as did executives at other automakers, who were funneling most of their political contributions to George W. Bush.

The auto press and Michigan lawmakers were upset after the annual meeting in Atlanta. "Ford Admits Its Trucks Hurt Earth," was the large headline in *The Detroit Free Press*. A columnist for *The*

Detroit News warned that the automaker was emboldening environmentalists. The industry's favorite lawmakers in Washington were alarmed that Ford was undercutting their efforts. "It does make it more difficult for us to propose reasonable standards," said Paul F. Welday, the chief of staff for Representative Joe Knollenberg, a Michigan Republican on the Appropriations Committee. "The company is trying to find itself right now, and we're not sure where it is."

Ford's corporate citizenship report also drew a lot of snide comments from other automakers, who observed that while the report acknowledged the shortcomings of SUVs, the company had nothing new to announce to address these shortcomings. Even some Ford executives were irked, with one quipping that the message of the report seemed to be that, "We hate ourselves, but we're going to make as many as we can."

Bill Ford himself was defensive about the Excursion at the annual meeting, criticizing it while at the same time pledging to continue making it. "If we didn't provide that vehicle, someone else would, and they wouldn't provide it as responsibly as we do," he said.

He had a point, too. Other automakers would have been delighted if Ford stopped making the Excursion. "If they withdraw from that market, we'll continue to sell the Suburban," GM's Lovejoy said.

Two months after the Atlanta annual meeting, Ford Motor dropped its biggest bombshell of all. At the National Press Club in Washington, Nasser announced that the company would increase the average gas mileage of its sport utilities by 25 percent, almost 5 miles per gallon, within five years. He and his aides also vowed that they would accomplish this feat without any gimmicks: not by increasing the production of dual-fuel vehicles or producing more SUVs over 8,500 pounds or any of the other tricks automakers had learned over the years. The Excursion would be included in the plan. A third of the improvement would be achieved by changes in the mix of SUVs that Ford sold, notably the introduction of the car-based Ford Escape and possibly the termination of the Excursion someday. But the rest of the gains would come from raising the gas mileage of existing models.

For years, Ford and other automakers had insisted that the technology to improve fuel economy did not exist and that American consumers did not care about gas mileage anyway. All of a sudden, top Ford executives were saying the opposite. "Everything we're doing is something already tested and proven, and some of it is already in production elsewhere" within Ford, said Kelly Brown, Ford's director of vehicle environmental engineering. Ford Motor planned a similar pledge to improve the gas mileage of its minivans and pickup trucks as soon as some technical details could be worked out, he added.

Janet Mullins Grissom, Ford's vice president for Washington affairs, chimed in that fuel economy was important to the public after all and that previous market research showing otherwise had not been accurate. Market research, she said, "is just like polling—it depends on how you ask the question." Nasser himself said repeatedly that making Ford Motor the industry leader in SUV fuel economy would so improve the company's image that the effort would pay for itself in increased sales.

Executives at rival automakers were aghast. For a quarter of a century they had been quietly and very profitably building ever more light trucks with gas mileage that was considerably inferior to the mileage of cars. Suddenly, Ford was drawing attention to the poor fuel-efficiency of the most profitable segment of the market. Ford was not saying how it would improve gas mileage, but all of the proven approaches were expensive: substituting high-strength, lightweight alloys for steel, using more electric motors and installing more sophisticated engines.

DaimlerChrysler refused to say anything publicly the day of Nasser's announcement, while GM simply said that it had no plans to make any such commitments. But Ford Motor's commitment received so much attention that Harry Pearce, GM's vice chairman, became worried that the Ford strategy of positioning itself as an environmental leader was actually succeeding. Detroit had not been too worried about quality in the 1970s and 1980s, until Japanese competition forced the domestic industry to focus on the issue. Now, Ford seemed to be starting a competitive free-for-all over who could produce the greenest vehicles.

A week after Nasser's announcement, Pearce called a hastily organized press conference in suburban Detroit at GM's truck engineering center, a vast warren of offices with twice the floor space of the Empire State Building. His public relations staff parked several GM pickups and SUVs equipped with experimental, fuel-saving technology in a white-walled, concrete-floored workroom, and put out several rows of metal chairs for reporters. Pearce stood behind a lectern, his white hair cropped short and his posture ramrod straight, a legacy of his early career as an Air Force lawyer.

Pearce started by pointing out that GM actually had slightly better average gas mileage than Ford for its SUVs and for its light trucks overall. In an extraordinary example of corporate one-upsmanship, he then declared that no matter how much Ford increased the gas mileage of its SUVs over the next five years, GM would make sure that its SUVs would have even better average mileage. He proceeded to broaden the challenge, saying that no matter how much Ford increased the average mileage of all its light trucks, GM would achieve better mileage for all its light trucks, too.

"GM will still be the leader in five years, and in 15 years for that matter," he said, chin jutting.

Pearce made clear that it was the competition with Ford that prompted him to speak out. "What annoys me is the perception that seems to come from that press conference that Ford is somehow the environmental leader," he said. GM was the real environmental leader, with its ambitious research programs on hybrid gasoline-electric cars and fuel cells, he contended.

It was a bold claim, which did not stand up to close scrutiny.

Ford had voluntarily and deeply reduced air pollution from its entire lineup of light trucks; GM had not even bothered to match Ford's example. Ford had broken ranks with the industry and committed itself to improving SUV fuel economy; GM was merely saying "me too," albeit while widening the competition to minivans and pickups.

A few months later, GM held a press conference in its environmental policy planning room. The walls happened to be covered with internal charts showing, among other things, projected fuel economy in future years for various models, so I wandered over and read them after the speeches. Some of the charts had notations forecasting the fuel-economy gains that Ford would have to make to achieve its 25 percent target, along with comments that GM's future models were not yet on course to match Ford's projected improvements.

Chrysler, the American unit of DaimlerChrysler, conspicuously refrained from matching with its Jeeps and other light trucks either Nasser's or Pearce's pledges to improve gas mileage. "We'll let them do the tit for tat," a Chrysler spokesman said. The company was even more dependent financially on light trucks than Ford or GM, and its executives tended to be the most hostile in the auto industry to government safety and environmental regulations. It was also mulling the introduction of a Suburban-sized giant SUV based on the Dodge Ram pickup truck, which would push down the average fuel economy of its SUVs and of its light trucks overall.

Eight months later, however, Jürgen Schrempp, the German chairman of DaimlerChrysler, came to New York City and held an off-the-record meeting with senior editors at *The New York Times*. I did not attend, but asked my editor to inquire on my behalf why Ford and General Motors had pledged to improve their fuel economy voluntarily while Chrysler had not. Schrempp was surprised by the question and responded that his company would absolutely keep up with any improvements that Ford and GM made.

When I heard of this response, I called Schrempp's personal

spokesman, a German who had accompanied his boss to the meeting and then flown back to Germany. He cheerfully put Schrempp's comment on the record, adding that DaimlerChrysler had long experience with voluntary commitments in Europe, where automakers and regulators tended to be chummier than in the United States. DaimlerChrysler had taped the meeting with the editors with the permission of everyone present, and provided an official version of Schrempp's comment. "We are committed to improving the fuel efficiency of all our vehicles," Schrempp had said. "Our fleet will match or exceed those of other full-line manufacturers."

Schrempp had not specified a time frame, nor had he said how he was measuring the fleet; a Chrysler spokesman said that he had been referring to cars and to light trucks, but not to SUVs separately. Like Pearce, Schrempp had also put his comments in terms of keeping up with the competition. In other words, if Ford failed to keep its pledge, everyone else would be off the hook, too. GM and Chrysler officials told reporters anonymously that they doubted Ford could pull it off; Ford officials insisted they could and would manage to increase the gas mileage of their SUVs by 25 percent by 2005.

Chrysler officials were nonetheless angry when they learned what Schrempp had volunteered them to do. "It's going to be news to a lot of people who are toiling in the fields on our fuel economy and on our future products," said an American executive at Chrysler who insisted on anonymity. "I really don't think that's something the company has to do to sell cars."

As it turned out, however, nobody at Chrysler or GM had to worry about Ford Motor's deriving any marketing advantage from its safety and environmental initiatives. Exactly a week after Pearce responded heatedly to Ford Motor's plans for improving fuel economy, a crisis engulfed Ford that would eclipse everything else the company had done to project a public-spirited image for its SUVs.

15

THE FORD EXPLORER-
FIRESTONE TIRE DEBACLE

No automaker's leaders had ever endured anything like the drubbing that Ford executives faced at two Congressional hearings on September 6, 2000.

Through the 1980s and 1990s, Congress had seldom taken much interest in investigating the auto industry. In the 1960s and 1970s, auto executives were frequently called to task before Congressional committees, but in that more decorous era of Washington politics, witnesses were typically warned of the questions in advance and the hearings were often fairly courteous. But for the Ford executives on September 6, there would be no warning of the questions, and the denunciations would start at 10 A.M. and last far into the night.

The interrogation began in one of the less prepossessing Senate hearing rooms, a very modest, white-walled room with no windows on the first floor of the Dirksen Building, across Constitution Avenue from the Capitol. Throngs of lobbyists and reporters showed up, and most were forced to watch the proceedings on a closed-circuit television from an adjacent room. Several dozen lobbyists were allowed into the seats at the back of the room because they had lined up very early that morning—or, in some cases, had hired people to wait in line for them. High-intensity television lights were pointing in all directions, and before the hearing had even begun, the room was sweltering hot. Many in the room took off their suit jackets, but as the cameras rolled, executives from the Ford Motor Company and Bridgestone/Firestone Inc. had to keep their jackets on. Facing the senators from seats in the front row of the hearing room, the executives formed a dark gray and blue phalanx with the exception of Helen Petrauskas, Ford's vice president for safety and the environment, who defiantly wore a canary-yellow suit.

Senator Richard C. Shelby, the Alabama Republican who chaired the Transportation Subcommittee of the Appropriations Committee, set the tone for the meeting with his opening remarks. He ran through a litany of early signs that Firestone tires installed on Ford Explorers were failing and causing catastrophic rollovers, signs that Ford, Firestone and NHTSA had ignored or even concealed. A State Farm insurance analyst had notified NHTSA's Office of Defects Investigation in July 1998 of a growing number of tire failures on Explorers. A Ford dealer in Saudi Arabia repeatedly warned the automaker the same year that Firestone tires were failing on Explorers. A Ford memo in March 1999 said that Firestone's legal staff did not want to replace tires in Saudi Arabia for fear that doing so would require Firestone to notify NHTSA, and added that a Ford lawyer had worries "similar to the Firestone concerns."

Shelby scornfully berated the Ford and Firestone officials sitting quietly before him. "We are here because Ford and Firestone had at a minimum a moral obligation to make sure that the products they sell to the American public and other people in other countries are safe," he said. "And yet they both failed to bring this issue to consumers and the federal government's attention, at the cost of dozens of lives, I am afraid."

Six more senators took turns piling on, adding similar comments about the conduct of Ford and Firestone. They were followed by Joan Claybrook, the president of Public Citizen and a former NHTSA administrator, and by David Pittle, the technical director of Consumers Union, who also condemned Ford, Firestone and NHTSA.

Only then were Petrauskas and Masatoshi Ono, the chairman and chief executive of Bridgestone/Firestone, the American unit of Bridgestone of Japan, allowed to speak, along with Dr. Sue Bailey, the acting NHTSA administrator. Despite a warning from Senator Shelby not to blame each other, the Ford and Firestone officials did just that.

Petrauskas pointed out that Explorers equipped with Goodyear tires were not having problems. Ono responded that the problem lay in Explorers that were rolling over. "I come before you to apologize to you, the American people and especially to the families who have lost loved ones in these terrible rollover accidents," Ono said in halting English.

The finger-pointing continued when the Ford and Firestone executives went across Capitol Hill that afternoon and were joined by Jacques Nasser for an additional eight hours of testimony before a House panel. The mutual recriminations were typical of an episode that was a debacle not just for Ford and Firestone but for the whole auto industry. Also typical of the debacle was the condemnation on Capitol Hill from politicians, and the massive media coverage. But at the heart of the whole fiasco lay a remarkable series of mistakes and missed opportunities by everyone involved in the debacle.

Most of the mistakes, if they had occurred separately, would not have caused a problem. But coming in succession, year after year, they allowed a significant safety problem to develop that caused as many as 300 deaths worldwide and nearly a thousand injuries. The victims were unsuspecting drivers and occupants of Ford Explorers.

*

Daniel P. Van Etten was 19 when he hopped into a friend's Explorer for the long trip back to West Virginia University after spending spring break of his freshman year with his family in southern Florida in March 1997. He was big, 285 pounds, and West Virginia had actively recruited him to play offensive or defensive line on its football team. He was tall, popular and handsome, with a great future.

Making several stops along the drive up Interstate 95, the Explorer became more and more full. By the time the group stopped to refill the gas tank just short of the Georgia border, there were five people stuffed in the two-door Explorer: four football players from West Virginia University, including Van Etten, and a girlfriend of one of the other players, who was wedged between two of the players in the back seat. The cargo area at the back of the vehicle was crammed with luggage.

Van Etten took the wheel at midnight, after the Explorer had been refueled, and continued the drive up the interstate highway. His friends were dozing when, at 1:25 A.M. in southern Georgia, the left rear tire, a Firestone ATX, came apart, the tread peeling off like the skin of an orange.

The vehicle began weaving back and forth sharply, then rolled over. The football player in the front passenger seat was wearing his seat belt and suffered only minor injuries. The two football players and the young woman in the back seat were wedged in so tightly that not one was ejected from the vehicle even though they were not wearing their seat belts. They escaped serious injury. But Van Etten, who was not wearing his seat belt, was thrown from the vehicle and killed.

"He was just a young kid coming back from spring break," said Doc Holliday, the football coach who had recruited Van Etten for West Virginia University. "You don't know how far he would have gone."

For a long time after the crash, Danny Van Etten's mother, Kim Van Etten, left his room untouched. She would go in there, sit down, close her eyes and breathe, convinced that she could still smell him. She would hold his baseball glove, which still had his scent. But after four years, she finally took his clothes out of the room and repainted it.

"I feel like I'm betraying him," she said. "He was beautiful, he looked like he walked out of *GQ*."

Danny Van Etten's untimely death was one of the early ones in Explorers equipped with Firestone tires that came apart, and many more would follow. Yet for the first seven years that the Explorer was on the road—all the way up until Van Etten died—Explorer occupants actually had a lower rate of tire-related deaths than occupants of other SUVs.

Through the early 1990s, occupants of other SUVs died in tire-related crashes at a rate of 5.5 per million SUVs on the road, an analysis of federal fatality data would show.[1] The rate for other SUVs declined slowly through the decade, as tire quality improved and more of the SUVs on the road were larger models that were less prone to flipping over and were likely to be driven by older, more careful drivers. By 1999, the death rate for other SUVs was 3.5 per million vehicles.

Car occupants had a death rate of about 3 per million vehicles per year in the early 1990s, and this rate also fell slowly to 2.2 per million by 1999. Explorer occupants had virtually no deaths related to tires in the early 1990s, partly because their tires were new. But the tire-related death rate in Explorers rose to 3.6 per million Explorers in 1995, fell slightly to 3.4 in 1996 and then increased to 5.3 in 1997, the year of Danny Van Etten's death. The death rate climbed further in 1998, then leaped to 18.7 per million Explorers in 1999—one-sixth of all rollover deaths in Explorers that year.

One person who took notice of the problem and started tracking it in earnest was Sean Kane, a very bright, young traffic safety consultant for personal-injury lawyers. Unlike most safety consultants, who specialized in big-money issues like rollovers or fires, he was interested in tires. As an undergraduate at Stonehill College in Easton, Massachusetts, Kane had earned money by working in his spare time at tire stores. After graduation in 1989, he worked for a year for a tire distributor in Boston, where he says he learned how poorly data is collected on tire problems. He moved to Washington and took a 60-percent pay cut to work for the Center for Auto Safety, a low-budget, non-profit group in Washington that has championed many improvements in regulations. After a year and a half there, he went to work for another legend in automotive safety, Ralph Hoar, who ran his own consulting firm that helped trial lawyers sue automakers and other manufacturers. Kane became a specialist in the arcane art of mining government databases for evidence of safety defects.

NHTSA maintains several databases on crashes, using clerks who enter data from crash reports supplied by state and local law enforcement agencies. The best of these databases, the Fatality Analysis Reporting System, or FARS, covers every fatal crash in the country, gathering 114 different details about each of the nearly 42,000 deaths on the nation's roads each year, including the angle of impact of each crash, the speed of the vehicles, the sobriety of the drivers and so forth. Less detailed databases cover small samples of less serious crashes. These crash databases are invaluable for researchers looking at broad safety trends.

The crash databases only cover the kind of fairly basic information to be found on every crash report, like the number of occupants of each vehicle, how many people were hurt, whether or not any of the vehicles rolled over and so forth. So the data is seldom of use in identifying rarely occurring flaws with specific models. One exception is that FARS does have a category for tire-related deaths. But even the FARS data on crashes in each year does not become available until autumn of the following year, making it of little use in spotting problems quickly.

Another database, relied on by NHTSA and lawyers alike, keeps track of complaints about specific models. Many of these complaints come from consumers calling the agency's toll-free number,

1-888-327-4236. But the information from these calls is often fragmentary, with consumers sometimes unsure of their vehicle model,
and especially unsure of details like their tire model. Much more
detailed complaints come from personal-injury lawyers around the
country, who voluntarily fill in the forms in great detail about cases
that they file. NHTSA engineers keep track of complaints and open
investigations if they see a pattern of problems, or sometimes if
they receive even a single complaint about a potentially important
vehicle part.

Through the early 1990s, however, lawyers became more and
more disgusted with NHTSA. Many were deeply unhappy when
the agency closed the Bronco II rollover investigation in 1990 and
some agency officials left the government and became expert witnesses for Ford in Bronco II litigation. The dismay of lawyers
increased when NHTSA opened investigations into certain General
tires, especially on Ford Bronco IIs, in 1993 and certain Michelin
tires on various light trucks two years later, only to close each
investigation without any finding of wrongdoing, helping the tire
makers defeat lawsuits against them.

In 1994, NHTSA basically abandoned a case alleging that the
fuel tanks on GM pickups were prone to rupture and catch fire during crashes. The Transportation Department said that the fuel tanks
were potentially lethal, but GM denied this and was allowed to settle the case by spending $51 million on safety programs while
doing nothing to repair the pickups themselves. In 1995, NHTSA
closed a huge investigation into rear liftgate latches on Chrysler
minivans after the company agreed to ask minivan owners to bring
in their vehicles for repairs, provided that the government did not
call it a formal recall or find that the latches were defective. NHTSA
defended the deal as the fastest way to get millions of minivans
repaired quickly, since Chrysler was determined to fight any recall
in court. But the outcome did nothing for personal-injury lawyers
with cases against Chrysler, or for their clients.

The outcomes of the pickup and rear liftgate investigations especially infuriated personal-injury lawyers because GM and Chrysler each used their connections in Congress to bring considerable political pressure to bear on NHTSA not to impose harsher sanctions. Agency officials were sometimes openly contemptuous of the lawyers, too, describing them as more interested in their fees than in public safety. Angry at what they viewed as a fickle regulator too close to the automakers, the lawyers became less inclined to keep filling out complaint forms on their cases.

Sean Kane was already accustomed to mining the complaint database for information when he began hearing from lawyers in Texas in the spring of 1996 about problems with Firestone ATX tires on Ford Explorers. That November, he helped KPRC, a local television station in Houston, produce a damning two-part report on the tires, and the station subsequently referred callers with tire problems to him. But as often happens with local television reports far from major media centers like Washington or New York, the documentary attracted no broader attention.

At the end of 1996, Kane and two of Hoar's other aides left and set up their own consulting firm, Strategic Safety, to work for trial lawyers in competition with their former boss. Kane says he began checking the NHTSA complaint database every week for tire complaints, even when he did not have any lawyers paying him to do so. He painstakingly sifted through the often fragmentary complaints from consumers to figure out which tire models and vehicle models were actually involved.

Kane's clients were mainly lawyers in Texas. Motorists there drove long distances at high speeds in very hot weather, the worst possible conditions for any tire, since overheating weakens the chemical bonds that hold a tire together.

One of the Texas lawyers was Rob Ammons, who recalls that a pattern had developed by 1997. "I began to see pictures of Explorers lying upside [down] on the road with a tread nearby, and it dawned on me that we had a problem," he said.

Kane approached television news magazine shows in 1998 and

asked if they would be interested in doing a story on defective tires. He had earlier culled several dozen complaints from the database and pieced together that they involved Firestone ATX tires, often installed on Ford Explorers. But he also had a problem: Firestone in particular had been settling cases practically as soon as they were filed, so personal-injury lawyers had done little legal discovery. As a result, the lawyers and Kane had obtained few incriminating documents showing that Ford or Firestone knew of a broader problem. The few documents that were obtained, notably in the Van Etten case, were under court seal at Firestone's insistence as part of settlement agreements.

No television show took Kane up on the story. Auto-safety stories were still in disrepute at television networks after NBC's "Dateline" had aired footage in November 1993 of a GM pickup bursting into flames in a side-impact collision. The show did not disclose that the consultants who staged the test had rigged the pickups with model rocket engines to ignite the fuel. NBC later apologized, but the incident cast a cloud over auto-safety coverage on television.

Firestone's sealing of records meant that the lawyers did not have many documents that they could show to reporters or to NHTSA to demonstrate that a problem existed. The legal "gag orders" would not have prevented the lawyers from filling out NHTSA's complaint forms, however, and NHTSA has the legal authority to demand any document from any manufacturer of automotive equipment once the agency hears that an incriminating document exists.

Kane did not tell NHTSA safety investigators about the tire problems, although he says that he spoke to them practically every week on other issues. Nor did Kane or the Texas lawyers submit complaints to the agency's database. "Everyone was very leery of the agency getting involved with this because a number of plaintiff lawyers have been burned when an investigation has been opened and closed without a finding of a defect—basically, it's an agency that has a long history of being swayed by political winds," Kane said. "Everybody was like, 'If the agency gets involved in this, that could be a real problem.'"

Ricardo Martinez, the safety agency's administrator from 1994 to 1999, would later say the agency might have acted if it had been told of a problem. But Kane doubts this. Alerting the regulators to an issue without documents in hand to prove a broad problem would only result in a whitewash investigation that would have hurt the interests of people injured in crashes, he contends. "Would it have made much of a difference if NHTSA knew of some lawsuits? I doubt it."

While Kane was working with lawyers in Texas and with the Van Etten family's lawyers in south Georgia, a few lawyers elsewhere were also beginning to sue Firestone. Tab Turner, a flamboyant Arkansas lawyer who drove a big Chevrolet Suburban and bought his own jet airplane, a Cessna, with his winnings from lawsuits on other automotive issues, especially rollovers, says that his staff mailed two Firestone-related complaints to NHTSA in the mid-1990s but that the agency never put them into the database. Bruce Kaster, who is based in Ocala, Florida, and is the chairman of the national committee of plaintiffs' lawyers specializing in tire cases, says that he did not tell the government about the problem or fill out complaint forms because he doubted NHTSA would do anything about it. "I'm cynical is why I didn't talk to them," he said. "As long as big business and bankers run the government of the United States, regulation is not going to be effective."

As trial lawyers and their consultants geared up from 1996 through 1998 to fight Firestone, the tire maker was beginning to receive warnings that something was wrong with its tires. State officials in Arizona, where the blazing summer heat is an ordeal for any tire, notified the company in the summer of 1996 that the tread had peeled off two Firestone ATX tires, causing crashes. Firestone dismissed the problem by saying that the tires were inadequately maintained. As it happened, Firestone was already in the process of discontinuing the ATX tires then, manufacturing instead Wilderness AT tires of the same size and similar, but not identical, design.

State Farm began asking Firestone in 1998 to reimburse it for the cost of insurance claims involving tire failures on Explorers, after drawing its own conclusion that the tires were failing with excessive frequency. Firestone agreed to pay; it later said that the claims were all small and it was cheaper to pay than to pick a quarrel with State Farm.

Another warning for Firestone lay in the growing volume of lawsuits involving the tires. While Firestone settled most of these cases, it won the only case that actually produced a verdict. That case involved a young woman in Texas who died when her Explorer crashed after a tire came apart. The woman had set off on a drive to New Mexico despite strong warnings from her Ford dealership that her tires were about to fail. The dealership refused to rotate the tires because they were in such bad shape and even called her at home to urge her to get new tires when she declined to buy them at the dealership.

Firestone made an important change in the design of the Wilderness AT tire in May 1998, doubling the thickness of a rubber wedge inside the corners of the tire near where the sidewall met the tread. Such wedges, found in many tires, are designed to stop cracks from spreading across the width of the tire in a way that can cause the tread to peel off. Firestone insists to this day that the thicker wedges were a routine improvement that it also made to other tire models through the late 1990s. But the plaintiffs' lawyers and later Ford would seize upon the change as evidence that the company knew of a problem at least by early 1998 and was trying to fix it.

Ford had somewhat less warning of a problem. It was not always named as a defendant in the early lawsuits—Kane said that he and the lawyers with whom he worked paid little attention to the automaker. Ford also left all of the warranty and repair of tires to Firestone, to the point that buyers of new Explorers actually received two warranties in their glove compartments, one from Firestone for the tires and one from Ford for the rest of the vehicle.

But by late 1997, Ford was beginning to receive letters from dealers in the Persian Gulf, warning that Explorer tires were failing during prolonged driving in very hot weather and that some of the SUVs had rolled over as a result. Ford engineers asked Firestone if there was a problem, and the tire maker insisted there was not and refused to replace the tires. But the problem persisted, and at the end of the summer of 1999, as problems began to crop up in Venezuela as well and Firestone continued to resist doing anything about it, Ford began replacing tires in Saudi Arabia at its own expense. But the automaker did not tell NHTSA about the tire problems or about the replacement effort. NHTSA had never actually required automakers to tell it about overseas recalls of products also sold in the United States. While the manufacturers had voluntarily informed the agency of such sales in the 1970s, they had gradually stopped doing so as the agency's clout and interest dwindled.

As the Firestone tire problem grew, NHTSA was asleep. The agency had never recovered from the budget cuts at the beginning of the Reagan Administration, and its annual spending was still almost 25 percent lower than it had been in the late 1970s, after adjusting for inflation. The National Resource Council estimates that the 41,000 deaths and 3 million injuries in crashes each year carry an economic cost of $150 billion, mainly from lost wages. That is as much as cancer and heart disease together. Yet NHTSA had a budget of just $300 million through the mid-1990s, compared with federal spending of $2.6 billion for cancer research and $972 million for research into heart disease and strokes.[2]

The agency had fewer than 20 safety defect investigators to conduct dozens of extensive engineering investigations each year and keep an eye out for any new problems in a national fleet of more than 200 million vehicles. When a State Farm analyst sent an e-mail to the agency's Office of Defect Investigations in July 1998 documenting that the insurer had received 21 claims regarding Explorer tires over the preceding six and a half years, the agency never replied, nor was the information copied into the complaint database.

Yet through 1998 and 1999, the litigation and the deaths were piling up. According to FARS, there were 11 tire-related deaths in Explorers in 1997, 18 in 1998 and 51 in 1999. Much later, NHTSA would receive complaints of even more deaths during these years that had not been counted as tire-related in the police reports. Lawsuits against Firestone were also accumulating: Hoar's SafetyForum.com would later tabulate that the tire maker, and in some cases Ford as well, had been sued by the end of 1998 for crashes involving 22 deaths and 69 serious injuries.

By early autumn of 1999, top management at Ford was becoming concerned about the Firestone tires on its Explorers. Firestone kept assuring the company that the tires were fine, but was refusing to share its warranty data. Internal Ford documents obtained by Congressional investigators show that the automaker's engineers overseas checked the NHTSA complaints database to see if there were a problem in the United States. But their simple computer searches for complaints that clearly mentioned Explorers and tires found very little.

There is no evidence that Ford engineers checked FARS, which is not normally used in safety investigations because the information is so general. Yet Ford had the vehicle identification numbers of all three million Explorers on the road and could have run them through the database; Ford later released the identification numbers to news organizations so that they could run their own safety investigations. If Ford had checked the database in late 1999, it would have found a somewhat disturbing jump in tire-related deaths in the 1998 data. It also would have found a jump in rollovers with no clear evidence of tire problems, as Ford ramped up sales of two-door models. The big surge in tire-related deaths and in overall rollovers in 1999 did not become available in the FARS database until the autumn of 2000, however, after Firestone tires had already been recalled.

One of many missed opportunities at Ford can be found in a perplexing two-paragraph memorandum dated September 15,

1999. Written by Carlos Mazzorin, Ford's group vice president for purchasing, it was addressed to Jacques Nasser, Ford's chief executive and president; Wayne Booker, vice chairman for international operations; and six vice presidents responsible for sales, manufacturing, quality control, vehicle engineering, Asian operations and public relations.

The memorandum said that the tread sometimes separated from the rest of the tire when Explorers were driven for long periods at high speeds in Saudi Arabia, Oman, Qatar and Venezuela. The tread separations had caused 19 rollovers and some deaths in the Middle East, where Ford had just recalled the tires, and an unspecified number of deaths in Venezuela. But Mr. Mazzorin concluded the memorandum with a horribly inaccurate statement: "No known instances have occurred in other markets."

The memorandum's distribution list mysteriously failed to include two executives who might have told Mr. Mazzorin that he was wrong, had they received the note and then checked records. One was John M. Rintamaki, Ford's general counsel; the company had already been included in some of the lawsuits against Firestone. But Ford paid little attention, because automakers are almost routinely sued after serious crashes. The other executive was Helen Petrauskas, whose safety engineers might have warned that good tires were essential to the stability of SUVs.

Despite Firestone's repeated assurances that the tires were fine, Ford executives became increasingly suspicious through the autumn of 1999, especially because Firestone was refusing to hand over the warranty records that Ford was requesting. Ford engineers gave away several hundred new tires to Explorer owners in Southwestern states in late autumn in exchange for used tires, and then visually examined the tires, looking for problems. But only a few tires were actually cut apart for close examination.

This anemic effort failed to find a problem. The shortcoming of the project, Ford later decided, was that it did not check enough tires.

What was extraordinary about the evolving problem was that a small number of tire failures—fewer than 1 in 5,000 tires—was killing so many motorists. The previous big tire recall in the United States, involving Firestone 500 tires in 1978, was linked to 40 deaths, even though it involved roughly the same number of tires that Firestone would recall in August 2000. Moreover, the Firestone 500 tires were much worse tires than the ATX and Wilderness tires that produced deadly crashes in Explorers.

Firestone replaced 17 percent of the Firestone 500 tires in the year before the recall because they were excessively worn. But Firestone warranty and production records obtained by Congressional investigators in 2000 showed that less than four-tenths of a percent of the recalled ATX and Wilderness tires were replaced under warranty in 1998 and 1999. The ATX and Wilderness tire failures were proving especially deadly because the tires were mostly failing during high-speed driving and the Explorers were then rolling over. But neither Ford nor Firestone appeared to have understood this in 1999.

The tire problem was about to gain greater visibility, however. A television reporter for another Houston television station, KHOU, called a local lawyer in late 1999 looking for story ideas. The lawyer did not normally handle tire cases but had just taken a Firestone case and told the reporter, Anna Werner, all about it. "We just sort of fell into it," she recalls.

Werner and her producer, David Raziq, began calling other lawyers and gathering copies of lawsuits against Firestone across the South. They called NHTSA and asked to deliver the documents to the agency's officials with the cameras rolling. NHTSA's press office was wary of staging such an event and refused. KHOU began airing a series of reports on the tires in February, and included NHTSA's toll-free number for complaints, urging viewers to call the agency if they had experienced any problems with the tires on Explorers.

The televised reports had two quick results. Firestone angrily denied that there was anything the matter with the tires and sent a letter to KHOU's corporate parent with a thinly veiled warning that it might sue. And 20 consumers called the NHTSA hotline within two weeks with complaints.

NHTSA began looking at the tire problems, finding the same complaints already in its files that Sean Kane had discovered years earlier. But the agency still had a problem: Most of the complaints were from consumers who had suffered minor crashes or no crash at all after their tires had failed. The more serious cases, in which Explorer owners had retained lawyers, were not in the database.

NHTSA asked KHOU and the lawyers for help. Both provided some help, but not enough to satisfy the agency. KHOU refused to provide the documents that it had previously offered or a computer database it had compiled of fatal Firestone crashes. Most media organizations have policies against sharing with anyone any notes or information that they gather in the course of an investigation, because in doing so they lose the right to protect the notes from subpoena if they are later sued. Raziq says that the station was afraid of being sued by Firestone and that station officials were asking themselves, "Do we act as a fifth column for the government?"

KHOU instead offered the agency the case numbers for lawsuits scattered around various courthouses across the South. While there are services that will retrieve such lawsuits, they are expensive and NHTSA did not use them.

Strategic Safety also began telling NHTSA about the tire problems then. But Kane says that he and the various tire lawyers around the country were still leery of sharing all they had with the agency. "You submit certain things and they end up in the public record," Kane said. "You don't want to be tipping your hand to the defendants."

A reporter for the *Chicago Sun-Times*, Mark Skertic, ran a good series of stories on April 30 and May 1, 2000, describing the dangers of tire failures. The series gave little attention to Firestone tires and Explorers, however, which had not posed a problem in northern states. The series nonetheless helped prompt NHTSA to turn its informal inquiry into a formal investigation on May 2.

With another potentially bloody summer of tire-related crashes approaching, KHOU became concerned about the slow pace of the investigation. The station reversed its decision to withhold its database of fatal crashes from regulators. But Anna Werner had put many of her personal notes into the same database, and was understandably reluctant to make them public. She began deleting the notes from the database, but was not done by the time the Firestone tire problems had become a national issue, and KHOU never had to share its data with regulators.

More complaints poured into NHTSA over the summer from law offices across the South. Kane learned on July 27 that Ford was replacing Firestone tires on Explorers in Venezuela and announced this in a press release on July 31. *USA Today* picked up the story and public criticism of the tires began to build. Several large retailers soon refused to sell the tires.

Ford had been separately tracking the growing number of complaints to NHTSA with rising alarm. After repeatedly refusing to share its data on warranties or injury claims with Ford, Firestone finally agreed to do so in late July. Ford statisticians ran the data through their more sophisticated computers in Dearborn. Within several days, they found a serious problem: Injury claims were unusually high and rising for 15-inch Firestone ATX and ATX II tires of the P235/R75 size—the main size used on Explorers, as well as a few Ranger pickups and Mercury Mountaineer SUVs. The Ford statisticians also found growing problems with Firestone Wilderness AT tires of the same size that had been made at Firestone's oldest factory in Decatur, Illinois. In a series of acrimonious meetings with Firestone officials, Ford executives began demanding that Firestone recall these tires. But the statisticians did not find a problem with 15-inch Wilderness tires made at factories in cities other than Decatur, nor did they find any problem with 16-inch or 17-inch Wilderness tires, so Ford did not ask that these tires be recalled.

Bill Ford was late in learning of the developing crisis. During a routine gathering of the Ford board before the annual meeting at the Atlanta Zoo, a Ford executive had mentioned in passing that the tires on Explorers were being investigated internally and by NHTSA. But Bill Ford's candid comments at the zoo about the drawbacks of SUVs produced considerable wariness and even criticism of him within the company, especially in the public relations department, as well as from Ford dealers around the country. Bill Ford says that he only heard briefly about the tire issue in mid-July and only learned of its seriousness by accident in late July. It was then that he mentioned to Rintamaki, Ford's general counsel, that he planned to attend the hundredth anniversary of Firestone in mid-August along with other descendants of Harvey Firestone.

"John said: 'Oooooooh. You might want to rethink that because I think this thing's about to blow sky-high,'" Bill Ford later told a magazine writer.[3] Bill Ford went with his family to the extended Ford clan's estate on Long Island for a summer vacation, but left his family there and came back to Ford headquarters in early August to be available for any questions when it became clear that a recall was inevitable.

Firestone finally announced a recall on August 9, 2000. It was one of the largest recalls ever, covering 13 million tires: ATX tires produced at various factories and 15-inch Wilderness tires made in Decatur. Firestone and Ford estimated at the press conference that half the tires, or 6.5 million, were still in use. Tire serial numbers face inwards on a vehicle, so to determine whether a Wilderness tire had been made in Decatur or not, consumers were asked either to climb under their Explorers or else take them to a dealership or tire store—a considerable inconvenience either way.

But both companies insisted that there were no safety problems with the 15-inch Wilderness AT tires that had been produced at factories other than the one in Decatur, and many of these were used to replace the recalled tires. The two companies also said repeatedly that 16-inch or 17-inch Wilderness AT tires were perfectly safe. Personal-injury lawyers and consumer advocates contended that all 15-inch and 16-inch Wilderness AT tires posed risks and should be recalled, but were rebuffed. Only the 17-inch tires, of which a small number had been made, were uncontroversial.

The recall announcement triggered a media and political storm the likes of which the auto and tire industries had never seen before. For years, Ford and the rest of the auto industry had fought off critics of SUVs with little difficulty, and on issues involving a far greater loss of life than the tire-related crashes. But in the Firestone fiasco, Ford met its match in the trial lawyers. The trial lawyers retained public relations companies and peppered reporters with offers of bedside interviews with paralyzed crash victims. They faxed out hundreds of pages of internal Ford and Firestone documents that they had obtained through discovery in court cases. They produced a more detailed chronology than Ford or Firestone ever provided of the entire development of the tires and what went wrong, then shrewdly had Public Citizen release the text, which gave it more credibility. For reporters who wanted to go into extra detail, the lawyers made available an index of hundreds of Ford and Firestone documents stored in warehouses, photocopying them and sending them overnight by Federal Express. Ford and Firestone played into the lawyers' hands by bitterly blaming each other for the crashes, with each side providing documents and statistics to show that the other was at fault. As a result, the Explorer tire saga remained in the news for nearly a year, far longer than previous automotive-safety issues.

The Explorer's status as the favorite vehicle of American yuppies through the 1990s, and of many reporters and politicians in particular, suddenly turned into a liability for Ford. Representative Billy Tauzin, the Louisiana Republican who led the House investigation into the mess, announced that his dark green Explorer with recalled tires would stay parked in his garage, and he turned down discreet offers from Ford to give him priority on replacement tires. At Congressional hearings, member after member either talked about their own Explorers or their friends' Explorers.

Unlike the fuel-tank problems in GM pickups or the rear liftgate latches in Chrysler minivans, to say nothing of the threat that SUVs posed to car occupants, this was a hazard that struck close to home for the nation's elite. As Fred Baron, the president of the Association of Trial Lawyers of America, bluntly and perhaps callously declared, "The SUV has become such a popular vehicle, and we're not talking about poor people in the ghetto getting killed, we're talking about white people in the suburbs."

The saturation media coverage had an immediate and sad result. Ford and Firestone had initially announced that they would replace all tires first in Sun Belt states, where almost all of the fatal crashes had occurred, usually in hot weather. They then planned to offer replacements in colder states in a process that could take all winter. The slow schedule was partly because Firestone insisted at first on replacing as many tires as possible with other Firestone tires, and partly because other tire makers did not have the equipment to start supplying large numbers of tires of the right size quickly. Yet daily newspaper stories and nightly television coverage prompted Explorer owners to mob dealerships and tire stores all the way up to the Canadian border. In Michigan, where virtually no tire-related crashes had occurred, the local media gave frequent and prominent coverage to local Explorer owners' fears of becoming the next victims and described fast-dwindling supplies of replacement tires. With dealers and tire stores nationwide demanding replacements for the recalled tires, Ford and Firestone were unable to direct the replacements to hot-weather states. Through the autumn, there was a string of further fatal, tire-related rollovers in southern states of Explorers still equipped with tires that had been recalled.

What had gone wrong and why were so many people dying? Little by little, the problems dribbled out through the autumn and winter. Put simply, Ford chose tires with a slender safety margin for a tall vehicle that was prone to rolling over if the tires failed, and Firestone then made the tires badly.

The Explorer used some of the same tires as the Ranger on which it was based. But the Explorer weighed 600 pounds more than a Ranger, mainly because the Explorer had a much longer, plusher passenger compartment with an extra row of seats.

The weight-carrying capacity of tires depends partly on their size but mostly on how much air they have inside. For the Ranger, Ford recommended a pressure of 30 pounds per square inch (usually abbreviated p.s.i) for the front tires and 35 for the rear tires, on the assumption that Ranger customers would be more accepting of the hard, bouncy ride that goes with high-pressure tires than SUV customers would be. GM recommended a tire pressure of 35 p.s.i. for the Chevrolet Blazer SUV, which used the same size of tires as the Explorer and Ranger, which meant that the Blazer's tires could carry 8,112 pounds. But when Ford chose a pressure of just 26 p.s.i. for the Explorer's tires in 1989, partly because a higher pressure would have increased the risk of rollovers, the same four tires could carry only 7,012 pounds.

The Explorer weighed 4,000 to 4,400 pounds when empty. Ford recommended that the vehicle carry a payload of not more than 950 to 1,350 pounds, depending on whether it was a two-door or four-door model and how many heavy options it had, like four-wheel drive or air conditioning. So even at the recommended pressure, the tires could have a carrying capacity reserve of less than 1,300 pounds. That works out to a reserve of a little over 300 pounds per tire. Overload the vehicle, or load it unevenly, and the weight reserve could drop to zero.

Worse yet, the tires had no reserve at all if they dropped much below 20 p.s.i. Tire pressure can drop one or even two p.s.i. per month through many tiny leaks. But low tire pressure was hard to notice on the Explorer tires because, like most tires these days, they were radial tires, which always bulge somewhat at the sides even when properly inflated. The virtual disappearance of full-service gas stations, which used to check tire pressure, made it even less likely that tires would be fully inflated to the recommended pressure.

Ford's engineers were also too confident that Explorer owners would not overload their vehicles. I once asked Lee Carr, a vehicle dynamics engineering consultant on the Explorer and former Ford engineer, about the possibility of overloading and he was downright dismissive. "It provides you on the label the gross vehicle weight rating—you can't load it so that you exceed 3,000 pounds on the rear axle either," including the weight of the back half of the vehicle, he said.

Yet the Explorer looks like such a sturdy vehicle that few people would guess that its suspension could not safely carry any more weight than a Ford Taurus sedan. Ford advertised heavily the Explorer's cavernous interior as offering motorists a way to carry plenty of people and cargo, without mentioning the limited payload. Making matters worse was the fact that the label cited by Carr was a sticker in the doorjamb that did not actually give how much weight the Explorer could carry. Indeed, nowhere on an Explorer or in the owner's manual was the buyer actually told the vehicle's maximum payload of people and cargo.

The sticker inside the doorjamb gave the Explorer's gross vehicle weight, the weight that it could carry when fully loaded. The label gave no indication how much the vehicle weighed when empty. Explorers varied in weight by hundreds of pounds depending on what options they had, but Ford did not actually weigh them before they left the factory.

Explorer buyers—or at least the tiny minority who read their owner's manuals cover to cover—were instructed instead by the owner's manuals to weigh the vehicle themselves, then subtract that amount from the gross vehicle weight on the sticker in the door jamb to calculate the maximum payload. And how do you weigh a two-ton SUV? The owner's manuals in Explorers gave this unhelpful advice which Ford had been providing to its truck customers for many years: "To obtain correct weights, try taking your vehicle to a shipping company or an inspection station for trucks."

David Champion, the auto-test director at Consumers Union, pointed out this absurd advice to me after the tire recall became national news, and I resolved to try it out. I checked out an

Explorer from the Ford press fleet and began looking for a place to weigh it. Local shipping companies had little interest in letting me use their scales. The state police in Michigan and New York told me I was not supposed to visit the truck weighing stations next to interstate highways because I did not have a freight truck. Lt. Jamie Mills of the New York State Police suggested that I try nearby garbage dumps, which weigh all the trash coming in and bill municipalities by the ton. So I drove to the dump closest to my home in Michigan and dutifully waited in a short line of garbage trucks. When I reached the front of the line, I drove onto a long metal plate next to a single-story white building, stepped out of the vehicle and walked off the plate. The amused manager standing in an alcove printed out the vehicle's weight on a piece of paper and handed it to me, and I drove off.

Checking the doorjamb and doing a little subtraction, I calculated that I had been driving an Explorer that could carry 1,100 pounds. I called Ford's Jon Harmon, pointed out the inadequate advice in the owner's manual, asked him for comment and began drafting a scathing description of the owner's manual and door-jamb sticker for a comprehensive feature I was writing on the tire debacle. Ford beat me to the punch, however. It responded to my question a couple weeks later by announcing that it would start calculating the weight of all new vehicles at the factory and would give the recommended payload on the door jamb sticker, while revising the language in the owner's manuals.

When tires are overloaded, either because a vehicle is too heavily laden or because the tires do not have enough air inside, the tires tend to bulge slightly more at the sides. The extra bulging causes the sides to flex during driving, which causes them to become hotter. Heat, in turn, is the greatest enemy of tire strength, because it can cause the chemical bonds that hold the tire together to begin to break down. And it is extremely difficult to tell from the outside of a tire when it is coming apart inside.

To make matters worse, the Firestone ATX and ATX II tires that

Ford initially chose, and the similar Firestone Wilderness AT tires that succeeded them, were inexpensive models that were not very good at withstanding heat. They carried a "C" temperature rating, the lowest on the government's tire-rating scale of A to C, meaning that they were the most susceptible to damage at high temperatures.

The Firestone tires chosen by Ford also had a speed rating of "S," which means that they were certified by the government to last at least 10 minutes at a speed of 112 miles per hour when fully inflated. The rating system assumes that a fully inflated tire had a pressure of 35 p.s.i. But at 26 p.s.i., an S-rated tire was only certified to last for 10 minutes at a speed of 106 miles per hour.

That seemed to Ford engineers to offer an ample margin in the late 1980s. Explorers had computerized engine controls to prevent them from going more than 99 miles per hour and the federal speed limit was 55 miles per hour. But the federal speed limit was repealed on December 8, 1995. Western and southern states in particular began raising their speed limits to 70 or 75 m.p.h., and sometimes did not even enforce those standards. At the same time, Ford had not properly programmed the computers in some of the engines, so that drivers could actually go as fast as 120 miles an hour. Ford officials only realized the problem after the Firestone tire crisis broke and they had to recall 110,633 Explorers and Mercury Mountaineers to replace the computers. While the automaker insisted that it was not aware of any crashes that had actually occurred at such speeds, tire experts pointed out that even reaching those speeds once could damage the tires in ways that could cause them to fail later.

The Explorer's modest margin of safety proved adequate when the SUVs were equipped with Goodyear tires, as half of them were for the 1995, 1996 and 1997 model years. There have been very few tire-related crashes in Goodyear-equipped Explorers. But the SUV's narrow margin of safety was not nearly adequate to cope with Firestone's shoddy design and manufacturing of tires for the SUV.

Firestone's own internal investigation found a design problem with all of the ATX tires along with manufacturing problems at an aging factory in Decatur, Illinois, that affected ATX and Wilderness tires produced there. The ATX tires, but not the Wilderness tires, had deep grooves at the sides that were supposed to give a macho, outdoorsy look. The ATX's grooves resulted in the rubber being too thin where the tread met the sidewall. This let cracks appear that could spread into the tire, allowing the tread to peel off. At the factory in Decatur, Illinois, old equipment produced rubber of inconsistent thickness for the ATX and Wilderness tires alike so that the rubber in some tires could be even thinner in places than called for by the design specifications. And the rubber pellets used to make the tires in Decatur had been sprayed by old machinery with excessive quantities of lubricants that kept the pellets from sticking together during the manufacturing process but also interfered later with the rubber's ability to form strong chemical bonds in tires.

Personal-injury lawyers accused Firestone of hiding other problems, which Firestone denied. The lawyers contended that the design of the Wilderness tire was also flawed, especially for tires produced before May 1998 without the thicker rubber wedges. The lawyers also found former Firestone workers who said that managers under pressure to meet quotas had forced them to produce tires that did not even meet Firestone's own quality standards.

All of the tire problems and Explorer design problems might not have posed a big threat to safety had it not been for one other danger: rollovers. A computer analysis of FARS found that 97 percent of the tire-related deaths in Explorers in the 1990s had occurred in vehicles that rolled over.[4] Rollovers were a factor in 84 percent of the 377 tire-related deaths that occurred in all other sport utility vehicles during those years, but in only 38 percent of such deaths in cars. Intriguingly, the Explorer's close rival in tire-related deaths was its predecessor, the Ford Bronco II equipped with General tires, which NHTSA had investigated in 1993 without finding a defect. Also interesting was that there were virtually no tire-related deaths in Jeep Grand Cherokees, one of the most stable SUVs on the market.

Yet the tire failures could have been even worse if they had occurred on another SUV. Data from the Insurance Institute for Highway Safety shows that among midsize SUVs on the road in large enough numbers for the crashes to be counted reliably, only Grand Cherokee occupants have a lower death rate in rollovers than Explorer occupants. Yet Explorer occupants still had double the rollover death rate of occupants of Ford Taurus midsize sedans. Firestone tire failures had only a small effect on the overall rollover statistics.

The bigger problem was that the Explorer, like many other SUVs, was too tall in relation to the distance from left to right between its wheels (known as the wheel track). Using the stability formula that the government had rejected in 1986, of comparing the wheel track to twice the height of its center of gravity, an Explorer carrying just a driver would have more than a 30 percent likelihood of rolling over in a single-vehicle crash, while a fully loaded Explorer would have more than a 40 percent chance of flipping over. Virtually all cars and minivans have less than a 20 percent chance, and many cars have less than a 10 percent chance.

Firestone later claimed that as the deaths and injuries piled up in Explorers in the late 1990s, the trend was hard to spot partly because SUVs roll over even when the tires are fine. The regulations "do not address this vehicle population, a population which has exploded in the past 10 years," said John Lampe, Firestone's executive vice president of sales and later Ono's successor as CEO, in testimony before Congress on September 12, 2000. "These issues have been difficult for us. We are not vehicle experts. And these issues may have made it harder for us to see the problems we had and that we now recognize in our tires."

The rollover controversy did have one salutary effect: NHTSA finally did something to address the problem, although not enough to satisfy safety advocates. The agency had coincidentally announced in the spring of 2000 that it planned to begin rating the stability of cars and light trucks by assigning them one to five stars, much as it assessed vehicles' sturdiness in side and frontal impacts. Taking up the formula rejected in 1986, the agency said that it would divide the wheel track of each vehicle by twice the height of its center of gravity.

Vehicles with a five-star rating would be fairly wide and low, and were predicted to roll over in less than 10 percent of single-vehicle crashes. Vehicles with four stars would be predicted to flip over in 10 to 20 percent of single-vehicle crashes, and so forth, with one-star models expected to roll over in more than 40 percent of single-vehicle crashes. Most cars would receive four or five stars, minivans would tend to receive four stars and SUVs and pickups would receive one to three stars.

The auto industry strenuously objected to NHTSA's plan. Consumers Union also criticized the ratings as inadequate, for two reasons. The ratings did not bar the sale of the most unstable models, as an actual safety standard would. And the ratings would not help consumers distinguish enough within categories of vehicles, so as to separate the more stable SUVs, like the Jeep Cherokee, from the rest. Indeed, unlike most SUVs, the Cherokee did not fit NHTSA's statistical model well at all, in that it only had two stars but seldom rolled over.

Consumers Union called instead for the government to try again to develop a driving test for rollovers. NHTSA had made considerable progress toward devising a reliable test, including the development of computer-controlled robotic steering devices that could ensure that different vehicles were driven through the same course in exactly the same way every time. Unlike a statistical comparison of a vehicle's track width to the height of its center of gravity, a driving test would provide an incentive for automakers to install electronic stability systems, which use antilock brakes and various sensors of tire and vehicle motion. These systems automatically slow one or two wheels when a vehicle starts to slide sideways, so that the vehicle instead travels in whatever direction the driver points it using the steering wheel. This reduces the risk of rollovers by making it less likely that a motorist will slide onto a shoulder or into a guardrail.

Senator Shelby, whose home state of Alabama was home to the DaimlerChrysler factory where Mercedes M-Class SUVs were built, seized on the criticisms of Consumers Union. He amended NHTSA's budget in the summer of 2000 to bar the agency from releasing any rollover ratings until more research could be done on driving tests of vehicle stability. But the Firestone controversy swept away those objections, and Shelby's amendment was removed before final passage of the NHTSA budget. When NHTSA finally began releasing the ratings in late autumn, the Explorer received just two stars.

To the auto industry's relief, however, the agency based its ratings solely on a vehicle's stability with only one occupant, instead of evaluating them when loaded with the maximum recommended payload. Putting more people or cargo into a car has little if any effect on its stability, NHTSA research found, because the seats and trunk of a car are close to the vehicle's center of gravity. But putting more people and cargo into an SUV actually makes it less stable, because the seats and rear cargo area tend to be above the vehicle's center of gravity. A NHTSA study showed that if the Explorer had been evaluated for rollover propensity when fully loaded, it would have received a single star.

Responding to public indignation about the tire-related deaths, Congress passed legislation on November 1, 2000, requiring NHTSA to draft tougher standards in several areas. The agency was ordered to try again to come up with a driving test that could reliably predict vehicles' propensity to roll over, instead of just comparing the width between the wheels to twice the height of the center of gravity. The agency was directed to tighten its weak tire-safety regulations, which had been written in the late 1960s and were even more lenient for light trucks than for cars (although the Explorer's tires happened to meet the car standards anyway).

Finally, automakers, tire makers and other manufacturers of automotive equipment were required to notify NHTSA of any recalls or safety-related replacement efforts overseas, and to notify the agency if they noticed any pattern of warranty claims or litigation that signaled a safety problem.

It was an ambitious attempt to make sure nothing like the Firestone debacle would ever happen again. But there was no sign that consumers were paying nearly as much attention to the rollover ratings as they had to the Firestone tire problem, even though Firestone tires had accounted for less than 1 percent of the rollover deaths on American roads in 1999, the last full year of crashes before the tires were recalled.

The auto industry, and Ford in particular, nonetheless hoped by the end of 2000 that the tire mess was mostly behind it. But they were wrong, as it turned out that even more Firestone tires had problems than they had realized.

Through the winter and spring of 2001, Ford engineers and statisticians continued to track closely the performance of Firestone tires. They had required Firestone to start handing over all of its warranty data on tire models installed on Ford vehicles. They also analyzed in great detail the failure rate for other companies' tires. In mid-April, they reached an ominous conclusion: The rest of the Wilderness tires installed on Explorers, including tires that had been installed as replacements the previous autumn, were failing at a rate triple the industry average, and the failure rate was rising. Problems were occurring in 16-inch Wilderness tires, a size that had not previously been recalled at all, as well as in 15-inch tires from factories other than the one in Decatur. Only the few 17-inch tires were free of problems.

With summer approaching, and with it the potential for more hot-weather tire failures, the question facing Ford was what to do about the problem. Ford executives found themselves reliving a nightmare, and it could not have come at a worse time. In early April, they and Firestone had publicly declared again that there was no problem with any tires beyond those already recalled. Firestone had rolled out a new advertising campaign to rehabilitate its reputation, hoping that consumers' memories were beginning to dim. Ford itself had just introduced an all-new Explorer, which no longer shared the same underbody as the Ranger. The 2002 Explorer had wheels mounted 2.5 inches farther apart than on earlier models, although Ford claimed that this design decision had been made several years earlier for occupants' comfort rather than because of any concern about rollovers. Ford desperately wanted the new Explorer to succeed.

There were some variations in the new data uncovered by the Ford statisticians in April—tires from some of Firestone's newest factories were more reliable than tires from older factories. The newer tires, with thicker wedges to prevent tread separation, also had fewer failures than older tires. So as Ford executives secretly mulled the data, they faced three options. They could ask Firestone to do a second recall covering all Wilderness tires, even the 17-inch tires, so as to avoid any confusion among consumers. They could ask Firestone to recall only those Wilderness tires showing elevated failure rates—but asking people to crawl under their vehicles again to check serial numbers for the factory where each tire had been manufactured seemed like a recipe for mass confusion. Or they could ignore the problem and hope for the best through the summer.

Growing increasingly upset with Firestone, Ford began quietly asking other tire companies how quickly they could make large numbers of replacement tires if they were needed. By Thursday, May 17, Ford engineers had exhaustively analyzed the company's options and Ford executives and directors were preparing to make a decision. An annual charity benefit was to be held that weekend at the Atlanta Zoo, and an executive jet had been scheduled to take some of the company's leaders to the event. But the flight was cancelled to make sure that everyone would be available for the big decision. Ford continued to keep Firestone in the dark.

I heard a rumor that Thursday that Ford had found a problem with more tires. I called Firestone officials, who said they had heard nothing. Jason Vines, Ford's vice president for communications, simply told me that Ford was constantly reviewing tire data and working closely with the National Highway Traffic Safety Administration, and declined to elaborate.

I ended up finding three other people who, after insisting that I protect their identities, said that Ford had found a problem with further Firestone tires beyond those already recalled. "We've got another problem that might be bigger than the last one" in how many tires might need recalling, said one person close to Ford's review. Another person close to the discussions was more cautious, saying, "There is a general conclusion that there are some models that have problems with them beyond those recalled, and the question is whether the problems are bad enough to justify a recall."

Vines still declined to say anything. But in what Ford officials later said was a coincidence, a group of Ford experts visited NHTSA's headquarters that evening, when the agency was normally closed, and informed regulators who were working late that they had found statistical evidence of a broader tire problem.

My story ran at the top of the front page of the next day's business section. It stressed that the additional tires in question did not appear to have as high a failure rate as those already recalled. But the article said that Ford was "leaning toward demanding that Firestone recall more tires."

Firestone officials were livid, and not just because Ford had not mentioned any of its findings to them. Because my story mentioned that I had three sources, which seemed like a lot, they wrongly assumed that I had been deliberately leaked the information by Ford. Firestone's new CEO, John Lampe, had attended a party that Thursday night for Mexican Firestone dealers, complete with a mariachi band, at a Firestone factory in Cuernavaca, Mexico. An assistant read the article to him over the phone early Friday morning, and he was appalled, immediately telling his driver to take him back to the Mexico City airport and ordering his office to book him on the first available commercial flight back to the United States, which left for Dallas at 10:30 A.M. (Unlike Ford, Firestone did not have a fleet of corporate jets.) He tried to reach Nasser by phone, but Nasser did not take the call.

When Lampe arrived in Dallas, he had a few minutes before his connecting flight to Nashville, so he called Nasser's office again. Once again, Nasser did not take his call. Instead, Carlos Mazzorin, Ford's group vice president for purchasing, called Firestone headquarters to say that he wanted to fly down as soon as possible to talk to Lampe in person. Firestone executives, convinced that Ford was trying something sneaky, told Mazzorin that Lampe was busy over the weekend with social obligations and could not speak with him until Monday morning at the earliest. Lampe did have some family obligations, but they did not fill the weekend. The truth was that Firestone officials were playing for time while they weighed their options.

In Dearborn, Nasser was outraged that such sensitive information had leaked from anyone, much less three people. The automaker's large security staff was ordered to conduct an immediate investigation of the leak.

To trace the leak, Ford security officials used computer software to pore through the records of thousands of calls passing through the automaker's phone system, Vines said in a call to me soon afterward. The security staff was trying to figure out who might have made or received a phone call from any of my phone numbers in the days immediately preceding the leak. "If we find out who it was, they will be dealt with severely—as severely as is possible in a corporation," Vines said, adding that this would involve immediate dismissal.

To me, this sounded like an attempt to intimidate people out of raising safety issues, with Vines using me to convey a threat to sources whom he could not find. Vines denied this. While my article had not caused a consumer panic because it said that the second batch of troubled tires appeared less dangerous than the first, the potential for a panic had been there and the company had an obligation to prevent such panics, he said.[5]

Ford's press office declined to comment about my article through most of Friday. But late in the afternoon, one of Vines' deputies foolishly said "No" when asked by a wire service reporter if the article were true. This prompted a spasm of stories in some newspapers on Saturday that Ford thought the tires were fine. Since Mazzorin was still asking to visit Nashville as soon as possible, this only deepened the suspicions of Firestone officials.

Firestone executives met through the weekend. They concluded that the only way to preserve the viability of the Firestone brand was to lash out at Ford before Ford could hurt them. When Mazzorin flew down to Nashville on a Ford corporate jet early Monday morning, Lampe personally drove to the airport to pick him up and bring him to Firestone's headquarters, where the two men met for less than an hour. Mazzorin presented Ford's statistical analyses and asked Firestone to conduct a second, much broader recall. Lampe countered that Firestone's own analyses did not show that its tires were any worse than those of any other tire manufacturer. Then Lampe handed Mazzorin a letter to Nasser, drawn up over the weekend, stating that Firestone would no longer sell tires to Ford, other than to complete existing contracts. A nearly century-old business relationship, one of the oldest in the corporate world, had been severed.

Mazzorin was emotionless in accepting the letter. "He was a gentleman, very professional," Lampe said. Firestone promptly announced its decision, saying that any safety problems had to be the result of defects in the Explorer and not in the tires.

Ford executives and directors were caught completely off guard. Ford's board discussed the matter at length on a conference call and finally came to a difficult conclusion: Ford would have to pay for the replacement of every Firestone Wilderness tire on every Ford light truck around the world, including those that had only been installed the previous autumn as replacements.

Like the August 2000 recall, the replacement effort would officially apply to roughly 13 million tires. But because the Wilderness tires were a fairly new model, most of them were still in use. So the actual number of tires to be removed from vehicles and replaced with new tires would be much higher—as many as 11 million tires. This would be spectacularly expensive, forcing Ford to set aside $3 billion to pay for the labor at dealerships and for the new tires, which would be made by other manufacturers.

Nasser was combative as ever at the press briefing at Ford headquarters on Tuesday morning, May 22. The Firestone tires were at fault, he said, stating that the failure rate was 15 per million tires, compared with 5 per million for other manufacturers' tires (and 60 to 200 failures per million tires of the models recalled the previous autumn). Bill Ford, sitting near Nasser at the press conference, was pale and grim and looked almost as though he were suffering from food poisoning. "I grew up with Firestone as part of my family," he said. "It's my family name, my mother's family name certainly. . . . It taints a lot of family memories and a lot of the family legacy."

Firestone quickly conducted a blistering assault on the Explorer's safety. "Our tires are safe," Lampe said in a statement soon after the Ford press conference. "When we have a problem, we admit it and we fix it. We've proven that. The real issue here is the safety of the Explorer."

In the following days, Firestone tried energetically to portray the Explorer as an unusually unstable vehicle that was just too vulnerable to tire failures. On May 31, Firestone asked NHTSA to open a formal safety investigation into the Explorer. A researcher retained by Firestone, Dennis A. Guenther, a professor of mechanical engineering at Ohio State University, contended that when a tire failed on an Explorer, the SUV was prone to "oversteer." When a vehicle oversteers, a small turn of the steering wheel produces a sharp turn of the vehicle. With oversteering, the back end of the vehicle swings out during the turn; if a vehicle's tires have enough traction to dig into the road suddenly while sliding sideways, they can cause a rollover.

To reduce the risk of rollovers, SUVs are usually designed to understeer, so that the steering wheel must be turned hard to make a fairly sharp turn. Guenther's calculations showed that the Explorer problem increased with the load of people and cargo in the vehicle, and he contended that the Explorer was more prone to oversteer following a tire failure than a Jeep Cherokee or Chevrolet Blazer.

Ford's response was predictable. The company had already tested the Explorer and five other SUVs over the winter and found that after a tire failure, all of them were susceptible to oversteer if the driver turned the steering wheel fairly sharply. The tests included the Blazer, which Ford, unlike Firestone, found no different from the Explorer. Ford conspicuously refrained from including the extremely stable Cherokee in its tests, however.

Once again, Ford was defending the Explorer by saying that it was like other SUVs. Indeed, that was Ford's response to every criticism leveled against the Explorer. Many other SUVs also had fairly low-pressure tires that did not have a large reserve for carrying extra weight. Many SUVs rolled over when their tires failed, too. And many other car and SUV tires were certified for no higher speeds than the Explorer's tires.

NHTSA finally closed its 18-month investigation into Firestone tires on October 4, 2001. Firestone agreed to recall 3.5 million Wilderness tires manufactured without the thicker wedges before May 1998, though it estimated that only 768,000 of these tires were still in use.[6] As it happened, Ford had already replaced most of these tires anyway, because it had quietly given priority to customers with older tires at the greatest risk of failure.

At the same time, NHTSA also said that it had found no evidence of a special problem with Explorers. "Claims and complaint data indicate that a tread separation on an Explorer is no more likely to lead to a crash than on other SUVs," the agency said.[7]

This was truly a case of damning with faint praise, given the rollover records and tire-failure records of other SUVs. Once again, the agency had been stymied in declaring an SUV problem to be a safety defect because there were so many other SUVs also on the road with exactly the same problem. By not setting stringent safety standards early in the development of SUVs, the agency was repeatedly confronted with broad problems affecting so many models that recalls were difficult or impossible to mandate. The effect of these errors on public safety had been limited somewhat through the 1990s because the first buyers of most SUVs were the safest drivers around. But with the used SUV market burgeoning, and with cheap new models like the two-door Ford Explorer Sport being marketed to young drivers, this respite seemed unlikely to last.

PART THREE

THE FUTURE OF THE SUV

16

THE NEXT DRIVERS OF SUVS

Sitting at the wheel of her family's bright red Chevrolet Suburban sport utility vehicle in a high school parking lot on a bright autumn afternoon, April reached over to the front passenger seat and grabbed a plastic tiara. Brandishing it out the window, she explained how she had just been chosen as one of five homecoming princesses at her high school in a wealthy Los Angeles suburb partly because of the popularity she enjoyed by driving the biggest vehicle of any student.

"I love big trucks because they just look cool and have big tires," she said. "Everybody knows me as the girl who drives the big red truck."

She never needed its four-wheel drive, but the vehicle's high ground clearance had given her the confidence to take occasional shortcuts across medians and lawns. "I'll go behind the bushes and along the railroad tracks," she explained. "I drive it to school every day—I feel safe, I feel like I'm the queen of the road because I'm up high and can see everything for miles."

April said she was 5 foot 6, but felt much taller in the SUV. Her father had jacked up the Suburban's suspension by six inches. That made the tall vehicle even taller, although also more likely to roll over and more likely to pass over cars' crumple zones in a collision.

"Up here, I'm probably 6 foot 10," she said, staying in the driver's seat. "I love it, it just makes me feel powerful—if someone disses me, I can tailgate the crap out of them."

But as she kept talking, April confessed that the size of her vehicle also frightened her. Her voice fell somewhat and her initial bubbly enthusiasm ebbed as she began talking about her concerns of ending another person's life in a crash. These fears had grown ever since she had recently struck her neighbor's parked Chevrolet Astro van.

"I'm worried about if I might kill someone—I hit my neighbor's truck and lifted it up, and I barely hit it," she said. "That's one of my biggest fears, I might kill someone."

It is an appropriate fear, and one that unfortunately seems to dissuade few parents from allowing their children to drive SUVs. Of the students who drove their own vehicles to the high school that day, at least a quarter seemed to be in sport utilities. By contrast, I couldn't help noticing that there were no SUVs in the section of the parking lot reserved for the teachers, who probably earned less than many of their students' parents.

There are lines of sport utility vehicles parked these days outside the affluent fraternities and sororities at the University of Michigan and other big universities across the country. High school parking lots are beginning to look the same way. Young people are the next big market for SUVs, especially used SUVs, with alarming consequences for traffic safety. With more than half of the nation's SUVs less than five years old, and with very few SUVs more than 12 years old, their drivers until now have tended to be their first owners—responsible, middle-aged people. Many of the initial owners have been married people who drive in the daytime and early evening, when crashes are far less frequent per million miles traveled than late at night.

Automakers' difficulties in keeping up with demand for new SUVs have kept the prices of used SUVs unusually high. Through the late 1990s, this allowed buyers of full-size SUVs to resell the vehicles within two or three years for as much as 90 percent of what they paid for them. This, in turn, helped fuel the sale and leasing of new SUVs, by making it easy for SUV owners to afford to trade in their vehicles for newer models on a regular basis.

But the high prices for used models also discouraged their purchase by young people and by hard-core drunk drivers, who tend to buy the oldest, cheapest vehicles on the market. Many states now have programs that impound temporarily the vehicles of people convicted of drunk-driving offenses. But some of these programs have had financial difficulties, because the large majority of the impounded cars turn out to be old junkers, and the drivers simply abandon them instead of paying the storage fees at the end of the impoundment in order to recover them.[1]

Especially worrisome is the sheer durability of SUVs. Through the 1980s and 1990s, Detroit gradually got serious about quality, and in recent years the Big Three automakers have produced vehicles of all types that are almost as reliable as those of their foreign competitors. Better steel is now used in vehicle bodies, so that they no longer rust out. Not surprisingly, vehicles are lasting longer, and the average age of vehicles on the nation's roads rose through the 1990s despite an economic boom; during previous economic booms, the average age of vehicles tended to fall as Americans scrapped the junkers in favor of the latest models.

Used-vehicle prices have stayed low for old models: vehicles that are more than 10 years old seldom fetch more than $2,500 and often much less. The result is a huge and growing pool of old, very cheap vehicles. But while the galvanized-steel exteriors of these vehicles may be durable, the mechanical workings are not immortal. Without proper servicing, brakes and other critical components will wear out.

There are still very few SUVs in this vast pool of older vehicles, but there will be far more over the coming decades. Indeed, SUVs built now may be especially likely to stay on the roads for a long time, and to keep inflicting heavy damage on cars and rolling over at an alarming rate through those years, too. Detroit's SUVs fare better than its cars in reliability surveys by groups like *Consumer Reports*, possibly because SUVs are of simple, heavy-duty construction and have had a lot of money and managerial attention devoted to them lately. Even an SUV that has been in a fatal collision, killing a car occupant and injuring its own occupants, can sometimes be in fairly good driving condition, requiring repairs only to the surface metal and passenger compartment, but not to the heavy steel underbody, according to police investigators of crashes. The only thing scarier than a drunk or teenager at the wheel of a shiny, new full-size SUV will be a drunk or teenager at the wheel of a 15-year-old full-size SUV with failing brakes. The more than 20 million SUVs that have already been built, with too little regard for stability and for the safety of other road users, will be roaming the roads for a very long time to come.

Automakers do not try to attract drunks to SUVs, but they do market SUVs to young people, both as a way to sell them new SUVs and as a way to keep demand strong and prices high for used SUVs. This is a bad idea, although the safety implications have not yet received much attention. The teenaged SUV driver incident that has drawn the most attention so far has not even involved a person as the victim, but a dog. On January 2, 2002, President Clinton's dog, Buddy, ran into the street in Chappaqua, New York, while chasing a contractor's truck and was struck and killed by a high school student driving an SUV. The police ruled the canine death an accident, and did not bring charges. But the case highlighted that SUVs have begun to catch on among the segment of the population with the worst driving record.

This trend is ominous for three reasons: An unusually large proportion of the American population is in its teens and early 20s these days, and their ranks are growing daily for demographic reasons; tastes in automobiles tend to form in the early teens and often last for life; yet no age group is less suited to drive SUVs than people in their teens and early 20s.

There are more teens in the United States now than there have been in a generation. The number of babies born annually soared during the baby boom, from 1946 to 1964, and plunged from the late 1960s through the mid-1970s, until the baby boomers themselves began to have vast numbers of their own kids. The number of births rebounded from 1977 to 1990 and has been at a high plateau ever since, almost matching the baby boom. These children include the teenagers and early 20-somethings who are now so obsessed with SUVs.

Researchers for various automakers and their consulting firms have consistently found that today's young people love the feeling of power of SUVs, and are more likely than people in any other age bracket to prefer SUVs to cars. Indeed, influential market researchers like Jim Bulin, the longtime Ford strategist, say that affection for SUVs varies inversely with age. Men and women who grew up in the Depression or World War II very seldom buy sport utilities. Baby boomers are deeply split in their attitudes toward SUVs, with some preferring cars and minivans while others have embraced four-wheel-drive vehicles. Drivers in their twenties and early thirties like SUVs but have had surprisingly little influence on the auto market because their numbers are limited and because they have not yet reached their peak earning years.

Teenagers and college students, though, love SUVs with an extraordinary unanimity. Automakers conduct focus groups with teens as young as 13 with their parents' permission. According to GM, 90 percent of teens interviewed in 1999 said they preferred SUVs to any other class of vehicles. That is an alarming figure given that SUVs are still roughly 17 percent of the market. The affection that young people hold for dangerous-looking SUVs should not be surprising. Children's entertainment has become much more violent in recent years. Cartoon shows now feature battling robots instead of the cute animals of Warner Brothers and Disney. The Happy Meals that McDonald's distributes to three-year-olds include Lego toys that, when assembled, turn out to be armored space-alien warriors. When Microsoft introduced its XBox video game system in 2001, the television commercial for one of the games, "Halo: Combat Evolved," showed the hero not only shooting humanoid aliens but also splattering them by driving through them in a vehicle that resembles a large SUV.

Automotive preferences seem to be a lot like tastes in music: They form early, often in rebellion against parents' tastes, and they last for life. Baby boomers who came of age in the 1960s have never shaken their love of groups like the Beatles, the Grateful Dead and the Rolling Stones. Some of their younger brothers and sisters retain an incomprehensible love of disco music from the 1970s. Similarly, men and women who lusted after big cars in the 1930s and 1940s are still buying large cars today. People seem to form their strongest, most enduring attachments to music and to automobiles between the ages of 12 and 15, Ford officials say. The disheartening implication of all this is that people who have entered the auto market since the mid-1980s may go on buying SUVs for life.

Auto-market researchers have taken notice of young people's interest in SUVs. "It's surprising, the appeal in younger genera-tions," said Ed Molchany, the Ford brand manager for Explorers. "All of our SUVs are very strong with Generation Y, it's a very pop-ular brand and imagery."

Ford's youth strategy did not get started until late 1997. Through the early and mid-1990s, the Ford factories in St. Louis and Louisville that assembled Explorers could not come close to meeting demand, so they mostly built bigger Explorers with four doors. The four-door models had larger profit margins than two-door models. Ford was building 430,000 Explorers a year, but only 30,000 to 50,000 a year had only two doors.

But the market for four-door, midsized sport utility vehicles had changed by the end of 1997. Chrysler had introduced the four-door Dodge Durango and Mercedes had come out with its four-door M-Class, partly relieving the shortage that had kept Explorer factories working around the clock. A flood of foreign sport utility vehicles was starting to come on the market, both truck-based and car-based. Ford itself had introduced the larger Ford Expedition in 1996, and many well-heeled families began choosing Expeditions instead of Explorers.

So Ford introduced a "Sport" options package for the two-door Explorer, with spiffier wheels and other details calculated to attract buyers in their 20s and even younger. It was an instant success. "There was this younger group, more singles, more females," said Douglas W. Scott, Ford's group marketing manager for all sport utility vehicles, and Molchany's predecessor as the marketing manager just for Explorers. "It was a younger buyer really interested in the look."

The new version was so popular that Ford later labeled it a different model, the Explorer Sport. To go with it, Ford created an Explorer Sport Trac, which has an open, 4-foot pickup truck bed in the back. Both were virtually identical to the Explorer beneath the sheet metal, and continued to be made on the same assembly lines. Annual production of two-door versions zoomed to 100,000 a year, as Ford sold fewer four-door models and more two-door models.

With these inexpensive Explorer variants, Ford has succeeded in lowering sharply the overall average age of Explorer buyers. "I'm working really hard to target youth," said Drew Cook, a Ford marketing manager for the Sport Trac and Ranger small pickups. Compared to Ranger pickups, he said, "The Sport Trac is positioned a little bit earlier, firmly entrenched among Gen Xers."

This is particularly important in Detroit. The bane of the domestic industry is that its models are mostly popular with older Americans who may soon buy their last car, as younger Americans have gravitated toward European and Asian models. The average age for buyers of Buick cars is nearly 70. Buyers of Explorer Sport and

Sport Trac may be coming back to dealerships for as many as 15 additional vehicles over their lifetimes. "It's a lot of folks just out of college," Scott said.

But the goal is only partly to sell more vehicles now. Ford also wants to convince people at as early an age as possible to become interested in Explorers, in the hope that they will buy more Explorers of various sizes and configurations throughout their adult lives.

"We want to bring people in younger than ever before, and that's driving the product offering," Molchany said. Toward that goal, Ford has used direct-mail campaigns, tapping commercially available databases of prosperous households with young residents, said James G. O'Connor, the president of the Ford brand division. Ford has also provided promotional vehicles of the Explorer, Explorer Sport and Explorer Sport Trac for sports events that cater to younger television viewers.

Ford has not been alone in promoting SUVs to younger buyers. Executives at other automakers say that the fastest growth in SUVs at the expense of cars over the next decade will come in models that will cost less than $20,000 and be affordable for young people. "The next inroads we really see in trucks are really here," said Paul Ballew, GM's top market researcher, while adding that Ford was ahead of GM in this area. "A large part of Ford's youth strategy is to leverage their truck strength."

GM is nonetheless active too, beginning with its licensing division. My three-year-old son has a children's book about a police rescue of a dog during a hurricane. The book features a Chevrolet Tahoe full-sized SUV painted and equipped as a police vehicle, and even comes with a three-inch-long matching toy Tahoe in police colors. When we recently walked by a police station, he pointed excitedly to a real police Tahoe and said, "Look, there's a police truck!"

Chrysler ran an extensive radio and television advertising campaign in the summer of 1996 aimed at persuading parents and grandparents to buy the small, inexpensive Jeep Wrangler for their children and grandchildren. Chrysler's market research had found that while many teenagers and early 20-somethings loved the Wrangler, they could not afford it and were buying cheap used vehicles instead. But Chrysler noticed that their elders could afford the Wrangler. So Chrysler ditched its previous, long-standing ad campaign, a macho series of television ads that featured Wranglers in fights with bulls and other adventures that nervous parents and grandparents might not want Junior to try.

Instead, Chrysler began running ads in which a clean-cut young man sat near a clean-cut young woman at a campfire on a beautiful mountainside while a Jeep Wrangler sat parked nearby in the gathering dusk. The message, Chrysler marketing officials said, was that buying a Wrangler was a good way for parents and grandparents to help young people visit the pristine wilderness. There was no suggestion of sex in the ads to frighten the elders—the young men and women in these ads were not sitting too close together. There were not even any tents in sight, so perhaps the youngsters were supposed to drive back down the apparently roadless mountainside in the dark. Radio ads for the Wrangler were even more carefully tailored to parents, with one ad featuring a young woman who goes for a drive with her mother and has a cheerful chat about the young woman's boyfriend, whom the mother likes.

Whether the campaign worked is hard to judge. Statistics on teen ownership of vehicles are highly unreliable, because vehicles are often registered in the names of the teens' parents. There are no publicly available statistics at all on how teens pay for their vehicles. But whatever the reason, the Wrangler has sold well over the last five years, as have other small sport utility vehicles, which tend to draw young drivers.[2]

Teens and people in their early 20s may love SUVs, but should they be driving them? A wealth of recent research says that any parent who really cares about the safety of a son or daughter should not allow him or her to drive a sport utility vehicle, and should discourage that child from riding in SUVs driven by friends.

The death rate for young people in auto accidents has been

extraordinary even without the recent rise of SUVs. A third of all deaths of Americans from ages 15 to 24, about 10,000 deaths a year, occur in motor vehicle accidents. That roughly equals all deaths in this age group from all diseases, and exceeds the number of deaths in this age bracket from homicides and suicides combined.[3]

Surprisingly little work has been done on exactly how young people die in crashes, particularly in comparison with the research done on homicides. The existing research does show, however, that young people die disproportionately in single-vehicle crashes, apparently because of their inexperience, rather than perishing in collisions with other vehicles. And many of these single-vehicle crashes involve rollovers—the kind of crashes to which SUVs are especially vulnerable, accounting for three-fifths of all deaths in SUVs. Since rollovers appear to be the biggest single cause of paralysis, and since people who are paralyzed in their teen years lose more years of mobility than those paralyzed later in life, allowing a teen to drive an SUV can be an especially sad mistake.

Insurers are becoming fed up with paying the bills from hospitals and repair shops when young people drive SUVs. When Brian O'Neill, the president of the industry's Insurance Institute for Highway Safety, heard of the enthusiasm of auto marketers for selling SUVs to young people, he was appalled. "If manufacturers are deciding that they should target people in their teens and early 20s for purchases of SUVs, it's a dumb and irresponsible thing to do because these are not safe vehicles, their rollover and handling characteristics are different," he said. "For teenagers, the appropriate vehicles are not small, they're not large and they're not SUVs—they're middle-of-the-road sedans."

The highway safety group issued a press release warning parents against allowing young drivers behind the wheel of SUVs: "Don't let your teen drive an unstable vehicle. Sport utility vehicles, especially the smaller ones, are inherently less stable than cars because of their higher centers of gravity. Abrupt steering maneuvers—the kind that can occur when teens are fooling around or overcorrecting a driver error—can cause rollovers in these less stable vehicles. A more stable car would, at worst, skid or spin out."

Indeed, even auto-industry safety officials are wary of recommending SUVs for young people. Helen Petrauskas, the longtime Ford vice president for safety and environment, said at a retirement lunch with reporters at Henry Ford's Fairlane Estate in the spring of 2001 that she had insisted her own daughter drive a Ford Tempo compact car when she was learning to drive. Petrauskas even insisted that her daughter not choose an exciting color, like red. Parents should choose cars that look like they would not be very interesting to drive, she suggested.

Sue Cischke, her successor, said at the same event that for teens, "probably a midsized sedan is good advice—what their image is, and what they want to do, is often different from what their parents want."

A few celebrities have taken an interest in what will happen as the next generation of SUV drivers takes over. The most prominent is Paul Newman, an actor who is also a racecar driver and understands the value of nimble steering and excellent brakes.

"In 1973, everybody's running around buying Volkswagen diesels," Newman said in 1999. "And now they're buying Expeditions. And this is the thing that I don't understand about the government. As this fad grew, why they didn't insist on certain bumper heights—I mean, it's criminal. And when an Expedition is eight years old and it goes down to 7,000 bucks, there'll be a lot of kids buying them and, unfortunately, it's the younger generation that's responsible for a lot of accidents. So you put a 17-year-old kid behind a 5,500-pound car and have them run into your blue-haired lady driving her Tercel Toyota. You know, it's going to be mayhem."[4]

CROSSOVER UTILITIES

Visitors to the Detroit and Los Angeles shows in January 1997 saw two oddities among the many SUVs of various sizes on display. The oddities were the Toyota RAV4, which had just gone on sale, and the Honda CR-V, which was to go on the market a month later. Both had fairly tall, boxy designs that made them look like small, four-door SUVs. Four-wheel drive was standard on the CR-V and optional on the RAV4.[1] Both were priced and sized to compete with the smaller midsize SUVs, like the Jeep Cherokee, although the RAV4 was somewhat smaller than the CR-V or Cherokee.

What made the RAV4 and CR-V unusual was that they each had carlike bodies in which the underbody, sides and roof were all welded together to form a single unit. This architecture, known as a unitized body, made them lighter and more fuel-efficient than traditional SUVs, which were still being built by bolting bodies onto the same heavy, steel underbodies used for pickup trucks. Japanese automakers had been very slow in the 1990s to take heed of the SUV boom in the United States, partly because they were barely active in the pickup market because of the old chicken tax and partly because they had dismissed SUVs as a short-lived fad. Indeed, some Japanese executives expressed incredulity that people could prefer poor-handling, modified trucks over better-performing cars. When Toyota and Honda did enter the market, it made sense for them to experiment with carlike designs because they no longer had much expertise in building body-on-frame vehicles, having largely rejected this old technology because of the lousy fuel economy it produced.

The ride of the RAV4 and CR-V was a little smoother than that of traditional SUVs because they did not have the same stiff, heavy underbodies. They were somewhat easier to drive because they were not quite so big and heavy as traditional SUVs. And they were a little easier on the wallet—a CR-V with an automatic transmission got a respectable 22 m.p.g. in the city and 25 on the highway, while a smaller RAV4 with a stick shift and two-wheel drive had a window sticker showing an impressive 24 m.p.g. in the city and 28 m.p.g. on the highway. But their lack of stiff, steel-frame underbodies meant that they were less useful than traditional SUVs for off-road driving or towing. Toyota and Honda nonetheless had both vehicles certified as light trucks by NHTSA. They argued that the two vehicles had the high ground clearance and at least optional four-wheel drive needed for off-road travel. The agency lets automakers decide whether a vehicle should be regulated as a car or a light truck and did not question the decisions by Honda and Toyota.

The CR-V and the RAV4 were both immediately popular, and Honda and Toyota struggled to produce enough of them. Women buyers in particular liked the handling and accessibility of the new vehicles. The RAV4 and CR-V, with carlike underbodies and light-duty all-wheel drive, allowed lower, easier ingress and egress than traditional SUVs, whose high floors require motorists to take a long step up and into the vehicle, which can be difficult in a skirt.

Detroit automakers, with four-fifths of the domestic market for light trucks, were alarmed by the immediate popularity of the

RAV4 and CR-V and accelerated efforts they had already begun to produce similar vehicles. Most of the new vehicles, from the Ford Escape to the Buick Rendezvous, were also hits, creating a market segment that grew from nothing in 1995 and a few thousand RAV4s in 1996 to a million vehicles in 2001, or 5.91 percent of all the vehicles sold in the United States that year. By comparison, the entire minivan segment was only 6.93 percent of the market in 2001.[2] The explosive growth was partly propelled by enormous advertising spending to make buyers aware of the new models, climbing from $33 million in 1996, when Toyota began promoting its new RAV4, to $413.6 million in 2000.[3]

The extraordinary growth in sales raised a question of what to call the new segment. The automakers contended that all of their new models were simply SUVs, and argued that no new segment was even needed. This stance fit their marketing and political agenda: They wanted to make sure that these vehicles, essentially tall cars with all-wheel drive, would continue to be called SUVs because consumers were buying anything called an SUV and regulators were certifying all SUVs as light trucks. Some data services, like the Polk Company, obliged the automakers and have never separated car-based utility vehicles from pickup-based utility vehicles in their statistics on SUVs. *Automotive News* tried referring to the carlike utility vehicles as "sport wagons" and kept statistics on them separately, but the term never caught on and was deeply disliked by the automakers. The best of the industry's data services, Ward's, which tabulates auto sales for use in economic indicators by the United States Commerce Department, tracks sales of the carlike models separately and calls them crossover utility vehicles.

Automakers have portrayed the shift toward crossover utilities not just as a way to meet consumer demands for better-riding vehicles, but as a response to safety and environmental concerns about traditional SUVs. The reality is that crossover utilities have become yet another way for automakers to take advantage of light-truck loopholes in government regulations. The auto-industry's market research shows they are bought primarily by people who otherwise would have bought a car, so the effect of the rise of crossover utilities has been to put even more vehicles on the road that are covered by the more lenient safety, fuel-economy and smog regulations that apply to light trucks.

Indeed, the biggest fuel-economy loophole of all, exceeding even the ethanol loophole, is simply to equip fairly high-mileage cars like the Toyota Camry or Ford Contour with four-wheel drive, give them a facelift and tell regulators that they are light trucks. By including these vehicles in the average fuel economy of their light trucks, automakers can sell even more behemoths while still being able to tell the government that their laboratory average is 20.7 miles per gallon or better. By raising the percentage of all new vehicles that get a lab average of 20.7 m.p.g. and lowering the percentage of all new vehicles that achieve an average of 27.5 m.p.g., the crossover utilities have actually hurt the overall gas mileage of the American fleet.[4]

Ford even promoted the introduction of the Ford Escape, the best-selling crossover utility on the market, as eventually providing up to a third of the 25 percent improvement it plans in the average gas mileage of its SUVs. Yet the Ford Escape gets worse mileage than the slow-selling sedans it replaced, the Ford Contour and Mercury Mystique, which were a little smaller than a Ford Taurus.[5] In 1999, the Ford Motor Company closed its assembly plant in Kansas City, where the Contour and Mystique were manufactured, and reopened it a year later with a combination of new and old equipment to produce the Escape. The discontinued Contour's window sticker showed it getting 20 m.p.g. in the city and 28 m.p.g. on the highway. The Escape's window sticker put its fuel-economy performance at just 18 m.p.g. in the city and 24 m.p.g. on the highway—good for a light truck, but not for a car. The Escape's mileage is worse mainly because it has a larger engine, generating 200 horsepower compared with the Contour's 170. Ford says the Escape needs the larger engine because its tall body makes it less aerodynamic than the Contour and because it can tow up to 3,500 pounds while a Contour could tow only 1,000 pounds. Since the Escape has outsold the former Contour and Mystique by a wide margin, Ford announced plans in early 2002 to close one of its two Taurus assembly plants, the one in Chicago, and retool it to make a Taurus-based crossover utility vehicle instead, the Ford Cross Trainer.

Over the last several years, automakers have become increasingly bold in labeling new models as light trucks and NHTSA has done nothing to stop them, saying that laws written in the 1970s give automakers considerable discretion. The Lexus RX-300, for example, is essentially a high-riding Toyota Camry wagon with an unusually tall front end and all-wheel drive. When Toyota, the parent company of Lexus, introduced the RX-300 in March 1998, it certified the vehicle as a car for fuel-economy and emissions purposes. But when Detroit automakers began classifying all their crossovers as light trucks, even the ones that looked like wagons, Toyota quickly followed their example. When the Toyota Highlander was introduced in January 2001, Toyota officials acknowledged that it was virtually identical to the RX-300, but they chose to certify the Highlander as a light truck.

Few of these crossover vehicles are ever likely to be driven up a rocky mountain trail. "Every crossover vehicle is being called a sport utility even if they can't go up a wet driveway," said Jamie Jameson, the vice president for North American sales and marketing at DaimlerChrysler.

Yet the most egregious offender in pushing the light-truck definition to the limit is Chrysler's PT Cruiser, which went on sale in 1999. It started off as a Dodge Neon compact sedan that was turned into a high-backed wagon and had the front reshaped to give it the appearance of a 1930s gangster getaway car. Its look is so unconventional that on several occasions, Chrysler's management almost cancelled the vehicle. The program survived because it had one very persistent, powerful patron, Chrysler's president and then vice chairman, the ubiquitous Bob Lutz.

Chrysler was determined to have the Cruiser labeled a light truck. Lutz and other executives wanted to use the Cruiser's small-car mileage to offset the dismal mileage of the Dodge Durango SUV and Dodge Ram pickup. They also wanted the rear windows of the Cruiser to hold tinted glass for a more menacing image. (As previously mentioned, federal regulations ban factories from installing tinted glass in the rear windows of cars but not light trucks.) The problem lay in the fact that the Cruiser had the same meager six-inch ground clearance as the Neon, making it very hard to classify as an off-road vehicle even if all-wheel drive were offered. So Chrysler engineers came up with an ingenious solution. To qualify for labeling as light trucks, minivans must have a flat load floor extending from behind the front seats to the back of the vehicle, with the rear seats either removed or folded down. Like most cars, the Neon had a design that did not permit this, but Chrysler engineers did not let that stop them. They designed the Cruiser's rear seats to fold down, then put brackets on the walls of the rear cargo area at the same height as the top of the folded seats and put a removable plastic plate across the brackets. Voilà, the Cruiser had a floor that extended from the back of the front seats to the rear door, and so met the regulatory definition of a van—although Chrysler ended up classifying it as an SUV anyway in its monthly sales report.

BMW faced a different problem when designing its all-wheel-drive X5 in the late 1990s. BMW had been complaining that it paid penalties because its powerful cars did not meet the federally mandated averages for car fuel economy, while Detroit automakers did not pay penalties while building powerful SUVs. So while the X5 was to be built using a carlike unit body so as to preserve as much as possible the nimble handling that is the hallmark of BMW cars, BMW did not want to pay the fuel-economy penalties that would ensue if it classified the vehicle as a car. The German automaker claimed no significant off-road capabilities for the X5, calling it a "sport activity vehicle" instead of an SUV. But BMW still ended up telling NHTSA that the X5 was a light truck, not a car, so as to qualify the vehicle for more lenient fuel-economy treatment. "That's the major reason: Why should we pay punitive penalties that Mercedes and Lexus do not [on their SUVs]?" said Victor Doolan, who was BMW's president for North American operations at the time. "It's the rules that are wrong, not the way we play the game."

The big question about crossover utilities lies in what their safety performance will be. Some have been doing very well in government crash tests because of their carlike designs, with the CR-V earning five stars for protecting both front-seat occupants in a frontal crash and five stars for protecting front- and rear-seat occupants in a side impact. The CR-V obtained a respectable three stars for rollover resistance, as have many other crossover utilities. The Pontiac Aztec, a GM crossover based on a minivan design, achieved a minivan-like four stars for rollover resistance.

While crash tests are a fairly good indication of how crossovers will protect their occupants in collisions with other vehicles, nobody really knows how much damage crossovers will inflict on other vehicles. There have not been enough crossovers on the road long enough to be involved in enough crashes to form statistically valid patterns. The most likely bet, however, is that they will be better than traditional SUVs but more hazardous than cars. Crossover utilities do not have the stiff frames of traditional SUVs, but their hoods are often within a couple of inches of being as tall as the pickup-based models that they ape.[6] The 1986 NHTSA study that involved slamming a dozen 3,000-pound barriers into the sides of Volkswagen Rabbits showed that hood height is considerably more important than stiffness in determining the damage inflicted in side impacts, suggesting that crossover utilities will be nearly as deadly as traditional SUVs in side impacts. Further evidence that crossover utilities will be nearly as deadly in side impacts comes from British research suggesting that the height of a vehicle's front end is more important than its weight in side impacts (although American researchers, especially at the automakers, dispute this). But because crossover utilities weigh less than pickup-based SUVs, the crossover models do appear less likely to kill car occupants in frontal collisions, for which weight matters more than in side collisions.

The overall effect of the rise of crossover utilities on everything from rollovers to fuel-efficiency will depend primarily on whether they replace cars or traditional light trucks. As mentioned, the evidence is discouragingly strong that crossover utilities are attracting people who used to buy cars and have avoided SUVs until now because they disliked the many drawbacks of driving a clumsy, uncomfortable truck. While the market share of crossover utility vehicles has burgeoned since 1997, the market share of traditional SUVs has stayed remarkably stable at 17 percent. According to J. D. Power & Associates, 62.4 percent of the vehicles traded in by Escape buyers are cars, for example, while another 8.4 percent are vans, 10.3 percent are pickups and 18.9 percent are sport utilities.

James O'Connor, the president of Ford brand cars and trucks at the Ford Motor Company, says that most people keep buying the same kind of vehicle over and over, so that defections from traditional SUVs to crossover utilities will be minimal. This suits the automakers, too, for having gone to the trouble and enormous expense of equipping factories for body-on-frame production, they are loath to convert them again.

"The crossover market is basically going to attract current car buyers," declared Rick Wagoner, GM's chief executive officer and president, in June 2001. "SUV buyers are content with SUV-type products."

18

THE SCHWARZENEGGER
DIVIDEND

Grinning broadly and wearing an impeccably tailored, light-gray suit, Arnold Schwarzenegger, the movie star and bodybuilder, drove the bright orange Hummer down Seventh Avenue into Times Square. In the front passenger seat, waving to the crowds, was Mayor Rudolph Giuliani of New York. It was lunchtime on a sunny April day in 2001, and the sidewalks were mobbed with tourists.

Police had closed the avenue to traffic. Arnold, as his screaming fans called him, rumbled down the road at practically a walking pace. For anyone used to the fleets of yellow taxis in Times Square, the Hummer was an incongruous sight. The windshield was practically vertical, not sloped, and the vehicle's sides were vertical too, meeting the hood and roof at crisp right angles and giving the whole vehicle a boxy, armored look that aped the Humvee military transport that the Army uses. Perched on the roof above the driver was a short black pillar with a foot-wide black disk on top—a night vision system connected to a screen inside the vehicle, next to the driver's sun visor, that could display people and vehicles in a 360-degree circle around the vehicle even in the dark.

Yet the Hummer's vivid orange paint made it look like an oversize piece of candy. Strapped to the back of the Hummer were two mountain bicycles, one yellow and the other red—the manufacturer's way of suggesting that the vehicle should appeal to people who saw themselves as young and athletic.

Broadway slices diagonally across Seventh Avenue in Times Square, and an Armed Forces recruiting station stands on the long, triangular traffic island in between. The Marines had parked a dark green armored personnel carrier—a Light Armored Vehicle, or LAV—at the apex of the triangle, touching 44th Street, and a half-dozen Marines in battle fatigues were standing next to it.

When the Hummer crossed 44th Street, Arnold turned the steering wheel to the left, away from the LAV, and the Hummer climbed the curb onto a stretch of sidewalk that had been cleared by the police in front of ABC Studios. Arnold and the mayor clambered out and walked to the back of the vehicle to shake a few of the outstretched hands, prompting a wave of squeals from young fans.

A huge, street-level window of the studio had swung out of the way on giant hinges. Rock music blared inside, and a hundred or so reporters, auto executives and public relations people waited. A professional driver carefully maneuvered the vehicle through the opened window and onto a narrow stage. Arnold and the mayor turned to stride in after it.

"I'll be back," Arnold growled as he left his fans, triggering more squeals. The famous line from *The Terminator* was appropriate—in the movie, he played a half-robot, half-human killing machine who spoke the words to a police officer who refused to allow Arnold's character into a police station; the cyborg returned moments later by driving a truck up over a sidewalk and through the front wall of the station.

Inside ABC Studios, a chain-link fence had been mounted behind the stage, to give what the auto executives hoped would be a gritty, urban backdrop to the gumdrop-hued Hummer. Arnold paced to the front of the stage with a microphone and began pointing out the muscular lines of the Hummer. "Look at those deltoids, look at those calves," he quipped.

Then he began telling the audience how he became a Hummer lover. He had been in Washington state a decade earlier, filming the movie *Kindergarten Cop*, when he had seen a convoy of 50 military Humvees on the road. "I stopped my car and said, 'I've got to have this car,'" he said. "I saw myself driving in the mountains in this car, I saw myself driving in the desert in this car."

So Arnold had the movie's transportation manager call AM General, the military contractor that built the Humvee in South Bend, Indiana, to demand one of the vehicles. AM General refused to provide one, on the grounds that the Humvee was a military vehicle that did not meet federal standards for sale to the public. To titters from the audience, Arnold recounted his reaction when the manager informed him of this: "I said, wait a minute, are you telling me, the Terminator, I can't have something? That's impossible."

Arnold personally called AM General executives repeatedly, and even flew to Indiana to lobby them in person. Military budgets were falling and the contractor eventually agreed to build a civilian version, the Hummer. Arnold related to the audience in ABC Studios how he bought the first one off the assembly line in late 1992, and still had it.

Continuing his banter, Arnold recounted that when General Motors bought the Hummer brand from AM General in December 1999, he spoke frequently with GM executives to make sure that they would not ruin the brand's aggressive appearance. They persuaded him that they would not.

Finishing his remarks, Arnold passed the microphone to Michael DiGiovanni, the GM market researcher who had persuaded the world's largest automaker to buy the Hummer brand, and had become GM's general manager for Hummer operations. "Mike, how was my rap, could I make it as a car salesman?" Arnold asked with a big smile.

A middle-aged General Motors bureaucrat with thinning black

hair, DiGiovanni looked short and scrawny next to Arnold (who wouldn't?) and seemed surprised not to receive whatever cue he had been told to expect in the automaker's rehearsal of the event that morning. He mumbled something inaudible to Arnold and then, still facing Arnold, recited the next line from his script.

"Hummer strives for excellence in everything we do," he intoned loudly with his back to most of the audience.

Arnold gently but firmly took DiGiovanni by both shoulders and turned him around to face the audience. "Hummer strives for excellence in everything we do," DiGiovanni repeated in a monotone to the crowd.

While the ending to the event might have been a little flat, the public reaction to Arnold's appearance was everything that GM had hoped for. In an age when the latest versions of Microsoft Windows software receives far more attention than new car models, the Hummer introduction made the evening news broadcasts of television stations across the country. Magazines about glamorous celebrities ran lots of photos taken by the cloud of paparazzi at the event. Best of all for the bean counters who run GM—the company has long been run by finance experts instead of car guys—Arnold did the whole event for free.

"I'm doing this whole thing because I'm part of the Hummer family—I was there from the beginning and I will always be there for Hummer," Arnold said.

Arnold's passion about the Hummer brand made sense. It strengthened his personal image of extreme machismo and allowed him to identify himself with a symbol of American military muscle—not a bad idea for a bodybuilder who grew up in Austria and never lost his accent after moving to the United States. His enthusiasm for Hummers not only helped create the brand but made it an international hit. He also helped rescue AM General in the process.

By a strange coincidence, AM General was yet another product of the duck-hunting trips of Roy Chapin Jr. and Stephen Girard in the 1960s. Kaiser Jeep had consisted of an unprofitable retail business, selling Jeeps to consumers, and a very profitable military business, selling Jeeps and other military vehicles to various armies around the world. Soon after Chapin bought Kaiser Jeep in 1969, he split it into two parts. The retail side of the business became the Jeep division of American Motors. The military business became AM General. American Motors sold AM General to raise money in 1982, and AM General has gone through a long list of owners since then.

When Arnold began calling in 1990, AM General was in trouble and its leaders knew it. The company had converted a transit bus factory in 1983 to assemble 20,000 big Humvees a year as part of the Reagan defense buildup. But then the Cold War began to thaw and the Berlin Wall fell. Military budgets plunged, and military orders for Humvees had fallen below 4,000 a year by the time Arnold picked up the phone and suggested a peace dividend for AM General.

Although the sport utility boom had begun by then, the Humvee was still an unlikely choice to turn into a civilian vehicle. Designed in 1979 and little changed since then, it was usually equipped with fabric doors and a fabric roof. It had no sound insulation, and virtually no heat insulation to protect the soldiers from the hot engine. The dashboard was not padded for crashes and the only seat with any springs in it was the driver's—the other three seats were just thick cloth pads on hard metal.

But the Humvee did have an extremely wide body that made it unlikely to roll over during a crash. It was so sturdy that when the American military dropped Humvees by parachute into Panama during the removal of dictator Manuel Noriega in 1989, those vehicles that landed upside down in a swamp were flipped over by Army Rangers and driven away without difficulty.

To turn a Humvee into a Hummer, AM General started by not including such Humvee options as turret-mounted grenade launchers and heavy-caliber machine guns. Instead, it installed a padded dashboard, lots of insulation, steel doors and a steel roof. A huge transmission housing still ran down the middle of the passenger compartment, but AM General installed modern car seats on each side of it.

The Hummer's doorways are so high that climbing in and out is like an exercise in rock climbing. I shall never forget coming out of an opening night performance at the Detroit Opera with my wife several years ago, and watching a parking valet try to help two gray-haired couples in tuxedos and evening dresses struggle up into their Hummer.

The list of Hummer buyers has come to read like a who's who of athletes and tough-guy celebrities, from Andre Agassi, the tennis star, to Mike Tyson, the boxer, and the rapper Coolio. AM General began selling 1,000 Hummers a year, despite a price tag of almost $100,000 apiece, and the Hummer turned into a cultural sensation, a symbol of American nationalism and excess used to sell everything from movies to toys.

Automakers commonly provide Hollywood studios with free vehicles to use in movies, television shows and music videos, hoping that the extra exposure for new models will increase sales. Sometimes the automakers pay millions of dollars for their vehicles to be used, as when BMW persuaded the producers of the James Bond series that the British secret agent should abandon Aston Martins, an English brand of extremely expensive sports cars, in favor of their German-built cars.

What was extraordinary about the Hummer was that studios began begging AM General to borrow Hummers, and were even willing to pay the Indiana company for the privilege. In 1999 and 2000, Hummers appeared in 32 feature-length movies, from *The Siege* to *Three Kings*, and in 48 television series.

"Hummers out here rent for $500 a day," said Danny Thompson, the president of Creative Entertainment Services Inc., a firm in Burbank, California, that specializes in getting commercial products used in movies. "When you're dealing with macho films, your macho videos, the rappers, they all want Hummers. It's the number one off-road vehicle requested in Hollywood."

For some movies, like *The General's Daughter*, producers were unable to persuade the military to lend them actual Humvees, so they rented Hummers that were painted to look like the real thing. The way to tell whether a Humvee in a movie is authentic is to look at the roof. A Hummer has three yellow lights mounted in the middle of the roof at the top of the windshield and at the top of the back window. These warning lights, commonly seen on delivery trucks, are required by federal regulations for all civilian vehicles wider than 6 feet 8 inches (the Hummer is 7 feet 2 inches wide). But military vehicles are exempt from the rule and do not have the lights.

Hollywood was not alone in taking note of the Hummer. Car's the Star, a store in Kansas City, Missouri, that sells model cars to children and collectors all over the country, sold more models of Hummers than any other vehicle in 1998. The Hummer had fallen to third by 2001, mainly because adult collectors moved on to newer models, said Phillip L. Schroeder, the store's president. But teenagers and even younger children continued buying more Hummers than any other model. The only limit to sales was that model Hummers only came in a 13-inch-long, die-cast edition that sold for a pricey $35.

"We could sell a lot more if we could get smaller ones," Schroeder said.

Many buyers of model Hummers were teenage boys like Cooper Schwartz, a 17-year-old in Bellevue, Washington, who was co-captain of his high school football team. As a young boy, he had collected sports cars—Porsches, Ferraris and Corvettes. But by high school, he had a black Hummer on the shelf next to his bed and dreamt of the day when he might afford a real Hummer.

"I love the fact that the Hummer is a tank; it's like a tank with fashion, it's like having your own war toy," he said. "I like something where I can look down into another car and give that knowing smile, that 'I'm bigger than you.' It makes me feel powerful."

The prospect that teenagers might be driving Hummers is terrifying yet real. Jason Frankel, a Texan who owns a factory that makes what he describes as "hillbilly" novelty teeth, has bought two Hummers and plans to buy another for his 9-year-old daughter when she turns 16. "I think it's a great first car for a kid," he said. "They can't destroy it, and they'll be the envy of all their friends."

This trend among future customers was spotted in 1999 by DiGiovanni, a shy man who sometimes seems more comfortable studying survey results than talking to other people. But when it comes to spotting changes in what consumers want, he has few equals in the world of market research.

DiGiovanni designed a "Teen Wheels Research" study. Market researchers contacted hundreds of youths, ages 13 to 18, in 10 cities and interviewed them by phone. Then they flew to eight cities and spoke in person with 65 "interview friendship pairs"—pairs of teenaged friends who were interviewed together in the hope that this would put them more at ease and make them more candid.

The results were startling: Hummer was the most popular brand overall, first among teenaged boys and third among teenaged girls. DiGiovanni decided that young Americans would want what he labeled as the "militaristic look" as they enter the vehicle market over the next decade, and became convinced that GM should provide it. "Having not grown up with Vietnam, they've been influenced by smaller points, like Desert Storm, in which America has been strong," he said. "It's not a bad thing in their minds, this militaristic look. It's a very militaristic vehicle, the current Hummer, and that appeals to these kids, it's muscular."

At the same time, AM General was beginning to realize that the Hummer brand had become too big a marketing hit for a medium-sized military contractor to exploit properly. The company tried to tap the widening market by offering some variations of the original, boxy Hummer. One offering was a "slant-back" Hummer resembling a military Humvee model that had the roof slanting down to the back bumper, to prevent the rear third of the roof from melting during the launch of roof-mounted antitank missiles. But with a cost structure designed for $100,000 vehicles and with little experience in mass markets, AM General was earning only modest profits from the Hummer's success.

DiGiovanni took his research to GM's top executives, who quickly became intoxicated with the idea. The automaker bought the Hummer brand from AM General in December 1999, for a price that was never disclosed. "For GM, a brand like Hummer is a marketer's dream," Ronald Zarrella, GM's president of North American operations, enthused at ABC Studios 16 months later. "It's an automotive icon with high recognition value, a loyal customer base and strong aspirational appeal, particularly among young people, creating another opportunity for us to connect with young buyers."

Under GM's agreement to buy the Hummer brand, AM General continues actually assembling the vehicles under contract, mainly because AM General has a surprisingly low-wage, 10-year agreement with the United Auto Workers union. But GM puts the marketing power of the world's largest automaker into promoting the new vehicle. GM is giving franchises to its 130 biggest, most successful car dealers around the country.

The marriage of GM and AM General has been odd. For a dinner the night before the ABC Studios event, five GM executives, two AM General executives and a retinue of public relations people invited a half-dozen reporters to AZ, a fashionable restaurant in the Flatiron neighborhood of Manhattan. There were two choices of entrees in the private dining room: sautéed sea bass with a rock shrimp croquette and watercress, or a very rare, inch-thick slab of beef with an asparagus salad. All five of the fairly urbane GM executives chose the sea bass, while both of the burly AM General executives sawed their way through the half-raw beef, blood running all over their plates.[1]

Hummer joined the ranks of other GM divisions like Buick, Chevrolet and Cadillac. The first new GM marketing group since the creation of Saturn and Geo in the late 1980s, Hummer is supposed to embody the nation's spirit today just as Saturn reflected a widespread desire in the 1980s for more harmonious relations between labor and management. GM's goal is ambitious: to be selling 140,000 Hummers a year within a decade, close to the level of annual sales of Cadillacs.

GM has renamed the original Hummer as the Hummer H1, and plans to continue selling 1,000 or 2,000 a year for $100,000 apiece to people whom DiGiovanni classifies as "rugged individualists." These are very affluent sport utility owners who care a lot about the vehicle's off-road performance, although only 5 to 10 percent of them actually engage in off-road driving, DiGiovanni said.

"The rugged individualists are people who really seek out peer approval," he noted.

But GM sees the real money in selling lots of slightly smaller Hummers at stiff prices. Bringing in consultants to make the work go faster and reusing the underbody of its existing full-sized SUVs and pickups, the automaker has quickly designed a Hummer H2 and hopes to sell 40,000 a year for roughly $50,000 apiece, beginning in July 2002. It was a prototype of an H2 that Arnold Schwarzenegger drove into Times Square.

Not quite as long as a Chevrolet Tahoe full-sized sport utility vehicle but three inches wider, four inches taller and with an extra inch of ground clearance, the H2 is designed to appeal to buyers who are still teenaged boys at heart. The leather front seats and dashboard are modeled on the Corvette. The gearshift, located between the front seats, resembles the throttle of a jet fighter. Prototypes even had the word "fire" on the button that drivers push to start the engine, although production models will not have this feature.

"The lawyers wouldn't let us do that," DiGiovanni said wistfully.

The Hummer H2 is being designed for "successful achievers," whom DiGiovanni describes quite cynically: "They're daring in the sense they may take a big stock market position, like buying 20,000 shares of an e-commerce stock. They really have not much intention of going off road, but it's really important for them that people tell them how successful they are."

Like the H1, the H2 bears Arnold's imprint. GM initially designed the vehicle with a sloping windshield and fairly conventional-looking tire treads. Arnold persuaded GM to make the H2 windshield practically vertical, which gives it the look of an armored car that delivers money to banks, and to adopt tires with an aggressive off-road appearance. "He didn't like the wheels we had, he thought they were too wimpy—we made some changes," said Ronald Zarrella, GM's president of North American auto operations.

GM plans to introduce a Hummer H3 midsized sport utility vehicle in 2004 or 2005, hoping to sell 80,000 to 100,000 a year for $25,000 apiece. GM executives make no secret of their desire to sell this vehicle to drivers as young as they can find them, notwithstanding the concerns of safety experts. "That will be a vehicle youth can buy, and they'll buy it because they aspire to the Hummer cachet," Zarrella said in an interview after the ABC Studios event. And beyond the H3, still on the drawing boards of GM designers and not yet approved for production by senior management, lies an even smaller and cheaper H4, which would be the size of a Jeep Wrangler and even more affordable for young buyers.

Hummers tend to appeal to people who never performed military service but wished they had, GM found in its market research. Some veterans are understandably irritated. "It bothers me that some people who never served in the military want to wear military clothing and drive military vehicles," said Bruce Harder, a retired Marine colonel who is the national security director of Veterans of Foreign Wars of the United States. "It's like someone who always wanted to be a cowboy and who goes out later in life and buys a hat and horse—well, that doesn't make you a cowboy."

Where would all these Hummers be driven? GM calculated that households earning over $200,000 a year would buy the H1 and H2 because the Hummers were indulgences rather than practical family vehicles. Fully 70 percent of the franchises are going to Cadillac dealers, instead of GMC truck dealers, in recognition of Hummer's appeal mainly to the very affluent. Astute market researcher that he is, DiGiovanni also decided that because Manhattan has more high earners than any other place in the country, it will be a hub of GM's push to market Hummers. So he is negotiating with car dealers for a ring of Hummer dealerships to surround the city, plus one in Manhattan.

"Where you see Land Rover, Lexus dealerships, those will be the areas we'll be targeting," he said. "You'll see a lot in New York City, places like Manhattan where your affluent buyers are."

Yet some of the buyers, especially young buyers, could prove to be tough characters. When GM held its first exhibit of the H2 at the Detroit auto show in January 2001, there were two fights among spectators on the first night. A cry of "shots fired" during the second fight prompted a small stampede as visitors raced out of the convention center. The police did not find a gun, however, and the exhibit proceeded, although with heavy security.

GM has not been alone among automakers in noting the appeal and profit potential of giant, military-based vehicles, although its plan is by far the most ambitious. Executives at Freightliner, one of the world's largest makers of 18-wheelers, had been watching the trend toward ever-larger SUVs with great interest. In the summer of 2000, they were ready to act. Their choice to enter the market was the Unimog.

Dr. James Molloy III, a family physician who lives on a 97-acre farm in Sheridan, Oregon, waited outside his house on the morning of Valentine's Day 2001. With him were his family and friends, including several friends who shared his passion for Unimogs, a hulking German military transport. They had all bought aging Unimogs from Europe, and sometimes gathered on Dr. Molloy's farm to practice driving them up and down a steep, muddy hillside, putting to work the Unimogs' extremely powerful four-wheel-drive systems. Dr. Molloy so loved his 1963 Unimog that he drove it every day for the 13-mile commute each way to his clinic, tooling up and down the highways at about the same speed as a logging truck and sometimes driving into downtown Portland and parking it on the street.

When the new Unimog came into view, they were awed—especially Dr. Molloy's 18-year-old son, Jimmy, and his teenaged friends. For starters there was the Unimog's size: at 9 feet 7 inches tall, it was nearly the height of a basketball net and almost 3 feet taller than the tallest SUV. It was 2 feet taller than Dr. Molloy's aging Unimog. A three-step ladder was mounted on the side, for reaching its 6-foot-high front seat. The Unimog was 20 feet long, outstripping even the immense Ford Excursion by a foot. It was 2 feet wider than a typical car and 3.5 inches wider than a Hummer H1, and carried truck-warning lights across the front and back of its roof as a result.

The Unimog had every amenity a pampered SUV lover could want. Walnut interior trim. Mood lights. Leather seats. A 1,000-watt stereo. Four beverage holders in each door. Even a vertical exhaust pipe, just like on real 18-wheelers. But it could only seat three in the cab, with a pickup truck bed behind.

Jimmy loved it, although he was a little discouraged by the estimated price: $150,000. "I thought it was incredible," he breathed in a telephone interview the next day, adding that his friends had shared his reaction. "They were all pretty thoroughly impressed—it all sounded like they wanted one."

According to the official web site maintained by Freightliner's corporate parent, Daimler-Benz, the first plans for the Unimog were made in a Berlin suburb by Daimler-Benz officials in 1942. Daimler officials refuse to elaborate on the truck's origins, and I have never found a reliable outside history. But by an intriguing coincidence, development of the Unimog began the year after an extraordinary humiliation for the German truck-building industry. Countless German trucks had become stuck in deep mud during the Nazi invasion of the Soviet Union in 1941, creating a logistical nightmare for Hitler and his generals as they tried to keep their troops supplied with ammunition, fuel and food.

Whether because of the Nazi experience on the Eastern front or for some other reason, Daimler-Benz began designing the under-body for a new truck that would be especially able to wallow through deep mud without getting stuck. The underbody would feature an extremely heavy, watertight transmission and axles, a heavy frame and a powerful four-wheel-drive system, which would allow it to be driven through knee-deep mud without breaking down.

Allied bombers shattered most of Nazi Germany's manufacturing capacity soon after Daimler-Benz made its plans, and Unimogs did not begin to be assembled until 1948. They were built then as farm tractors—Germany had been demilitarized after World War II. Marketed by Mercedes, a Daimler-Benz division, the Unimog subsequently became popular as a fire and rescue vehicle in remote areas and as a sturdy snowplow and road maintenance vehicle, as well as seeing service in the German and Swiss armies.

All of those sturdy, heavy-duty truck components weigh a lot, literally tons, and they have only become heavier and sturdier over the years. Even when empty, the latest Unimog weighs in at an extraordinary 12,500 pounds, or six and a quarter tons, more than two Chevrolet Suburbans or four Honda Accords.

Daimler-Benz bought Freightliner in 1981, and for many years Freightliner prospered. Sales rose quickly in the late 1990s when Freightliner agreed to sell and then buy back large numbers of 18-wheelers from customers at fairly generous prices after two or three years of use. For a while, Freightliner was able to resell these trucks in the used-truck market, a strategy that worked fine as long as used trucks were commanding steep prices. But then the market for heavy-duty trucks slumped in 2000 as the American economy slowed, used-truck prices plunged, and Freightliner was stuck with thousands of used trucks it could not sell.

Casting around for a way to generate new revenues and profits, Freightliner decided in August 2000 to import the Unimog from Mercedes, its sister company in what by then had become Daimler-Chrysler. Mercedes had been making and selling Unimogs in Germany for half a century, but had not exported them to the United States because they did not meet American safety and environmental rules.

Off-road driving enthusiasts like Dr. Molloy had imported hundreds of used Unimogs anyway, using a loophole in the safety and environmental regulations that exempts vehicles at least 25 years old. The loophole exists to help people bring antique Rolls Royces and so forth into the country, but the off-road enthusiasts used it to buy and import 25-year-old Unimogs that German and Swiss armed forces and fire departments had declared as surplus. While most of these enthusiasts were responsible drivers who stuck to existing trails when they visited state and federal parks, a few engaged in the pernicious sport of "tree whacking"—using the power and weight of a Unimog to knock down trees with trunks up to four inches in diameter.

Freightliner executives decided that with a few safety and environmental modifications, they could import new Unimogs from their corporate sibling, Mercedes, and sell them. They hatched a plan to sell 1,000 a year, up to 250 of them for wealthy individuals and the rest for fire departments and municipalities, as rescue trucks and snowplows.

Freightliner opted to certify the Unimog as having a gross vehicle weight of 26,000 pounds. This was a sly move. State and federal regulations require drivers to obtain commercial drivers' licenses for anything that can weigh 26,001 pounds or more when fully loaded. The vehicle actually had the mechanical strength to carry 27,000 pounds or more when fully loaded, but as long as the vehicle was not certified to carry even one pound over 26,000, it was completely legal as a personal vehicle, said Bruce Barnes, the Unimog's marketing manager.

While the Unimog has a four-wheel-drive system designed to scale dirt tracks twice as steep as the steepest road in San Francisco, it is more of an off-road truck then a true SUV. The most basic version, slated to cost $80,000 at the vehicle's introduction in 2002, consists of a three-seat truck cab and an empty chassis in back; getting even a pickup truck bed is an extra $4,000. The Unimog bears more than a passing resemblance to a monster truck that escaped from a truck rally somewhere. But Mercedes has been supplying Unimogs for years as hunting vehicles in Persian Gulf countries like Oman, for which they are outfitted by outside contractors with sleeping quarters and other amenities for prices ranging from $250,000 to $600,000. A luxury expedition model was even displayed at the Museum of Modern Art in New York City as part of an exhibit of unusual work and living spaces.

Freightliner unveiled the sport version for individuals at the Great American Truck Show in Dallas in November 2000, trying to persuade Freightliner dealers to sell it and stock the parts for it. "The Unimog adds a new dimension to both the North American 4X4 truck and SUV markets," said Jim Hebe, Freightliner's chief executive and president, in a press release. "It's incredibly adaptable and can maneuver in the toughest conditions imaginable—in high water, over the roughest terrain, and under wild weather conditions. Yet along with all its rugged ability, the sport recreational driver also gets an interior designed for comfort, style and easy access."

The sales brochure was even more provocative. "You don't need roads when you can make your own," it said on the cover, which showed a Unimog perched on a rocky crag in the mountains.

"Wanting to conquer the great outdoors is simply not a good reason to give up leather and air conditioning," it said inside. There was a photo of a Unimog driving past an office building and a Unimog diagram labeled, "Here's what SUV's and other so-called 4x4's will see as you drive by."

Perhaps most ominous for other drivers was the text on the back of the brochure: "Aggressive and bold. That's you in the Unimog."

Incredibly, no one noticed. The national media does not cover truck shows. Freightliner executives moved forward with their plans, sending photographs of the machomobile to Arnold Schwarzenegger's agent in the hope of persuading Arnold to take the first one off the assembly line (the agent did not return their calls). They began contacting collectors of used Unimogs to drum up interest in the new model. They staged their first consumer clinic, to gauge market reaction, at Dr. Molloy's home.

I heard about the Unimog from a friend a couple of months after its unveiling and wrote a fairly critical story that ran on the front page of the *Times*'s business section on February 21, 2001. A chart on the front page of the newspaper, with a caption referring readers to my story in the business section, used scale drawings to compare the Unimog to a Honda Insight coupe, an M1 tank and a Tyrannosaurus Rex. The Unimog weighed as much as a T. Rex, the text of the chart noted.

The result was a frenzy of media coverage, especially by cable television and radio programs but also some newspapers. The Internet site of "Car Talk," a National Public Radio show, held a contest to come up with a more apt name for the vehicle—Unimog is short for universal motor *gerät*, which is German for universal engine-driven apparatus. The winner was Dodgezilla, followed by Whatinthehellweretheythinkingog, The Compensator and, tied in fourth place, Frankensmog and Testostosaurus Rex.

A columnist in the New York *Daily News* was particularly dismayed by Freightliner's approach to Arnold. "Gee, do you think having an Austrian drive a German tank through America is really the best marketing plan?" her column asked. (Schwarzenegger revealed a year later that he did own a Unimog that he kept at a ski vacation home in Idaho. "It's like 9 $1/2$ feet tall," he told the *Milwaukee Journal Sentinel*. "People in Sun Valley were kind of freaking out seeing me drive around in this stupid vehicle. I can't get it into my garage, but my kids love it because it has this huge loading area in the back and I drove them to the ski slopes in it.")[2]

DaimlerChrysler officials in Germany welcomed the attention to the new model in the first few hours after my story appeared. "This thing makes the Hummer look anemic," a company spokesman in Germany said.

But when DaimlerChrysler's Washington lobbyists reached their offices that morning, after hearing about the Unimog repeatedly on the radio that morning, they had a fit. They feared that the attention would embolden lawmakers interested in restricting SUVs. I received an apologetic phone call that afternoon from Freightliner's press office to say that while nothing in my story was wrong, the company would issue a press release implying that it was wrong anyway.

The subsequent release said that Freightliner would sell a mere 300 Unimogs in 2002 as commercial trucks. The only allusion to the family market was a terse statement, "The Unimog is not intended to compete in the mass sport-utility vehicle markets." The company swiftly deleted from its Internet site the press release quoting its CEO on the Unimog. It also refused to give other reporters any copies of the sales brochure, and even refused to share the brochure with DaimlerChrysler lobbyists in Washington. Freightliner released a photo of a Unimog equipped as a fire engine, while refusing to release photos of the sport version.

A couple of weeks after the frenzy had died down, a Freightliner spokeswoman said that the company would sell 1,000 Unimogs in 2003 and that the retail market would be "10 percent, 5 percent or 25 percent; we're talking just a handful." The mention of 25 percent sounded suspiciously like the company was still hoping to sell 250 a year to prosperous individuals, just as it said in the beginning.

But a month later, Daimler pushed out the top American managers at Freightliner and replaced them with Germans, while announcing heavy losses because of the buyback program. The new executives put on hold the plan to import any Unimogs at all, even for use by fire departments and snow-plowing services.

That left them with the awkward question of what to do with the luxury sport model that they had shown to the Molloys, and which reporters around the country were still clamoring to see. The truck could not be shipped back to Europe because it had been fitted to meet American safety standards and no longer complied with some European rules. But it also had not been certified to meet American environmental regulations, a costly process required for the vehicle to be sold in the United States.

Freightliner came up with an imaginative response: It leased the Unimog, mood lights and leather interior included, for a dollar a year to the fire department of the Pima Indian Reservation in Arizona, for use as a rescue vehicle and to carry firefighters and their equipment to wildfires on remote hillsides. Firefighting vehicles on Indian reservations are exempt from environmental regulations. And the move made it likely that fairly few people—and very few reporters—would ever see the vehicle again.

The broader significance of Hummers and Unimogs lies in the fact that they are legal as family vehicles at all. They are the most egregious examples of the loopholes in federal regulations big enough to drive a truck through.

Start with fuel economy. The Hummer H1 and H2 get 13 miles to the gallon in a combination of city and highway driving while the Unimog gets 10. The H1 and Unimog manage even that only because they have diesel engines, which provide one-third better fuel economy than gasoline engines (the H2 has a 6-liter gasoline engine). All three vehicles are so heavy that they are classified as medium-duty trucks and exempt from fuel-economy standards.

Then there's air pollution. You don't burn that much diesel without emitting a lot of soot particles and smog-causing gases. But medium-duty trucks are allowed to emit a lot more of both than light-duty trucks.

What about safety? Anyone hit by a Hummer H1 or Unimog in particular is going to be in bad shape, and not just because of their great weight. They both ride unusually high off the ground and have enormous steel rails in their underbodies that do not give at all in a crash. The ground clearance of a Hummer H1 is 16 inches and it is designed to climb a vertical wall 22 inches high. The Unimog is taller still. Federal regulations require cars to have bumpers that can withstand an impact between 16 and 20 inches off the ground.

GM and Freightliner have given little attention to the compatibility of either vehicle in crashes with cars. Barnes, the Unimog marketing manager, was surprised even to be asked about it, replying, "I just couldn't speculate on that—good question."

Terry Connolly, GM's director of North American vehicle safety, candidly told me in the summer of 2000 that his office had played little role in the design of the Hummer H2, a design process that had been dominated by GM marketers and outside consultants. A few months later, Terry Henline, Hummer's design director, told me that to make sure the H2 was more capable of off-road driving than any other SUV except the H1, GM had mounted the thick steel rails in a prototype's underbody two inches higher than in a Chevy Tahoe.

Raising frame rails is one of the most dangerous design decisions of all when it comes to crash compatibility, and I began mentioning to GM executives that I thought this was a truly lousy idea. Somebody inside GM must have reached the same conclusion, because Jim Queen, GM's vice president for engineering, told me in the summer of 2001 that the height of the frame rails was being reviewed with an eye to crash compatibility. GM would also offer the H2 with somewhat smaller tires for the mass-production version, and this would help for crash compatibility, too, he said.

There is a popular theory that the aggressive appearance makes Hummers safer than cars. It is a myth, but has many adherents, like Marcie Brogan, a Detroit advertising executive. Every weekday for years, she has made her 40-mile round-trip commute in a bright red Hummer H1.

"I've always said I'd like to drive a tank," she said. "There are lots of nutty people on the road, including myself—I'm a very absent-minded driver, so safety was very important to me."

This perspective is not only self-centered but wrong, safety experts say. As a medium-duty truck, the Hummer H1 is exempt from many safety regulations and lacks basic features like air bags (although the H2 has them). The H1 also lacks crumple zones.

Keri Quinn, a 44-year-old software designer and Hummer enthusiast who lives near Dallas, proudly told me about a collision he once had with a Mercedes car. Quinn had been driving his Hummer in stop-and-go traffic on a highway on a rainy afternoon. The Hummer was a metallic green 1994 model that he had nick-named Lucy, after a truck-stop waitress he once met. Preparing to exit the highway, he was leaning forward and to his right, peering across his wide vehicle at the side-view mirror, when he was hit from behind by a large Mercedes sedan. The car's front end was destroyed but the Hummer suffered only $150 in damage.

So I asked what happened to the people inside the two vehicles. Quinn then acknowledged to me that while the woman in the Mercedes had been unhurt, the shock of the impact had whipped his head back past the side of the head restraint, injuring the base of his neck and damaging three disks at the top of his spine. He has had extensive medical treatment since then, including acupuncture, with limited results. "My neck hurts all the time, my head hurts all the time, my shoulders hurt all the time," he said.

Not the litigious sort, Quinn never filed any lawsuits after the incident, so the crash was never the subject of a rigorous review by crash analysts. But Quinn estimated that he had been rolling forward at 5 or 10 miles an hour when he was hit, and that the Mercedes behind him could not have been going more than 20 miles an hour.

While the Mercedes crumpled, the Hummer had only scratches on its bumper and a bent license-plate frame. The bumper had no give to it at all because it was a specially reinforced, steel bumper designed to be so sturdy that a helicopter crew could attach hooks to it and airlift the entire vehicle. When the Mercedes hit, Quinn felt every motion as the two vehicles came together.

"Let me put a steel pipe against your head and hit it with a rubber mallet—the pipe may not be scratched, but your head will hurt," Quinn explained.

I described the incident to James A. Armour, the CEO of AM General, during the dinner at AZ. While not familiar with Quinn's crash, he defended the overall safety of the Hummer, and said that it was tough to protect occupants' necks during rear impacts.

As for Quinn, he is still driving Lucy and remains enthusiastic about Hummers. But the crash gave him a renewed appreciation of the damage that a large, stiff Hummer could also inflict if it ever hit a car.

"I generally try to drive like a friend put it, like an elephant among kittens," Quinn said, "because you could hurt someone pretty easily."

THE TRIUMPH OF SUVS

If ever there were a city unsuited for SUVs, it is Paris. The old streets are narrow and throng with pedestrians, especially in the tourist season, when they spill off the meager sidewalks and into traffic. The cars are small and low, the result of steep gasoline taxes that more than triple the price compared to what American motorists pay. Parking places are tiny, if you can find one at all. And there is no place for off-road driving—environmentalists have persuaded local officials across the length and breadth of France to ban such activities on public lands.

Yet on a beautiful weekday morning in a wealthy Paris neighborhood in early summer, Franck Romens's Land Rover dealership was bustling. The service area was full of SUVs, some of them new and being prepared for delivery. The clients are wealthy—one is making do with his Ferrari and BMW 7-series sedan while his Range Rover is fixed. The dealership sells grille guards, and at least one of the SUVs in the service area has one. Romens's Jaguar dealership around the corner, by contrast, was comparatively quiet.

The Land Rover showroom has the usual fake woodsy feel, but

the decorator of Romens's office upstairs has taken a jarringly modernist approach, with everything in the room either black or white. Romens is candid about the opportunities in France for using four-wheel drive.

"In France, it's complicated to do," he says. "We do not have the spaces of the West" in the United States.

So the dealership makes its own arrangements. There are hunting trips to private estates, horse-riding forays and even golf trips. Four-wheel drive is unnecessary even for these activities, Romens explains, but customers want the feature anyway. "It's also a lifestyle, like an advantage in your mind—[even] if you don't do it, you can do it," he said.

Automakers in the United States like to say that consumer demand prompted them to build more SUVs. But Romens has no such illusion, saying that it is the ever-increasing luxury of SUVs that make people want to own them. "It is the product that has created the demand, it's more the vehicle that has changed than the people," he said in French.

"*C'est la mode*—fashion," he said, injecting the English word for emphasis.

SUV dealers like Romens are thriving these days, as their sales in France rose 148 percent between 1995 and 2000 even as the overall French auto market showed virtually no growth. SUVs were still just 3.3 percent of the French market in 2000, even including car-based crossover utility vehicles, but the trend toward more SUVs is clear. Nor is France alone.

While the United States remains the land of SUVs, the off-road vehicles are starting to become more common everywhere. Market researchers say that affluent families around the globe increasingly have more in common with each other, in terms of consumer tastes in everything from food to perfume, than they have in common with their less prosperous countrymen. SUVs are becoming a good example of this.

In Mexico, prosperous families have long bought Chevrolet

Suburbans to carry their families and maids between their city residences and their rural estates. But now that fashion is being followed by middle-class urban families, to the delight of General Motors, which has also been introducing smaller models to cater to those with thinner pocketbooks.

In Brazil, high crime rates have made SUVs popular, partly because they have heavy-duty suspensions that allow the vehicles to be encased in bulletproof armor. Visiting a dealership in Sao Paolo in 1997, Michael M. O'Mara, Chrysler's executive director of sales and marketing in Brazil then, told of the plainly dressed man who had recently showed up at a Chrysler dealership with his wife and adult son. Without bothering to bargain, the man ordered three armor-plated Jeep Grand Cherokees for $110,000 apiece, simply pulling out his bank checkbook to pay for them immediately. Most of the Brazilian auto market consists of very cheap cars smaller than any sold in the United States, and the results of SUV collisions with these cars will be frightful in the years ahead.

In Australia, SUVs now claim 13 percent of the market. Ford, which does a booming business in Explorers there, predicts SUVs could reach 20 percent of the market as soon as 2006. Australia protects domestic car manufacturers with steep import taxes, but sets much lower tariffs for imported trucks, a category into which SUVs have been placed. Like the United States, Australia also allows SUVs to emit more air pollution than cars, allowing manufacturers to install less expensive kinds of catalytic converters. Rapaille, who has studied the market for Chrysler, says that SUVs appeal to Australians' reptilian instincts. "Australians are survivors, that's the key," he said. "They love the feeling they can survive anywhere."

In China, which is likely to become the world's largest auto market in a decade, Toyota is preparing to build big Land Cruisers while a glossy new magazine dedicated to SUVs is now being published in Chinese. Ford is aggressively promoting its Escape in Taiwan, even perching one at the edge of the 12th floor of a building damaged by an earthquake, a publicity stunt that drew complaints of tastelessness. In the impoverished southern Philippines, successful fishermen aspire to buy used "Jeeps," as SUVs are known, although most of these vehicles are actually Japanese models.

SUVs were briefly a hit in Japan in the early 1990s but then faded, making Japan the only big country in which this has happened. Crossover utility vehicles like the Toyota RAV4 are now gaining popularity, but large, pickup-based models have not. Fujio Cho, the president of Toyota, told me when he visited the United States that this reflected the weakening of the Japanese economy, which made people less able to afford expensive models. But Honda officials have a different assessment. They say that the strong sense of community in Japan led to powerful social pressures against neighbors who chose vehicles that took up too much space for parking and blocked the views of other motorists. As in Brazil, the auto market in Japan is also dominated by small cars that are vulnerable in collisions with SUVs.

Germany has started to go the other direction, as a national leeriness of aggressive-looking vehicles seems to be fading. Seldom seen on German roads until recently, SUVs and crossover utility vehicles accounted for 2.92 percent of new-vehicle sales in 2001, more than double their proportion a decade earlier. J.D. Power and Associates, the automotive consulting firm, forecasts that these vehicles will jump to 4.7 percent of the German market by 2005 as automakers step up their output.

In Britain, Land Rover officials tell with amazement of customers who get their vehicles as muddy as possible in the countryside and then drive them proudly around London for months without washing them. Land Rover has even been running billboard ads in London simply showing an SUV covered with mud, to suggest the vehicle's owner must have a rural estate since off-road driving is as widely prohibited in Britain as in France. But while some customers use their SUVs to tow horse trailers on weekends, many are used simply to catch the train.

"Most of them you'll see parked up at the station," said Mark Pocock, the general manager of a Land Rover dealership in the London suburbs that has a short, manmade hill on which prospective buyers can try out the vehicles' off-road capabilities.

While no market has gone as gaga over SUVs as the United States, sales are clearly rising overseas. J. D. Power and Associates graciously did an extensive analysis of overseas SUV market shares for this book, and found them climbing practically everywhere except South Africa. From 1995 to 2001, the SUV share of family vehicle sales in western Europe rose from 2.6 percent to 3.3 percent, in South America the proportion climbed from 2.4 percent to 3.6 percent, and in Asia (including Australia) it increased from 6.4 percent to 8.3 percent.[1] Even with these increases, however, the United States alone still accounts for more than two-thirds of the entire world's SUV sales.

The biggest SUVs are still confined to the United States and other countries with wide open spaces, high levels of income inequality and low gasoline prices—notably Mexico, Venezuela and the Persian Gulf countries. Midsized and small models sell better in East Asia and Europe, with the Mercedes M-Class, BMW X5 and Jeep Grand Cherokee faring especially well.

The progenitor of SUVs in most markets around the world is the Jeep. The American military used it across Europe and Asia in World War II, and sturdy military surplus Jeeps found a ready market in less developed regions after the war as well. Kaiser Jeep built small factories in more than a dozen countries in the 1950s and 1960s, partly because automobile-import tariffs were still so high in most of the world then that exporting from the United States was uneconomical. Kaiser Jeep erected an enormous factory in Argentina, shipping there a lot of surplus equipment from the United States, and became one of the largest competitors in Argentina and Brazil. "We struggled like hell to sell Jeeps all over the world," said Stephen Girard, the longtime president of Kaiser Jeep.

The Jeep image from World War II, reinforced by international production and by countless Hollywood movies, endures to this day in almost every country, says Clotaire Rapaille, the psychoanalyst-designer. He traveled the globe to do studies for Chrysler of consumer attitudes toward Jeep in more than a dozen countries, and consistently found the vehicle associated with liberation. "Jeep is an American icon and because of Hollywood and American movies, it is the American liberator," Rapaille said, adding that during market research in Germany, "The Germans said you came to liberate us from ourselves. . . . Even if you're in South America and in Asia, you have this image, the idea that you can go anywhere and rescue anybody."

Among the world's major auto markets, only in Britain does the Jeep lack this image, perhaps because Britain was never liberated by American troops. Rapaille found that public perceptions of SUVs there were shaped by the Land Rover, which has long had an elite image in Britain because it was developed for the wealthy gentry to use in touring their muddy estates after World War II.

Mid-sized and small SUVs are virtually certain to spread rapidly outside the United States in the years ahead. Automakers have gone to the trouble of designing dozens of new SUV models over the last several years for the American market, which is a third of the global automobile market. Now automakers are looking to recover their investment by selling as many SUVs as possible globally. Ford has designed variations of the Explorer so as to meet different regulatory standards all over the world, and now sells it in 93 countries. High gas prices and narrow streets overseas will probably prevent SUVs from ever reaching the same market share in most countries as in the United States, but their market share will rise.

One reason why SUV sales have not grown more quickly outside the United States until now is that manufacturers have been running their factories flat-out to meet American demand and do not have a lot of extra production capacity available to supply foreign markets. General Motors ships Chevrolet Blazers to Russia from a factory in Brazil, even though a Blazer factory in Ohio is much closer to Russian ports, because the Ohio factory can barely make enough Blazers for the American market. Half of Porsche's Cayenne crossover utility vehicles are slated for the American market even though they are built in Leipzig, Germany.

But with so many SUV models now coming on the market in the United States and with a half-dozen large assembly plants now being built or converted to SUV production in North America and Europe, additional capacity is becoming available to supply other markets. If the American market for SUVs ever slows, the wave of SUVs bound for foreign markets will be even larger.

This will cause serious environmental problems. The air pollution from large-engine, less-regulated SUVs will worsen smog. More SUVs will undermine the fight against global warming, although the total number of SUVs sold overseas will likely remain smaller than the number in the United States for quite a few years.

Even scarier are the safety problems that SUVs will cause overseas. As Ford's own research with the Explorer shows, even a mid-sized SUV can inflict terrible damage on any car that it hits. The damage is likely to be even worse on European, Latin American and Asian streets clogged with subcompact cars, which tend to have even lower doorsills and hoods than most cars in the United States. Most regulators outside North America are also woefully behind in setting rules to mitigate the harm caused by rollovers. Only Canada and Saudi Arabia have started regulating automobiles' resistance to roof crush, for example, although both have simply adopted the anemic roof-crush regulations of the United States. Europe and Japan still have no standards at all.[2]

Worst of all is the threat to pedestrians. The great bulk of the pedestrian deaths in motor vehicle collisions occur in developing nations, where many roads lack sidewalks, pedestrian overpasses and other features to protect people on foot or on bicycles. Only 13 percent of the traffic deaths in the United States are pedestrians or bicyclists, while estimates for developing countries run as high as 40 percent. Putting SUVs onto badly designed roads with no sidewalks, lots of people on foot and poor medical care for the wounded is a recipe for disaster.

The United States has led the way into a highway arms race. But the body count and the environmental damage in the years ahead may actually be as high or higher far from America's shores. Since SUVs are an American creation, and since the United States has traditionally set the world's pace for safety and environmental regulations covering automobiles, the United States logically should take the lead in fixing the problems of SUVs. Yet after facing strong criticism of SUVs in the late 1990s and 2000, automakers are now emerging triumphant, with plans to build ever bigger, more aggressive, gas-guzzling SUVs with few government restrictions at all.

For a few short weeks in the summer of 2001, it seemed as though Washington might actually wipe out the biggest SUV loophole of all: the rules that allow light trucks to meet much less stringent fuel-economy standards than cars. High gasoline prices for the second summer in a row had frightened millions of Americans. The Bush Administration was pushing hard to open the Arctic National Wildlife Refuge in Alaska for drilling by its oil industry allies in Texas, and was casting about for other measures to mitigate environmentalists' opposition. Conservation had gained new public support after electric power shortages in California had been resolved through energy-saving strategies, higher retail electricity prices and regulatory limits on wholesale electricity prices.

The auto industry was beginning to run out of ways to stave off tighter rules. From 1996 through 2000, the Republican majority in Congress had put provisions in the Transportation Department budget each year to prevent any money from being spent on fuel-economy issues, thereby barring any increase in light-truck standards. But in the spring of 2000, gasoline shortages and high prices had produced considerable controversy and made it very hard to renew the provision. Michigan's Congressional delegation had fought off tighter standards only by agreeing to have the National Academy of Sciences conduct a comprehensive, year-long study into the feasibility of raising standards.

The academy ended up choosing a panel heavy on auto-industry consultants and retired oil and auto-industry officials to write the report, with no representatives of environmental groups. So in early 2001, the auto industry told its members in Congress not to bother renewing the budgetary ban on any Transportation Department examinations of energy policy.

Renewing the ban would have provoked a nasty political fight, and the industry thought there was little chance the newly elected Bush Administration would raise standards. President George W. Bush and Vice President Dick Cheney had each said that their position on fuel economy would be guided mainly by the report from the National Academy of Sciences, and that report was expected to say that limited improvements in fuel economy were possible. The industry had heavily favored Bush in its political donations the year before, having given $126,850 to Bush and just $21,765 to his opponent, Al Gore.[3]

Two longtime auto-industry allies had also taken top jobs in the new Bush Administration. Andrew Card, the president of the American Automobile Manufacturers Association from 1993 to 1998 and then General Motors' top lobbyist in Washington in 1999 and 2000, had become George W. Bush's chief of staff—indeed, he was the very first person whom Bush named for his new Administration. Bush then named Spencer Abraham, a Republican senator from Michigan who had fought ferociously in Congress against auto regulations in general and fuel-economy rules in particular, to join his Cabinet as Energy Secretary. Abraham had been the biggest single recipient of automakers' cash in 2000, collecting $185,450 from the manufacturers in an unsuccessful fight to keep his Senate seat.[4]

But the auto industry's plans unraveled in the late spring and early summer of 2001 when gasoline shortages and soaring prices returned. Refinery capacity was again proving inadequate to supply the nation's thirsty SUVs with enough fuel. Representatives and senators from California in particular began calling for higher fuel-economy standards.

To head off the pressure, Representative John Dingell, the Michigan Democrat, worked out a plan with Representative Billy Tauzin, a Louisiana Republican, and Representative Joe L. Barton, a Texas Republican who is the chairman of the House Energy and Air Quality Subcommittee. Tauzin's and Barton's districts are longtime bases for the oil and gas industry. Barton's district also has many homes of UAW workers from a vast, nearby GM factory in Arlington, Texas, that made full-sized cars for many years but was converted in 1997 to the production of full-sized SUVs. The factory itself lies not in Barton's district but in the adjacent district of Representative Martin Frost, the most senior Democrat on the powerful House Rules Committee, which controls the flow of legislation to the House floor.

Dingell, Tauzin and Barton drafted an energy bill that superficially appeared to do something about light-truck fuel economy. While allowing drilling in the Arctic refuge, it also required the Transportation Department to raise light-truck fuel-economy standards by enough to save 5 billion gallons of gasoline between 2004 and 2010.

Putting the savings in billions of gallons of gasoline was a cagey maneuver, because it sounded like a big number. But the bill also had a lot of special deals in the fine print, like extending the loophole for calculating the mileage of vehicles that could burn either gasoline or ethanol. The net effect of the bill would be to ask the Transportation Department to raise standards by an anemic 1 mile per gallon. Barton's subcommittee nonetheless approved the meager fuel-economy compromise on July 12 by a vote of 29 to 3, with most Democrats joining Republicans on the subcommittee in supporting the provision.[5] Environmentalists and their allies in Congress called for another vote on the House floor on whether to amend the energy bill so as to raise light-truck standards to the same standard of 27.5 m.p.g. that applied to cars.

Yet the auto industry's lobbyists and its Congressional allies were operating in the dark on one important question: What was really in the report being produced by the National Academy of Sciences panel? The panel had held public hearings around the country to gather technical information and gauge public sentiment. But because of the political sensitivities, the 13-member panel prepared the report with elaborate secrecy. The panel members, scattered around the country, exchanged paper copies of drafts by Federal Express instead of relying on e-mail messages that might be intercepted. They shared nothing with the White House, Congress, the Transportation Department or the auto industry.

Congress had asked that the report be completed by July 1, but the panel was not ready by then. By mid-July, however, the panel had completed its draft and asked nine anonymous technical specialists on gasoline mileage to review it; they liked it.

The draft report did not recommend specific increases in fuel-economy standards. But the executive summary clearly stated that the average fuel economy of new vehicles, especially sport utility vehicles and pickup trucks, could be raised with existing technologies by as much as 8 to 11 miles a gallon over the next 6 to 10 years.

The panel looked at the extra costs of using more lightweight, high-strength steel alloys and modern engine technologies like variable valve timing, which were already available on some cars made in Japan and Europe, where gasoline prices were high. Then the panel calculated all the improvements in fuel economy that would pay for themselves in the United States in gasoline savings over the typical 14-year life of a vehicle if gasoline stayed at $1.50 a gallon, the price prevailing that summer. The report concluded that it would be cost effective for midsize SUVs to get an average of 26 to 30 m.p.g. instead of 21 m.p.g. (using lab calculations of fuel economy, not window-sticker values). Large SUVs could get 24 to 26 m.p.g., instead of 18, an improvement of 35 to 49 percent.

Those were eye-popping numbers for anybody who had followed the endless political struggles over fuel-economy averages, although still not as high as the environmentalists wanted. Yet the improvements would not be especially expensive. The mileage gains for midsize SUVs could be achieved at a cost of $1,100 a vehicle, the panel said, while the gains for large SUVs would run about $1,400 a vehicle.

Best of all, many changes could be made without affecting the safety of the driving public. Encouraging automakers to build more small cars might cause more traffic deaths, the report warned. But encouraging automakers to build fewer large SUVs and pickups was different, the report said, adding "the adverse safety impact could be minimized, or even reversed, if weight and size reductions were limited to heavier vehicles (particularly those over 4,000 pounds). Larger vehicles would then be less aggressive (damaging) in crashes with all other vehicles and thus pose less risk to other drivers on the road."[6]

Auto executives hit the roof when I wrote a front-page article for *The New York Times* based on a copy I had obtained of the key sections of the report. A frenzy of activity ensued, with GM in particular contacting a few panel members at their homes as well as staff at the National Academy of Sciences. Paul Portney, the panel's chairman, has maintained that changes were subsequently made strictly for scientific reasons. But others close to the panel disagree, with one saying, "Some members of the committee heard from the auto industry and got more nervous as a result."

Whatever the reasoning, key sections of the report were redone. The document finally made public on July 30 was somewhat less optimistic than the draft. The fuel-economy gains could only be made over 15 years, not 6 to 10 years, and they would be slightly smaller than previously predicted. Environmental groups and their Congressional allies demanded that the National Academy release the earlier draft, but the Academy refused, saying that doing so would chill future research. The panel members agreed to destroy their own copies of the draft, and other journalists and environment-minded members of Congress were never able to obtain copies of the draft either. Even so, environmentalists still thought they had the votes to pass an increase in light-truck standards to 27.5 miles per gallon. They had not reckoned, however, on the power of the UAW.

While the automakers were lobbying the Academy panel, they were also reaching out to the UAW. The union had sat out the fuel-economy debate through the spring and most of the summer, reluctant to antagonize environmentalists. GM stepped up the pressure in late July by warning publicly that if light-truck standards were raised to car standards, it might have to close 16 of its 26 assembly plants in North America. Chrysler said that it would have to close two of its 13 assembly plants, while Ford said that it might not have to close any factories. Since all three automakers sold light trucks with very similar gas mileage, GM's dire prediction seemed odd at best, for it was based on an assumption that light-truck standards would be raised overnight, instead of over six years, as Democrats were proposing.

The UAW decided at the end of July to oppose any increase in fuel-economy standards beyond the Dingell-Tauzin-Barton plan. All of the union's powerful regional directors, often political power barons in their states, began calling Democratic congressmen in the four days before the energy bill finally came to the House floor on August 1.

The amendment to raise light-truck standards to 27.5 m.p.g. was decisively defeated, 269 to 160, so the Dingell-Tauzin-Barton plan stayed in the bill. "We got 80-some Democrats to vote against the amendment, and 40 of them were because of the UAW," Rob Liberatore, who had become DaimlerChrysler's top lobbyist in Washington, chortled afterwards. The House then voted to open the Arctic refuge to oil drilling and passed the entire energy bill, a huge victory for President Bush.

Some of the most powerful Democrats decided at the last moment to vote against the environmentalists, including Representative Dick Gephardt, the House Democratic leader, whose district in St. Louis, Missouri, is home to a Ford Explorer factory. Another key defector was Martin Frost of Texas, whom environmentalists had considered an ally on fuel-economy questions for years until GM converted the factory in his district to building full-sized SUVs. Frost's central role on the House Rules Committee meant that his defection posed a serious long-term problem for environmentalists.

Representative Dingell and his wife, Debbie, held their annual Labor Day Weekend party four weeks after the House vote. The party is an institution in Michigan politics. Politicians, auto executives and a few journalists gather to hobnob on the back deck of the Dingells' brick home in a gated community in Dearborn, less than 2 miles from Ford headquarters. It was a Hawaiian-theme party in 2001 with a catered buffet, and the crowd spilled off the deck in both directions, into the house and onto the backyard below.

The cream of Michigan's politics was there, some of them wearing garishly bright Hawaiian shirts. Jennifer Granholm, the state attorney general and a Democrat, was pressing the flesh on the deck and cheerfully talking about her hopes to become governor. Representative David E. Bonior, the second-ranking Democrat in the House of Representatives as the Minority Whip, had come back from Washington and was telling people about his gubernatorial ambitions, although in his usual serious, almost somber tones. Representative Sandy Levin, a powerbroker on the House Ways and Means Committee, was giving carefully balanced assessments of free-trade issues.

Inside the house, in the white-walled living room with white furniture, Representative Joe Knollenberg, a senior member of the House Republican Policy Committee, was bubbling happily about the subject that had really preoccupied Michigan politicians through the summer, defeating a big increase in fuel-economy standards for light trucks. "I would never have counted on Gephardt's vote until the last day or two," he said.

John Dingell himself, the longest-serving member of the House and still powerfully built at 75, wore a very loud, orange, short-sleeved shirt with a palm-tree print on it. Standing on the deck near the buffet table, he put a meaty left arm around my shoulders and relished his latest success, especially the unexpected support of Congressman Frost from the Rules Committee. "Marty's a smart fellow," he said. "You're supposed to represent your constituents."

Dingell added that he looked forward to more such votes, telling me with an amused smile that, "I see these things with great objectivity, and a strong auto industry is in the interests of this country."

By coincidence, another big event for SUVs happened a day after the House vote: Bob Lutz returned to power in the auto industry. He had retired from Chrysler in July 1998, unwilling to report to the company's new German masters. Retirement quickly bored him, and he became chairman and chief executive of the Exide Corporation, the world's largest maker of automotive batteries, like the DieHard brand. But his skills as a designer and marketer of automobiles were clearly wasted at Exide.

So the auto industry was electrified on August 2, 2001, when he showed up at a press conference at GM's monolithic headquarters next to the Detroit River for the announcement that he had been made vice chairman of the company with total authority over the development of all future vehicles. For stodgy GM to choose the ultimate car guy for such a top job was huge news in Detroit. The city's two daily newspapers, the *Detroit Free Press* and *Detroit News*, were ecstatic. Both ran banner headlines across the top of the paper the next day; indeed, every single story on the front page of the *Detroit News* on August 3 was about Lutz and the implications of his move.

The only GM model that Lutz wanted to talk about at his press conference was, predictably, the Hummer H2. He was effusive about how GM engineers had designed the H2 to be somewhat less unwieldy than the original Hummer but still pugnacious. "When I saw that, I thought, 'Boy, this is absolutely sensational—a reduced-size Hummer where you can garage it and get it through car washes,'" he said. "In an era where everybody has a sport utility vehicle and they all look the same, this one is different."

Lutz was 69 years old when he joined GM. The automaker has a policy that all senior executives must retire upon turning 65, but the company's lawyers reviewed the policy and declared that there was no retirement rule covering people who joined the company after turning 65. Lutz himself joked that, "As someone said, 69 in centigrade is only 18."[7]

He began prowling GM's design studios in Warren, Michigan, looking for good ideas for future vehicles. Within a week of his arrival, a call went out from GM's headquarters to Clotaire Rapaille's office in Boca Raton, Florida. The world's largest automaker wanted to hire the Frenchman who had advised Chrysler during Lutz's years there, and who had some very strong ideas about how to market sport utility vehicles.

Lutz quickly began redesigning some models and canceling others. To his credit, he gave considerable attention to GM's dwindling car sales. He particularly looked for ways to create the sort of crisp-handling, nimble cars that he and other auto executives liked to drive instead of the burly SUVs that the public wanted to buy. But he made some last-minute changes to the company's SUV lineup, too, notably to make the Hummer H2 even scarier, and prepared to unleash them that winter at the Detroit auto show. He also moved swiftly to consolidate his power at GM, and was named chairman of the company's entire North American operations on November 13 while remaining GM's vice chairman for worldwide development of future vehicles.

The press previews at the Detroit auto show are held at the most dismal time of year in Michigan, early January, just when some of the worst blizzards hit. The show is never quite ready on time, so the towering back doors of the vast convention center are left open for the latest car and SUV prototypes to be brought in, admitting arctic blasts of cold air. Journalists and auto executives dodge fork-lift trucks and try not to trip over the miles of cables that workmen are connecting to the many exhibits.

The show is nonetheless the Cannes Film Festival and the Comdex technology show of the auto industry all wrapped into one. It is a can't-miss event that draws 6,000 journalists and 22,000 auto executives and engineers from all over the world, followed by 700,000 paying visitors when it opens to the public. Big automak-ers spend as much as $50 million to mount huge exhibits of their latest models, complete with artificial hills and waterfalls for the SUVs and even executive meeting rooms on specially constructed platforms overlooking the show floor. The companies bring in acro-bats, mimes, entertainers like Jay Leno and phalanxes of beautiful women to introduce their latest models, often using the television footage later in advertisements.

The automakers try to create a favorable impression of their lat-est models, in the hope that this will percolate out to the general public. In January 2002, most of the latest models were SUVs and crossover utility vehicles. Each manufacturer also seeks at the show to persuade the press that it has momentum: it stands on the cut-ting-edge of design with rising sales and strong morale. And at the 2002 show, there was little doubt that General Motors had the momentum.

Bob Lutz strutted on stage, showing off the Pontiac Solstice sports car and other prototypes with a big grin on his face, and later led a throng of reporters around the show floor, giving his dismis-sive evaluations of competitors' models. Rick Wagoner and other top GM executives stood nearby and were a little more subdued, but beaming like new parents.

They had good reason to be pleased, for they were surrounded by success. Upon becoming the company's CEO a year and a half earlier, Wagoner had promised to increase the company's market share by selling more SUVs and pickups. Everyone had been skeptical then. GM's market share had been fairly steadily eroding since the early 1960s, when it held more than half the American market and mostly worried about antitrust regulators.

But in 2001, GM had finally managed to increase its market share. It had been a small increase, just a quarter of a percentage point, to 28.1 percent. But in a market where every tenth of a point was more contested than Helen of Troy, GM had shown that it could stop its slide.[8] To manage its feat, GM had cranked up SUV production and overtaken Ford to become the first automaker ever to sell more than a million SUVs in a single year in the United States.

The reasons for its comeback were prominently displayed in the exhibits of each of GM's divisions. Scattered through the Chevrolet, GMC and Oldsmobile exhibits were the mid-sized Trailblazer, Envoy and Bravada, respectively. All three SUVs had been introduced the previous spring with more aggressive-looking front ends but simpler, less expensive suspensions than Ford had chosen for the Explorer. The three GM models had gained tens of thousands of customers at the Explorer's expense.

In the Cadillac area was a full-sized Escalade, touted in a sign as the "most powerful SUV in the world" and extolled in a rap artist's song. With its very tall, toothy grille, it looked like a very large shark traveling down the road with jaws gaping. Escalade sales had jumped 34 percent in 2001 even as sales of Ford Motor's somewhat less sinister-looking Lincoln Navigator had slipped 16 percent.

Nearby was the all-new, equally menacing Escalade EXT, which was essentially an Escalade with a shorter passenger compartment to make room for a short, covered pickup-truck bed in the back. Cadillac was also preparing for introduction in 2003, although it did not actually display, a much larger Escalade EVT that would be an SUV similar to the Chevrolet Suburban. Also in the works was a mid-sized Cadillac SRX crossover utility vehicle. The Escalade, EXT and EVT were part of an extraordinary fleet of full-sized, pickup-based SUVs that GM was building. The Escalade, Escalade EXT and Escalade EVT all had the same mechanical underpinnings as the

Chevrolet Avalanche, Tahoe and Suburban, the GMC Yukon and Yukon XL and the Hummer H2, as GM kept breeding ever more ferocious looking bodies to bolt on underbodies originally designed for the Chevrolet Silverado and GMC Sierra full-sized pickup trucks.

Near the center of the GM exhibits was a hulking, black Hummer H2. It sat on a pedestal behind steel bars, with fog being blown around its base. A large box attached to the bars had a warning, "DANGER: High Voltage, 500,000 Volts, Authorized Personnel Only." There was no high-voltage equipment inside the exhibit, of course, but it added to the vehicle's sense of menace.

In a gesture to address crash compatibility, GM had installed a hollow steel beam across the front end of the H2's frame rails, just behind the bumper, to reduce the risk of overriding cars' bumpers and doorsills. After some careful design work, the frame rails were the same height as a Tahoe's rails—somewhat taller than a car's, although not as high as in some SUVs. But the front of the H2's hood measured a towering 51 inches high, 10 inches higher than even the hood of a Tahoe.

The frame rails and hood could have been a little lower were it not for Bob Lutz's last-minute intervention. During a visit several months earlier to the Hummer H2 factory in Indiana, Lutz had been shown versions of the H2 with and without the smaller tires. Jim Queen, GM's vice president for engineering, had been expecting the smaller, but still huge, tires to improve the vehicle's crash compatibility. Lutz decided on the spot that the smaller tires did not fit the H2 image and ordered that they not be used at all. He subsequently used the incident in interviews to illustrate how he was spicing up the design of GM vehicles. But the frame rails and hood rode four-fifths of an inch higher with the larger tires than the smaller tires, a classic example of how design and marketing considerations sometimes take priority over safety.

"He just liked the more aggressive appearance," said Bill Knapp, the H2 program engineering manager, as he hovered near his creation at the Detroit auto show.

The terrorist attacks on September 11, 2001, had played into GM's hands. Hummers consistently received strong scores when shown to small groups of consumers before the attacks, but the ratings soared after the destruction of the World Trade Center towers and the partial burning of the Pentagon. Standing near Knapp, DiGiovanni cheerfully predicted that the H2 would be sold out as soon as it reached dealerships.

The September 11 attacks had briefly threatened to turn a mild recession into a deep one, with severe consequences for the auto industry. Consumer confidence had plunged. Dealerships had been deserted. But GM responded with an extraordinarily successful discount program. Dubbed "Keep America Rolling," it offered zero-percent financing for three years on all GM models, including SUVs.

GM had offered rebates and low-rate loans before on its cars. But for the first time, GM was offering extremely generous deals on SUVs and GM had lots of SUVs to sell because it had been converting car factories to their production. With profits of $10,000 or more on each large SUV, there was a lot of room for discounting. Lending money to customers with no interest cost GM about $4,500 on a $35,000 model, so it was still making money. Ford and DaimlerChrysler were compelled to match GM's terms, and Americans thronged dealerships from coast to coast to buy SUVs in record numbers. October 2001 ended up being the best sales month in the American auto industry's history, and continued discounts in November and December produced strong sales in those months, too.

Auto factories, especially SUV factories and their suppliers, worked full tilt and their workers began going to restaurants again, buying new cloths and otherwise spending money. So important is the auto industry to the economy that in a front-page article, *The Wall Street Journal* credited GM's incentive program with having prevented a mild recession from turning into an economic nosedive—although the economy continued to show signs of serious long-term weaknesses into 2002.

GM could afford to offer the deep discounts even more than Ford or DaimlerChrysler. GM had been quietly pouring billions of dollars into converting car factories to SUV production while expanding and modernizing existing SUV and pickup truck factories. Wandering across the 2002 Detroit auto show, I happened to meet John Devine, GM's vice chairman and chief financial officer, and the former chief financial officer of Ford. He happily assured me that GM had been making money even when offering discounts on every model, and had been able to ratchet back a few of the discounts on better-selling models at the end of the year with little loss of sales.

Walking by the Porsche exhibit, I happened to find James Harbour, the famous manufacturing productivity consultant who evaluates assembly plants around the world. Sitting wearily in a metal chair left over after a press conference for the introduction of a new Porsche 911, Harbour waxed enthusiastic about how GM was changing the way automobiles were built.

Instead of each factory producing different models with different equipment, GM had transformed no fewer than eight of its two dozen vast assembly plants in North America to make full-sized SUVs and pickups by exactly the same processes. The potential for cost savings and quality improvements was huge.

"Every one of the air conditioners goes in the same place in every factory," Harbour marveled. "How would you like to have eight plants all the same? I find a problem in one, I fix it in all, it's all standard."

I strolled several times over to the Ford display, a two-floor extravaganza that covered the area of a football field with a few cars and a lot of SUVs. Only a few of the Ford executives seemed cheerful, notably those in the central location devoted to the company's Land Rover division, which was introducing a completely redesigned Range Rover. Large, flat-panel television screens mounted on the polished wood walls of the Land Rover display showed ads of the Range Rover on safari and traversing perilous terrain. A Range Rover hung diagonally from the wall, so that admirers could gawk at its heavy-duty four-wheel-drive system.

Stephen Ross, Land Rover's head of vehicle development and the former chief product planner for the Explorer, stood below the suspended vehicle and talked about its remarkable capabilities to extricate itself from bogs and ascend rock fields. But he was also frank about how many customers would ever try such activities in a luxury vehicle that would soon go on sale for more than $70,000. "Who's going to boulder crawl in this thing?" he asked. "But you have to be true to the brand, so you have to be able to boulder crawl."

In the nearby Ford brand area of the Ford complex, a few signs still promoted the automaker's slogan, "Cleaner, Safer, Sooner." The Expedition had been completely redesigned and the new ones were on display, to go on sale in the autumn of 2002. Ford also displayed a separate Expedition underbody, and a nearby sign helpfully explained that the new underbody had a Blocker Beam at the front to reduce damage to cars. Some of the underbody parts were painted bright blue, to indicate that they were made of lightweight alloys to improve fuel economy slightly. But the huge, boxy vehicle's window sticker, not yet printed at the auto show, would later show poor gas mileage: 14 m.p.g. in the city and 17 m.p.g. on the highway for the main version, equipped with four-wheel drive and a big 5.4-liter engine.

Across an aisle, Volvo, also a Ford division, was displaying its first crossover utility vehicle, a black XC90. It was equipped with a reinforced roof for rollovers—something that American automakers, including Ford, were still insisting was unnecessary for SUVs that they built in the United States. Using a carlike unit body instead of a body-on-frame design based on pickup trucks, the XC90 also had a front end that was designed to crumple and absorb energy in a crash. There was a hollow steel bar down low in the front to reduce the risk that it would ride over car bumpers and door sills.

But when I fished my tape measure out of my pocket, I found that the front of the hood was 38 inches high, lower than for most SUVs but still 8 inches taller than on the Volvo S80 sedan. I asked Christer Gustafson, Volvo's senior safety engineer, about the hood height. He responded that while Volvo had done a lot about crash compatibility, cars would simply have to be equipped with side air bags to defend their occupants against side impacts by the growing number of high-hood vehicles on the road. Since side air bags have only been available as options on a few new, fairly expensive models in the last three years—and since side air bags are almost impossible to find in the more affordable market for used cars—that advice seemed like faint comfort for most car drivers today.

A few Ford executives occasionally walked past the displays and they looked grim. They had good reason to be worried. The company had gone from a profit of $7.24 billion in 1999 and $3.47 billion in 2000 to a loss of $5.45 billion in 2001. Unlike GM, Ford had not been converting car factories to SUV production, and it had been slow to standardize production techniques. Ford's quality, measured by complaints per 100 vehicles, had slipped to last among the Big Three, and its market share began to erode.

Bill Ford had ousted Nasser as Ford's CEO on October 30, 2001, and declared that the company would pursue a more cost-conscious approach to doing business. With Bill Ford's backing, Nasser had made many mistakes. He had poured billions of dollars into everything from car dealerships to scrap yards to Internet marketing in the hope of turning the Ford Motor Company into a more diversified company like General Electric. These ventures not only lost money but distracted Ford Motor's management from the basic task of producing and marketing cars and light trucks. The company had serious trouble even manufacturing new models reliably, forcing an embarrassing series of recalls of the new Escape and the redesigned 2002 Explorer soon after each went on sale. While GM's design studios had been cranking out a wide range of increasingly menacing-looking vehicles, Ford had stuck with the less sinister looking Ford Expedition and had barely changed its appearance even for the new model displayed at the Detroit auto show. Expedition sales weakened as reptilian buyers flocked to GM showrooms instead, and Ford stopped running its Michigan Truck Plant around the clock, although it remained the company's busiest factory.

Bill Ford's dream of turning the Ford Motor Company into the world's most socially responsible automaker had been overturned by the Firestone debacle just as surely as an Explorer with tires that disintegrated. The Ford brand had been so tarnished that it would be nearly impossible to position it in the marketplace as the brand for people who wanted an especially safe or clean-running vehicle, so the financial justification for Bill Ford's strategy had collapsed. His mantra, "Cleaner, Safer, Sooner," had infuriated rival auto executives from 1998 to 2000 by gradually forcing them to compete in areas like fuel economy and air pollution, instead of just doing the bare minimum to meet government regulations. But now that slogan, while still used for signs at auto shows, largely disappeared from the lexicon of Ford executives, in favor of a cost-cutting mantra: "Back to Basics."

Especially bitter was the outcome of Ford Motor's massive purchases of palladium for the souped-up catalytic converters that made Ford SUVs and pickups less polluting than many rival vehicles. Ford had come to account for a fifth of global palladium consumption. Its heavy buying had driven up the rare metal's price tenfold in precious metals markets, to $1,100 an ounce in early 2001, nearly four times the price of gold. Research engineers at Ford and other automakers had watched the price spike and had come up with ways to use less palladium in each catalytic converter without any loss of effectiveness. But Ford's purchasing department had not kept abreast of the technical progress and went on signing contracts to buy more palladium, even paying top dollar for years of future production from palladium mines. In late 2001, the price of palladium collapsed below $400 an ounce and Ford's top management realized that the company had enough palladium sitting in vaults to satisfy its needs for at least a decade. Proving perhaps the cynical maxim that there is no reward for virtue, the automaker announced a $1 billion loss on its palladium stockpile on the last day of press previews at the Detroit auto show.

Ford Motor insisted that it still planned to improve the average gas mileage of its SUVs by 25 percent by 2005. But it had run into problems in that endeavor, too. The company had planned to start selling tens of thousands of gasoline-electric hybrid Explorers in 2005, but put the program on hold for technical reasons.

Washington's interest in pushing Detroit to address gas mileage was also flagging. Energy Secretary Spencer Abraham showed up at the Detroit auto show to announce that the Bush Administration would halt the Partnership for a New Generation of Vehicles. The partnership had required automakers to mass produce some high-mileage cars by 2004 in exchange for what had ended up being $1.5 billion in government research subsidies. The automakers were allowed to keep the subsidies while the Bush Administration set up a new program, called Freedom Car, that did not require actual production of vehicles. Freedom Car is to devote its subsidies to the development of fuel-cell vehicles, even though it will be many years before such vehicles account for a significant percentage of vehicle sales. Secretary Abraham nonetheless suggested that Freedom Car represented an alternative to fuel-economy standards.

Secretary Abraham's appearance was a brief diversion from the hyping of new models at the auto show, as journalists and executives spent most of their time in throngs around the many SUVs on display. The large cars and minivans sprinkled around the show at various automakers' exhibits, by contrast, might as well have been invisible. Most of them had not been updated for years, and almost nobody was even looking at them.

This was not surprising, since sales of large cars and minivans had been slowly eroding since the late 1990s as Americans bought SUVs instead. But it was also sad, because the large cars and minivans were safe, affordable, practical, reliable and surprisingly fuel-efficient.

The window stickers on large cars and minivans at the Detroit Auto Show were impressive. Large cars in particular have aerodynamic shapes and high-tech engines, and most have unit bodies too. A full-sized Dodge Intrepid with a 2.7-liter engine gets 20 m.p.g. in the city and 28 m.p.g. on the highway, according to the EPA calculation for its window sticker. A capacious Toyota Avalon, Japan's answer to Buick, gets 21 m.p.g. in the city and 29 m.p.g. on the highway. A full-sized Chevrolet Impala matches the Avalon in the city and gets 32 miles to the gallon on the highway. Minivans are not as efficient as large cars, but are still much better than SUVs. A Honda Odyssey gets 18 m.p.g. in the city and 25 m.p.g. on the highway.

As strong demand and aggressive marketing have pushed up SUV prices, reliable large cars and minivans are also available at very reasonable prices. When *Consumer Reports* listed its "Finds for under $25,000" for 2002, they included three minivans—the Dodge Caravan SE, Honda Odyssey LX and Mazda MPV LX. There were also 28 cars on the list, including large and fairly large models like the Chevrolet Impala, Dodge Intrepid SE, Honda Accord, Mercury Grand Marquis GS and Volkswagen Passat GLS. But only four SUVs made the list, and all of them were fairly small; the biggest was a two-wheel-drive version of the mid-sized Toyota Highlander equipped with a tiny four-cylinder engine.[9]

Perhaps most important, large cars and minivans inflict far less damage to other vehicles than SUVs do, yet provide excellent protection for occupants. NHTSA assigns new vehicles one to five stars for their performance on each of five different safety criteria: driver protection in a frontal crash, front passenger protection in a frontal crash, driver protection in a side crash, rear passenger protection in a side crash and vehicle resistance to rollover. No vehicle has received the highest possible rating, five out of five stars, on all five assessments, or 25 stars altogether. But three vehicles in the 2002 model year almost managed this automotive equivalent of a royal straight flush, receiving top scores on four out of five criteria, and falling just one star short of a perfect score on the fifth criteria, for a total of 24 stars.

Not one of these safety standouts is a sport utility vehicle. Indeed, no SUV even came close to being among the top-rated vehicles. The Ford Windstar minivan and the Honda Accord sedan and Lincoln LS sedan each managed the feat when equipped with side air bags. Three other models had a perfect 20 out of 20 on the frontal- and side-impact tests and probably would have four or five stars on the rollover resistance rating if NHTSA had assessed it for them: the Kia Sedona minivan, the Volvo S80 sedan and the Honda Civic compact coupe.

The star ratings for frontal- and side-impact crashes are only valid for comparing vehicles that do not differ in weight by more than 500 pounds. A Honda Civic coupe would be at a disadvantage in weight in many collisions, although its nimbleness might help a driver avoid a collision at all. But the larger cars and minivans are close to 4,000 pounds. Beyond that weight, further increases in weight offer few additional safety advantages for occupants while causing greater danger to other road users, according to the Insurance Institute for Highway Safety. So large cars and minivans not only fare well in the number of stars they earn but are close to the ideal weight for collisions with a wide variety of other vehicles.

By contrast, only two SUVs and one pickup managed to get even 22 stars: four-wheel-drive versions of the Lexus RX300 and Ford Escape SUVs when equipped with side air bags and the two-wheel-drive version of the Nissan Frontier pickup. Most other SUVs and pickups fared considerably worse, even while putting car drivers at great risk.

As the auto industry celebrated at the Detroit auto show, the National Highway Traffic Safety Administration was struggling along with anemic budgets. Research into crash compatibility had returned to the back burner where it had been for two decades. The flurry of interest from 1997 through 1999 had sent the annual budget for research into the issue up to $2.5 million. But then the overall agency's budget hit a Congressionally mandated ceiling and compatibility research was one of the first to get the axe, especially after the cost of the Firestone investigation soared. Hollowell's budget for crash-compatibility research plunged to $1 million a year, crippling his ability to hire outside statisticians like Joksch to look at real-world data, or computer programmers to update the agency's model of vehicle-to-vehicle crashes.

"All the things we wanted to do exceeded the ceiling," Hollowell lamented. "We're working at a slower pace than before."

The agency fell far behind schedule in drafting the new rules required by Congress after the Firestone debacle, but almost no one paid any attention. The Bush Administration budget for fiscal 2003 called for NHTSA spending to stay virtually flat, which meant a cut after inflation was included. NHTSA was still struggling to develop a driving test of rollovers, but faced the certainty of fierce industry opposition to anything it proposed.

At the same time, NHTSA's defect investigators remained reluctant to declare vehicles unsafe simply because they were prone to rolling over. Five weeks after the Detroit auto show, NHTSA denied Firestone's request for an investigation of the Explorer because, as NHTSA Administrator Jeffrey Runge put it, "The data does not support Firestone's contention that Explorers stand out from other SUVs with respect to its handling characteristics following a tread separation."[10]

But the agency did implicitly acknowledge that it had trapped itself by repeatedly insisting that any SUV model only be compared to other SUVs. Near the end of the fairly formulaic press release was a remarkable warning to the public: "The Ford Explorer decision aside, NHTSA reminds consumers that SUVs in general have a greater tendency to roll over during a crash than passenger cars. In 2000, 62 percent of all SUV fatalities were the result of rollover, compared to 22 percent for passenger cars."[11]

On March 1, 2002, the agency announced the appointment of a new chief counsel: Jacqueline Glassman, who had spent the preceding seven years as senior counsel for DaimlerChrysler. The revolving door between NHTSA and the companies it regulated had spun again. Six weeks later, DaimlerChrysler responded to the rollovers of Jeep Liberty in routine tests by two auto magazines by announcing that it would lower the suspensions on all future Liberties by three-quarters of an inch.[12] But the automaker audaciously declared that it had no plans to recall the 123,000 Liberties it had already sold in the previous nine months. While Daimler-Chrysler said that the stability problem was simply not that serious, the automaker's stance showed the weakness of regulatory pressures on manufacturers to address rollover concerns.

The end of the Firestone investigation did not mean the end of Ford's troubles—far from it. The automaker's market share continued sinking in the first half of 2002 and its losses mounted, presenting Bill Ford with a stark choice between preserving the company that was his family's heritage or clinging to his environmental principles.

In September 2000, at the height of Congressional inquiries into the Ford Explorer–Firestone tire controversy, he had defiantly declared that nothing would deter him from his emphasis on environmental responsibility because, "It's not a flavor of the month, it's a flavor of a lifetime, it's a flavor of a career." But with his company's financial health in steep decline, Bill Ford put his heritage before his beliefs. He recorded a series of four television ads, including one in which he spoke of his love of the outdoors while touting his company's SUVs, and he had Ford Motor lobby vigorously in March 2002 against a Senate proposal to raise fuel-economy standards. Ford even provided its employees with sample letters to send to Congress, opposing the proposed legislation. Environmentalists and journalists alike wondered how he squared all of this with his previous pronouncements, but Bill Ford had stopped talking to practically anyone except other auto executives. His family's ownership of Ford stock made it difficult for anyone to dislodge him from the top of the company, but he faced a difficult future. He was

distrusted by Detroit's old guard, which would never forget the sac-
rileges he committed from 1998 to 2000. And he was distrusted by
environmentalists, some of whom questioned whether his commitment to the environment was ever genuine (although those who
knew him well were adamant that environmental responsibility
has been one of his most passionate beliefs since boyhood).

The startlingly swift decline of the Ford Motor Company had little to do with Bill Ford's emphasis on social responsibility, but it
completely discredited the strategy in Detroit all the same. While
automakers continue to unveil the occasional prototype for a fuel-
cell vehicle or tout a few hybrid gasoline-electric models, it is
unlikely that any automaker in Detroit will commit itself in the
coming years to specific improvements in fleet-wide air pollution
or fuel economy beyond those required by federal regulations. Bob
Lutz now sets the pace for the industry, not Bill Ford.

For SUV critics, the final defeat came when the Senate's fuel-
economy proposal came up for a vote in mid-March. Since the
House had already made clear its opposition to higher standards,
the prospects for actual changes becoming law were not great. Two
Democrats, Senator John Kerry of Massachusetts and Senator
Ernest Hollings of South Carolina, nonetheless pushed legislation
to increase average fuel economy to as much as 35 m.p.g. for cars
and light trucks alike by 2013. The automakers and the UAW
responded with predictable fury and effectiveness. GM and the
union organized rallies of workers against the bill at the Chevrolet
Suburban factory in Janesville, Wisconsin, at a transmission factory
in Toledo, Ohio, and at a full-sized pickup-truck factory in the
Detroit suburbs. Even though Democrats controlled the Senate by a
slim margin (50 to 49, with one independent), the bill was soundly
defeated on March 13 by a vote of 62 to 38. Among those voting
against the bill were not just Democratic senators from the Midwest but also Tom Carper, who had attended the reopening of the
Dodge Durango factory in Wilmington, Delaware, nearly five years
earlier, and who had moved from Delaware's governor's mansion

to the United States Senate. For good measure, the Senate even passed a separate amendment barring NHTSA from increasing fuel-economy standards for pickups at all—a provision that the auto industry's lobbyists had not even requested.

The automakers, especially GM, stood triumphant. Their allies now walk the halls of the White House and NHTSA. Neither political party is willing to challenge SUVs seriously in Congress. Fuel-economy standards have been left largely untouched, although California regulators may set standards in that state in a few years because of global-warming concerns. While the trend toward Blocker Beams and crossover utilities has had some safety benefits, the crash-compatibility problem is still horrific and regulators are nowhere near setting standards. Sales of SUVs and crossover utilities are still strong despite the Firestone tire mess, global-warming concerns and pollution worries.

For as far as anyone can see into the future, America's roads and the world's are likely to become ever more crowded with SUVs.

20

FINDING A WAY OUT

The question posed by a reader to Randy Cohen, the ethics columnist of *The New York Times Magazine*, was straightforward: "I'm about to buy a cool SUV, but my friends act as if I'm some kind of criminal. Am I?"

Cohen's four-paragraph answer in his column was unusually vehement, especially by the cautious standards of the *Times*: "If you have no compelling need for the S.U.V.'s off-road features—i.e., if your sport utility vehicle has no utility—there's no way to justify endangering others so you can play cowboy. Why should your fellow motorists support your life style with their life span?" Cohen concluded, "So if you're planning to drive that S.U.V. in New York, pack a suitcase into your roomy cargo area, because you're driving straight to hell."[1]

SUVs represent the biggest menace to public safety and the environment that the auto industry has produced since the bad old days of the 1960s, before the advent of most safety and pollution-control devices in cars. They have already killed thousands of Americans who would still be alive today if the automakers had sold cars instead. They will kill many thousands more in the coming years. In the nation's homes and hospitals, they have left a trail of people suffering unnecessarily from rollover-induced paralysis or pollution-induced respiratory difficulties.

Perhaps the saddest part of the SUV boom is that it has been so unnecessary. Automakers have learned so much about designing more fuel-efficient, low-pollution engines that today's large cars burn as little gasoline as the subcompacts of the early 1980s, while emitting virtually no pollution. These large cars, like the Lincoln LS, Toyota Avalon and Volvo S80, also provide superb safety for their occupants, with extensive crumple zones, lots of air bags and scant susceptibility to rollovers.

If a family living through the oil crises of the early 1970s were to be magically transported to a present-day car dealership, they would be astounded to find that America had found a way to have its cake and eat it too—to have safe, roomy cars with decent gas mileage and negligible pollution. But the same time-traveling family might be aghast to walk out the doors of that car dealership and look out at a street today. Instead of driving large cars, the nation's best-educated, most affluent families have switched instead to tall, tippy monstrosities with mediocre brakes that block other drivers' view of the road and inflict massive damage during collisions.

Unfortunately, there are few easy answers to the problems posed by SUVs, which is why the problems have festered for so long and grown so serious. From Hollywood stars to Washington politicians to the national media, and through prosperous neighborhoods across the country, the nation's most influential people have been largely co-opted by automakers into driving SUVs instead of denouncing them. SUV manufacturing has become a cornerstone of the economies of Michigan, Ohio, Indiana and Wisconsin, states with outsized political influence because they are so closely fought in presidential elections. Building SUVs has also become a mainstay of employment for the nation's wealthiest and most politically powerful union, the United Automobile Workers.

Yet much could be done to address the problem. The example of the Jeep Cherokee shows that other SUVs need not roll over so easily. Some kind of minimum stability standard should be set before vehicles are allowed on the market. The National Highway Traffic Safety Administration should come up with a stringent driving test for the stability of new vehicles, a step that would provide a big incentive for automakers either to make their vehicles wider and shorter or else to equip them with the latest electronic systems to reduce the risk of rollovers. SUV roofs should not be allowed to crush so easily when SUVs do flip over. State highway departments should give priority to replacing low guardrails.

Congress should give NHTSA several million dollars a year—less than the price of building a mile of interstate highway—to develop crash-compatibility standards. The ideal standard would use a barrier, shaped like the front end of a midsized car, that would be smashed into the front end of any vehicle that an automaker proposes to put on the market. No vehicle should be allowed on the market if it inflicts unacceptable damage to the barrier. This would require automakers to design their SUVs and pickups in ways that will not override the front ends of cars.

At the same time, no vehicle should be allowed on the market if it suffers unacceptable damage from the barrier during the test, a rule that would put pressure on small-car makers to improve their designs too. Federal regulators already slam such barriers into the sides of new models to determine whether they adequately protect their occupants. Given the glacial pace of the underfunded research into crash compatibility now, however, no new crash-compatibility standard is likely to take effect until at least the 2010 model year, if at all. That is a sorry state of affairs, and Congress should be able to find the money in a $2 trillion budget to step up the pace.

Protecting car occupants in side impacts is more difficult. While a few SUVs, like the Excursion, now have Blocker Beams to prevent them from leaping over the low front ends of cars, they can still pass over the even lower door sills of cars. The best answer lies in redesigning the side-impact test. Instead of using a barrier that simulates being struck from the side by a compact car, the National Highway Traffic Safety Administration should use a taller, heavier barrier that simulates being hit from the side by a midsized or full-sized SUV. This would probably force manufacturers to turn side air bags into standard equipment on all their car models, instead of just offering it as an option.

The Insurance Institute for Highway Safety will begin slamming SUV-like barriers into the sides of cars in late 2002 and will release the results to the public, in the hope of shaming manufacturers into doing more about crash compatibility and in the hope of persuading more people to pay a few hundred dollars extra for optional side air bags. High-riding light trucks will withstand this test better than lower-riding cars, so every test result should be accompanied with a warning that rollovers kill more people than side impacts and rear impacts do.

In the meantime, insurers can and should play a big role in discouraging bad drivers from choosing especially homicidal vehicles. State regulators should be requiring them to adjust liability rates by model to the fullest extent justified by insurance claims. Car drivers sometimes ask me what they can do about the scourge of SUVs. One answer is to write a letter or e-mail to your insurer, asking that it use the widest possible adjustments by model for automotive liability insurance. Send copies to your state insurance regulator and state legislators while you're at it. If you are insured by a company that outright opposes adjustments, such as State Farm or USAA, you can probably cut your insurance bill by switching to Progressive or Allstate. If you switch insurers, be sure to explain your decision to your previous insurer and insurance agent.

The mere existence of liability insurance also reduces the incentives to buy a less homicidal vehicle. State legislators need to tighten the penalties for crippling or killing other motorists or pedestrians. Michigan now revokes the driver's license of anyone convicted of driving away from a gas station without paying, a provision that testifies to the political influence of gas station owners. But not until a driver has killed two other people in crashes where the fault is unclear does the motorist lose his or her license. That is inadequate. Ideally, there should be stiffer penalties for hurting others in crashes. Jail time should be imposed not just for drunks and the handful of people who deliberately cause crashes but for motorists who hurt or kill other people through negligence, too. Prosperous families might think twice about choosing the Suburban over the minivan if they thought that a jury would be more likely to send them to prison for manslaughter after a deadly crash if they were in an SUV that they did not need. This is unlikely to happen, however, until public perceptions of SUVs change enough that juries look askance at anyone who causes a death or serious injury while driving an SUV for a trip that could have been made in a car. That day is probably a long way off.

State licensing laws for teenagers should also be changed. Some states have reduced traffic deaths by experimenting with limits on licenses for 16 year olds, like only allowing them to drive by day at first. Another useful restriction would be to ban 16 year olds from driving SUVs or pickups. These are difficult vehicles to drive, and nobody should be acquiring early driving experience in a rollover-prone small SUV or in a Chevrolet Suburban that can demolish cars.

Small businesses that hire teens, like construction contractors and farmers, would likely object to restrictions on young drivers. A case might be made for exempting farmers from such limits. But if insurers fully adjust liability insurance by model then few cost-conscious business owners will put 16 year olds at the wheels of SUVs and pickups anyway. Drivers' education courses need to be rewritten as well, to include extensive warnings about the greater difficulty and danger in driving a taller vehicle.

The use of vehicles equipped with steel grille guards or bull bars should be banned within city limits. Grille guards are almost exclusively fashion accessories, and they are killers. They are also detachable, although some models are easier to detach than others.

If people want to spend an afternoon crashing through under-growth with a grille guard, that's fine, especially if they are doing it on private property. But they should take the accessory off the vehicle when they are done. (A more modest form of this rule would be for cities to ban steel grille guards while allowing rubber or plastic grille guards, which are less dangerous; this kind of a rule would be hard to enforce, however.) While the federal government regulates factory-installed automotive equipment, cities have the authority to regulate after-market products that affect safety. Some cities have banned the distracting rows of lights that some people put along vehicle underbodies, which make them look like UFOs. Such activist city councils should turn their energies to a real safety issue like grille guards.

Headlight height and the tilting of the beams also need to be tightly regulated. The glare from high-mounted headlights, shining straight into the eyes of oncoming car drivers or bouncing into their eyes from side mirrors, is one more reason why too many people are abandoning cars for SUVs. Automakers should be required to tilt slightly down any headlights mounted at a height of roughly 30 inches or more.

The Federal Trade Commission needs to investigate the advertising of SUVs and dissuade automakers from suggesting that four-wheel drive is a safety advantage. Any ad even hinting at such an advantage—by pointing out that four-wheel drive can extricate a vehicle from snow or a swamp—should contain some warning that SUV brakes are no more effective than car brakes on slippery surfaces, and may be less effective.

Federal tax loopholes for large light trucks need to be closed so as to end discrimination against luxury cars in the tax code. The depreciation rules should not allow accelerated write-offs against taxes for business people buying light trucks with a gross vehicle weight of a mere 6,001 pounds. The rules were written to limit excessive deductions by businesspeople who bought Cadillac DeV-illes and Lincoln Town Cars for personal use. But the rules are being abused by people who buy Cadillac Escalades and Lincoln Navigators, thereby ducking taxes that someone else ultimately has to pay (or else the federal government falls deeper into debt). The cutoff for accelerated depreciation should be raised to at least 10,000 pounds, and the rules for calculating personal use should match the car rules. If there is any loophole, it should be for full-size pickup trucks with an open bed at least six feet six inches long and only a single row of seats in the front, so as to accommodate commercial and agricultural users.

The luxury tax is being phased out in 2002 anyway. But if Congress ever revives it to close a budget deficit, the cutoff for light trucks should also be raised to a gross vehicle weight of 10,000 pounds, from 6,000 pounds now.

Emissions standards need to be strengthened for light trucks, especially SUVs. Under President Clinton, the EPA issued regulations requiring all SUVs with a gross vehicle weight up to 10,000 pounds to meet the same standards as cars by the 2009 model year. Automakers have accepted the first round of emissions cuts to achieve this, in the 2004 model year. But they have been coy about whether they will challenge the subsequent reductions in the 2007 and 2009 model years, either by lobbying EPA or filing lawsuits. Congress should preempt any such challenges by putting the stricter standards into legislation.

The toughest question of all lies in what to do about the poor gas mileage of SUVs. All of the available answers have drawbacks.

A big increase in gasoline prices would be the most effective way to prompt Americans to drive fewer miles and choose lighter, more aerodynamic vehicles with more efficient engines. This would reduce gasoline consumption and make at least a small contribution toward addressing global warming while curbing American dependence on oil from the Middle East or ecologically fragile areas like the Arctic National Wildlife Refuge. High gasoline prices would also discourage young drivers with thin wallets from buying gas-guzzling SUVs in the used-vehicle market. Some economists have suggested that the proceeds from a gas tax be used to reduce other taxes, such as income taxes, so that the higher gas taxes would not increase the overall tax burden for American workers.

But the auto industry's market analyses suggest that with SUVs being purchased by prosperous families who care little about the costs of filling a tank, it would take a permanent increase in prices to as much as $2.50 a gallon to have a big effect on sales of new SUVs. A price increase on that scale is very unlikely.

The likelihood of persistently low prices at American gas stations leaves the question of whether to tighten fuel-economy standards. Economists and other fans of free markets deeply dislike the standards. But leaving the standards the way they are, with different averages for cars and light trucks, has distorted the auto market. It is bad enough that over the last 27 years, the federal government has provided a big incentive for manufacturers to replace safe, low-pollution cars with dangerous, high-pollution light trucks that are less efficient. Fighting now to keep the light-truck standards unchanged cannot be justified as letting free markets work.

The work of the National Academy of Sciences panel suggests that fairly substantial fuel-economy increases are possible. Better gas-mileage technology would pay for itself in gasoline savings and would not cause vehicles to shrink much. Ford's own promise in 2000 to raise the average gas mileage of SUVs by 25 percent by 2005—and comments by Ford officials in 2000 that they were working on similar pledges for minivans and pickups, although these pledges were never actually made—demonstrates that significant improvements in light-truck fuel economy are possible.

Research by the National Highway Traffic Safety Administration and the Insurance Institute for Highway Safety has also shown that requiring better mileage from light trucks could actually save lives. Making the larger SUVs and pickups a little smaller and lighter would not hurt the safety of their occupants, while making the roads safer for everybody else. While insurers have long argued that cars should be as large as possible for safety reasons—an argument disputed by environmentalists and some liberal safety advocates—even the insurers are critical of full-sized SUVs.

Yet simply mandating higher fuel-economy averages for light trucks could pose dangers. The risk is that while adopting better engine technology and using more high-strength, lightweight alloys in their behemoths, automakers would also build a lot more small, cheap SUVs. That would increase their gas-mileage averages in a hurry, and such SUVs would find a ready audience among young Americans. There is a historical precedent for this. Partly to meet rising fuel-economy standards through the late 1970s and early 1980s, as well as in response to high gasoline prices, automakers built huge numbers of small cars and sold them at a loss to make sure that they could continue selling big cars at a profit.

Providing an incentive for automakers to subsidize sales of small SUVs so as to sell more full-sized SUVs would be a bad idea for traffic safety. Look at the combined death rates of vehicle occupants and other road users they hit—the broadest measure of safety—and small SUVs are deadlier than any other size of SUV, and deadlier than any size of car, van or pickup truck.[2] Small SUVs are much worse than small cars. A Toyota Celica small sedan has a rollover death rate of 14 per million registered vehicles and an overall driver death rate in all types of crashes of 73 per million. A two-door Explorer with two-wheel-drive has a rollover death rate of 150 per million registered vehicles and an overall driver death rate of 231. With its high front end and stiff, pickup-based underbody, the two-door Explorer is also far more likely than the Celica to kill other motorists in crashes.[3]

Steep increases in light-truck standards also run the risk that automakers will simply beef up the weight-carrying capacity of SUV suspensions, giving the vehicles a gross vehicle weight over 8,500 pounds so as to make them exempt from fuel-economy standards. GM did this for four-wheel-drive Suburbans in the 1999 model year when it had trouble meeting the fuel-economy averages.[4] If light-truck standards are to be increased at all, phe weight cap needs to be raised to the 10,000-pound mark set in the original 1975 legislation, so as to avoid giving automakers an incentive to sell behemoths.

Further increases in gas-mileage standards for cars are a poor idea as long as light-truck standards remain much lower. Large cars, like the Buick Park Avenue, have doorsills that are high enough to catch the front ends of many SUVs. Small cars do not. Americans like roomy vehicles even for small families. If Americans are to be lured away from SUVs and back to clean, safe, efficient cars, those cars need to be as large as possible. Since some of the biggest cars these days get better mileage than some small SUVs, anything that encourages people to switch back to cars is a plus, even if the cars are not the gasoline-electric hybrid compact and subcompact cars that the environmental movement so admires.

The Kerry-Hollings legislation in the Senate in March 2002 would have kept car and light-truck standards largely separate through at least 2010, and possibly permanently, by increasing each standard separately. That would have left the SUV loophole open, which is a bad idea for safety. At a minimum, Congress should eliminate the distinction between cars and light trucks before taking any further action on fuel economy. Then if fuel-economy standards are raised, automakers will at least have the flexibility to use small cars to offset large SUVs, rather than small SUVs.

If you combine the car and light-truck fuel-economy averages for various automakers, the results vary widely. This poses a big political obstacle to combining the categories. Chrysler now sells three light trucks for every car it sells, for example, while for Honda the proportion is reversed. As a result, the combined fuel economy for DaimlerChrysler was 21.8 m.p.g. in the 2000 model year and Honda's was 29.4 m.p.g., using laboratory averages.[5] Setting a single standard for cars and light trucks, perhaps 25 m.p.g., would be an enormous burden for Detroit's Big Three while allowing Honda and Toyota to ramp up sales of their own big SUVs.

There are a couple of ways to deal with this problem. One is to require each automaker to increase its combined car and light truck gas mileage by a fixed percentage over a decade. The increase could be anything from 10 to 50 percent, depending on how concerned regulators or members of Congress are about global warming and reliance on Mideast oil.

Honda bitterly opposes any approach based on percentage increases, arguing that it should not be penalized for having had better fuel economy until now. Honda has powerful allies in the environmental movement because Honda has often led the way in introducing cleaner-burning, more fuel-efficient engines. Environmentalists love Honda for its willingness to call for higher fuel-economy standards for the industry—which would be easy to meet for Honda and hard for most other manufacturers.

But while part of Honda's high fuel economy reflects advanced engine technology, it mostly reflects Honda's emphasis on car sales, especially sales of small cars like the Honda Civic. It is absurd to design an entire fuel-economy system around preserving Honda's ability to enter the full-size SUV market if it wants to do so.

Setting percentage increases by automaker could make a new regulatory system much more palatable to the United Automobile Workers union, which would greatly increase the odds of something actually happening. Environmentalists and their Congressional allies have wasted their time since the days of the Bryan bill by repeatedly bringing overly ambitious legislation to the floors of the House and Senate without first striking compromises with the UAW. The sad truth is that by tilting the playing field in favor of SUVs for a quarter of a century, government regulations have left the economy of the Upper Midwest addicted to the production of dangerous substitutes for cars. Any fuel-economy policy must recognize this huge social and economic problem.

Opposition to new standards from farmers, builders and other owners of small businesses also needs to be allayed. They could be partly accommodated by putting in a tightly circumscribed loophole for full-size pickup trucks, which could qualify for lower mileage. Just as for depreciation rules, there would need to be strict rules limiting the loophole to pickups with an open bed at least six feet six inches long and with no more than a single row of seats.

Combining car and light-truck standards and then requiring a percentage increase for each automaker will still leave a potential safety problem, however. Automakers still might build lots of small cars and lots of small SUVs while continuing to crank out plenty of lethal, full-sized SUVs.

The best fuel-economy system from a safety perspective would be one that encouraged Americans to drive large cars and mini-vans, since these vehicles have the lowest combined death rates for their occupants and other road users that they strike. A good sys-tem should also provide automakers with an incentive to sell mid-sized SUVs, not full-sized ones, to the small minority of Americans who really needed four-wheel drive and heavy-duty towing capa-bilities. Mid-sized and full-sized SUVs have similar death rates for their own occupants, while full-sized SUVs have the disadvantage of being even more deadly than mid-sized models to occupants of other vehicles that they hit.[6]

Providing an incentive for automakers to address safety as well as energy conservation and global warming is not easy, and would require a more complicated set of fuel-economy rules. The rules could get so complicated that they would become vulnerable to manipulation by the auto industry and its lobbyists. But if safety is the paramount goal, then regulators need to set separate fuel-econ-omy targets for categories of vehicles based not on whether they are cars or light trucks but on their weight or size.

The safety advantages of increasing vehicle weight seem to level off once cars and SUVs reach a weight without cargo of 4,000 pounds—the weight of a large car or a minivan or a mid-sized SUV. Above that weight, SUVs in particular are more likely to kill other motorists while they are no safer for their own occupants. So a strong case can be made on safety grounds for creating separate fuel-economy standards for a series of weight brackets up to 4,000 pounds and then a single bracket for all vehicles (except full-sized pickups) weighing, say, 4,000 to 10,000 pounds. The standard for these big vehicles could then be raised quickly for safety reasons over the next few years, while smaller improvements in gas mileage would be required of lighter vehicles. This would force automakers to use the bigger mid-sized SUVs or large cars or minivans to offset sales of large SUVs in the 4,000-pound-plus fuel-economy average, or else to make the large SUVs lighter and equip them with less primitive engines. These would all be good outcomes for safety.

Another possibility is to use vehicle size instead of weight as the determining factor. Multiply a vehicle's length by its width and you get what is known as the vehicle's footprint. Setting fuel-economy standards by footprint, allowing lower m.p.g. for large-footprint models, would give automakers an incentive to make vehicles as long and wide as possible, while still making them as light as possible. Extra width would make automobiles less prone to rolling over. Automakers would feel pressure to sell lightweight, unit-body cars that would be as big as possible, with very large crumple zones.

Environmentalists, however, oppose using size or weight guidelines. They fear that automakers would drastically cut back production of small cars and small SUVs and mostly sell large cars, minivans and midsize SUVs if there were separate rules for different sizes or weights of vehicles. While rules could be drafted to discourage this, environmentalists are convinced that automakers would find or create new loopholes. If small cars and small SUVs faded away, the result could be more oil imports, more pressure to drill in environmentally sensitive areas like the Arctic and more emissions of global-warming gases.

Looking at the complexity of the safety and environmental problems posed by SUVs, it is easy to despair of a solution. With the exception of raising gasoline taxes, changing the way liability insurance rates are calculated and restricting the use of grille guards, very few remedies exist for the 20 million SUVs that are already on the road and likely to remain in service for the next decade or more. With so many factories now geared up to produce SUVs, the problems are likely to become more serious in the coming years, not better. The only question is how serious the overall problems will become.

Yet something must be done. For most families, SUVs are terrible substitutes for cars. But badly designed government regulations—often shaped by industry lobbyists—have created huge incentives for automakers to build ever-growing numbers of SUVs anyway. The manufacturers have beguiled Americans into buying SUVs with lavish and sometimes misleading advertising campaigns, and by coming up with vehicle designs that appeal to the darkest shadows of human nature. As SUVs have multiplied in the United States and beyond, they have fed a highway arms race that has made the world's roads less and less hospitable for car drivers, worsening a trend that hurts safety and the environment alike.

Every year that the United States and the world wait to take action, the problems only become worse.

MYTHS AND REALITIES
ABOUT SUVS

Myth: SUVs are safer than cars.

Reality: SUVs are no safer than cars for their occupants, and pose much greater dangers for other road users. SUV occupants die slightly more often than car occupants in crashes. The occupant death rate in crashes per million SUVs on the road is 6 percent higher than the death rate per million cars. The occupant death rate for the largest SUVs, which tend to be driven by middle-aged families, is 8 percent higher than the occupant death rate for minivans and upper-midsize cars like the Ford Taurus and Toyota Camry, which are typically driven by similar families. SUV occupants are much more likely than car occupants to die in a rollover, which accounts for about 1,000 more deaths a year than if the same people had been in cars. In collisions with other vehicles, however, SUVs are nearly three times as likely as cars to kill other drivers, inflicting another 1,000 unnecessary deaths a year among motorists who would have survived if hit instead by cars of the same weight. SUVs also contribute much more than cars to air pollution, causing up to 1,000 extra deaths a year among people with respiratory ailments.

Myth: SUVs are good choices for young drivers.

Reality: Parents who care about their children should not let them drive SUVs. Compared to older drivers, teens' involvement in multivehicle crashes is above average. But their involvement in single-vehicle crashes is far above average, presumably because of their inexperience. SUVs are the worst vehicles to be driving for anyone concerned about single-vehicle crashes. They have limited crumple zones, providing less protection than a car in an impact with a solid roadside object like a bridge abutment. Worse, SUVs are several times more likely to roll over than a car. Rollovers are the main cause of paralysis in crashes and paralysis can be an especially heavy burden for a young person to bear.

Parents should also discourage their children from riding in SUVs driven by other young people. Not only are SUVs unsafe, but insurance industry statistics show the risk of a fatal crash increases swiftly the more occupants there are in a vehicle driven by a teen, probably because inexperienced drivers are more easily distracted.

Young people should drive mid-sized or full-sized sedans, which are unlikely to flip over, provide ample crumple zones and do not pose nearly the risk of an SUV to other motorists.

Myth: Rollovers happen to people who drive recklessly but are of little concern for responsible drivers.

Reality: While inexperienced drivers are more likely to flip vehicles than experienced drivers, rollovers can happen to anyone. Federal research, accepted by the auto industry, shows that 92 percent of all rollovers begin when a vehicle is "tripped." This can occur when the vehicle strikes a curb, guardrail or another, lower-riding vehicle. Tripping can also occur when the wheels on one side of the vehicle pass over a high-friction surface, like the mud or gravel of a soft road shoulder. While reckless drivers are more likely to trip their vehicles, any motorist can wind up in an emergency situation, such as swerving to avoid a pedestrian, in which tripping is a risk.

Myth: If a drunk driver starts drifting across the centerline toward you, you are better off in an SUV than in a car.

Reality: On a narrow, crowded or slippery road with no shoulder, it may not be possible to swerve out of the drunk's path. But drunken driving tends to be particularly a problem at night, when roads are less congested. You have a better chance of maneuvering out of a drunk's path in an agile car than in a tall, lumbering SUV, and you are less likely to roll over in a car than in an SUV if you swerve across the shoulder. If you are in a collision, an SUV will typically provide more protection than a car if it stays upright because of its greater weight and because its height may allow it to override bumpers and crush the softer passenger compartment of the drunk's vehicle. But SUVs are more likely to roll over in multi-vehicle collisions as well as single-vehicle crashes.

Myth: Vehicles with all-wheel drive or four-wheel drive have more effective brakes than two-wheel-drive vehicles.

Reality: All-wheel drive or four-wheel drive simply means that the engine is supplying power to turn all four wheels. These systems help a vehicle accelerate. But this has nothing to do with braking effectiveness. Indeed, all vehicles have brakes on all four wheels. Taller, heavier vehicles, including most SUVs, are harder to stop than shorter, lighter vehicles, including most cars. Because SUVs are less likely to slip while accelerating on wet or icy surfaces, their drivers are easily lulled into forgetting that they cannot stop any better than nearby cars. The most important factor in braking and steering is the surface area of contact that the tires have against the road. Many SUV tires actually have less contact with paved roads than car tires because they have deep, macho-looking grooves that are designed to let them sink deep into mud or snow to harder ground below.

Myth: SUVs must be safe vehicles because the overall rate of traffic deaths per 100 million miles driven in the United States has inched down during the last decade even as SUV sales have soared.

Reality: The SUV problem has snuck up on America because the percentage of all registered vehicles in the nation that are SUVs has been rising by less than a percentage point a year. Drunk driving has plunged, seat-belt use has soared and air bags have become widespread over the last decade, three changes that should have produced big improvements in American traffic safety. Yet the deadliness of the nation's roads has barely changed. Nearly 42,000 Americans still die on the nation's roads each year and 3 million are injured, making traffic accidents one of the nation's biggest public health problems.

Myth: Riding up high improves visibility and allows the driver to anticipate trouble ahead.

Reality: Like sitting on a thick phone directory at a theater, driving a tall vehicle does improve a motorist's view, but at the expense of those driving behind. Drivers of tall vehicles are able to avoid some crashes by seeing dangerous situations in advance. But they also increase their odds of rolling over, with all the risks of death or paralysis that this implies. Tall vehicles are no safer than short vehicles while putting others in danger.

Myth: The safety problems of SUVs are "growing pains" that will diminish as safer models come on the market in the next few years.

Reality: Small steps are being taken, like installing hollow steel bars below the front bumpers of SUVs to reduce the danger they pose to lower-riding cars. But even the newest SUVs are likely to prove less stable than cars and more dangerous to other road users. The biggest problems still lie ahead. The majority of the SUVs on the road today, including three-quarters of the full-sized SUVs, were built in the last five years and are still being driven mainly by middle-aged families. As these vehicles age, their mechanical parts will begin to deteriorate and they will become more affordable for young drivers and for drunks, who tend to choose inexpensive vehicles. At the same time, the proportion of vehicles on the road that are SUVs is set to nearly double in the next decade or so. SUVs make up only 10 percent of registered vehicles now, but this is likely to catch up eventually with the 17 percent of new vehicle sales that are SUVs.

Myth: Only an SUV can provide the room that families with children need.

Reality: Mid-sized and large cars provide the same seating room as mid-sized SUVs. The trunks of the larger cars often have just as much floor space for groceries, although they are not as tall as the cargo areas of SUVs. Minivans, which are built like tall cars, offer seating for seven as well as tall cargo areas. Very few families need the slightly greater interior space offered by the very largest SUVs.

Myth: SUV air pollution does not matter because they are less dirty than the cars of a generation ago.

Reality: Big SUVs are allowed to emit up to 1.1 grams per mile of smog-causing nitrogen oxides, which is less than the 3 to 4 grams a mile from cars of the early 1960s but still a lot worse than today's cars, which are only allowed to emit up to 0.2 grams per mile. The air quality in most American cities has been improving, but further improvements require constant effort. Before leaving office in 2001, President Clinton issued regulations requiring that cars and SUVs emit no more than 0.07 grams per mile by 2009, a rule that ought not to be relaxed.

Myth (version 1): The rise of SUVs is a principal cause of global warming.

Myth (version 2): SUVs are unimportant to global warming.

Reality: The truth lies somewhere in between. Most scientists say that human activity is helping to tip the balance of nature toward a warming of the Earth's climate, the so-called greenhouse effect, but the extent of the human contribution is uncertain. Automobiles emit 19.5 pounds of carbon dioxide, a global-warming gas, for each gallon of gasoline they burn, as carbon from the gasoline is combined with oxygen from the air passing through the grille. SUVs, with their gas-guzzling ways, account for less than 1 percent of all human emissions of global-warming gases. But SUVs are nevertheless an especially wasteful contributor to global warming. Switching from a mid-sized car to a large SUV for a year consumes as much energy as leaving a refrigerator door open for six years. Americans' attachment to their SUVs has helped make it very hard for presidents to commit the United States to steep reductions in total emissions of global-warming gases, and this has crippled international efforts to address global warming.

Myth: SUVs need to have primitive, gas-guzzling engines to provide the necessary power for towing large objects.

Reality: Automakers' lobbyists have used this argument for years to fight tougher fuel-economy rules, but many of their own engineers disagree. Many SUV engines still have just two valves for each cylinder, an antiquated, gas-guzzling design often defended by lobbyists as necessary for providing extra power. But with careful design of the combustion chamber, engines with four valves for each cylinder can be very effective for towing. "You can take a four-valve engine and soup it up at the low end," said Tanvir Ahmad, GM's engine director. Some of the newest SUVs on the market have four-valve engines, including the full-sized Toyota Sequoia and GM's mid-sized Chevrolet Trailblazer, GMC Envoy and Oldsmobile Bravada. Using four valves instead of two not only produces an immediate improvement in fuel economy but allows the introduction of further technologies that are just emerging from laboratories and save even more gasoline, like variable valve timing. The problem is that designing new combustion chambers is very expensive. Compared to two-valve engines, four-valve engines also have more parts, making them slightly more costly to manufacture. Automakers have been reluctant to invest the money in switching existing SUV models to four-valve designs. "I don't think there is any conversion to four-valve that is cheap," Ahmad said.

Myth: If you can't beat 'em, join 'em.

Reality: For the truly self-centered person who cares nothing about hurting other people in crashes, obscuring other drivers' views of the road, making smog worse and contributing to global warming, this might seem a viable option. But such drivers need to be aware that they are not improving their own safety, and must endure the aggravation of driving a vehicle that is harder to drive and harder to park than a car.

THE FAMILY TREE OF AUTOMOBILES

SUVs are not cars. They are descendants of pickup trucks, but with a long passenger compartment and an extra row or two of seats instead of a pickup's open cargo bed. SUVs have flourished in the marketplace to a great extent because they benefit from many regulatory loopholes. Together with pickup trucks and minivans, new SUVs are categorized as light trucks and allowed an average gas mileage of 20.7 m.p.g. in the United States and Canada, compared with 27.5 m.p.g. for cars. SUVs and other light trucks are allowed to emit up to 5.5 times as much smog-causing gases per mile as cars. There are no government standards for the two main safety problems posed by SUVs—rollovers and damage inflicted on other vehicles—although federal regulators have begun providing consumers with ratings of vehicles' resistance to rollovers. Federal regulators have repeatedly required cars to meet stricter safety standards many years before light trucks on everything from air bags to brakes to seat headrests.

The following is a brief description of each class of vehicle mentioned in this book along with a representative but not exhaustive list of examples. At the end is a brief history of early off-road vehicles.

FULL-SIZED PICKUPS:	Cadillac Escalade EXT	Ford F-Series
	Chevrolet Avalanche	GMC Sierra
	Chevrolet Silverado	Lincoln Blackwood
	Dodge Ram	Toyota Tundra

These are vehicles with a passenger compartment and a long, open cargo bed in the back. Pickups used to be spartan vehicles with two doors and a bench seat in the front, but are now available with four doors and separate "captain's chairs." The cargo beds are typically 6 feet 7 inches long, or 8 feet 2 inches for extended-bed models. Automakers build pickups using what is known as "body-on-frame" architectures, in which the body of the vehicle is manufactured separately from the underbody, which is composed of a thick steel frame with the wheels, suspension and so forth attached. The body is then bolted onto the underbody near the end of the assembly line.

SMALL PICKUPS:	Chevrolet S-10	GMC Sonoma
	Dodge Dakota	Nissan Frontier
	Ford Ranger	Toyota Tacoma

Also known as compact pickups, these were seldom seen in the United States until the oil crises of the 1970s made fuel economy more important. These pickups are built on shorter frames than full-size models, with shorter cargo beds. The cargo beds are 6 feet long for two-door models and as short as 4 feet 7 inches for four-door models.

FULL-SIZED SUVS:	Cadillac Escalade	GMC Yukon XL
	Chevrolet Suburban	Lexus LX470
	Chevrolet Tahoe	Lincoln Navigator
	Ford Excursion	Toyota Landcruiser
	Ford Expedition	Toyota Sequoia
		GMC Yukon

These are SUVs that are built on underbodies originally developed for full-sized pickups, and share the body-on-frame architecture of full-sized pickups. They are heavy-duty vehicles that can tow or carry heavy loads, but are poorly adapted for family use. They nonetheless became extremely popular among affluent families beginning in the mid-1990s, partly because of their size and menacing appearance, partly because plusher models were introduced and partly because of tax advantages available to buyers of large light trucks.

MID-SIZED SUVS: Chevrolet Blazer   Land Rover Range Rover
                Chevrolet Trailblazer   Mercedes M-Class
                Ford Explorer   Nissan Pathfinder
                GMC Envoy   Nissan Xterra
                Jeep Cherokee   Oldsmobile Bravada
                Jeep Grand Cherokee   Toyota 4Runner

These are mostly SUVs that share the underbodies and body-on-frame construction of small pickups. These models became extremely popular in the late 1980s and early 1990s and remain popular today. Also included here are three Jeeps with "uniframe" construction—they have extremely heavy underbody frames, but were assembled as a unit like cars, with the roof, sides and floor all welded together.

SMALL SUVS: Chevrolet Tracker   Ford Explorer Sport
                Ford Bronco II   Jeep Wrangler

A favorite of recreational users for many years, these two-door models are too small for most families and tend to have bouncy rides. They are built using body-on-frame construction, often with underbodies even smaller than those found in most small pickups.

CROSSOVER UTILITY
VEHICLES: Acura MDX   Lexus RX300
                        BMW X5   Pontiac Aztec
                        Chrysler PT Cruiser   Saturn Vue
                        Ford Escape   Toyota Highlander
                        Honda CR-V   Toyota RAV4

These are essentially tall cars that have been built to look like traditional, pickup-based SUVs. They have the unit bodies of cars, but have taller front ends and a higher seating position. They are very carefully designed to qualify for the more lenient regulations that apply to light trucks, but are not really made for off-road travel. Instead of traditional four-wheel drive, they usually have all-wheel drive, which means that they do not have the very low gear, "below" first gear, that is needed for descending steep inclines. The first crossover utility was the Toyota RAV4, introduced in late 1996, and this market segment has become hugely popular since then.

MINIVANS: Chrysler Town & Country   Honda Odyssey
                        Dodge Caravan   Pontiac Montana
                        Ford Windstar   Toyota Sienna

The most practical vehicles for families with lots of people or gear to move, minivans are built like large cars. Because they seldom have all-wheel drive and are not designed for off-road travel, they ride lower than SUVs or crossover utility vehicles. Most minivans have unit bodies like cars. They provide the high, chairlike seating that many motorists like for maximum visibility and comfort, but they block the view of car drivers. The ample crumple zones of minivans provide superb protection for their occupants during crashes while limiting damage to other vehicles.

LARGE CARS: Cadillac DeVille   Mercury Grand Marquis
                        Ford Crown Victoria   Toyota Avalon
                        Lincoln Town Car   Volvo S-80

These provide better handling than a light truck with lots of room inside and plenty of trunk space. They have better gas mileage than even a mid-sized SUV and emit far less pollution. But stringent fuel-economy regulations on cars have caused automakers to sell fewer of them and make them less tall. Some motorists dislike bending down to climb into a car, and dislike low seats that make them feel like they are sitting on a cushion with their legs out in front of them. The generous crumple zones of most large cars make them safe for their occupants and for other road users. Most have unit bodies; Ford still builds its large cars with body-on-frame construction, but they ride low enough that they have not posed a serious threat to other motorists.

MID-SIZED CARS:	Chevrolet Lumina	Pontiac Grand Prix
	Ford Taurus	Toyota Camry
	Honda Accord	Volkswagen Passat

American families used to buy more mid-sized cars than any other category of vehicles, but SUVs as a group overtook them in sales in 2001. Like large cars, mid-sized cars are safe, fairly fuel-efficient and pollute very little. They are unit-body vehicles.

SMALL CARS:	Acura RSX	Honda Civic
	Audi TT	Toyota Celica
	Chevrolet Cavalier	Volkswagen Jetta
		Ford Focus

These provide affordable transportation for young people but are a little cramped for families. Invariably built as unit-body vehicles, they typically have good handling that can help motorists avoid crashes. But if a crash does occur, they offer less protection than larger cars.

EARLY OFF-ROAD VEHICLES

These were sold in limited numbers through the 1970s and tended to have spartan interiors. Mainly purchased by outdoorsmen and businesses, they were slow to catch the attention of families.

Chevrolet Carryall Suburban. An eight-passenger sedan with three rows of seats but just one door on each side of the vehicle. Based on the Chevy pickup. Introduced in the spring of 1935, halfway through the 1935 model year. Initially available with a surprisingly luxurious interior, but a better-selling commercial version had just two seats in the front and a large cargo area behind, and became popular with funeral homes, flower shops and other small businesses. Used on Navy bases during World War II, it weighed 3,625 pounds and was 16 feet 6 inches long. Four-wheel drive became an option in 1958. A second door was added on the right-hand side in 1967. The ancestor of today's Chevrolet Suburban full-sized SUV, which has become 18 feet 3 inches long and weighs 5,220 pounds because of more comfortable seats, more sound insulation, and other amenities.

World War II Jeep. Designed for the U.S. military in 1940 and 1941. Only 11 feet long, 4 feet high and weighing 2,160 pounds. The distant ancestor of today's Jeep Wrangler and Jeep Liberty small SUVs.

Jeep Station Wagon. Introduced in 1946. With one door on each side, it seated seven: three across the front, three in a middle row and one more facing sideways in the back. Had very straight, angular body panels because the panels were stamped out of sheet metal at a former washing machine factory that could not accommodate very curvy shapes.

International Harvester Scout. Introduced in 1961 and discontinued in 1980. A small, four-wheel-drive vehicle that was slightly larger than the basic Jeep but considerably smaller than a Suburban or Jeep Station Wagon.

Jeep Wagoneer. Introduced in 1963, as a successor to the Jeep Station Wagon. Available as a two-door or a four-door, and with either two-wheel or four-wheel drive.

Ford Bronco. Introduced in 1965 as a 1966 model. A large, two-door SUV with a spartan interior. Based on a Ford full-sized pickup truck. The ancestor of today's full-sized Ford Expedition SUV.

Chevrolet K-5 Blazer. Introduced in 1969. A large, two-door SUV with a spartan interior, just like the Bronco. Based on a Chevy full-sized pickup truck. The ancestor of today's Chevrolet Tahoe full-sized SUV.

Jeep Cherokee. Introduced in 1974, it was basically a renaming of the two-door version of the Jeep Wagoneer, with a somewhat sportier exterior and more luxurious interior. American Motors later reused the name for the completely different, four-door Jeep Cherokee that sold from late 1983 to 2000 and was the first true SUV.

NOTES

INTRODUCTION

1. Statistics from the Insurance Institute for Highway Safety. These figures will be covered in greater detail in Chapter 8, on rollovers.
2. The extra deaths in rollovers are based on comparing the proportion of rollovers that occur in SUVs (about 20 percent, although it varies slightly from year to year) to the proportion of all vehicles on the road that are SUVs (under 10 percent). There were 2,049 rollover deaths in SUVs in 2000, according to federal statistics; if the rollover death rate in SUVs had matched the rate in cars, there would have been more like 1,000 deaths. The extra deaths inflicted by SUVs on occupants of cars are calculated by Hans Joksch, a University of Michigan statistician who did a federal safety study under contract in 1998 that found that the designs of SUVs, pickup trucks and minivans were causing 2,000 more deaths in other vehicles than if those vehicles had been struck by cars. Joksch estimates that half these deaths were caused by SUVs, although this breakout of the data did not appear in his report. The EPA estimated in late 1999 that tighter standards for air pollution would save 4,000 lives a year; the agency provided me the figure of 1,000 lives for SUV pollution alone just before the Clinton Administration left office. Each of these calculations is dealt with again later in the book.

CHAPTER 1: EARLY RUMBLINGS

1. The 1936 catalog and information on the 1935 model come from the private collection of James K. Wagner, Society of Automotive Historians.
2. Patrick R. Foster, *The Story of Jeep*, Iola, Wisc.: Krause Publications, 1998, pp. 22–37. Full of technical information and photos, this is an excellent resource for Jeep collectors seeking to research the history of their vehicles.
3. "Archives of Business," *The New York Times*, Mar. 15, 1987, sec. 3, p. 4.
4. Foster, p. 41.
5. Ibid., p. 47–49.
6. Ackerson, Robert C., *Standard Catalog of 4x4s: 1945–2000*, 2d ed., Iola, Wisc.: Krause Publications, p. 522.
7. Foster, p. 86
8. Ibid, p. 93.

CHAPTER 2: REVIVING A CORPSE

1. Meyers, Gerald, "I Didn't Know My Truck Would Hog the Road," *The New York Times,* July 30, 2000, sec. 3, p. 11.
2. Technically, the Transportation Secretary has this authority, rather than the department itself. In practice, the administrator of one of the department's agencies, the National Highway Traffic Safety Administration, actually handles the regulations, while consulting closely with his or her boss, the Transportation Secretary, and with the White House.
3. "Light Truck Fuel Economy Standards," Federal Register, Vol. 43, No. 57, March 23, 1978, p. 11997.
4. Ibid.
5. Ibid.
6. Historical market share statistics calculated from sales figures in *Automotive News The 100-Year Almanac,* Detroit, MI: Crain Communications, April 24, 1996, p. 105ff.
7. While developing its own small pickup, GM sold from 1979 to 1982 a small pickup called the Chevrolet LUV. This was actually a pickup manufactured in Japan by a partly owned GM affiliate, Isuzu, and shipped to the United States to be sold under the Chevy name.
8. Data provided to author by Ward's Auto Infobank.

CHAPTER 3: CREATING THE FORD EXPLORER

1. Vlasic, Bill, and Bradley A. Stertz, *Taken for a Ride,* New York: William Morrow, 2000, p. 32.
2. Ibid., p. 34–35.
3. Eisenstein, Paul A., "Body Builder: Bob Lutz Plans to Put Some Muscle Back Into GM's Cars," *Hour,* January, 2002, p. 53.
4. Lutz, Robert A., *Guts,* New York: John Wiley & Sons, 1998, p. 11–12.
5. One line of the Ford family has fallen into the confusing habit of naming first-born boys for their grandfathers. Henry Ford named his only son Edsel, and Edsel Ford named his eldest son Henry Ford 2d. Henry Ford 2d followed the pattern in naming his son Edsel Ford 2d, who in turn has named his son Henry Ford 3d, who is now in college.

   Henry Ford 2d's younger brother was named William Clay Ford Sr., and he is the father of Ford Motor's current chairman, William Clay Ford Jr., who grew up as Billy Ford but now prefers to be known as Bill Ford.

CHAPTER 4: PAVING THE ROAD TO EVER BIGGER SUVS

1. Center for Responsive Politics database, which relies on filings with the Federal Election Commission.
2. Fuel-economy standards and figures for specific corporations are from editions of "Summary of Fuel Economy Performance," a statistical report that the National Highway Traffic Safety Administration puts out three times a year.
3. Doyle, Jack, *Taken for a Ride: Detroit's Big Three and the Politics of Pollution,* New York: Four Walls Eight Windows, 2000, p. 265.
4. Remarks of Governor Bill Clinton, Drexel University, April 22, 1992, p. 5.
5. This was based on an exaggerated calculation by the automakers that if the standards were raised, the manufacturers would simply close every assembly plant producing anything bigger than a compact car, and lay off all the workers. More likely, automakers would shift some of these resources toward making smaller vehicles. But some job losses still would have occurred in Michigan to the extent that foreign automakers gained market share at Detroit's expense.
6. Gardner, Greg, et al., "CAFE Clash: Clinton Insists He's Flexible; GOP Ads Assail Him on Auto Fuel Economy," *Detroit Free Press,* Aug. 22, 1992, p. 9A.
7. Lenzke, James T., *Standard Catalog of American Light-Duty Trucks,* 3d ed., Iola, Wisc.: Krause Publications, 2001, p. 150.

8. Vehicle registration data provided by the Polk Company.
9. "National Transportation Statistics 2000," Bureau of Transportation Statistics, April, 2001.
10. More than 90 percent of the Insight's horsepower comes from its gasoline engine and not its electric motor. The Insight's superb mileage mainly reflects that it is a tiny aluminum car, and the market for tiny cars has been small. Weight still matters more than a hybrid engine in determining fuel economy—DaimlerChrysler plans to introduce a hybrid Dodge Durango SUV in 2003, but it will get only 18 m.p.g., compared to 15 for the gasoline-powered version. Hybrid-powered vehicles cost several thousand dollars more to manufacture than vehicles with conventional gasoline engines, because the hybrids require so much additional electrical hardware. While hybrids can pay for themselves in gasoline savings in Europe or Japan in less than a decade, they are not yet economical in the United States without substantial government assistance through tax breaks, which the auto industry has been seeking. Based on current industry plans, less than 1 percent of all registered vehicles will be hybrids by 2010—a smaller share than dual-fuel E85 vehicles already represent, and not enough to make any meaningful difference in overall gasoline consumption.

    Another will-o'-the-wisp lies in replacing all internal-combustion engines with fuel cells, which convert hydrogen efficiently and quietly into electric current to turn the wheels. This is not a new idea—General Motors showed a prototype of a fuel-cell car at auto shows in the late 1960s. Then and now, the problem has been in manufacturing a fuel-cell vehicle at a cost that is competitive with a gasoline-powered engine. Even today, the cost is still 20 or 30 times greater. The Energy Department is the biggest backer of fuel cells, yet its own statisticians currently forecast that just 32,000 fuel-cell cars and 25,000 fuel-cell light trucks will be sold in the year 2020. For statistics on projected sales of alternative-fuel vehicles, see the Annual Energy Outlook 2002, Energy Information Agency, Dec. 21, 2001, Supplemental Table 45.

CHAPTER 5: THE SUV ECONOMY

1. ExxonMobil and Wal-Mart passed the three automakers in total sales in 2000, and appear likely to stay ahead. But both of these companies arguably have less economic impact than the big automakers. ExxonMobil finds, pumps and distributes oil but does not actually make it, and has a smaller workforce than the leading automakers. Wal-Mart has a larger work force than any automaker but these are mostly clerks earning less than a third of an auto worker's wages, as Wal-Mart does not manufacture the goods it sells.
2. Figures supplied by the National Association of Realtors, using median prices for existing single-family homes.
3. The recent history of the Michigan Truck Plant mirrors that of the auto industry. The factory thrived in the 1960s and 1970s, but Ford laid off most of the work force in 1980 because of the recession and only 1,100 workers remained at the factory by 1987. By the late 1990s, thanks to the SUV boom, the work force had quadrupled. For an excellent portrayal of the despair that pervaded the factory in the late 1980s, read *End of the Line: Autoworkers and the American Dream* by Richard Feldman and Michael Betzold, Champaign: University of Illinois Press, 1988.
4. The sales and profits figures for Expeditions and Navigators are from Wall Street analysts who had been briefed at the time by the company. While Ford declines to provide sales and profit figures by factory or by model for competitive reasons, company officials have told me that the estimates here are about right.
5. Letters of Understanding Between UAW and the Ford Motor Company, Oct. 9, 1998, vol. IV, p. 95. The side letters to the Chrysler and GM labor contracts contained identical language. Ford and DaimlerChrysler both ran into severe financial difficulty when the economy slowed in 2001, but neither was able to persuade the union to let it close any factories. They both laid off thousands of workers, but had to keep paying these workers two-thirds of their pay for 42

weeks, after which they had to put back on full pay those who had not retired or found work elsewhere even if they had no work for them. Both companies hope to close factories as part of the next round of contract talks in September 2003.

6. A handful of companies, like Philip Morris and McDonalds, came close to the automakers if spending by auto dealers is excluded. But it is more fair to include the dealers, since they are advertising the same products, and by this measure the auto industry truly dominates ad spending.

CHAPTER 6: REPTILE DREAMS

1. Lutz, Robert A., *Guts,* New York: John Wiley & Sons, 1998, p. 71–72.

2. Concerned that some buyers might avoid SUVs because of the harm they caused to others, Chrysler secretly commissioned a study in early 1998. SUV buyers interviewed by market researchers proved to be a somewhat diverse group, depending on the models they chose. Buyers of burly Dodge Durangos expressed very little concern at all about causing pain and suffering for others, while owners of other models with a less menacing appearance gave more caring responses, according to a person with a copy of the report.

3. Ad spending is measured with extraordinary precision in the United States by a data service called CMR, formerly known as Competitive Media Reporting. Just as the Nielsen system measures the size of television audiences, CMR gauges advertising. It measures the duration or size of ads on all television and radio networks and hundreds of newspapers and magazines, then compares them to the pricing schedules that these media charge for various lengths or sizes of ads. Many media outlets, including television networks and outdoor billboard providers, also provide advertising spending data directly to CMR. Advertisers then pay large sums to CMR to find out exactly what their competitors are spending to promote certain products. For this book, I provided a list of 51 SUVs based on pickup-truck designs and CMR graciously had its computers crank out the annual spending for each of them. The calculations covered spending in every medium, from broadcast television and newspapers to magazines and outdoor billboards, for every model.

4. Data calculated for me by the Polk Company, which tracks vehicle registration data nationwide.

5. This is an average for all of 1981; prices were even higher in some months and in some states.

6. The share of purchases by top earners is from J. D. Power and Associates. The extrapolations of gas prices are mine, based on data from the American Petroleum Institute and the Census Bureau.

7. Cobb, James G., "Behind the Wheel/2002 Cadillac Escalade," *The New York Times,* July 15, 2001. Also Roberts, Selena, "Some Winter Stars Prefer Green to Gold," *The New York Times,* Feb. 7, 2002.

CHAPTER 7: THE MYTH OF FOUR-WHEEL-DRIVE SAFETY

1. There were different versions of this ad. Chrysler declines to discuss the ad.

2. Sophisticated "leveling" devices in some suspensions partly address this problem by diminishing forward lean somewhat.

3. It may not be intuitively obvious why most of the slowing should occur near the end of the stopping distance, so here is a simple explanation. An automobile's brakes can slow it by 15 to 22 miles per hour for each second that the brakes are fully applied. But the vehicle goes farther in the first second of braking than the last because it is traveling faster. A 2002 Explorer stops in about 3 seconds from 60 miles an hour. In the first second, the speed drops to 40 miles an hour but the Explorer travels 75 feet, or more than half the total stopping

distance. During the next second, the speed drops to 20 miles an hour while the Explorer travels another 42 feet. During the final second the speed drops to zero as the Explorer travels only about 18 feet.

4. *Consumer Reports* performed this calculation for this book. These figures were not published in the magazine.

5. Shultz, Gregory A., and Michael J. Babinchak, "Final Report for the Methodology Study of the Consumer Braking Information Initiative," U.S. Army Materiel Command, March 1999. The report included a disclaimer that the results should not be used to judge specific models, and did not suggest that the Expedition was any worse or better than other large SUVs. A fully loaded Expedition can also carry more weight than a fully loaded car.

6. Csere, Csaba, "Avoiding Crashes or Surviving Them?" *Car and Driver,* September 1998, p. 11.

7. To save money, regulators actually crash test the least expensive in a group of essentially identical models. The Chevrolet Tahoe, GMC Yukon and Cadillac Escalade are all essentially the same vehicle, although the Yukon and Escalade have cosmetically different front ends and more opulent passenger compartments. Research has shown that the opulence of a passenger compartment has little effect on safety. So regulators actually crashed a Tahoe, but say that the results are valid for the Yukon and Escalade as well. Earlier versions of these models actually did slightly better on crash tests, before a redesign in 2000 to make them more luxurious.

CHAPTER 8: ROLLOVERS

1. More recent research in Arkansas has found that 45 to 50 percent of paralysis cases are caused by motor vehicle crashes and half of these were rollovers. Arkansas used a somewhat more stringent definition than Utah for how far over a vehicle had to turn before the crash was counted as a rollover. Oral communication, Thomas Farley, Arkansas Spinal Cord Commission.

2. Wilson, Kevin A., "A Jeep Rollover Proves Hard to Understand," *AutoWeek,* Nov. 26, 2001, p. 10.

3. Friedman, Donald, and Carl E. Nash, "Advanced Roof Design for Rollover Protection," Seventeenth International Conference on the Enhanced Safety of Vehicles, 2001.

4. Partyka, Susan C., "Roof Intrusion and Occupant Injury in Light Passenger Vehicle Towaway Crashes," NHTSA, 1992.

5. Rains, Glen C., and Michael A. Van Voorhis, "Quasi Static and Dynamic Roof Crush Testing," NHTSA, 1998.

6. "Federal Motor Vehicle Safety Standards; Roof Crush Resistance: Docket No. NHTSA–1999–5572; Notice 2," NHTSA, 2001.

7. Insurance Institute for Highway Safety, annual death tables by model. Note that the rollover death rates for bigger midsize SUVs would be even higher if the Grand Cherokee were not included in that category.

8. Farmer, Charles M., and Adrian Lund, "Characteristics of Crashes Involving Motor Vehicle Rollover," Insurance Institute for Highway Safety, 2000, p. 6.

9. These death rates by vehicle category are not comparable with the rollover death rates by model earlier in this chapter. The Insurance Institute for Highway Safety calculates driver death rates for specific models, and the most up-to-date figures for this are for 1999. The institute calculates death rates for all occupants, not just drivers, for entire classes of vehicles, like cars and SUVs, and has done so most recently for 2000.

10 The Cato Institute's *Regulation* magazine published a computer calculation by two economists in 2001 claiming that SUVs and other light trucks had higher death rates than cars in the mid-1990s because they were more likely to be driven on rural roads. But traffic safety experts discounted this conclusion because they were skeptical of the methodology.

CHAPTER 9: KILL RATES

1. Chillon, "The Importance of Vehicle Aggressiveness in the Case of a Transversal Impact," First International Conference on Enhanced Safety of Vehicles, 1971.
2. Ventre, Phillippe, "Homogenous Safety Amid Heterogeneous Car Population?" Third International Conference on Enhanced Safety of Vehicles, 1972.
3. Kossar, Jerome M., "Big and Little Car Compatibility," Fifth International Conference on Enhanced Safety of Vehicles, 1974.
4. Wolfe, Arthur C., and Oliver M. Carsten, "Study of Car/Truck Crashes in the United States," Highway Safety Research Institute, University of Michigan, 1982.
5. Terhune, Kenneth W., and Thomas A. Ranney, "Components of Vehicle Aggressiveness," 28th Annual Proceedings of the American Association for Automotive Medicine, 1984.
6. Monk, Michael W., and Donald T. Willke, "Striking Vehicle Aggressiveness Factors for Side Impact," National Highway Traffic Safety Administration, 1986. Lowering the hood height did create a new problem. The barrier hit the Rabbit so low that the crash dummy in the Rabbit swiveled, so that its pelvis went toward the center of the car while its head swung like an inverted pendulum, coming out the Rabbit window and hitting the top of the barrier. But regulators had conducted the test using a low-cost dummy that was not designed to simulate the actual movements of a real person's neck or head, so the accuracy of this outcome is unclear.
7. Hollowell, William T., and Hampton C. Gabler, "NHTSA's Vehicle Aggressivity and Compatibility Research Program," Fifteenth International Conference on Enhanced Safety of Vehicles, 1996. The paper did not calculate separate kill rates for different sizes of SUVs, lumping them all into a single category instead for comparison to other categories of vehicles. The federal crash data is arranged in a way that makes it difficult to assess the size of SUVs involved in crashes.
8. Hollowell, William T., and Hampton C. Gabler, "The Aggressivity of Light Trucks and Vans in Traffic Crashes," National Highway Traffic Safety Administration, 1998. The new analysis was also limited to drivers killed in other vehicles, instead of all occupants in other vehicles, as in the Melbourne paper. Every vehicle has a driver, but minivans, for example, tend to have more occupants than pickup trucks. If a certain class of vehicles disproportionately hits minivans for some reason, that might inflate its kill rate for other vehicle occupants without affecting its kill rate of other drivers. Since minivans are mainly found in cities, classes of vehicles mainly used in cities would be more likely to hit them than classes of vehicles used mainly in rural areas.
9. Eisenstein, Paul A., "The Truck Jihad: America's popular press wages a holy war on trucks, putting the squeeze on SUVs. Why?" *AutoWeek*, May 25, 1998, p. 18. The magazine's cover showed a powerful fist crushing an SUV in its grip, next to a front page of *The New York Times* that had been doctored by computer to show nothing but articles of mine about the dangers of SUVs.
10. "Special Issue: Vehicle Compatibility in Crashes," Status Report, vol. 34, no. 9, Insurance Institute for Highway Safety, 1999.
11. I had some firsthand experience with these dangers. My college scholarship had paid for me to spend the summer of 1983 with the police department in Rochester, New York. I rode on midnight patrol for weeks in some of the city's highest-crime neighborhoods (yes, Rochester has some, although it is a mostly safe city). One night I was riding in a squad car with a rookie cop when we received a call on the radio that a motorist had fled when another police car tried to pull him over. Just then, the sought-after car went roaring by us, so we gave chase. The motorist went roaring up the exit ramp of an interstate highway, so we followed him and began hurtling down the wrong side of the highway at top speed. Fortunately, it was the wee hours of the morning and there

was virtually no traffic. The fleeing driver hooked around at the next exit ramp and got off the highway and we did the same. The driver pulled into a housing project and brought the car to a screeching halt; the police officer with me pulled to a halt so close to the driver's door that it could not be opened. A passenger with the driver hopped out and the officer with me ran after him and caught him. The driver crawled out of the other side of the car and ran around the corner straight into the arms of a very beefy policeman who had never caught a suspect before in a foot chase; the officer grabbed the driver and pinned him to the ground. I later asked the rookie police officer how he had learned to engage in high-speed chases. He responded that he had been terrified during the chase, partly because he had never been trained in high-speed chases and had never done one before. The city was so leery of litigation and uncertain about the best way to train for such chases that it simply offered no training for them at all.

12. Barbat, Saeed, Xiaowei Li, and Priya Prasad, "Evaluation of Vehicle Compatibility in Various Frontal Impact Configurations," Seventeenth International Conference on the Enhanced Safety of Vehicles, 2001.

13. The arithmetic is fairly simple. Leave aside SUVs for the moment and consider just the number of drivers killed per 5,000 crashes in which a large car hits another car of any size. In such crashes, an average of 2.2 drivers die in the large cars and 5.5 drivers die in the other cars that were struck. Add these numbers together and it works out to 7.7 deaths per 5,000 crashes. Why are the deaths lopsidedly occurring in the other cars instead of in the large cars? The large cars are heavier than most of the cars they hit, so the drivers of the large cars tend to fare better. Now look at the crashes involving Explorers. The good news is that only 1.2 drivers die in Explorers in the same number of collisions with cars. Compared to the 2.2 drivers who died in the large cars, the Explorers are actually saving a life. The bad news is that when hit by Explorers instead of large cars, the death rate zooms for the drivers in the other cars. Indeed, it doubles, to 11 deaths. That means 5.5 extra deaths in the cars. The combined death rate for drivers on both sides of the collision has now risen too. It is 12.2 for collisions involving Explorers, compared with 7.7 when there were just large cars hitting the other cars.

14. For a discussion of how such a barrier test might work, see: Summers, Stephen, William T. Hollowell, and Aloke Prasad, "Design Considerations for a Compatibility Test Procedure," Society of Automotive Engineers, March 2002.

CHAPTER 10: THE SUV INSURANCE SUBSIDY

1. Collision insurance is calculated partly on the basis of a vehicle's cost. The owner of a new, $35,000 SUV would typically pay higher collision insurance premiums than the owner of a 10-year-old car worth only $2,000. But for a car and an SUV of equal value, the collision insurance would tend to be higher for the car.

CHAPTER 11: TROUBLE FOR CITIES

1. The Polk Company analyzed SUV registration data by metropolitan area for this calculation.

2. Kockelman, Kara M., and Raheel A. Shabih, "Effect of Vehicle Type on Capacity of Signalized Intersections: The Case of Light-Duty Trucks," *Journal of Transportation Engineering* 126 (6), p. 506–512. Minivans might take a long time to get through intersections because they attract cautious drivers who may accelerate slowly when the light turns green. The researchers did not distinguish between

full-sized pickups and compact pickups; had they done so, the figure for full-sized pickups might have been somewhat closer to the large SUV figure and the figure for compact pickups might have been closer to the number for small SUVs.

3. I developed a habit of carrying a tape measure in my parka pocket, and found it useful for many articles. The only time it embarrassed me was when I attended a Christmas Eve midnight mass at the National Cathedral in Washington with my family. The Clintons were there by coincidence, and the Secret Service had set up metal detectors. I could not figure out at first why I was setting off the machine even though I had taken all my keys and coins. When an agent ended up finding the tape measure by using a scanning wand, he was initially quite suspicious of why anyone would be carrying a tape measure to church. He eventually gave it back; this was before the September 11 attacks, after which I probably would not have gotten the tape measure back.

4. Kahane, Charles J., and Ellen Hertz, "The Long-Term Effectiveness of Center High Mounted Stop Lamps in Passenger Cars and Light Trucks," National Highway Traffic Safety Administration, March 1998.

5. "Surface Vehicle Draft Technical Report J2338: Recommendations of the SAE Task Force on Headlamp Mounting Height," Society of Automotive Engineers, November 1996.

6. GM also ended up sending an engineer out in a parking lot for me with a digital device to measure the height of the headlights on their full-sized pickups and SUVs more precisely. The four-wheel-drive vehicles had the low-beam headlight bulbs between 36.5 and 38.78 inches off the ground, while the bulbs in two-wheel-drive vehicles were 34.45 to 35.5 inches high. This illustrates again how vehicles ride higher with four-wheel drive, which creates dangerous consequences for other motorists during crashes as well as the inconvenience of extra glare.

7. Lefler, Devon E., and Hampton C. Gabler, "The Emerging Threat of Light Truck Impacts with Pedestrians," Seventeenth International Conference on Enhanced Safety of Vehicles, 2001, p. 3. Large vans and pickup trucks were even deadlier than SUVs. The percentage figures here differ somewhat from those in the article; I rely on updated figures that Gabler provided after the article had been published.

8. Attewell, R., and K. Glase, "Bull Bars and Road Trauma," Australian Transport Safety Bureau, December 2000.

9. Holland, Andrew J. A., et al., "Driveway Motor Vehicle Injuries in Children," *Medical Journal of Australia* 173, p. 192–195.

10. Urban Land Institute and National Parking Association, *The Dimensions of Parking,* 4th ed., 2000, p. 45.

11. "Carjackings in the United States, 1992–1996," Bureau of Justice Statistics, March 1999, p. 1.

12. The National Insurance Crime Bureau releases an annual list of the most-stolen automobiles, and it tends to be led by the Toyota Camry and Honda Accord. But the list fails to allow for the fact that there are more Camrys and Accords on the road than any other models. Adjusting for the number of vehicles of each model on the road, SUVs and large luxury cars stand out.

13. Rochman has since changed jobs to become the top spokesperson for the property and casualty insurance industry.

CHAPTER 12: GLOBAL WARMING, GASOLINE MILEAGE, AND A GENTLEMEN'S AGREEMENT

1. "Light-Duty Automotive Technology and Fuel-Economy Trends 1975 Through 2001," Environmental Protection Agency, September 2001, p. 15.

2. Ibid., p. F–1, F–3.

3. Ibid.

4. Ibid.

5. Ibid., p. 3.

6. Data from Steven Plotkin, Argonne National Laboratory.

7. Each carbon atom has an atomic weight of about 12, and each of the two oxygen atoms has an atomic weight of roughly 16. The atomic weight of a carbon dioxide molecule is 44, with $^{12}/_{44}$ of the weight coming from the carbon in the gasoline and the rest from the oxygen in the air. Depending on how gasoline is refined, it may have slightly more or less than 5.4 pounds of carbon per gasoline. So carbon dioxide emissions can range from 19.4 to 19.7 pounds per gallon of gasoline burned.

8. This remark came in the prepared text of a speech that was labeled as off the record. But I am not bound by this because I was not invited to the speech and was not there; copies of the speech later circulated in the auto industry and I obtained one four years later from someone in the industry.

9. DeCicco, John, and James Kliesch, "ACEEE's Green Book: The Environmental Guide to Cars & Trucks, Model Year 2001," American Council for an Energy-Efficient Economy, Washington, D.C., 2001, p. 117.

10. 2001 Inventory of Greenhouse Gas Emissions and Sinks, Environmental Protection Agency, Box ES–4. Car and light-truck emissions of all types of greenhouse gases—mainly carbon dioxide—rose 7.8 percent in the United States from 1995 to 1999.

11. However, the lease costs may be higher if the lessor, typically an automaker or bank, concludes that the vehicle is such a gas-guzzler that it will have little resale value at the end of the lease. Used-vehicle shoppers with lower incomes may be more sensitive to gasoline prices, and this could affect resale values.

12. In calendar 2001, pickup-based SUVs were 17.24 percent of the light vehicle market, car-based utility vehicles were 5.91 percent, vans were 8.97 percent and pickups were 18.67 percent, for a total of 50.79 percent of the market, according to Ward's.

13. German, John, "Emission Inventory: Planning for the Future," Proceedings of a Specialty Conference Cosponsored by the Air & Waste Management Association and the U.S. EPA, Oct. 28–30, 1997, Research Triangle Park, NC. Vol. II, p. 676.

14. Salpukas, Agis, "Shell, Texaco to Merge Some U.S. Refining," *The New York Times,* Mar. 19, 1997, p. D1.

15. Cushman, John H., "U.S. Would Need to Cut Use of Fuel Drastically," *The New York Times,* Dec. 11, 1997, p. A10.

16. "State Motor Fuel Tax Rates 1/1/2002," American Petroleum Institute.

17. German, "Emission Inventory," p. 678.

CHAPTER 13: SEDUCING THE PRESS

1. Robinson, Aaron, "Reinventing 4-Wheel Drive," *Automotive News,* Oct. 11, 1999, p. 2i.

2. *The New York Times* is practically the only news organization that also reimburses automakers for the use of test cars, too.

3. All the ad figures here were generously calculated for me by CMR. Automakers spent a total of $1.92 billion advertising SUVs and car-based utility vehicles in 2000, which might seem at first glance to be less than their market share would justify compared to total auto industry advertising of around $13 billion. But much of the industry's advertising cannot be assigned to specific models. Many ads by automakers tout rebates and cut-rate loans or are designed to burnish the image of an entire brand, like Cadillac or Lexus. Many ads by dealers either promote the entire dealership or list so many models for sale that they are not counted as specific SUV or car-based utility vehicle advertising.

CHAPTER 14: THE GREEN PRINCE

1. The special class of stock accounted for 5 percent of the equity in Ford and 40 percent of the votes. The family holds another 1 percent of the common stock. So its total voting power, as mentioned earlier, is 41 percent.

2. Collier, Peter, and David Horowitz, *The Fords: An American Epic,* London: Futura Publications, 1989, p. 354.

3. Ibid., p. 411.

4. When the special shares are sold to anyone outside the Ford family, they are automatically converted into common stock with no extra voting rights. But the voting power of the entire class of special stock declines if enough shares are converted. When Bill Ford set up the family fund, the number of shares in family hands had fallen perilously close to the minimum needed for the family stock to have 40 percent of the voting rights at the company. Below that minimum, the class of family-controlled stock would only have 30 percent of the voting rights, and with a significant further drop the voting rights would drop to 20 percent and eventually zero. The creation of the family fund, which uses part of each family member's dividend income to buy any shares of special stock that come up for sale, has stabilized the family's holdings and there is no immediate threat that the family's voting power will drop from 40 percent to 30 percent.

5. Morris, Betsy, "This Ford is Different: Idealist on Board," *Fortune,* April 3, 2000, p. 134.

6. Ibid.

7. Taylor 3d, Alex, "Behind Bill's Boardroom Struggle: The Fight at Ford," *Fortune,* April 3, 2000, p. 141.

8. Bill Ford speech to 5th annual Greenpeace Business Conference in London, Oct. 5, 2000, p. 7.

CHAPTER 15: THE FORD EXPLORER–FIRESTONE TIRE DEBACLE

1. This was one of several superb analyses by Josh Barbanel, a gifted statistician for *The New York Times.*

2. Plungis, Jeff, "Money, Clout Key to Fixing NHTSA," *The Detroit News,* Mar. 6, 2002, p. A1.

3. Sherrill, Martha, "The Buddha of Detroit," *The New York Times Magazine,* November 26, 2000, p. 113.

4. This analysis was also performed by Josh Barbanel of *The New York Times.*

5. As it turned out, Ford's goons never found any of my sources. Long before Vines told me of the effort to hunt down the sources for the tire-problem article, I had been aware that the automaker sometimes traced calls through its phone system. It is legal for a company to keep track of the phone numbers that employees call, or receive calls from, while using company phones, although it is illegal to record those calls without the knowledge of everyone on the call.

6. Gilpin, Kenneth N., "Firestone Will Recall an Additional 3.5 Million Tires," *The New York Times,* Oct. 5, 2001, p. C3.

7. NHTSA Press Release 51–01, Oct. 4, 2001.

CHAPTER 16: THE NEXT DRIVERS OF SUVS

1. Minnesota has come up with a shrewd solution to this problem. It impounds the license plate and puts a steel boot on the vehicle at the owner's home to prevent it from being driven. This avoids the need for any storage fees at all, and gives the vehicle owner an incentive to redeem the license plate later by paying any relevant fines.

2. It is a measure of my initial naivete about sport utility vehicles that at the time of the Wrangler ad campaign, I thought it was a great idea. Indeed, I even wrote an advertising column saying so. Thankfully, the column never ran because I reworked it into a broader feature on how automakers pursued young buyers. I was new to Detroit then and still covered the industry purely as a business reporter, having not yet become concerned about the broader safety and environmental issues of SUVs.

3. "Deaths: Final Data for 1998," July 24, 2000, National Vital Statistics Report, vol. 48, no. 11, Centers for Disease Control and Prevention, p. 26.

4. Kitman, Jamie Lincoln, "Blue Eyes on the Set, Blue Streak at the Wheel," *The New York Times,* Nov. 13, 1999. Newman meant: So you put a 17-year-old kid behind the wheel of a 5,500-pound *SUV* .... Like many people even in the auto industry, Newman was being imprecise in referring to an SUV as a car. A typical Expedition does weigh around 5,500 pounds, however, showing that Newman follows automotive developments more closely than most people do.

CHAPTER 17: CROSSOVER UTILITIES

1. Four-wheel drive later became optional on the CR-V, but most continued to be sold with it.

2. Market segment data in this chapter is exclusively from Ward's Auto Infobank. This figure for minivans excludes large vans, which accounted for another 2.04 percent of the auto market in 2001.

3. These are CMR calculations performed for this book. I provided a list of 17 vehicles that were defined by Ward's as crossover utility vehicles, and CMR added up the advertising in every medium for these models. From 1996 through September 2001, automakers and their dealers spent $1.13 billion to advertise crossover utility vehicles.

4. Crossover utilities undermine the overall average gas mileage as long as automakers barely meet the light-truck standard. If automakers use crossover utilities to raise their light-truck mileage above the minimum then the net effect on overall fuel economy would be more ambiguous, but this has not happened yet.

5. The Contour and Mystique were actually based on a model developed by Ford's European operations, the Ford Mondeo, which was very successful in the mid- and late 1990s. Higher gas prices, a greater willingness to be squished together by transportation and perhaps lower rates of obesity have made Europeans more receptive to sedans that are slightly smaller than typical American models in this segment.

6. There is no accepted industry standard for how to measure hood height, and automakers do not provide such figures. Recent hood heights in this book are based on my measurements at auto shows with a tape measure, a practice I began in January 1998 and continued until my departure from Detroit in March 2002. I try to measure hood height from the ground to the front edge of the hood. If the hood goes nearly straight up from the front edge to a crease and then curves back, then I measure the height from the ground to the crease.

CHAPTER 18: THE SCHWARZENEGGER DIVIDEND

1. The three GM spokeswomen at the event took their cue from the AM General executives, however, and all ordered the bloody beef, as did I.

2. Daly, Sean, "Arnold's Latest Film Finally Sees the Light," *Milwaukee Journal Sentinel,* Feb. 6, 2002, p. 1E.

CHAPTER 19: THE TRIUMPH OF SUVS

1. No data is available for Africa except in South Africa, where the SUV market share is creeping down slightly, to 8.6 percent in 2001, as more small cars become available. The J. D. Power data does not distinguish between SUVs and crossover utility vehicles, lumping them all together as SUVs.

2. "Federal Motor Vehicle Safety Standards; Roof Crush Resistance: Docket No. NHTSA–1999–5572; Notice 2," NHTSA, 2001.

3. Center for Responsive Politics database, accessible at www.opensecrets.org.

4. Ibid.

5. Kahn, Joseph, "Panel Calls for Higher Mileage Standards," *The New York Times,* July 13, 2001, p. A12.

6. Unpublished draft report, Committee on Impact and Effectiveness of Corporate Average Fuel Economy. The parentheses here are the report's, not mine.

7. This conversion from Fahrenheit was a little off: 69 degrees Fahrenheit is 20.6 degrees centigrade.

8. James Bennet, my predecessor in Detroit for *The Times,* was the first to compare the fight for market share to the contest for Helen of Troy.

9. "Finds for under $25,000," *Consumer Reports,* April, 2002, p. 7.

10. NHTSA Press Release 11–02, Feb. 12, 2002.

11. Ibid.

12. The Liberty rolled over in tests by *AutoWeek* magazine in the United States and *Auto Bild* magazine in Germany. DaimlerChrysler said that it was lowering the suspension not just in response to the rollovers but also because its customer research showed that even fewer drivers than expected ever took the vehicle off-road, so they did not need high ground clearance. The lower suspension also made the ride more comfortable, the company said. *Consumer Reports* gave the Liberty a "good" rating on its emergency handling test while NHTSA assigned the vehicle a two-star rating for stability, meaning that it would be expected to roll over in 30 to 40 percent of single-vehicle crashes.

CHAPTER 20: FINDING A WAY OUT

1. Cohen, Randy, "The Ethicist: Departure Delays," *The New York Times Magazine,* May 2, 1999, p. 26.

2. Lund, K. Adrian, "CAFE Standards Statement Before the U.S. Senate Committee on Commerce, Science and Transportation," Jan. 24, 2002, p. 3.

3. Ibid. The Celica is one of the safer small cars, while the two-door Explorer with two-wheel drive is one of the less safe lightweight SUVs, so the numbers given here provide an especially lurid comparison. But look at the safety statistics for broader categories and the problem remains clear. The combined death rate for occupants and other road users struck by the vehicle is 275 for the smallest cars and 424 for the smallest SUVs.

4. The K1500 Suburban went back below 8,500 pounds gross vehicle weight for the 2000 and subsequent model years, however. The heavy-duty K2500 and K3500 versions of the Suburban have been well above 8,500 pounds for many years, but make up only a tenth of the sales volume of Suburbans and are mainly marketed to businesses.

5. "Light-Duty Automotive Technology and Fuel-Economy Trends 1975 Through 2001," Environmental Protection Agency, September 2001, p. 27.

6. Lund, "CAFE Standards Statement," p. 3.ß

INDEX